TEACHER'S BOOK
with Digital Pack

2

CEFR
B1

TH!NK
SECOND EDITION

Brian Hart

CAMBRIDGE
UNIVERSITY PRESS

CONTENTS

PRONUNCIATION	THINK!	SKILLS
Intonation and sentence stress	**Values:** Human qualities	**Reading** Online survey responses: Who do you admire most? Article: Human moles **Writing** A short passage about someone you admire **Listening** Guessing game
Word stress	**Values:** Learning for life **Train to THINK** Learning about texts	**Reading** Article: The loneliest schoolboy in Britain Article: The power of 'yet' **Writing** An email describing your school routine **Listening** Conversation about a summer activity list
B1 Preliminary for Schools Exam practice		
Words ending in /ə/	**Values:** Preconceived ideas	**Reading** Article: A new kind of superhero Article: The history of watching TV **Writing** A paragraph about your TV habits **Listening** Interview with a teenage filmmaker
The short /ʌ/ vowel sound	**Values:** Responsible online behaviour **Train to THINK** Logical sequencing	**Reading** Article: Leaving footprints Short texts: Different types of messages **Writing** A web page giving advice **Listening** Conversation about falling for online scams
B1 Preliminary for Schools Exam practice		
been: strong /biːn/ and weak /bɪn/	**Values:** Following your dreams	**Reading** Magazine article: A bright star Article: The future of live music **Writing** The story of your favourite band **Listening** Interviews about music
/f/, /v/, /b/ consonant sounds	**Values:** Caring for the world **Train to THINK** Different perspectives	**Reading** Magazine article: Hot topic: saving the Earth Leaflet: Energy matters **Writing** An article for the school magazine **Listening** Interview about a town project
B1 Preliminary for Schools Exam practice		
Intonation of question tags	**Values:** Believe in a better future	**Reading** Newspaper article: Today's world Group chat: Arranging a party **Writing** An invitation to a party **Listening** Interview with a singer and a journalist
The /juː/ sound	**Values:** How science helps people **Train to THINK** Using criteria	**Reading** Magazine article: Curious minds Web forum: What invention or discovery would make your life better? **Writing** A blog entry **Listening** A science lesson
B1 Preliminary for Schools Exam practice		
/tʃ/ and /dʒ/ consonant sounds	**Values:** What's important in a job?	**Reading** Article: The perfect job? Article: Technology in the workplace **Writing** A short essay about jobs in the future **Listening** Interview with Marina Stuart
/tʃ/ and /ʃ/ consonant sounds	**Values:** Never give up **Train to THINK** Logical conclusions	**Reading** Article: 8,000 birds to see before you die Article: 3D printing – it can change lives **Writing** A story **Listening** Conversation about health and exercise
B1 Preliminary for Schools Exam practice		
Intonation: rude or polite?	**Values:** Reacting to jokes	**Reading** Article: It's all fake news Article: The danger of live TV **Writing** A news report **Listening** Profile of an extreme weather journalist
Silent consonants	**Values:** The importance of rules **Train to THINK** Being creative	**Reading** Article: Hard times to be a kid Website contest: The best 50-word stories **Writing** A set of rules **Listening** The rules of chess
B1 Preliminary for Schools Exam practice		

Welcome to TH!NK, the course that develops your students' communication and critical thinking skills, values and life competencies so they can successfully meet the challenges ahead.

Have you ever asked yourself: "how can I be expected to prepare my students to succeed in a world that's changing so fast?" While it's impossible to predict what specific skills will be in demand by the time our students enter the workforce, there are some things that we as educators can do to ensure our students are as well prepared for their futures as they can be. We know there is an ever-increasing need for individuals to be able to work together effectively with others around the world, and to be able to think creatively and solve problems collaboratively. They also need to be able to analyse and process sources of information more critically, communicate and support their views more effectively, and they need to maintain a positive mindset in challenging environments.

With **TH!NK** you can be certain you're giving your learners the tools they need to build a brighter future for themselves and a better world for us all.

What's new in the Second Edition?

We've kept everything that teachers loved about TH!NK First Edition:

- The high-interest, relevant and thought-provoking topics
- The development of critical thinking, positive values and self-esteem
- A syllabus built upon the Cambridge English Learner Corpus and English Profile
- The inclusion of Cambridge Exams practice sections

The second edition builds and expands on these strengths:

- The **globally focused content** will appeal to teens' natural curiosities and interests, and feed their growing sense of the world around them.
- The **Life Competencies** strand, supported by entertaining student vlogs and correlated to the Cambridge Life Competencies Framework, will help them develop the vital capabilities they'll need to be successful throughout their lives.
- The authentic, **real-world documentary-style videos** will captivate student interest and provoke meaningful thought and lively classroom discussion.
- Powerful, all-in-one digital tools and support will empower teachers to deliver dynamic and effective lessons.

The story of TH!NK

TH!NK Second Edition was developed using the latest research into teen cognitive science and best practices and methodologies for the secondary classroom. To learn more, visit **cambridge.org/think2e** or scan this QR code with your smartphone or tablet.

Cambridge Life Competencies

A framework to develop skills for life

There have been many initiatives to address the skills and competencies our students need for the 21st century – each relating to different contexts. At Cambridge, we are responding to educators who have asked for a way to understand how all these different approaches to life competencies relate to English language programmes.

The Cambridge Framework sets out to have three dimensions:

BREADTH	DEVELOPMENT	DEPTH
Complete view of transferable skills within one system	How the skills develop across stages of the learning journey	Enough detail to guide teaching and assessment in practical ways

We have grouped the different competencies into six main areas.

- **Creative Thinking**
- **Critical Thinking**
- **Learning to Learn**
- **Communication**
- **Collaboration**
- **Social Responsibilities**

These are supported by three foundation layers that underpin the Framework:

- **Emotional Development**
- **Digital Literacy**
- **Discipline Knowledge**

What Are 'Competencies'?

We call these 'competencies' rather than 'skills', because competencies are more than just skills. The competencies in this Framework are complex and require development in three areas:

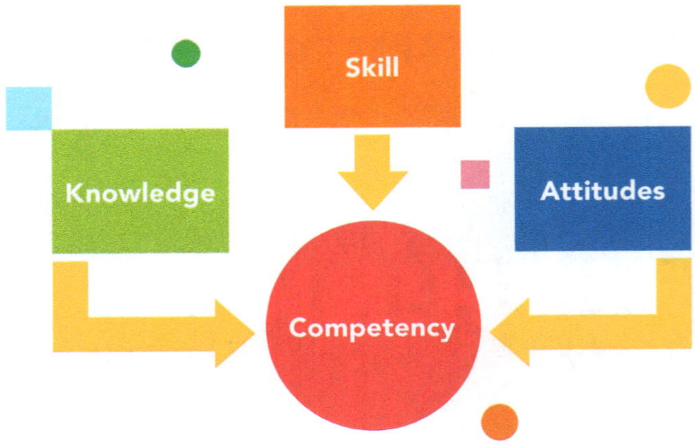

Competencies are defined as a combination of knowledge, skills and attitudes, where:

a) knowledge is composed of the facts and figures, concepts, ideas and theories which are already established and support the understanding of a certain area or subject;

b) skills are defined as the ability and capacity to carry out processes and use the existing knowledge to achieve results;

c) attitudes describe the disposition and mind-sets to act or react to ideas, persons or situations.

Council of the European Union, 2018, p14.

Core areas

Core area				
Creative Thinking	Participating in creative activities	Creating new content from own ideas or other resources	Using newly created content to solve problems and make decisions	
Critical Thinking	Understanding and analysing links between ideas	Evaluating ideas, arguments and options	Synthesising ideas and information	
Learning to Learn	Practical skills for participating in learning	Taking control of own learning	Reflecting on and evaluating own learning success	
Communication	Using appropriate language and register for context	Managing conversations	Participating with appropriate confidence and clarity	
Collaboration	Taking personal responsibility for own contribution to a group task	Listening respectfully and responding constructively to others' contributions	Managing the sharing of tasks in a project	Working towards a resolution related to a task
Social Responsibilities	Understanding personal responsibilities as part of a group and in society – including citizenship	Taking active roles including leadership	Understanding and describing own and others' cultures	Understanding and discussing global issues – environmental, political, financial and social

Foundational layers

- Emotional Development
- Digital Literacy
- Discipline Knowledge

cambridge.org/clcf

See page ix for an example of how Life Competencies are covered in **TH!NK**.
For a full correlation to the Cambridge Life Competencies Framework, visit **www.cambridge.org/think2e**

TH!NK and the Cambridge Life Competencies Framework

Although **TH!NK** focuses on both the *Social Responsibilities* and the *Emotional Development* competencies in the *Cambridge Life Competencies Framework*, all of the six Life Competencies are explored throughout the course.

The table below shows, at a glance, where you can find an activity which concentrates on a particular Core Area.

The following table shows which *competencies* are developed in this level.

Competency	Core Area	U1	U2	U3	U4	U5	U6	U7	U8	U9	U10	U11	U12
Social Responsibilities	Understanding personal responsibilities as part of a group and in society - including citizenship	✔					✔			✔	✔		✔
	Understanding and discussing global issues - environmental, political, financial and social				✔	✔	✔						
	Understanding own and others' cultures		✔		✔		✔		✔		✔		✔
Emotional Development	Empathy and relationship skills	✔	✔	✔		✔	✔	✔				✔	
	Managing own emotions			✔								✔	
Critical Thinking	Evaluating ideas, arguments and options		✔	✔	✔		✔	✔	✔	✔	✔		✔
	Understanding and analysing links between ideas	✔	✔		✔		✔		✔	✔	✔	✔	
	Synthesising ideas and information		✔					✔					
Learning to Learn	Practical skills for participating in learning	✔	✔	✔	✔	✔	✔	✔	✔	✔	✔	✔	✔
Communication	Managing conversations							✔	✔			✔	
	Participating with appropriate confidence and clarity											✔	
Creative Thinking	Creating new content from own ideas or other resources											✔	✔
	Participating in creative activities					✔							✔
Collaboration	Listening respectfully and responding constructively to others' contributions	✔	✔	✔	✔	✔	✔	✔	✔	✔	✔	✔	✔

Here are a few examples of how activities can help your students develop particular Can Do Statements:

Competency: Critical Thinking

Core Area: Evaluating ideas, arguments and options

Can Do Statement: Assesses strengths and weaknesses of possible solutions.

In this **TH!NK** *Values section, students are encouraged to compare points and arguments from different sources.*

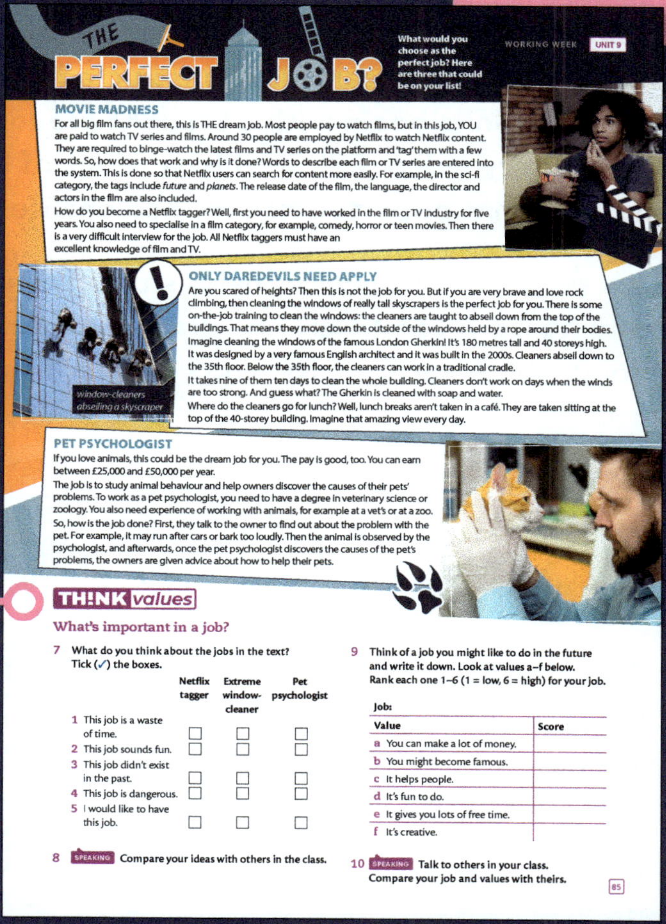

WORKING WEEK UNIT 9

THE PERFECT JOB?

What would you choose as the perfect job? Here are three that could be on your list!

MOVIE MADNESS

For all big film fans out there, this is THE dream job. Most people pay to watch films, but in this job, YOU are paid to watch TV series and films. Around 30 people are employed by Netflix to watch Netflix content. They are required to binge-watch the latest films and TV series on the platform and 'tag' them with a few words. So, how does that work and why is it done? Words to describe each film or TV series are entered into the system. This is done so that Netflix users can search for content more easily. For example, in the sci-fi category, the tags include *future* and *planets*. The release date of the film, the language, the director and actors in the film are also included.

How do you become a Netflix tagger? Well, first you need to have worked in the film or TV industry for five years. You also need to specialise in a film category, for example, comedy, horror or teen movies. Then there is a very difficult interview for the job. All Netflix taggers must have an excellent knowledge of film and TV.

ONLY DAREDEVILS NEED APPLY

Are you scared of heights? Then this is not the job for you. But if you are very brave and love rock climbing, then cleaning the windows of really tall skyscrapers is the perfect job for you. There is some on-the-job training to clean the windows: the cleaners are taught to abseil down from the top of the buildings. That means they move down the outside of the windows held by a rope around their bodies. Imagine cleaning the windows of the famous London Gherkin! It's 180 metres tall and 40 storeys high. It was designed by a very famous English architect and it was built in the 2000s. Cleaners abseil down to the 35th floor. Below the 35th floor, the cleaners can work in a traditional cradle.

It takes nine of them ten days to clean the whole building. Cleaners don't work on days when the winds are too strong. And guess what? The Gherkin is cleaned with soap and water.

Where do the cleaners go for lunch? Well, lunch breaks aren't taken in a café. They are taken sitting at the top of the 40-storey building. Imagine that amazing view every day.

window-cleaners abseiling a skyscraper

PET PSYCHOLOGIST

If you love animals, this could be the dream job for you. The pay is good, too. You can earn between £25,000 and £50,000 per year.

The job is to study animal behaviour and help owners discover the causes of their pets' problems. To work as a pet psychologist, you need to have a degree in veterinary science or zoology. You also need experience of working with animals, for example at a vet's or at a zoo.

So, how is the job done? First, they talk to the owner to find out about the problem with the pet. For example, it may run after cars or bark too loudly. Then the animal is observed by the psychologist, and afterwards, once the pet psychologist discovers the causes of the pet's problems, the owners are given advice about how to help their pets.

TH!NK values

What's important in a job?

7 What do you think about the jobs in the text? Tick (✓) the boxes.

	Netflix tagger	Extreme window-cleaner	Pet psychologist
1 This job is a waste of time.	☐	☐	☐
2 This job sounds fun.	☐	☐	☐
3 This job didn't exist in the past.	☐	☐	☐
4 This job is dangerous.	☐	☐	☐
5 I would like to have this job.	☐	☐	☐

8 SPEAKING Compare your ideas with others in the class.

9 Think of a job you might like to do in the future and write it down. Look at values a–f below. Rank each one 1–6 (1 = low, 6 = high) for your job.

Job:

Value	Score
a You can make a lot of money.	
b You might become famous.	
c It helps people.	
d It's fun to do.	
e It gives you lots of free time.	
f It's creative.	

10 SPEAKING Talk to others in your class. Compare your job and values with theirs.

85

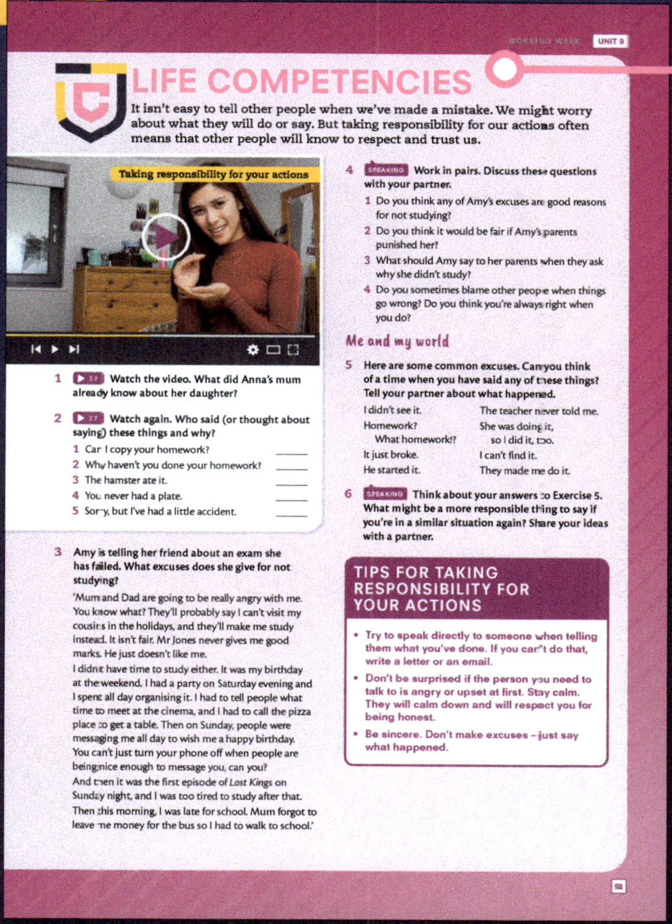

WORKING WEEK UNIT 9

LIFE COMPETENCIES

It isn't easy to tell other people when we've made a mistake. We might worry about what they will do or say. But taking responsibility for our actions often means that other people will know to respect and trust us.

Taking responsibility for your actions

1 ▶ 27 Watch the video. What did Anna's mum already know about her daughter?

2 ▶ 27 Watch again. Who said (or thought about saying) these things and why?

1 Can I copy your homework? ____
2 Why haven't you done your homework? ____
3 The hamster ate it. ____
4 You never had a plate. ____
5 Sorry, but I've had a little accident. ____

3 Amy is telling her friend about an exam she has failed. What excuses does she give for not studying?

'Mum and Dad are going to be really angry with me. You know what? They'll probably say I can't visit my cousins in the holidays, and they'll make me study instead. It isn't fair. Mr Jones never gives me good marks. He just doesn't like me.

I didn't have time to study either. It was my birthday at the weekend. I had a party on Saturday evening and I spent all day organising it. I had to tell people what time to meet at the cinema, and I had to call the pizza place to get a table. Then on Sunday, people were messaging me all day to wish me a happy birthday. You can't just turn your phone off when people are being nice enough to message you, can you?

And then it was the first episode of *Lost Kings* on Sunday night, and I was too tired to study after that. Then this morning, I was late for school. Mum forgot to leave me money for the bus so I had to walk to school.'

4 SPEAKING Work in pairs. Discuss these questions with your partner.

1 Do you think any of Amy's excuses are good reasons for not studying?
2 Do you think it would be fair if Amy's parents punished her?
3 What should Amy say to her parents when they ask why she didn't study?
4 Do you sometimes blame other people when things go wrong? Do you think you're always right when you do?

Me and my world

5 Here are some common excuses. Can you think of a time when you have said any of these things? Tell your partner about what happened.

I didn't see it. / The teacher never told me. / Homework? What homework!? / She was doing it, so I did it, too. / It just broke. / I can't find it. / He started it. / They made me do it.

6 SPEAKING Think about your answers to Exercise 5. What might be a more responsible thing to say if you're in a similar situation again? Share your ideas with a partner.

TIPS FOR TAKING RESPONSIBILITY FOR YOUR ACTIONS

- Try to speak directly to someone when telling them what you've done. If you can't do that, write a letter or an email.
- Don't be surprised if the person you need to talk to is angry or upset at first. Stay calm. They will calm down and will respect you for being honest.
- Be sincere. Don't make excuses – just say what happened.

Competency: Social Responsibility

Core Area: Managing own emotions

Can Do Statement: Managing stress by employing strategies

The following exercises demonstrate and model how to prioritise problems and manage the outcomes effectively

Student's Book

Each unit of TH!NK builds students' knowledge and skills through a series of carefully constructed learning inputs and activities. Units begin with a thought-provoking question and introductory video, followed by a series of high-interest readings and abundant opportunities for personalised speaking practice.

Each sequence of exercises helps students unlock the text, while contextualised vocabulary and grammar concepts recycle and build throughout the unit, sharpening students' language proficiency.

Objectives

Learning objectives clearly show unit aims at a glance, including language functions and target vocabulary and grammar concepts.

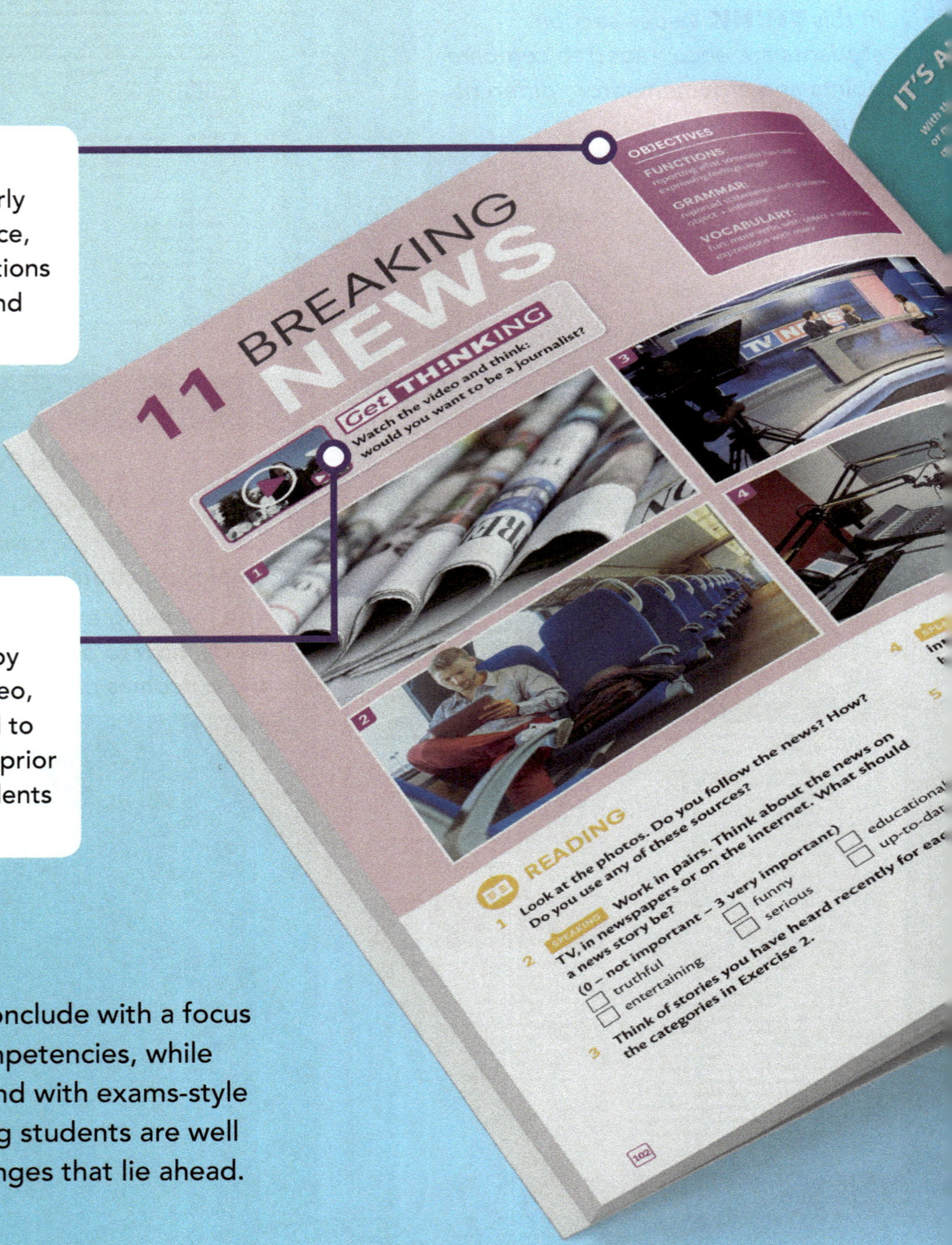

Get THINKING

Each unit is introduced by a documentary-style video, with questions designed to pique curiosity, activate prior knowledge and get students thinking critically.

Odd-numbered units conclude with a focus on developing Life Competencies, while even-numbered units end with exams-style practice pages, ensuring students are well prepared for the challenges that lie ahead.

THINK values

This feature encourages students to reflect on and discuss a wide range of important values, helping to develop their character as well as their sensitivity to others.

GRAMMAR

Grammar presentations use a scaffolded inductive approach to help students understand the features and structures of English grammar.

Grammar rap!

These short but catchy videos help illustrate and explain grammar concepts in an innovative and memorable way.

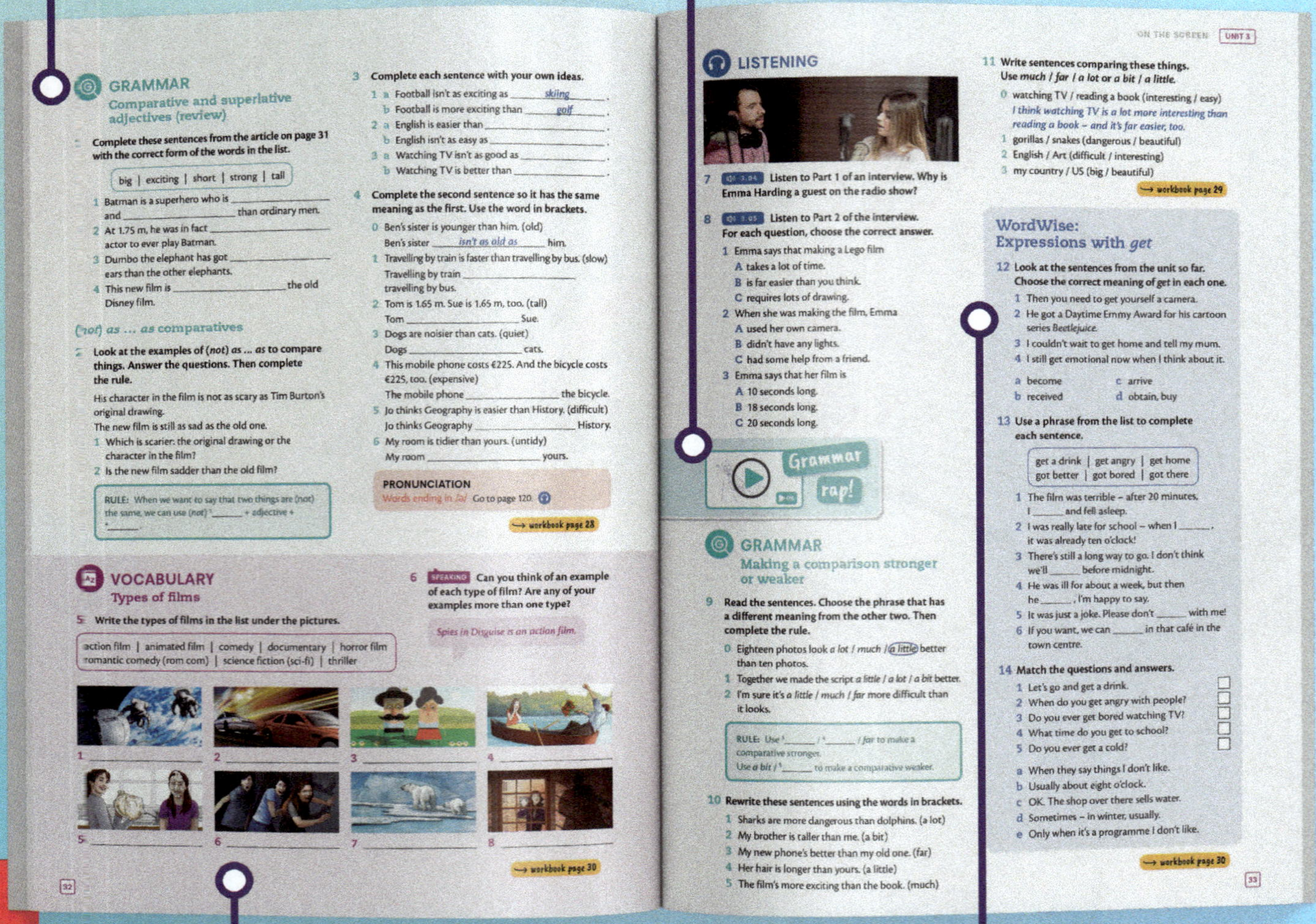

GRAMMAR
Comparative and superlative adjectives (review)

1 Complete these sentences from the article on page 31 with the correct form of the words in the list.

big | exciting | short | strong | tall

1 Batman is a superhero who is ______ and ______ than ordinary men.
2 At 1.75 m, he was in fact ______ actor to ever play Batman.
3 Dumbo the elephant has got ______ ears than the other elephants.
4 This new film is ______ the old Disney film.

(not) as … as comparatives

2 Look at the examples of (not) as … as to compare things. Answer the questions. Then complete the rule.

His character in the film is not as scary as Tim Burton's original drawing.
The new film is still as sad as the old one.
1 Which is scarier: the original drawing or the character in the film?
2 Is the new film sadder than the old film?

RULE: When we want to say that two things are (not) the same, we can use (not) ______ + adjective + ______.

3 Complete each sentence with your own ideas.
1 a Football isn't as exciting as *skiing*.
b Football is more exciting than *golf*.
2 a English is easier than ______.
b English isn't as easy as ______.
3 a Watching TV isn't as good as ______.
b Watching TV is better than ______.

4 Complete the second sentence so it has the same meaning as the first. Use the word in brackets.
0 Ben's sister is younger than him. (old)
Ben's sister *isn't as old as* him.
1 Travelling by train is faster than travelling by bus. (slow)
Travelling by train ______ travelling by bus.
2 Tom is 1.65 m. Sue is 1.65 m, too. (tall)
Tom ______ Sue.
3 Dogs are noisier than cats. (quiet)
Dogs ______ cats.
4 This mobile phone costs €225. And the bicycle costs €225, too. (expensive)
The mobile phone ______ the bicycle.
5 Jo thinks Geography is easier than History. (difficult)
Jo thinks Geography ______ History.
6 My room is tidier than yours. (untidy)
My room ______ yours.

PRONUNCIATION
Words ending in /ə/ Go to page 120.

→ workbook page 28

VOCABULARY
Types of films

5 Write the types of films in the list under the pictures.

action film | animated film | comedy | documentary | horror film
romantic comedy (rom com) | science fiction (sci-fi) | thriller

6 SPEAKING Can you think of an example of each type of film? Are any of your examples more than one type?

Spies in Disguise is an action film.

→ workbook page 30

32

ON THE SCREEN UNIT 3

LISTENING

7 1.34 Listen to Part 1 of an interview. Why is Emma Harding a guest on the radio show?

8 1.35 Listen to Part 2 of the interview. For each question, choose the correct answer.
1 Emma says that making a Lego film
A takes a lot of time.
B is far easier than you think.
C requires lots of drawing.
2 When she was making the film, Emma
A used her own camera.
B didn't have any lights.
C had some help from a friend.
3 Emma says that her film is
A 10 seconds long.
B 18 seconds long.
C 20 seconds long.

Grammar rap!

GRAMMAR
Making a comparison stronger or weaker

9 Read the sentences. Choose the phrase that has a different meaning from the other two. Then complete the rule.
0 Eighteen photos look a lot / much / a little better than ten photos.
1 Together we made the script a little / a lot / a bit better.
2 I'm sure it's a little / much / far more difficult than it looks.

RULE: Use ¹______ / ²______ / far to make a comparative stronger.
Use a bit / ³______ to make a comparative weaker.

10 Rewrite these sentences using the words in brackets.
1 Sharks are more dangerous than dolphins. (a lot)
2 My brother is taller than me. (a bit)
3 My new phone's better than my old one. (far)
4 Her hair is longer than yours. (a little)
5 The film's more exciting than the book. (much)

11 Write sentences comparing these things. Use much / far / a lot or a bit / a little.
0 watching TV / reading a book (interesting / easy)
I think watching TV is a lot more interesting than reading a book – and it's far easier, too.
1 gorillas / snakes (dangerous / beautiful)
2 English / Art (difficult / interesting)
3 my country / US (big / beautiful)

→ workbook page 29

WordWise:
Expressions with *get*

12 Look at the sentences from the unit so far. Choose the correct meaning of *get* in each one.
1 Then you need to get yourself a camera.
2 He got a Daytime Emmy Award for his cartoon series Beetlejuice.
3 I couldn't wait to get home and tell my mum.
4 I still get emotional now when I think about it.

a become c arrive
b received d obtain, buy

13 Use a phrase from the list to complete each sentence.

get a drink | get angry | get home
got better | got bored | got there

1 The film was terrible – after 20 minutes, I ______ and fell asleep.
2 I was really late for school – when I ______, it was already ten o'clock!
3 There's still a long way to go. I don't think we'll ______ before midnight.
4 He was ill for about a week, but then he ______. I'm happy to say.
5 It was just a joke. Please don't ______ with me!
6 If you want, we can ______ in that café in the town centre.

14 Match the questions and answers.
1 Let's go and get a drink.
2 When do you get angry with people?
3 Do you ever get bored watching TV?
4 What time do you get to school?
5 Do you ever get a cold?

a When they say things I don't like.
b Usually about eight o'clock.
c OK. The shop over there sells water.
d Sometimes – in winter, usually.
e Only when it's a programme I don't like.

→ workbook page 30

33

GRAMMAR and VOCABULARY

Each unit includes grammar and vocabulary sections that are presented in context and supported by additional practice in the Workbook.

WordWise

These features provide valuable practice with words or phrases that often have multiple uses or meanings in English.

WRITING

Each unit includes scaffolded writing activities presented in a real-world context, as either an informal activity or a more academically focused task.

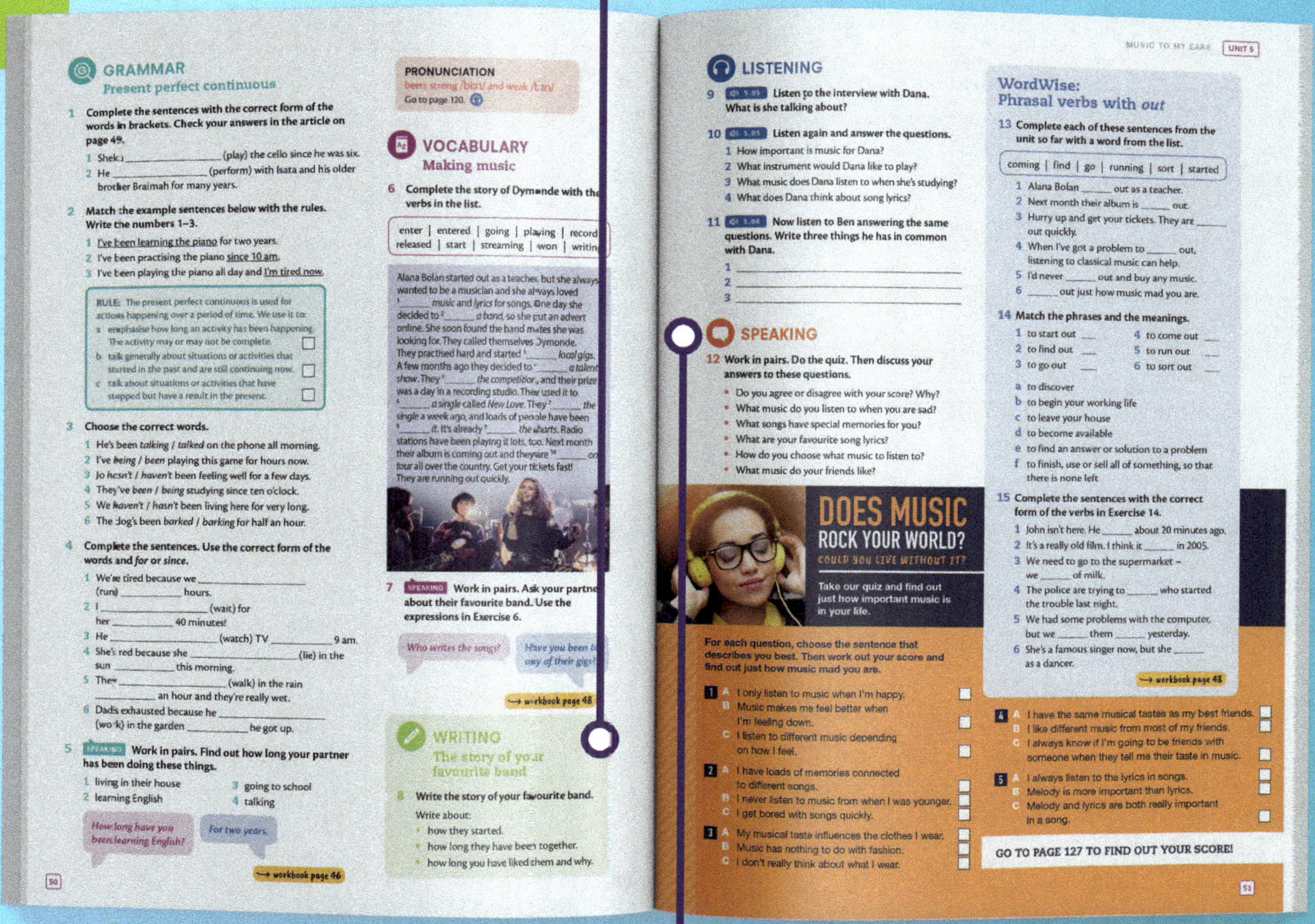

SPEAKING

Frequent opportunities for speaking practice build on students' prior knowledge and encourage them to relate the text to their own experience, personalising the speaking tasks.

DEVELOPING **SPEAKING**

These modelled speaking activities provide abundant practice to help students build their speaking confidence while Phrases for Fluency tips focus on authentic language to help them sound more natural.

LIFE COMPETENCIES

These lessons focus on developing a key competency area from the Cambridge Life Competencies Framework. The competencies that students develop throughout **TH!NK** will serve them throughout their lives within their communities and in the world at large.

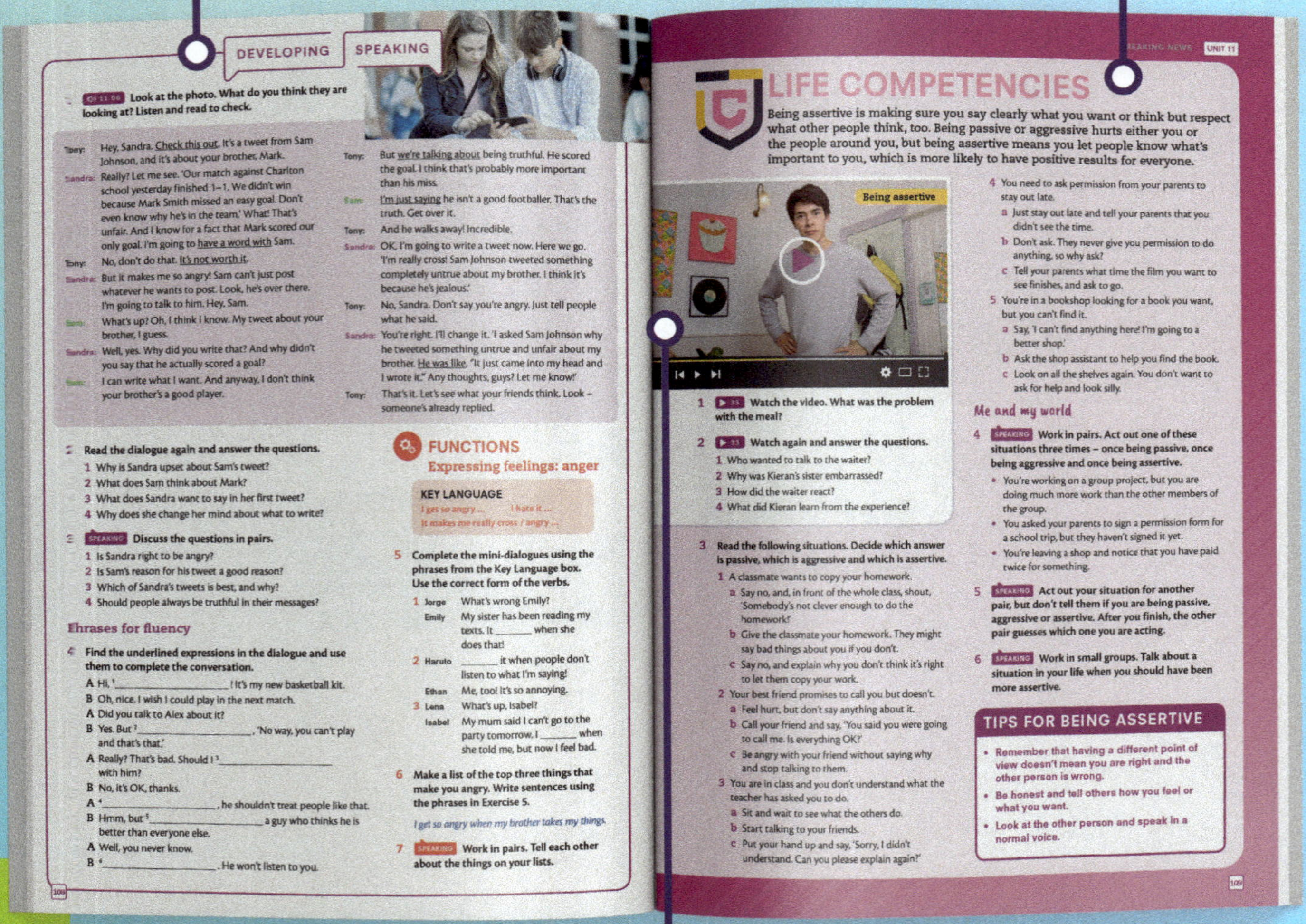

Life Lessons videos

Each Life Competency is introduced by a Life Lessons vlog recorded by a student. These videos help introduce the competency area in a natural and accessible way and serve as a springboard to the activities that follow.

Train to TH!NK

Train to **TH!NK** sections encourage students to reflect on the topics presented in the readings and to express their opinions on meaningful issues, as well as requiring them to work together to achieve consensus or to solve a problem.

Culture

The Culture sections introduce interesting topics and information about people and places around the world and spark discussion in a speaking task that requires students to make use of the information presented in the text.

WRITING

An extended writing section guides students through the writing process for a variety of text types. Students are presented with a model text for analysis of the task and purpose, and to practise the useful language they will need, before they move on to produce and share their own compositions.

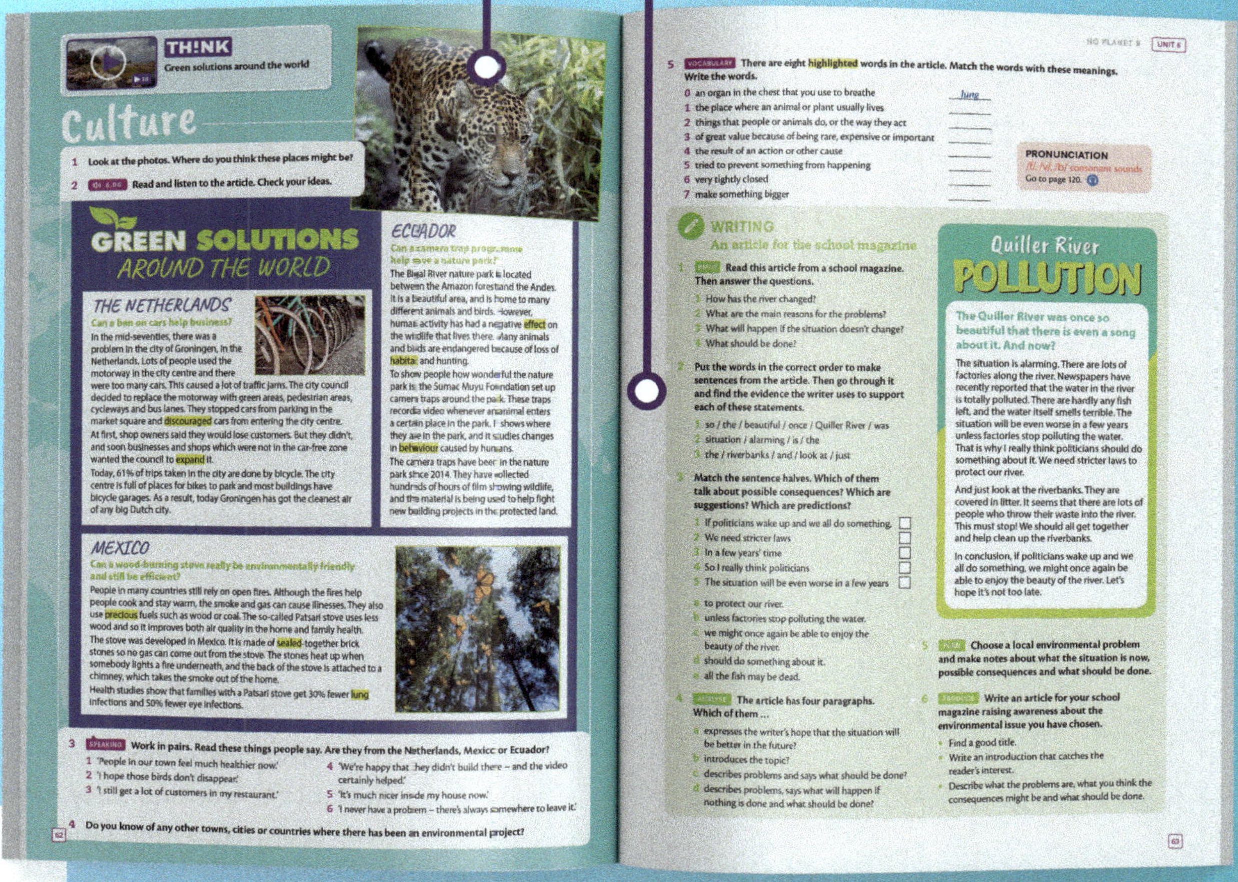

Exams

Exercises on these pages replicate the format of tasks from the Cambridge English Exams.

Cross-references to the Workbook lead to additional exams practice and useful test-taking tips.

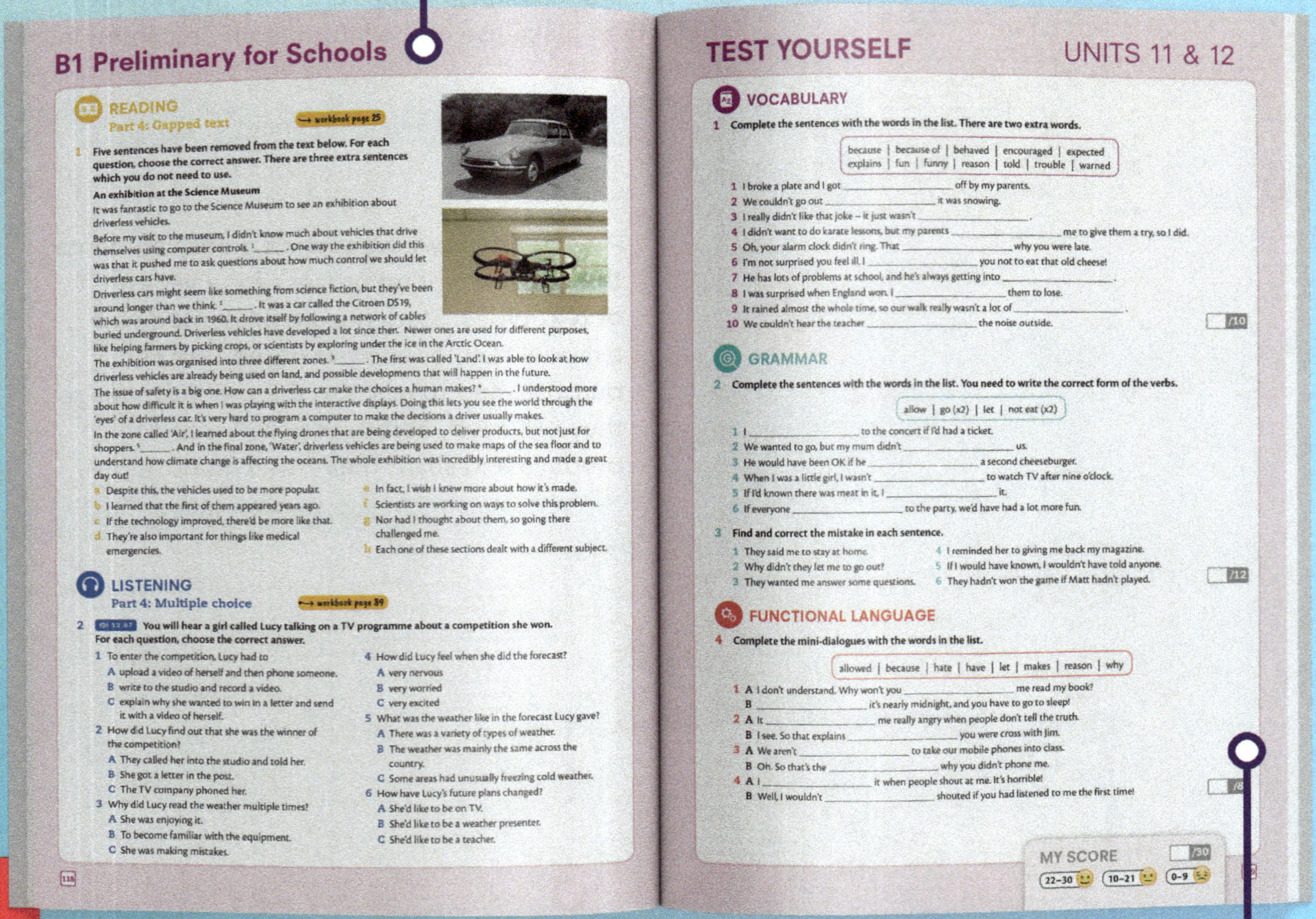

Test Yourself

The Test Yourself page allows students to check their progress and is based on the language presented in the previous pair of units.

The "emoji" scoring key encourages students to continuously monitor their progress as they move through each level.

Pronunciation

This handy reference at the back of the Student's Book covers sounds that are likely to pose a challenge for English learners and provides additional practice and support via the classroom audio program.

Get it Right!

Cross-references in the Teacher's Book indicate appropriate points within the unit to direct students to this section in the back of the Student's Book. Get it Right! activities help students avoid common errors as identified by the Cambridge English Learner Corpus*.

Cambridge English Corpus

*What is the Cambridge English Learner Corpus?

The Corpus comprises a 50 million-word collection of real-life learners' written and spoken English, derived from actual students taking the Cambridge English exams. We use this information to determine which word structures are more easy or more difficult for English learners, and, ultimately, to determine how best to support students when they encounter them.

Workbook

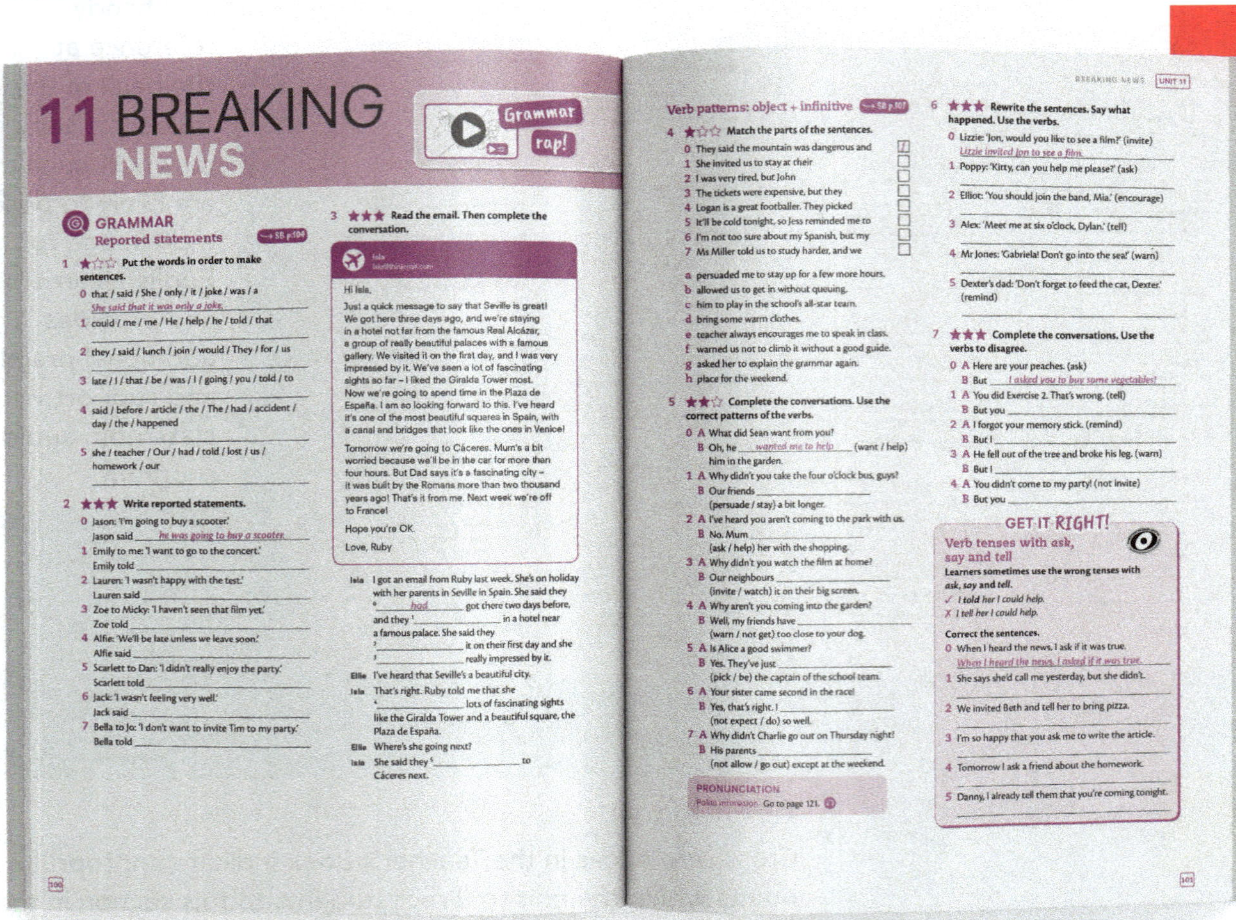

The Workbook offers extra practice of the language and skills presented in the Student's Book. Handy cross-references immediately following activities in the Student's Book direct students to corresponding pages in the Workbook, where they can get additional practice.

Cambridge Exams Practice

The Cambridge Exams sections provide useful tips and practice to help students prepare for Cambridge English as well as other high-stakes international exams.

THINK Digital Support

Presenting all your digital tools together in one place!

With **TH!NK**, everything you need is at your fingertips, including Presentation Plus, the powerful front-of-class presentation tool with complete course content, the entire classroom audio and video programs, Teacher's Resource Bank, and Test Generators.

Presentation Plus

- Student's Book and Workbook with interactive exercises
- Embedded links to classroom audio and video
- Additional games and activities
- Accessible online and offline.

Teacher's Resource Bank

- Online teacher resource area with support for projects, graded grammar and vocabulary practice worksheets, video worksheets, writing templates, extra speaking activities and more!
- Test Generator: an easy-to-use tool to customize and create end of unit, end of term, and end of year tests, as well as exam practice tests.

Collaboration Plus

- Students can work together on digital projects online using the Collaboration Plus tools and teachers can set, view, support and grade the work.
- Teachers can share students' project work with the class in the Showcase area.

Practice Extra

- Mobile-friendly platform and content
- Bite-sized learning activities with audio and video
- Online speaking tasks
- Performance tracking.

For updated information on **TH!NK**'s Digital Tools, visit **cambridge.org/think2e** or scan this QR code.

How to use the Teacher's Book

The TH!NK wraparound Teacher's Book is designed to help you plan and deliver highly effective lessons easily and seamlessly.

White panel side notes provide guided lesson support and include model student responses in activities and answers to questions.

Light blue panel notes provide additional background information and optional suggestions for building and expanding on lessons.

Purple panels identify lesson objectives and assist with unit navigation.

Yellow panels identify potential homework and flipped-classroom ideas.

Red panels alert teachers to available teaching resources and point out areas where students are likely to struggle.

Warmer

Ideas to introduce students to the unit's topic help activate their prior knowledge and experience and encourage classroom discussion.

Get TH!NKing

Strategies to help teachers get the best use out of the Get **TH!NK**ing videos and activities ensure students are primed to discuss the unit topic.

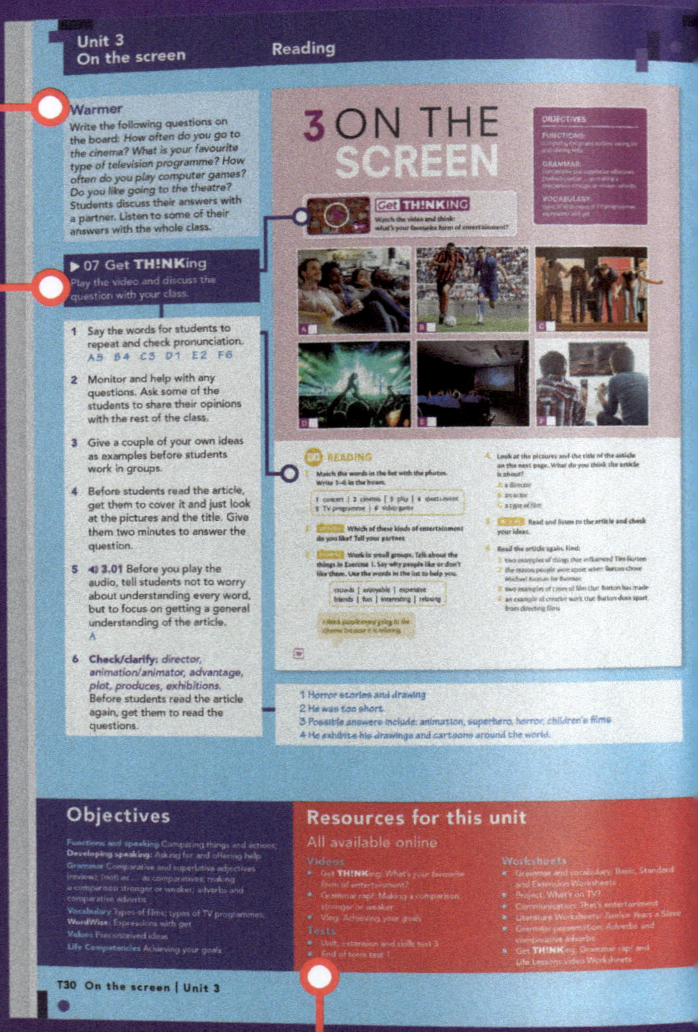

Resources for this unit

An at-a-glance listing of all the lesson support available for the unit appears in the bottom panel, including available teaching resources, video, digital support and assessment tools.

Alternative Activities

Ideas for alternative classroom activities give teachers additional flexibility and freedom to dive deeper into rich language-building opportunities.

Homework

Useful ideas for activities that students could do at home to consolidate in-class learning and encourage independent study.

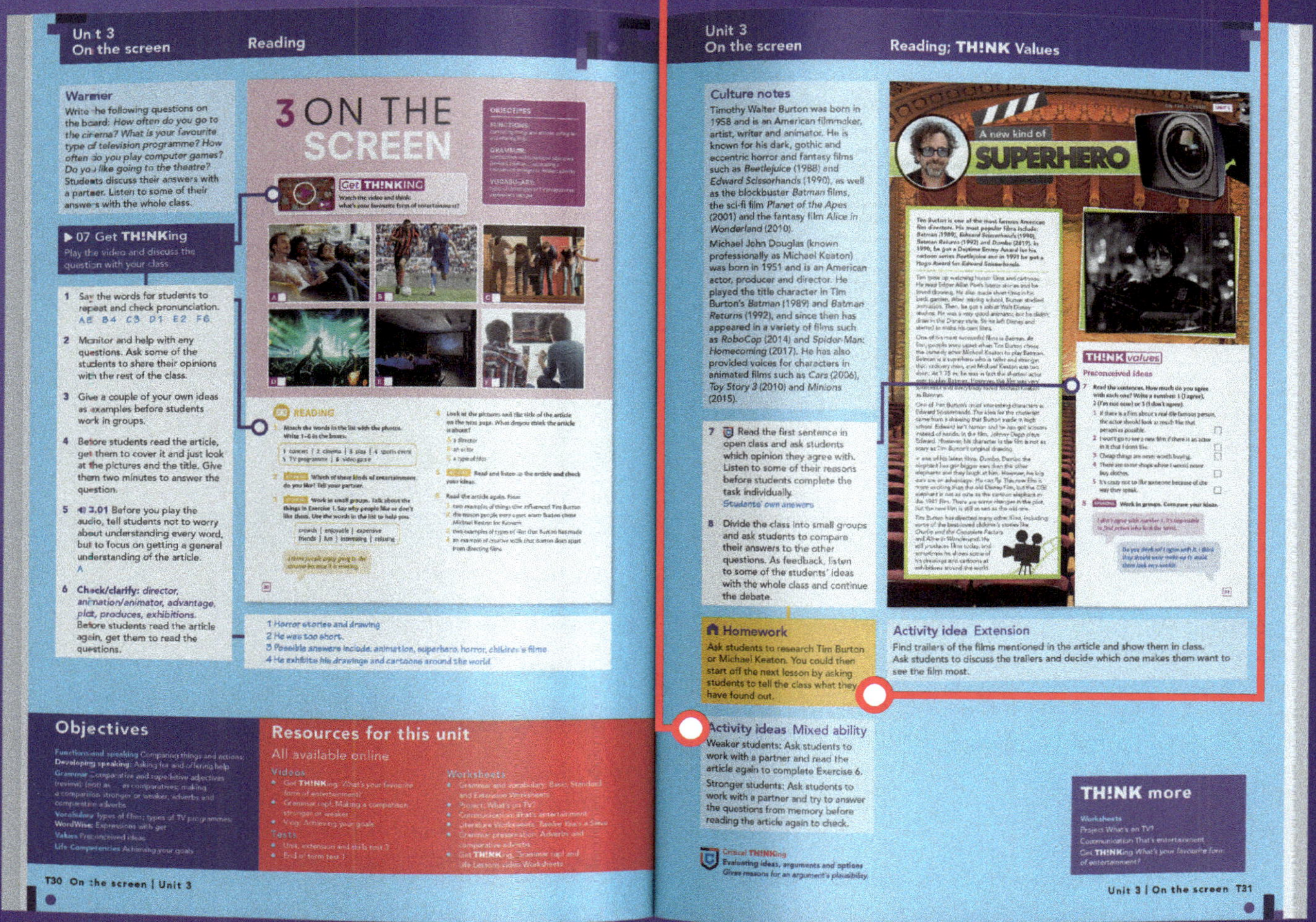
Unit 3 On the screen Reading

Warmer
Write the following questions on the board: How often do you go to the cinema? What is your favourite type of television programme? How often do you play computer games? Do you like going to the theatre? Students discuss their answers with a partner. Listen to some of their answers with the whole class.

07 Get TH!NKing
Play the video and discuss the question with your class.

1 Say the words for students to repeat and check pronunciation.
2 Monitor and help with any questions. Ask some of the students to share their opinions with the rest of the class.
3 Give a couple of your own ideas as examples before students work in groups.
4 Before students read the article, get them to cover it and just look at the pictures and the title. Give them two minutes to answer the question.
5 3.01 Before you play the audio, tell students not to worry about understanding every word, but to focus on getting a general understanding of the article.
6 Check/clarify: director, animation/animator, advantage, plot, produces, exhibitions. Before students read the article again, get them to read the questions.

3 ON THE SCREEN

Objectives

Resources for this unit
All available online

T30 On the screen | Unit 3

Unit 3 On the screen Reading; TH!NK Values

Culture notes
Timothy Walter Burton was born in 1958 and is an American filmmaker, artist, writer and animator. He is known for his dark, gothic and eccentric horror and fantasy films such as Beetlejuice (1988) and Edward Scissorhands (1990), as well as the blockbuster Batman films, the sci-fi film Planet of the Apes (2001) and the fantasy film Alice in Wonderland (2010).
Michael John Douglas (known professionally as Michael Keaton) was born in 1951 and is an American actor, producer and director. He played the title character in Tim Burton's Batman (1989) and Batman Returns (1992), and since then has appeared in a variety of films such as RoboCop (2014) and Spider-Man: Homecoming (2017). He has also provided voices for characters in animated films such as Cars (2006), Toy Story 3 (2010) and Minions (2015).

7 Read the first sentence in open class and ask students which opinion they agree with. Listen to some of their reasons before students complete the task individually.
Students' own answers
8 Divide the class into small groups and ask students to compare their answers to the other questions. As feedback, listen to some of the students' ideas with the whole class and continue the debate.

A new kind of SUPERHERO

Homework
Ask students to research Tim Burton or Michael Keaton. You could then start off the next lesson by asking students to tell the class what they have found out.

Activity idea Extension
Find trailers of the films mentioned in the article and show them in class. Ask students to discuss the trailers and decide which one makes them want to see the film most.

Activity ideas Mixed ability
Weaker students: Ask students to work with a partner and read the article again to complete Exercise 6.
Stronger students: Ask students to work with a partner and try to answer the questions from memory before reading the article again to check.

TH!NK more

Unit 3 | On the screen T31

Get it Right! and Pronunciation

These notes help alert teachers to potential problem areas for English learners and offer mitigation and/or remediation strategies and tools.

Cambridge Framework for Life Competencies

This icon identifies which Life Competency is being developed and what teachers should expect students at this level to be able to do via a Can-Do statement.

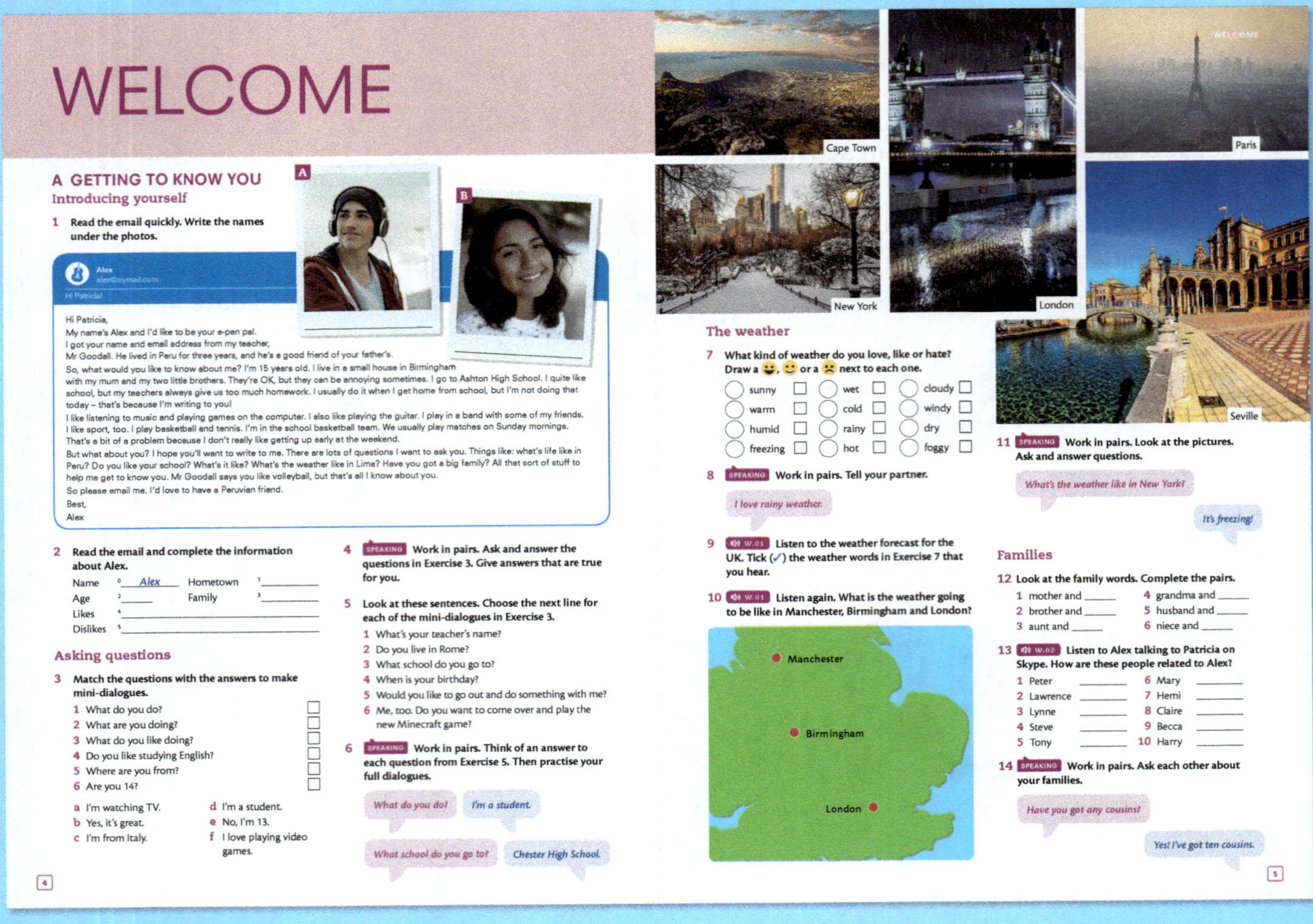

WELCOME

A GETTING TO KNOW YOU

Introducing yourself

1 Read the email quickly. Write the names under the photos.

A

B

Alex
alex@mymail.com
Hi Patricia!

Hi Patricia,
My name's Alex and I'd like to be your e-pen pal.
I got your name and email address from my teacher, Mr Goodall. He lived in Peru for three years, and he's a good friend of your father's.
So, what would you like to know about me? I'm 15 years old. I live in a small house in Birmingham with my mum and my two little brothers. They're OK, but they can be annoying sometimes. I go to Ashton High School. I quite like school, but my teachers always give us too much homework. I usually do it when I get home from school, but I'm not doing that today – that's because I'm writing to you!
I like listening to music and playing games on the computer. I also like playing the guitar. I play in a band with some of my friends. I like sport, too. I play basketball and tennis. I'm in the school basketball team. We usually play matches on Sunday mornings. That's a bit of a problem because I don't really like getting up early at the weekend.
But what about you? I hope you'll want to write to me. There are lots of questions I want to ask you. Things like: what's life like in Peru? Do you like your school? What's it like? What's the weather like in Lima? Have you got a big family? All that sort of stuff to help me get to know you. Mr Goodall says you like volleyball, but that's all I know about you.
So please email me. I'd love to have a Peruvian friend.
Best,
Alex

2 Read the email and complete the information about Alex.

Name [0] *Alex* Hometown [1] ______
Age [2] ______ Family [3] ______
Likes [4] ______
Dislikes [5] ______

Asking questions

3 Match the questions with the answers to make mini-dialogues.

1 What do you do? ☐
2 What are you doing? ☐
3 What do you like doing? ☐
4 Do you like studying English? ☐
5 Where are you from? ☐
6 Are you 14? ☐

a I'm watching TV.
b Yes, it's great.
c I'm from Italy.
d I'm a student.
e No, I'm 13.
f I love playing video games.

4 SPEAKING Work in pairs. Ask and answer the questions in Exercise 3. Give answers that are true for you.

5 Look at these sentences. Choose the next line for each of the mini-dialogues in Exercise 3.

1 What's your teacher's name?
2 Do you live in Rome?
3 What school do you go to?
4 When is your birthday?
5 Would you like to go out and do something with me?
6 Me, too. Do you want to come over and play the new Minecraft game?

6 SPEAKING Work in pairs. Think of an answer to each question from Exercise 5. Then practise your full dialogues.

What do you do? *I'm a student.*

What school do you go to? *Chester High School.*

4

Cape Town
Paris
New York
London
Seville

The weather

7 What kind of weather do you love, like or hate? Draw a 😃, 🙂 or a ☹ next to each one.

sunny ☐ wet ☐ cloudy ☐
warm ☐ cold ☐ windy ☐
humid ☐ rainy ☐ dry ☐
freezing ☐ hot ☐ foggy ☐

8 SPEAKING Work in pairs. Tell your partner.

I love rainy weather.

9 W.01 Listen to the weather forecast for the UK. Tick (✓) the weather words in Exercise 7 that you hear.

10 W.01 Listen again. What is the weather going to be like in Manchester, Birmingham and London?

Manchester
Birmingham
London

11 SPEAKING Work in pairs. Look at the pictures. Ask and answer questions.

What's the weather like in New York?

It's freezing!

Families

12 Look at the family words. Complete the pairs.

1 mother and ______ 4 grandma and ______
2 brother and ______ 5 husband and ______
3 aunt and ______ 6 niece and ______

13 W.02 Listen to Alex talking to Patricia on Skype. How are these people related to Alex?

1 Peter ______ 6 Mary ______
2 Lawrence ______ 7 Hemi ______
3 Lynne ______ 8 Claire ______
4 Steve ______ 9 Becca ______
5 Tony ______ 10 Harry ______

14 SPEAKING Work in pairs. Ask each other about your families.

Have you got any cousins?

Yes! I've got ten cousins.

5

1 A Alex B Patricia

2 1 Birmingham 2 15 3 mum, two little brothers 4 (quite like) school, (listening to) music, (playing) computer games, (playing) the guitar, (playing) sport, (basketball and tennis) 5 getting up early at the weekend

3 1 d 2 a 3 f 4 b 5 c 6 e

4 Students' own answers

5 Dialogue 1 (d) – 3 Dialogue 2 (a) – 5 Dialogue 3 (f) – 6 Dialogue 4 (b) – 1 Dialogue 5 (c) – 2 Dialogue 6 (e) – 4

6 Students' own answers

7 Students' own answers

8 Students' own answers

9 W.01
sunny ✓ wet ✓ cloudy ✓ warm ✓ cold ✓ windy ✓ humid ✓ rainy ✓ dry ✓ hot ✓

10 W.01
Manchester: cold, windy, rainy, wet
Birmingham: warm, dry, cloudy
London: hot, clear, sunny, humid

11 Students' own answers

12 1 father 2 sister 3 uncle 4 grandad 5 wife 6 nephew

13 W.02
1 brother 2 brother 3 mum 4 uncle 5 uncle 6 aunt 7 cousin 8 cousin 9 cousin 10 grandad

14 Students' own answers

TH!NK more

Workbook
A Getting to know you p4–5, Ex.1–8

B EXPERIENCES

Meeting people

1 **Put the parts of the dialogue in order. Write 1–10 in the boxes.**

- ☐ **A** Really! Where? When?
- ☐ **A** What book was it?
- ☐ **A** Did she give you one?
- 1 **A** Have you ever met a famous person?
- ☐ **A** Did you say anything to her?
- ☐ **B** It was my English course book, believe it or not. I had it with me to help me with my English.
- ☐ **B** Well, I realised that I didn't have my phone with me, so she signed a book that I was carrying.
- ☐ **B** It was last summer. We were on holiday in LA. We were walking out of a restaurant when she walked in.
- ☐ **B** Yes, I did. I asked her for a selfie.
- ☐ **B** Yes, I have. Millie Bobby Brown.

2 W.03 **Listen and check your answers.**

3 SPEAKING **Work with a partner. Practise the conversation. Change names, places and other details.**

4 **Find examples of the following tenses in Exercise 1.**

1 A past simple positive statement.
2 A past simple negative statement.
3 A past simple question.
4 A past simple short answer.
5 A past continuous statement.
6 A present perfect question with *ever*.
7 A present perfect short answer.

Irregular past participles

5 **Write the past participles of these irregular verbs.**

1 think	______	7 eat	______
2 drink	______	8 make	______
3 wear	______	9 run	______
4 see	______	10 win	______
5 lose	______	11 read	______
6 hear	______	12 ride	______

6 **Complete the questions with past participles from Exercise 5.**

0 Who's the most famous person you've ever *seen* ?
1 What's the strangest food you've ever ______ ?
2 What's the best book you've ever ______ ?
3 What's the funniest joke you've ever ______ ?
4 What's the most expensive thing you've ever ______ and never found again?
5 What's the best prize you've ever ______ ?
6 What are the most embarrassing clothes you've ever ______ ?
7 What's the longest phone call you've ever ______ ?
8 What's the longest distance you've ever ______ ?

7 **Answer the questions in Exercise 6 with your own information.**

The most famous person I've ever seen is Usain Bolt.

8 **Work in groups. Each person takes one of the questions from Exercise 6 and thinks of two questions to add.**

Who's the most famous person you've ever seen?
Where did you see him/her?
Did you say anything to him/her?

9 **Ask the other students in your group your questions.**

10 **Report back to the class.**

The most famous person Giovanni has seen is Usain Bolt. He saw him outside a shop in London. He didn't say anything to him.

Losing things

11 **Read Liam's story. What was in the wrong container?**

People often complain about airline companies losing their suitcases when they fly. It's never happened to me, but something a lot worse happened to my family recently.

About ten years ago my mum got a job teaching at a university in Thailand. At first she only went for six months, but she really liked it and agreed to stay longer, so we all went to live with her. We had a great time, but last year my parents decided that they wanted to return to the UK. Because we'd been there so long, we had loads of things we wanted to take back with us – all the furniture from our house, in fact.

So Mum and Dad went to a shipping company and arranged to take everything back in one of those big containers that you see on ships. The company packed everything into it: the armchairs and sofas, the TV, wardrobes, desks, even all the rugs and curtains. Our whole house was inside that big green metal box.

We flew back to the UK and waited for the container to arrive. About ten weeks later, we were having breakfast one morning when a big lorry arrived outside our house. On the back was a big green metal box. We were so excited. The men opened the container and started to take out our things. But they weren't our things. The container was full of gym equipment. It was the wrong one. We were so upset. But the story has a happy ending. The men took the container and gym equipment away, and about two months ago our things finally arrived.

12 **Read the story again and answer the questions. Use the word in brackets in your answer.**

1 When did Liam's mum start her job in Thailand? (ago)
2 When did the family move to Thailand? (later)
3 How long did they stay there? (about)
4 When did they decide to move back to the UK? (last)
5 How long after they got back to the UK did the first container arrive? (about)
6 When did the correct container finally arrive? (ago)

13 WRITING **Write a short story about something you lost. Use these questions to help you.**

- When did it happen?
- What was it?
- Where did you lose it?
- What did you do?
- How did you feel?
- Did you find it? If so, when and where?

Furniture

14 **Tick (✓) the items mentioned in the story.**

15 SPEAKING **Name the other items. Which of these do you think Liam's parents probably didn't put into the container?**

They probably didn't put the toilet into the container.

16 SPEAKING **Discuss in small groups.**

Your family is moving to the other side of the world. What five items from your bedroom or house do you want to take with you?

1 & 2 W.03
4, 10, 1, 8, 5, 9, 3, 7, 2, 6

3 Students' own answers

4 1 It was last summer. We were on holiday in LA. I asked her for a selfie. I realised that …… she signed a book …. It was my English course book … I had it with me … 2 I didn't have my phone … 3 Did you say anything to her? Did she give you one? What book was it? 4 Yes, I did. 5 We were walking out of a restaurant … … a book that I was carrying. 6 Have you ever met a famous person? 7 Yes, I have.

5 1 thought 2 drunk 3 worn 4 seen 5 lost 6 heard 7 eaten 8 made 9 run 10 won 11 read 12 ridden

6 1 eaten 2 read 3 heard 4 lost 5 won 6 worn 7 made 8 run / ridden

7 Students' own answers

8 Students' own answers

9 Students' own answers

10 Students' own answers

11 Gym equipment

12 1 About ten years ago 2 Six months later 3 About nine or ten years 4 Last year 5 About ten weeks 6 About two months ago

13 Students' own answers

14 desk ✓ sofa ✓ armchair ✓ curtains ✓ wardrobe ✓ rug ✓

15 Students' own answers

16 Students' own answers

THINK more

Workbook
B Experiences p5–7, Ex.1–11

Welcome
C Eating and drinking

C EATING AND DRINKING
Buying and talking about food

1 W.04 **Listen and complete each space with one word.**

Assistant Morning. Can I help you?
Customer Yes, please. Um, I want [1]______ onions.
Assistant OK, how [2]______ ?
Customer Two large ones, please. And can I have [3]______ mushrooms, too? About half a kilo?
Assistant OK, sure. Anything else?
Customer Oh, yes – tomatoes. A [4]______ of tomatoes, please. And some chillies.
Assistant Sorry, we haven't got [5]______ chillies today. Maybe try the supermarket across the street.
Customer OK, thanks.
Assistant So, [6]______ are your tomatoes. Are you making something special tonight?
Customer Yes, I'm going to make a vegetable curry. I had one in an Indian restaurant last week so I thought I'd try and make one, too.
Assistant What about lemons? Lemon juice is [7]______ good in a curry.
Customer That's a good [8]______! But I don't need any. I've [9]______ got lemons at home. So, how [10]______ is that?
Assistant Let's see. That's £4.15, [11]______.
Customer Here you are – £5.
Assistant And 85p [12]______. Thanks. Enjoy your dinner!

8

2 Complete each sentence with *some* or *any*. Then match the sentences with the pictures. Write the numbers 1–8.

1 There's ______ butter in the fridge.
2 There are ______ eggs in the kitchen.
3 There aren't ______ olives on the pizza.
4 I'd like ______ of those tomatoes, please.
5 Sorry, there aren't ______ eggs.
6 I'd like ______ water, please.
7 Oh, there isn't ______ milk.
8 No, I don't want ______ orange juice, thanks.

3 Which of these things would you always / never / sometimes use to make a sandwich? Write sentences.

butter | bread | cheese | chicken | coffee | eggs | milk | olives | onions | pears | tomatoes | yoghurt

You always use bread to make a sandwich – but you never use …

4 ROLE PLAY **Work in pairs. Use your sentences from Exercise 3 to do a role play.**

In a restaurant

5 W.05 **Read the sentences. Mark them W (waitress) or C (customer). Listen and check.**

1 Can we see the menu, please? ☐
2 Is everything OK? ☐
3 This soup is too cold! ☐
4 Can we have the bill, please? ☐
5 A table for two? This way, please. ☐
6 We'd like the soup to start. ☐
7 What soup have you got today? ☐
8 Are you ready to order? ☐

6 Complete each phrase with *much* or *many*.

1 too __________ butter
2 too __________ onions
3 too __________ things in your bag
4 too __________ milk
5 too __________ noise
6 too __________ cars

7 Complete the mini-dialogues with a phrase from Exercise 6.

1 **A** This coffee is horrible.
B I know! There's ______________________ in it.
2 **A** Ugh! I can't eat this toast.
B I know! There's ______________________ on it.
3 **A** This salad isn't very good.
B I know! There are ______________________ in it!
4 **A** This restaurant is horrible. We can't talk.
B I know! There is ______________________ here.
5 **A** It took me an hour to drive to work today.
B I know! There are ______________________ on our roads.
6 **A** I can't carry this. It's too heavy.
B There are ______________________. Take something out of it.

Shops

8 Look at the shops below. What things can you buy in each place? Think of as many things as you can.

coffee shop	☐	phone shop	☐
chemist's	☐	post office	☐
bookshop	☐	supermarket	☐
clothes shop	☐	sports shop	☐

9 W.06 **Listen. Which shop is each person in? Write the number of the dialogue next to the correct shop in Exercise 8. There are three shops you don't need.**

10 W.06 **Listen again. In which shop do you hear these sentences?**

1 You don't have to wait in a queue. ______
2 You have to wear them two or three times. ______
3 You have to fill in this form. ______
4 You don't have to pay for the third one. ______

Things you have to do

11 Read the sentences below. For each one, think of possibilities for a) who said it and b) who to.

1 *You don't have to read it.*
2 *You have to give it to me before the lesson.*
3 *I don't have to do what you say!*
4 *I have to finish this tonight.*
5 *You don't have to throw it away.*
6 *It's fantastic! You have to see it!*

12 SPEAKING **Work in pairs. Choose three of the sentences in Exercise 11. Act out a mini-dialogue for each sentence that you choose.**

This book is really boring.
Well, you don't have to read it.
I do. I have to read it for school.
Oh. When do you need to finish it by?
Tomorrow!

9

1 W.04
1 some 2 many 3 some 4 kilo 5 any 6 here 7 usually 8 idea 9 already 10 much 11 please 12 change

2 1 some, D 2 some, F 3 any, G 4 some, A 5 any, H 6 some, B 7 any, C 8 any, E

3 Students' own answers

4 Students' own answers

5 W.05
1 C 2 W 3 C 4 C 5 W 6 C 7 C 8 W

6 1 much 2 many 3 many 4 much 5 much 6 many

7 1 too much milk 2 too much butter 3 too many onions 4 too much noise 5 too many cars 6 too many things in your bag

8 Students' own answers

9 W.06
1 clothes shop 2 post office 3 bookshop 4 sports shop 5 coffee shop

10 W.06
1 coffee shop 2 sports shop 3 post office 4 bookshop

11 Students' own answers

12 Students' own answers

TH!NK more

Workbook
C Eating and drinking p7–8, Ex.1–10

Katy
katy@thinkmail.com
Party

Hi Lucy,

I was really happy to get your text saying that you're coming to visit us at the end of the month. I'm very excited, and you're going to be here at just the right time!

On the 29th our town is having its special weekend gala. There is one every year. What's a gala? Well, it's like a party but with sports and other events, too. There are lots of different activities. We're going to join in, so I hope you're ready for some fun!

It all starts on Saturday. There's an opening ceremony in the morning, and after lunch, there are things for kids – like races and games. And at five o'clock there's a football match – we're playing against a team from another town. Then in the evening, there's dancing in the town square. A famous DJ is playing the music! (I can't say who yet – it's secret!)

On Sunday morning there's a charity run – it's about five kilometres. It starts at the town hall and goes past the school and down the High Street to the park, where it finishes. And guess what? I'm running in the race! (Would you like to run, too? I think we can get you in – let me know ASAP, OK?) And on Sunday afternoon, there's a big street party with games and food. It's going to be great. The only problem is the weather forecast says it's going to rain, so I'm going to wear my raincoat.

We're looking forward to seeing you here. Oh, I almost forgot! On Sunday evening we're having a party at our place for my dad's 50th birthday! We're going to make it a really special party. Please say you don't have to leave on Sunday evening!

Anyway, let me know more about your plans. When are you arriving on Friday?

See you soon,

Katy

D LOOKING AHEAD

Plans and arrangements

1 **Read the email. Match the times and the events.**

1 Saturday morning ☐
2 Saturday afternoon ☐
3 Saturday evening ☐
4 Sunday morning ☐
5 Sunday afternoon ☐
6 Sunday evening ☐

a sports events
b party for Katy's dad
c opening ceremony
d dancing
e charity run
f street party

2 **Read the sentences. What do the underlined verbs express? Write A (arrangement) or I (intention).**

1 A famous DJ <u>is playing</u> the music. ☐
2 <u>I'm running</u> in the race. ☐
3 We<u>'re going to join in</u>. ☐
4 <u>I'm going to wear</u> my raincoat. ☐
5 We<u>'re going to make</u> it a really special party. ☐
6 We<u>'re having</u> a party at our place. ☐

3 **Find other examples of the present continuous for arrangements in Katy's email.**

4 SPEAKING **Work in pairs. Ask and answer questions about plans you have for next weekend.**

What are you doing on Saturday morning?

I'm going running. / I'm not doing anything.

Sports and sport verbs

5 **Complete the table with the sports in the list.**

athletics | football | gymnastics | karate
rock climbing | running | skiing | tennis

play	do	go

6 SPEAKING **Work in pairs. Which sports do you often / sometimes / never do? Talk to your partner.**

I often go running, but I never do karate.

10

WELCOME

Travel plans

7 W.07 **Put the parts of the dialogue in order. Then listen and check your answers.**

☐ A Great idea. OK, see you soon. We're going to have a lot of fun this weekend!
☐ A Ah, OK. 3.15 is difficult for me. Is it OK if I don't meet you at the station?
☐ A Hey, Connor. What time are you arriving on Saturday?
☐ A Well, sometimes the train's late. If it's late, I'll meet you.
☐ B OK. As soon as the train leaves Liverpool, I'll send you a text message.
☐ B 3.15 – I'm going to catch the two o'clock train from Liverpool.
☐ B I know. It's going to be great!
☐ B Of course. I can walk. No problem.

8 **Complete the sentences with the correct form of the verbs in brackets.**

1 If I ______ (miss) the bus, I ______ (catch) the next one.
2 If the bus ______ (arrive) late, I ______ (take) a taxi.
3 If there ______ (not be) any taxis, I ______ (walk) to your place.
4 I'll send you a text message when I ______ (get) to the station.
5 As soon as I ______ (get) to your place, we ______ (start) having a good time.
6 If we ______ (not have) a good time, I ______ (not visit) you again!

9 **Ellie travelled a lot last year. Complete the sentences with the past simple of the verbs in the list.**

catch | drive | fly | miss | ride | ~~take~~

0 She *took* a taxi in Paris.

1 She ______ the train in Vienna.

2 She ______ to Madrid.

3 She ______ the train in Berlin.

4 She ______ to Rome.

5 She ______ a bike in Athens.

10 **Complete the sentences with *be going to* and the verbs in the list.**

buy | get up | not visit | take | try | visit

1 We don't like flying so we ______________ a boat.
2 I want to go to Dublin. I ______________ my ticket online.
3 My train leaves at 5.00, so I ______________ very early tomorrow.
4 We'll only be in Madrid for one day, so we ______________ any museums.
5 When we're in Birmingham, we ______________ my cousins.
6 We love Italian food, so we ______________ all the best restaurants in Rome!

11 **Imagine you can go on a holiday to wherever you want, any time you want. Make notes about your plans:**

- where you're going to go
- where you're going to stay
- how long your holiday is going to be
- what you're going to do
- who you're going to go with
- what you're going to eat
- what time of year you're going to go

12 SPEAKING **Work in pairs. Ask and answer about the holiday you planned in Exercise 11.**

Where are you going to go on holiday?

Thailand. And I'm going to stay in a hotel on the beach.

11

1 1 c 2 a 3 d 4 e 5 f 6 b

2 1 A 2 A 3 I 4 I 5 I 6 A

3 … you're coming to visit us at the end of the month …
… our town is having its special weekend gala.
… we're playing against a team from another …
When are you arriving on Friday?

4 Students' own answers

5 play: football, tennis
do: athletics, gymnastics, karate
go: running, rock climbing, skiing

6 Students' own answers

7 W.07
3, 6, 2, 8, 4, 5, 1, 7

8 1 miss, 'll catch 2 arrives, 'll take 3 aren't, 'll walk 4 get
5 get, 'll start 6 don't have, won't visit

9 1 caught 2 drove 3 missed 4 flew 5 rode

10 1 're going to take 2 'm going to buy 3 'm going to get up
4 're not going to visit 5 're going to visit 6 're going to try

11 Students' own answers

12 Students' own answers

TH!NK more

Workbook
D Looking ahead p8–9, Ex.1–9

Warmer

Ask students to write three adjectives to describe their own personality. Read some out to the class (e.g. *This person is cool, friendly and intelligent*). The class guess which student wrote the adjectives.

▶ 01 Get TH!NKing

Play the video and discuss the question with your class.

1 Before students do the task, get them to cover Exercise 1 and just look at the photos. Give students two minutes to think about adjectives to describe the people in the photos. Bring the class together and compare their ideas with the words in the box. Check pronunciation and ask: *Which words can be negative?* (boring, serious).
Students' own answers

2 At the end of the exercise, listen to some of the students' ideas and encourage open class discussion.

3 Describe a famous person and ask students to guess who it is. Encourage students to do the same for people they know.

4 Give students two minutes to read the responses and write the names. Encourage them not to focus on every word for now.
1 Renata 2 Mr Ronay
3 Deming 4 Anna

5 🔊 **1.01 Check/clarify:** *marathon, operation, wheelchair.*
Give students time to read the responses and answer the questions. Encourage them to justify their answers.
1 T 2 F 3 T 4 F 5 T 6 T
7 T 8 F

1 INCREDIBLE PEOPLE

OBJECTIVES

FUNCTIONS: talking about things you have and haven't done; offering encouragement

GRAMMAR: present perfect with *just*, *already* and *yet*; present perfect vs. past simple

VOCABULARY: personality adjectives; collocations; phrases with *just*

Get TH!NKING Watch the video and think: what makes people incredible?

READING

1 **Look at the photos. What is your first impression of these people? What adjectives could you use to describe them?**

boring | caring | confident | cool | easy-going | friendly | funny | happy | intelligent | serious

2 SPEAKING **Discuss the photos in pairs.**

He seems friendly.

She looks like a happy person because she's smiling.

3 SPEAKING **Use the adjectives in Exercise 1 and other adjectives to describe people you know.**

My brother is very easy-going.

He doesn't get angry very often.

4 **Quickly read the responses to the survey question on the next page. Who do the respondents admire?**

5 🔊 1.01 **Read and listen to the responses again. Mark the sentences T (true) or F (false).**

1 Renata's got a daughter. ____
2 Renata works as a sports trainer. ____
3 Mr Ronay helps children to learn the piano. ____
4 Mr Ronay plays concerts all over the world. ____
5 Deming has never had lessons in painting. ____
6 Deming is very good at drawing pictures. ____
7 Anna's got a problem with her heart. ____
8 Anna never goes to school. ____

6 SPEAKING **Work with a partner. Correct the false sentences in Exercise 5.**

12

6 2 Renata works as a teacher.
4 Mr Ronay played concerts all over the world (when he was younger).
8 Anna goes to school when she can.

Objectives

Functions and speaking Talking about things you have and haven't done; **Developing speaking:** Offering encouragement
Grammar Present perfect with *just*, *already* and *yet*; present perfect vs. past simple
Vocabulary Personality adjectives; collocations; **WordWise:** Phrases with *just*
Values Human qualities
Life Competencies Recognising others' good work

Resources for this unit

All available online

Videos
- Get **TH!NK**ing: *What makes people incredible?*
- Grammar rap!: Present perfect vs. past simple
- Vlog: Recognising others' good work

Tests
- Unit, extension and skills tests 1

Worksheets
- Grammar and vocabulary: Basic, Standard and Extension Worksheets
- Project: Amazing characters
- Communication: Amazing people
- Literature Worksheets: *The Mill on the Floss*
- Grammar presentation: Present perfect vs. past simple
- Get **TH!NK**ing, Grammar rap! and Life Lessons video Worksheets

7 Ask students to try to write the words from memory first, before referring back to the texts to check.

1 cheerful 2 laid-back 3 creative 4 positive 5 talented 6 brave 7 charming

8 Go through the first sentence as a class, asking students to explain why the correct answer is *cheerful*. With stronger classes, you could ask them to complete the gaps from memory before referring back to Exercise 7.

1 brave 2 charming 3 laid-back 4 talented 5 creative 6 active 7 positive

9 Give your own example before students do the task. Encourage them to give reasons for their choice of adjectives.

10 In pairs, students describe the person they admire. Monitor and help as they complete the task.

Homework

Ask students to find a photo of a person they admire and upload the picture. You might like to give them some ideas, e.g., a Paralympian from your country, someone who has overcome adversity. Ask students to research this person. They can use the internet to find out more. Ask students to make a poster that shows their person and to write a short text about why they admire them or why they are admirable. As a follow-up, students can bring the poster to the next class, present it to the class and discuss who is the most admirable.

Activity idea Fast finishers

Ask students to close their books and write down as many of the personality adjectives as they can remember. Students open their books to check answers and spelling.

WHO DO YOU ADMIRE MOST?

1 My cousin Renata is an amazing person. She's 26 and she's got a little girl, Bruna, aged four. Her husband died three years ago, so she is bringing Bruna up on her own. Renata lives in São Paulo, where she works as a teacher. It's hard work, but she's always happy and smiling. Renata's a keen athlete, too – she's a very good runner and she trains a lot. She's already run two half-marathons, but she hasn't won a race yet. She hopes to run a marathon one day. Her life isn't easy, but she always stays **positive** about everything.

Juliana, 17

2 There's an elderly man who lives near us called Mr Ronay. He's very **charming** and I think he's just incredible. He's 85 and he has difficulty walking now, but that doesn't stop him being **active** and doing the thing he loves most: playing the piano. He has always been a very **talented** performer. When he was younger, he played concerts all over the world, but he can't do that any more. Now, he teaches the piano. He gives lessons at home, and he's just started to give free lessons to neighbourhood kids.

Urgun, 16

3 There's a boy at my school called Deming. He's 15 years old and he can be quiet and shy, but he's very interesting when you talk to him. He's also a wonderful artist with an amazing memory – he looks at a building for just a few minutes, then goes away and paints it exactly as it is in real life. He also paints things from his imagination. He's very **creative**. He has never studied art; he just knows how to draw and paint. He's already sold a lot of paintings, and he's just won a place at an art school in Beijing. But he's very **laid-back** about the success he's had.

Li Ju, 16

4 My best friend's sister, Anna, is amazing. She's 13 and she was born with a serious heart problem. She's already had about ten operations, but she is incredibly **brave**. She knows that there will be more operations, but she doesn't complain and always seems so **cheerful**. The problem makes her very weak, so she spends a lot of time in bed or in a wheelchair. But she goes to school when she can, and when she can't go to school, she studies in hospital or at home. She's just had another operation, but she's also just passed all her exams!

Luigi, 15

VOCABULARY
Personality adjectives

7 There are eight words in bold in the texts. Match the words with these meanings. Write the words.

0 is always doing things *active*
1 is usually happy ______
2 is very easy-going ______
3 has very original ideas ______
4 looks for the good in all situations ______
5 is very good at doing something ______
6 doesn't get scared easily ______
7 is very easy to like ______

8 Complete the sentences with the words from Exercise 7.

0 Why are you so *cheerful* today? Have you had some good news?
1 He stood up in the front of the whole school and read out his poem. He was really ______ .
2 She's very ______ and it's easy to see why she's got so many friends.
3 He's so ______ that some people think he's a bit lazy.
4 Have you seen him doing ballet? He really is a ______ dancer.
5 If you want to work in advertising, you need to be ______ and come up with really good ideas.
6 My dad is really ______ around the house. He's always cooking or fixing things or working in the garden.
7 He's had a really difficult life but he's really ______ about the future.

TH!NK values
Human qualities

9 Think about someone who is not famous but who you think is special.

a Think of three adjectives to describe them.
b Think about why you chose these adjectives. Make notes.

10 SPEAKING Tell your partner about the person you admire.

I really admire my sister. She's really confident in difficult situations.

TH!NK more

Worksheets
Project Amazing characters
Communication Amazing people
Get TH!NKing *What makes people incredible?*

Practice Extra
Vocabulary: Personality adjectives

Workbook
Vocabulary p12, Ex.1–3
Vocabulary Extra p13, Ex.1–2

Worksheets
Vocabulary Worksheets 1

Emotional Development
Empathy and relationship skills
Shows understanding of other people's perspectives and feelings.

Warmer

In pairs, ask students to imagine they are planning a birthday party for the weekend. Ask: *What things do you need to organise?* Set a three-minute time limit and ask them to make notes.

1 Students complete the example sentences and rules. Check understanding by asking: *Which word means a short time before now?* (*just*); *Which word means before now?* (*already*); *Which word do we use when something hasn't happened?* (*yet*).
1 already, yet 2 just
RULE: 3 yet 4 just 5 already

2 Students match the pictures with the sentences. Ask students to explain the reason for their choices.
A 2 B 3 C 1

3 Students work individually and write sentences with *already* and *yet*. Monitor to make sure students are writing complete sentences.
2 He's already sent out invitations.
3 He hasn't organised the music yet.
4 He's already chosen what to wear.
5 He hasn't decorated the room yet.
6 He's already bought the drinks.

4 Students' own answers

5 **Check/clarify:** *start a vlog, abroad, enter a competition.* Write *bucket list* on the board and ask students to guess what it means (a list of things somebody wants to do before they die). In pairs, ask students to discuss what they would put on their own bucket list.
Ask students to complete the exercise.

GRAMMAR
Present perfect with *just, already* and *yet*

1 **Complete the sentences with *just, already* and *yet*. Then complete the rules.**
1 She's ______ run two half-marathons but she hasn't won a race ______.
2 She's ______ had another operation.

RULE: In the present perfect, we often use
- [1]______ in negative sentences and questions to talk about something that hasn't happened but that we expect to happen soon. It comes at the end of the sentence.
- [4]______ to emphasise that something happened very recently. It goes before the past participle.
- [5]______ to show that something has been done or finished sooner than expected. It usually goes before the past participle.

2 **Match the pictures and the sentences. Write 1–3 in the boxes.**
1 He's just woken up.
2 He's already got out of bed.
3 He hasn't woken up yet.

A

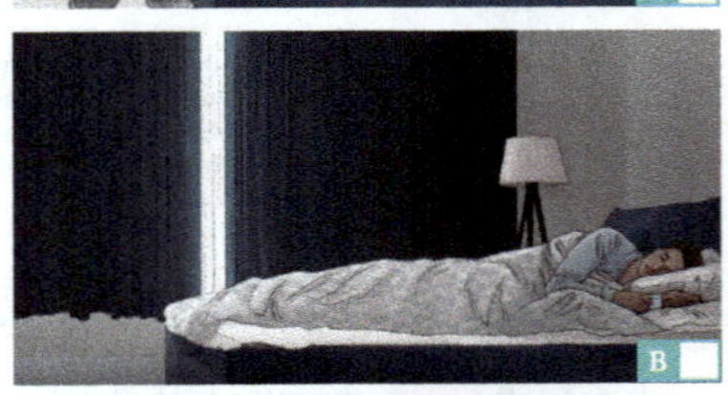
B

C

3 **Look at Jack's list of things to do for his party. Write sentences with *already* and *yet*.**

1 *He hasn't made the cake yet.*

4 **Use your imagination to answer the questions. Use the present perfect and *just* in each one.**
0 Why is Mum so angry?
Because Dad's just crashed her car.
1 Why is Jacob so sad?
2 Why is your face so dirty?
3 Why is Liam so scared?
4 Why is Dana so excited?
5 Why are you smiling?

5 **Tick (✓) the things you have already done.**

EIGHT THINGS TO DO BEFORE YOU'RE 20:
- ☐ start a vlog
- ☐ meet a famous person
- ☐ travel abroad
- ☐ write a song
- ☐ act on stage
- ☐ learn to play a musical instrument
- ☐ enter a competition
- ☐ climb a mountain

6 SPEAKING **Work in pairs. Ask each other questions.**

Have you started a vlog yet?
Yes, I've already done that. Have you?
No, I haven't done that yet.

→ workbook page 10

6 Focus on the sample dialogue and pay attention to pronunciation. Students should use a rising intonation for the first question, with a strong stress on *you* at the end of the second question. Divide the class into pairs or small groups to complete the exercise. Monitor and help with any questions. Listen to some examples in open class.

Workbook p10

Language note Present perfect with *just, already* and *yet*

Students may make the following types of error:
I just see my friend. I already have seen that film. I didn't go to Paris yet.
Remind them that we use the present perfect as follows:
have + *just/already* + past participle
have + *not* + past participle + *yet*

TH!NK more

Workbook
Grammar p10, Ex.1–3

Worksheets
Grammar Worksheets 1

7 1.02 **Check/clarify:** *your turn.* Before students listen, explain that they will hear Jack, Sarah and Ella playing a game.
1 never 2 what it is 3 both of you 4 a point 5 one of you 6 don't get 7 your turn

8 1.03
Jack: 0 Sarah: 0 Ella: 2

9 1.03
1 C 2 B 3 C 4 B

10 1 If the other people have done the things you say you haven't, then you get a point.
2 When she went to Italy.
3 Because they had spring rolls for lunch and she didn't know that they weren't Japanese.
4 She says she's bored. Students' own answers.

11 You may want to give an experience of your own as an example. Allow students six to eight minutes to play the game. Monitor to make sure all students are on task.

12 Write on the board: *I have just passed my driving test. There were just 12 people at the concert. The film was just brilliant.* Ask students to try to explain the different meanings of *just* in the three sentences (*a short time ago; only; really*).
1 b 2 a 3 c

13 1 a 2 b 3 c 4 a 5 b

14 1 c 2 a 3 b

Workbook p12

Homework

Ask students to write their own 'bucket list'. Include *Things I have already done* and *Things I haven't done yet*. As a follow-up, students can share their lists in the next class.

LISTENING

7 1.02 **Listen to three people: Jack, Sarah and Ella. They're going to play a game called *I've Never*. Complete the rules they describe.**

Ella It's a game called *I've Never*. So, I think of something that I've [1] ___ done but I think both of you have done.
Jack Right.
Ella Then I say [2] ___. And you say if you've ever done the thing or not. If [3] ___ say 'Yes, I've done that,' then I get [4] ___ and another turn. But if [5] ___ says 'No, I've never done that,' then I [6] ___ a point and it's [7] ___.

8 1.03 **Listen to the rest of the conversation and the game. How many points does each person get?**

9 1.03 **Listen again and choose the correct answer A, B or C.**

1 How did Ella's family travel to Spain?

2 What has Ella never worn?

3 What kind of food has Ella never eaten?

4 Who loses a turn of *I've Never* first?

Ella Jack Sarah

10 **Work in pairs. Answer the questions.**
1 How do you win a point in the game?
2 When did Sarah travel by plane?
3 Why does Sarah think Ella has eaten Japanese food?
4 Why does Ella say she wants to stop playing the game? Do you think this is the real reason she wants to stop playing?

SPEAKING

11 **Work in small groups. Play *I've Never*.**

OK, I've never travelled outside my country. And you?

I have / I haven't.

WordWise: Phrases with *just*

12 **Look at the sentences from the unit so far. Choose the correct meaning of *just* in each one.**
1 She's just had another operation. ☐
2 He looks at a building for just a few minutes, then goes away and paints it exactly as it is. ☐
3 I think he's just incredible. ☐

a only
b a short time ago
c really

13 **What does *just* mean in these sentences? Write a, b or c.**
1 Don't be angry. It's just a joke. ☐
2 I've just seen a fantastic film. ☐
3 It's cold today. The weather is just awful. ☐
4 No food, thanks – just a drink. ☐
5 She's just had some bad news. ☐

14 **Match the questions and answers.**
1 How many scoops of ice cream would you like? ☐
2 When did Paula get here? ☐
3 What do you think of Ariana Grande? ☐

a She's just arrived.
b She's just great.
c Just one, please.

→ workbook page 12

Activity idea Extension

In pairs, students write ten questions with *Have you ever …?*, then swap partners and ask and answer each other's questions. They can then compare answers with their original partner.

TH!NK more

Workbook
Listening p16, Ex.1–3
WordWise p12, Ex.5–6

Warmer

Give students two minutes in pairs to write down as many animals as possible. Go through the alphabet, asking students to offer animals beginning with each letter.

1 Ask students to look at the photo. Elicit what animal it is (a mole) and any adjectives to describe it.

2 Students' own answers

3 Before students read the task, get them to cover the article and just look at the title. Ask: *What do you think the article is about?*

Give students two minutes to read the article and write the answers. Encourage them not to focus on every word for now.

1 1985 2 Mexico, Nepal, Haiti, the Philippines, the United States, Indonesia 3 None of them

4 🔊 **1.04 Check/clarify:** *mole, tunnel, earthquake, buried, volunteer, tsunami, psychologist.* Before students read and listen to the article again, get them to read the questions.

1 in Mexico / Mexico City

2 In 2001, after the attack on the World Trade Center

3 It was the most difficult work they had ever done

4 They only go when local governments and rescue groups cannot manage alone.

5 They offer courses for people who want to become rescue workers.

READING

1 SPEAKING What animal is this? How would you describe it? What special characteristics does it have? Discuss with a partner.

2 SPEAKING Work in pairs. Look at the photos and discuss the questions.

1 What do you think has happened?
2 What are the people doing?
3 How do you think they are similar to a mole?

3 Read the article quickly. Name …

1 the year Los Topos began: ______
2 three countries where they have worked: ______
3 how many of Los Topos have died: ______

4 🔊 1.04 Read and listen to the article again and answer the questions.

1 Where did Los Topos begin?
2 When did Los Topos first work in the US?
3 What did they say about their work in Indonesia?
4 Why don't they go to every disaster?
5 What kind of training do Los Topos offer?

HUMAN MOLES

Moles are small animals that live underground and dig tunnels, looking for food. Sometimes humans also need to be like moles, but for a different reason – to save lives.

In 1985, there was a powerful earthquake in Mexico City. As often happens in earthquakes, many people were buried under fallen buildings and needed help. However, there weren't enough people to go and help them. So a group of young people decided to form a volunteer group. They started to dig into the rubble to try to find people and get them out. The group, who called themselves *Los Topos* ('the moles' in Spanish), quickly became well known for their bravery, and they started to travel to help at disaster zones in other places.

Since 1985 Los Topos have helped in places all around the world. At first they only worked in Mexico, but over the years they have been to Nepal, Haiti and the Philippines. In 2001, after the attack on the World Trade Center in New York, they came to the United States for the first time. And they went to Banda Aceh, Indonesia, in 2004, after the terrible tsunami that killed tens of thousands of people. They say that this was the most difficult work they have ever done. In 2017, they helped in Mexico City again, after another serious earthquake. Altogether, they have been to more than twenty countries.

The group has also grown – people in the group come and go, but on average it has about 40 members. It is very professional and includes doctors and other specialists, such as psychologists and engineers, but they are not paid for their work. They go to disaster areas when local governments and rescue groups cannot manage alone, and they also offer courses for people who want to become rescue workers. Los Topos members themselves pay most of what they need to travel to disaster zones – when they get there, they eat whatever they can and sleep wherever they can.

So far, not one member of Los Topos has lost their life – let's hope that this continues.

16

Culture note

Mexico City is the capital of Mexico and the most populous city in North America with approximately 8.9 million people in 2009. It is the oldest capital city in the Americas and was founded by the Aztecs in 1325. The historic centre is a UNESCO World Heritage Site. It is the largest Spanish-speaking city in the world. The city is approximately 2,240 metres above sea level and surrounded by mountains and volcanoes that reach over 5,000 metres. The area suffers from a lot of earthquakes.

TH!NK more

Workbook
Reading p14, Ex.1–3

▶ 02 Grammar rap! Present perfect vs. past simple

5 Ask students to try to answer the questions from memory before referring back to page 16 to check.
1 and 3.
RULE: 5 past simple
6 present perfect

6 During feedback, elicit the difference in meaning between the pairs.
1 a has, won; b won 2 a has met; b met 3 a recorded; b have recorded 4 a lived; b have lived 5 a has, signed; b signed

Workbook p11

Get it Right!
Present perfect vs. past simple
Student's Book p122

7 Do the first question in open class as an example and to introduce the concept of collocation (you can make a mistake or an appearance, but you can't make homework). Remind students that there are two correct answers.
1 b, c 2 a, c 3 b, c 4 a, c
5 a, c 6 a, b

8 Focus on the six words and ask students which words could collocate with them. Remind them that there may be more than one answer.
The verb *have* can go before all of them.

9 Ask students to decide which questions they need to ask to get the information. They should think of a *Have you ever …?* question and a 'details' question for each.

Workbook p12

10 Get students to make notes before they begin to write.

Homework
Ask students to write a short paragraph describing one of their experiences.

GRAMMAR
Present perfect vs. past simple

5 Look at the article on page 16 again. Which of the following events do we know happened at a specific point in time? Then complete the rules.
1 Los Topos formed?
2 Los Topos went to Nepal, Haiti and the Philippines?
3 Los Topos went to Banda Aceh?
4 Los Topos grew into a bigger organisation?

RULE: When we talk about a specific point in time in the past, we use the [5] __________.
When we don't refer to a specific point in time, we often use the [6] __________.

6 Complete the pairs of sentences. Use the past simple and the present perfect form of the verbs.
0 visit
a I _have visited_ Greece more than 20 times.
b I first _visited_ Greece in 1998.
1 win
a He __________ already __________ three gold medals, and he hopes to win more.
b He __________ a gold medal in the 2020 Olympics.
2 meet
a My mum __________ a lot of interesting people.
b My mum __________ Prince Harry ten years ago.
3 record
a They __________ their last album two years ago.
b They __________ more than 20 albums so far.
4 live
a We __________ in Samoa when I was young.
b We're living in Austria now, but we __________ in many different countries.
5 sign
a She __________ just __________ a contract with a new e-publishing company.
b She __________ the contract for her first book on her 21st birthday.

→ workbook page 11

VOCABULARY
Collocations

7 For each collocation, choose the two correct answers.
1 Which of these can you make?
a homework b a mistake c an appearance
2 Which of these things can you do?
a your best b a good time c work
3 Which of these things can you get?
a a bad day b a job c a reputation
4 Which of these things can you lose?
a a race b an idea c your life
5 Which of these can you take?
a a risk b a house c a photograph
6 Which of these can you form?
a a group b an opinion c a lesson

8 What verbs can go before the six words you didn't choose in Exercise 7? Think of at least one verb for each word.

9 SPEAKING Talk to other people in the class. Ask and answer questions and complete the table.

Have you ever … ? What happened?
Who did you ask?
What was the risk?
What did you lose?

Find someone who has …	Who?	Details
made a big mistake.		
done some chores at home this week.		
got a job.		
lost something important.		
taken a big risk.		
formed a group.		

→ workbook page 12

WRITING
Someone you admire

10 Write a short passage about someone you have admired for some time. Include:
- how long you have known (about) them.
- what you admire about them.

Activity idea Fast finishers
If any students finish the activity early, ask them to turn to page 128 in their Workbooks and test themselves on the past simple and past participle of irregular verbs.

TH!NK more

Practice Extra
Unit 1 Practise it!

Workbook
Grammar p11, Ex.4–6
Vocabulary p12, Ex.4
Developing Writing p15

Worksheets
Grammar Worksheets 1
Grammar presentation: Present perfect vs. past simple
Grammar rap! Present perfect vs. past simple

Warmer

Revise collocations by giving students a noun and eliciting a verb which collocates with it, e.g., *mistake – make a mistake.*

1 🔊 **1.05** Tell students to cover the dialogue and discuss the question in pairs before listening to check their answers.
They're talking about doing something for their music teacher who is leaving the school next month.

2 Have students underline the answers in the dialogue.
1 He's leaving the school.
2 Because he's a good teacher and his lessons are fun.
3 She doesn't think a concert is a good idea because none of them are good singers or musicians.
4 She likes his idea of making a recording.

3 *Students' own answers*

4 Write the sentences on the board. Ask students for an L1 translation before they complete the conversations in English.
1 I don't think so 2 Are you sure / You know what 3 that sort of thing 4 Let's face it 5 Are you sure 6 and that's that

5 *1 I'll help you if you want.*
2 That's a great idea.
3 You've got to make it happen.
4 You should definitely do it.

6 Allow students six to eight minutes to prepare their dialogues. Monitor to make sure all students are on task. Encourage them to use the key language.

DEVELOPING SPEAKING

1 🔊 1.05 **Look at the photos. What do you think the connection is between them? Listen and read to check.**

Mike: You know our music teacher, Mr Grimes? He's leaving our school next month.
Emma: Are you sure? I haven't heard anything.
Mike: Yes, I'm sure. Steve said so. Mr Grimes told his class in yesterday's lesson.
Emma: That's a shame. He's a good teacher. His lessons are fun – jokes, games, smiles, that sort of thing.
Mike: I know. He's one of the best. But he's leaving, and that's that. Still, I was thinking – maybe we could do something to thank him. He's taught us such a lot. It would be nice to say thank you.
Emma: That's a good idea. What kind of thing?
Mike: Well, maybe a little concert? We could play or sing something for him.
Emma: No, I don't think so, Mike. A concert is too much. Let's face it, none of us are really good singers or musicians.
Mike: I know. But I want to do something.
Emma: Oh, you'll think of something. You always do!
Mike: Well, here's another idea. We could each make a recording – well, those who want to – and say something that we remember from his lessons. Then we could choose a bit of music …
Emma: … that he told us about! Yes! Mike, that's great. You've got to make it happen.
Mike: Well, I'll start by talking to the others, and find out what they think.
Emma: I'll help you if I can. You know what? I think everyone's going to love this, Mike. Really. Well done.

2 Read the dialogue again and answer the questions.
1 What is the news about Mr Grimes?
2 Why does Mike think it would be nice to say thank you to him?
3 What does Emma think of Mike's first idea?
4 What does Emma think of Mike's second idea?

3 SPEAKING **Discuss the questions in pairs.**
1 Is Mike right to want to say thank you to the teacher?
2 Do you think the recording is a better idea than the concert? Why or why not?

Phrases for fluency

4 Find the underlined expressions in the dialogue and use them to complete the conversations.

1 A That new girl, Sally – she likes you!
B No, [1] ______________.
A [2] ______________ ? I have a feeling she likes you a lot.
B No. She never smiles at me. And she criticises me a lot, doesn't laugh at my jokes, [3] ______________.

2 A Oh, you got it wrong again!
B I know. [4] ______________, I'm no good at computer games.
A [5] ______________ ? We just need a rest. Let's go and watch some TV.
B OK, but I don't want to play this game again, OK? I'm useless at it, [6] ______________!

FUNCTIONS
Offering encouragement

KEY LANGUAGE
That's a great idea. You've got to make it happen.
You should definitely do it. I'll help you if you want.

5 Complete the mini-dialogues using the sentences from the Key Language box.

1 **Jake** I'm not sure I can do this homework on my own.
Paula ______________
2 **Carmen** Do you think Steve would like to have a party for his birthday?
Adrian Yes, I do. ______________
3 **Millie** I've got an idea to get money for the school. I'd like to put on a play.
Javier Oh, yes, brilliant! ______________
4 **Seb** You know I'm learning the guitar? Do you think I should enter the talent show?
Harry Yes! ______________

6 In pairs, write a new short dialogue, using the sentences from the Key Language box. Choose one of these ideas or your own idea.
- a surprise party for your mum
- an outing with your friends
- a present for someone in hospital

7 SPEAKING **Act out your dialogue from Exercise 6.**

PRONUNCIATION
Intonation and sentence stress Go to page 120.

18

7 If students have access to a recording facility (using their mobile phones, for example), they could record their conversation and play it back to check their own pronunciation and intonation. They can then repeat the exercise and listen for improvements.

Pronunciation
Intonation and sentence stress

Student's Book p120

Activity idea Disappearing sentences

Write the dialogue on the board. Put students in A/B pairs and get them to practise the conversation. Cover a small section of the dialogue, beginning from the right-hand side of the board. Students practise the dialogue again, including the part which is covered.

Students try to remember the part they can no longer see. Repeat the activity again and again, covering more and more of the dialogue each time. Continue until all the dialogue is covered and students are practising it from memory.

TH!NK more

Workbook
Pronunciation p118

Warmer

Write *recognising others' good work* on the board and elicit what it might mean. Encourage students to clarify its meaning through examples or explanation, rather than a translation. Ask students to read the introductory paragraph to check their ideas. Elicit examples of people recognising others' good work in Unit 1.

▶ 03 Life Lessons: Recognising others' good work

1 ▶ 03
Thank you

2 ▶ 03
1 c 2 d 3 a 4 b

3 **Check/clarify:** *litter, award.*
Give students one minute to read the poster and find the answer. Encourage them not to focus on every word.
It wants to give a special award to a community hero.

4 **Check/clarify:** *encouragement, lollipop lady.*
Julia: Her uncle – He does everything at football practice.
Milo: Mrs Wilkins – She has helped children cross the road for a very long time.

5 You may like to give your own example to get students started on this.

6 Monitor to help with any difficulties, but do not interrupt as this is a fluency activity.

Homework

Ask students to interview a family member about their own local hero. As a follow-up, students can present this hero to the class in the next lesson.

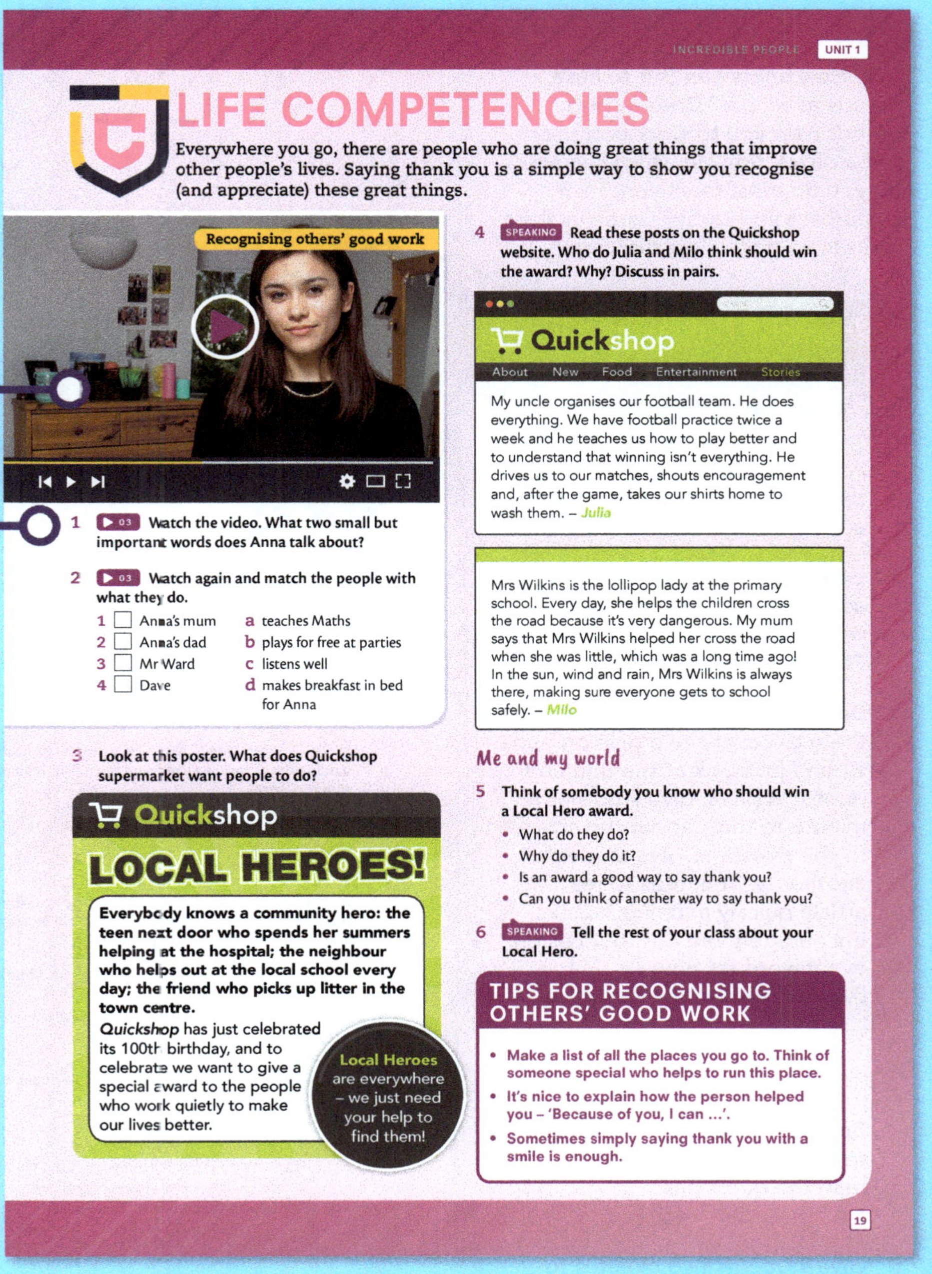

INCREDIBLE PEOPLE UNIT 1

LIFE COMPETENCIES

Everywhere you go, there are people who are doing great things that improve other people's lives. Saying thank you is a simple way to show you recognise (and appreciate) these great things.

Recognising others' good work

1 ▶ 03 Watch the video. What two small but important words does Anna talk about?

2 ▶ 03 Watch again and match the people with what they do.

1	☐ Anna's mum	a	teaches Maths
2	☐ Anna's dad	b	plays for free at parties
3	☐ Mr Ward	c	listens well
4	☐ Dave	d	makes breakfast in bed for Anna

3 Look at this poster. What does Quickshop supermarket want people to do?

Quickshop
LOCAL HEROES!
Everybody knows a community hero: the teen next door who spends her summers helping at the hospital; the neighbour who helps out at the local school every day; the friend who picks up litter in the town centre.
Quickshop has just celebrated its 100th birthday, and to celebrate we want to give a special award to the people who work quietly to make our lives better.
Local Heroes are everywhere – we just need your help to find them!

4 SPEAKING **Read these posts on the Quickshop website. Who do Julia and Milo think should win the award? Why? Discuss in pairs.**

Quickshop
About New Food Entertainment Stories

My uncle organises our football team. He does everything. We have football practice twice a week and he teaches us how to play better and to understand that winning isn't everything. He drives us to our matches, shouts encouragement and, after the game, takes our shirts home to wash them. – *Julia*

Mrs Wilkins is the lollipop lady at the primary school. Every day, she helps the children cross the road because it's very dangerous. My mum says that Mrs Wilkins helped her cross the road when she was little, which was a long time ago! In the sun, wind and rain, Mrs Wilkins is always there, making sure everyone gets to school safely. – *Milo*

Me and my world

5 **Think of somebody you know who should win a Local Hero award.**
- What do they do?
- Why do they do it?
- Is an award a good way to say thank you?
- Can you think of another way to say thank you?

6 SPEAKING **Tell the rest of your class about your Local Hero.**

TIPS FOR RECOGNISING OTHERS' GOOD WORK
- **Make a list of all the places you go to. Think of someone special who helps to run this place.**
- **It's nice to explain how the person helped you – 'Because of you, I can …'.**
- **Sometimes simply saying thank you with a smile is enough.**

19

Activity idea An interview

Students could act out an interview with either Julia's uncle or Mrs Wilkins. Divide the class into four groups: A (Julia's uncle), B (Mrs Wilkins), C (interviewer of Julia's uncle) and D (interviewer of Mrs Wilkins). Ask groups C and D to look at the relevant post again and write five questions to ask Julia's uncle / Mrs Wilkins. Ask groups A and B to look at the posts again and find key information about Julia's uncle / Mrs Wilkins in preparation for an interview. Monitor to make sure the students are making notes and help with ideas if necessary. Put the students in A/C and B/D pairs to act out the interview.

TH!NK more

Practice Extra
Unit 1 Master it!

Worksheets
Life Lessons: Recognising others' good work

Tests
Unit, extension and skills test 1

Social responsibility
Understanding personal responsibilities as part of a group and in society
Is aware of positive behaviour in different groups.

Warmer

Ask: *How important is it to have friends at school? Does having friends help you to work better or is it a distraction? In which subjects do you do most teamwork? Is it something you enjoy?* Listen to their ideas in an open class discussion.

▶ 04 Get **TH!NK**ing

Play the video and discuss the question with your class.

1 Ask students to describe what they can see in the photos and answer the question.

2 Give a couple of your own ideas as examples before students work in pairs.
Students' own answers

3 Before students do the task, get them to cover the article on page 21 and just look at the title and photo. In pairs, give students a minute to think about the answer to the question. Give students another two minutes to read the article quickly and check ideas. Encourage them not to focus on every word for now.
Because he's the only student at his school.

4 🔊 **2.01 Check/clarify:** *remote, private school, pier, factory.*
Before students read and listen to the article again, get them to read the questions.
1 C 2 D 3 C 4 D

5 Give students two minutes to think of and write the three questions.
Students' own answers

6 Demonstrate the role play with a stronger student before students work in pairs.

2 A GOOD EDUCATION

OBJECTIVES

FUNCTIONS: asking and giving / refusing permission to do something

GRAMMAR: present perfect with *for* and *since*; *a*, *an*, *the* or no article

VOCABULARY: school subjects; verbs about thinking

Get TH!NKING
Watch the video and think: how do you learn best?

READING

1 Look at the photos. Does your school have these rooms or places?

2 SPEAKING Write a list of all the things you think a school should offer as well as a good education. Then compare with a partner.

A school should offer students the chance to talk about any problems they might have in their lives.

3 Look at the photos and the title on the next page. Why do you think this boy is the 'loneliest schoolboy in Britain'? Read the text quickly to check your ideas.

4 🔊 2.01 Read and listen to the article again. Choose the correct answer to these questions.

1 What do we learn about the Out Skerries Islands from the text?
A They are on the coast of Scotland.
B There is a small airport.
C It takes two and a half hours to get to the nearest town.
D There is one shop on the island.

2 Why is Aron the only child at the school?
A No other children live on the islands.
B The government can't afford to send more children there.
C The other children are taught by their parents.
D The other children are too old for the school.

3 Why do some people complain about Aron's education?
A They think it's not good for him to have no friends at the school.
B They don't think he's learning the right things.
C They think it costs too much.
D They think he should be sent to private school.

4 How has the island changed over the last ten years?
A There are more shops.
B More families are coming to the island.
C It's not as safe as it was.
D There is less work there.

5 Think of three questions you would like to ask Aron and write them in your notebook.

What's the best part of your school day?
Do you miss your brothers?
Do you like always coming first in every test?

6 SPEAKING Work in pairs. Take turns to be Aron. Ask and answer your questions from Exercise 5.

What's the best part of your school day?

PE. I love being outside.

20

Objectives

Functions and speaking Asking and giving / refusing permission to do something; **Role play:** Asking permission
Grammar Present perfect with *for* and *since*; *a*, *an*, *the* or no article
Vocabulary School subjects; verbs about thinking
Values Learning for life
Train to TH!NK Learning about texts

Resources for this unit

All available online

Videos

- Get **TH!NK**ing: *How do you learn best?*
- Grammar rap!: Present perfect with *for* and *since*
- Culture: Schools with a difference

Tests

- Unit, extension and skills test 2

Worksheets

- Grammar and vocabulary: Basic, Standard and Extension Worksheets
- Project: A dream school
- Communication: The ways we learn
- Literature Worksheets: *The Mill on the Floss*
- Grammar presentation: Articles *a*, *an*, *the* or no article
- Get **TH!NK**ing and Grammar rap! video Worksheets

Reading; TH!NK Values

Culture notes

The Out Skerries Islands are an archipelago lying just east of the main Shetland Island group in Scotland, UK. Locally they are usually called just *Skerries*. Most of the Skerries place names are of Norse origin and the islands have been permanently inhabited from the Norse period. There is evidence of early Neolithic inhabitation. Currently around 70 people live on the two main islands.

Lerwick, the main town and port of the Shetland Islands, is 340 km north of Aberdeen and 357 km from Bergen, Norway. It is the most northerly and easterly town in the UK.

7 **Check/clarify:** *achieve, respect.*
1✓ 2✓ 4✓ 6✓

8 Read through the model dialogue with students. In pairs or small groups, ask them to compare their ideas. Listen to some of their answers with the whole class and encourage further discussion.

9 You could ask students to rank the statements in Exercise 7 in order of importance before discussing.

Homework

Ask students to write a list of ten things they would miss about their school if they had to live on an island in the middle of nowhere with no friends.

THE LONELIEST SCHOOLBOY IN BRITAIN

Imagine a school where you are the only student – where you come first in every test. Welcome to the life of ten-year-old Aron Anderson, who goes to school in Out Skerries, a group of small, remote islands in Scotland. Aron has been the only boy at his school for two months.

The Out Skerries Islands, which are around 280 km from the coast of Scotland, are home to about 70 people. The nearest town is Lerwick on the Shetland Islands. You can only get there by boat and it takes two and a half hours. Apart from Aron's school, there are two shops, a church and a community hall on the islands.

Aron isn't the only child on the islands and he hasn't always been the only student at the school. Until July there were several other children there, including Aron's two brothers. But now they are older, so they go to the secondary school in Lerwick. They only go back to their homes at the weekend. Aron has been the only student since September.

The school is very small. It has two classrooms, an art room, a music room and a library. Each week Aron studies Maths, English, Science and Art with the same teacher. She also gives him PE lessons. This is usually an hour-long walk around the islands. He also has the school playground all to himself. Of course, there is one problem. He has no one to play with.

What's more, Aron's education isn't cheap. It costs the UK government £75,357 each year. That is twice the price it costs parents to send a child to Britain's most famous private school, Eton. Some people want to close down the school. They think it is too much money to spend on one child's education.

Aron has lived in Out Skerries since he was born and loves the outdoor life. He enjoys exploring the islands on his bike and diving into the sea from the pier. Like most boys his age, he also likes watching TV and playing on his games console.

But his mother, who works in one of the shops on the islands, is worried that Aron might get lonely. She would like to see more families with children coming to live there. A lot of people have moved away since the local salmon factory closed ten years ago. That's why there are so few children on the islands and why Aron has found himself being known as the loneliest schoolboy in Britain.

TH!NK values

Learning for life

7 **Read the statements. Tick (✓) the things that you think Aron is probably not learning at his school.**

1 Everyone is different and that's a good thing. ☐
2 Teamwork is important to achieve things in life. ☐
3 We need to learn to respect the natural world. ☐
4 It is important to be friendly and help others. ☐
5 It is important to know how to spend time on your own. ☐
6 It's good to learn how to get on with people of different ages. ☐

8 SPEAKING **Compare your ideas with a partner.**

I think he is learning how to get on with people of different ages.
Why?
Well, he has all that time with just his teacher.
Yes, I agree with you.

9 SPEAKING **In small groups, discuss these questions.**

1 Which of the things from the list in Exercise 7 do you think are important to learn?
2 What would you add to your personal list of important things to learn?

Activity idea Extension

Ask students which of the six things in Exercise 7 they are actually taught at school. Ask: *In which subjects are you taught them? Do you learn them from teachers or from other students? If you are not taught them, do you think you should be?* Divide the class into small groups for discussion and after five minutes, appoint a spokesperson from each group to feed back some of their ideas to the class.

Critical TH!NKing
Evaluating ideas, arguments and options
Analyses causes and effects of problems.

Critical TH!NKing
Synthesising ideas and information
Selects key points from diverse sources to create a new account and/or argument.

TH!NK more

Worksheets
Project A dream school
Communication The ways we learn
Get TH!NKing *How do you learn best?*

Warmer

Test students on past participles.

▶ 05 Grammar rap!
Present perfect with *for* and *since*

1 As a follow-up, ask why the past simple is not used instead (the present perfect refers to an indefinite point in the past, or an action which started in the past and continues in the present).
Aron has been the only boy at his school for two months. He hasn't always been the only student at the school. Aron has been the only student since September. Aron has lived in Out Skerries since he was born. A lot of people have moved away since the local salmon factory closed ten years ago. Aron has found himself being known as the loneliest schoolboy in Britain.

2 1 since 2 for
RULE: 3 for 4 since

3 We use for with a period of time and since to mention a specific time.
for: a long time, an hour, a year, days, many years
since: Friday, I phoned you, 2014, yesterday, your birthday

4 1 've been, since 2 hasn't seen, for
3 haven't written, for 4 've had, since

5 1 They've been at the youth club for three hours. 2 Joanne and I have been good friends since primary school. 3 She's played in the volleyball team for two months. 4 I ought to see a doctor. I've been sick for a week. 5 I haven't heard from Silvia since last October.

Workbook p18

Grammar rap!

GRAMMAR
Present perfect with *for* and *since*

1 **Look again at the article on page 21. Find all the sentences in the present perfect.**

2 **Complete the sentences below with *for* and *since*. Then complete the rules.**

1 Aron has lived in Out Skerries ______ he was born.
2 Aron has been the only boy at his school ______ two months.

RULE: In the present perfect, we use:
- [3] ______ to talk about a period of time.
- [4] ______ to refer to the point in time when an action started.

3 **When do we use *for* and when do we use *since*? Complete the chart.**

~~a month~~ | ~~last summer~~ | a long time | an hour
a year | days | Friday | I phoned you | many years
2014 | yesterday | your birthday

for *a month* ______ ______
______ ______ ______

since *last summer* ______ ______
______ ______ ______

4 **Complete the sentences. Use the present perfect form of the verbs and *for* or *since*.**

1 I ______ (be) at my new school ______ last December.
2 Fatima ______ (not see) Michael ______ several weeks.
3 They ______ (not write) us an email ______ three months.
4 I ______ (have) this camera ______ I was ten.

5 **Write sentences using the present perfect with *for* or *since* and the words in brackets.**

1 They are at the youth club. (three hours)
2 Joanne and I are good friends. (primary school)
3 She plays in the volleyball team. (two months)
4 I ought to see a doctor. I'm sick. (a week)
5 I don't hear a lot from Silvia. (last October)

→ workbook page 18

VOCABULARY
School subjects

6 2.02 **Match the school subjects in the list with the photos. Write 1–12 in the boxes. Then listen and check.**

1 Science (Physics, Biology and Chemistry)
2 Music | 3 Art Education | 4 Drama
5 Design and Technology | 6 Geography
7 English | 8 PE (Physical Education)
9 ICT (Information and Communication Technology)
10 Maths | 11 History | 12 Spanish

7 SPEAKING **Answer the questions. Take notes. Then compare your answers with a partner.**

1 Which are your favourite subjects? Which don't you like? Why?
2 Which of the subjects are you studying this year?
3 How long have you studied each subject for?

→ workbook page 20

22

Get it Right!
Present perfect with *for* and *since*

Student's Book p122

6 2.02
A 6 B 12 C 9 D 3 E 5 F 10 G 2 H 8 I 4 J 7 K 1 L 11

7 You could ask students to rank the school subjects in Exercise 6 in their favourite order before discussing.

Workbook p20

TH!NK more

Workbook
Grammar p18, Ex.1–5
Vocabulary p20, Ex.1–2
Vocabulary Extra p21, Ex.1–2

Worksheets
Grammar Worksheets 2
Grammar rap! Present perfect with *for* and *since*
Vocabulary Worksheets 2

Activity idea Extension

Put the class into two groups and ask them to test each other. One group should say a sentence with *for*, e.g., *I have lived here for three years.* The other group have to say the same information in a sentence with *since*, e.g., *I have lived here since 2017.*

8 Before students do the exercise, elicit some ideas from the class.
A 6 B 5 C 8 D 10

9 2.03 Before students listen, explain that they will hear two people – Tom and his mother – discussing things Tom wants to do.
1 Watch the sun rise ✓ Climb a huge hill ✓
2 Eat an apple straight from a tree ✓ Feed a bird from your hand ✓

10 2.03 Complete question 1 as a class. Encourage students to think about the correct answer to the false statements.
1 T
2 F – He has until the end of the summer.
3 F – He found it online.
4 T
5 F – He wants his mum to take him.
6 F – She thinks it's a good idea.

11 You may want to talk about an experience of your own as an example.

12 Discuss ideas as a class.

13 Ask students to imagine that they are staying with an English family. They want to ask the family if they can borrow a bicycle. Ask: *What would you say?* Listen to their ideas and try to elicit: *Can I borrow a bicycle? Will you let me use your bicycle?*
2, 4, 3, 1
3, 1, 4, 2

14 You may like to do the first question with the whole class as an example.
1 AP, GP 2 AP, RP 3 AP, GP
4 AP, GP

ROLE PLAY Allow students six to eight minutes to prepare their role plays. If students have access to a recording facility (using their mobile phones, for example), they could record their conversation and play it back to check their own pronunciation and intonation.

Homework

Ask students to make a list of five subjects they would like to be included at school and to write a sentence for each explaining why they would like to be taught them.

LISTENING

8 Read the list of ten things to do this summer. Match four of the activities with the pictures.

A

B

C

D

9 2.03 Listen to Tom talking to his mother.
1 Which things on the list does he want to do tomorrow?
2 What other things on the list does he mention?

TEN THINGS TO DO THIS SUMMER!

GET OFF YOUR PHONE AND GET OUTSIDE. THERE'S A WORLD OUT THERE. GO AND EXPLORE!

1 Climb a tree
2 Camp out in the wild
3 Run around in the rain
4 Eat an apple straight from a tree
5 Swing on a rope swing
6 Watch the sun rise
7 Climb a huge hill
8 Feed a bird from your hand
9 Swim in a river
10 Cook on a campfire

10 2.03 Listen again. Mark the sentences T (true) or F (false).
1 Tom's mum is surprised he wants her alarm clock. ____
2 Tom has less than two weeks to finish the challenge. ____
3 Tom found the list in a magazine. ____
4 Tom's mum thinks the challenge is a good idea. ____
5 Tom wants to climb the Malvern Hills with his friends. ____
6 Tom's mum isn't happy to take him to the Malvern Hills. ____

11 SPEAKING Have you done any of the things on the list? Tell your partner.

12 Think of more things you could put on the list.

FUNCTIONS
Asking and giving / refusing permission

13 Put the dialogues in the correct order. Write the numbers 1–4.

1
☐ Dad Yes?
☐ Dad I'm afraid I need to use it, too.
☐ Nick Will you let me use your laptop?
☐ Nick Dad?

2
☐ Annie Can I watch the football match tonight?
☐ Annie Can I ask you something, Mum?
☐ Mum Yes, of course you can.
☐ Mum Go ahead.

14 Mark the sentences AP (asking permission), GP (giving permission) or RP (refusing permission).
1 Will you let me use your mobile? ____
Yeah, sure. Of course I will. ____
2 Can I borrow your bike, please? ____
No, sorry. I need it. ____
3 Can I use your laptop, please? ____
Yes, you can, but I want it back tomorrow. ____
4 Is it OK if I borrow this necklace? ____
Yeah, but be really careful with it, OK? ____

ROLE PLAY Work in pairs. Act out short conversations. Ask each other for permission. Use the ideas below, or come up with your own idea.

borrow £20 | come with him/her
copy his/her homework
get some help with homework
use his/her tablet

Activity idea Extension

If students only used the ideas in the book, as an extension you could ask each student to prepare their own three questions asking for permission to do something. Students then mingle and ask their questions to other members of the class, who should respond with one of the phrases for giving or refusing permission.

THINK more

Workbook
Listening p24, Ex.1–2

Warmer

Revise school subjects. Present images to represent subjects from page 22 and ask students to name them.

1 Before students read the text, get them to cover it and just look at the photos and answer the questions.
Students' own answers

2 2.04 **Check/clarify:** *motivation, failure, mindset.*
Write on the board: *growth mindset*. Ask students what they think it might mean. Give students two minutes to read the text quickly and find out. Encourage them not to focus on every word for now.
1 Because it changes the impossible into possible.
2 They stopped putting F for fail on the exam papers and put 'Not yet' instead.
3 They don't concentrate on failure.
4 They focus on the failure.
5 Stop believing that you can't do something and realise you just can't do it yet.

3 Give a couple of your own ideas as examples before students work in pairs. At the end of the exercise, listen to some of their ideas and encourage open class discussion.

4 During feedback, ask students to say why the other descriptions are incorrect.
C

5 Get students to underline the language in the text that helped them choose their answers.
1 D 2 A 3 E 4 B

READING

1 **Look at the photos and answer the questions.**
1 What do you think these people are thinking?
2 What would you say to them?

THE POWER OF 'YET'

1 **Does life sometimes seem to be full of impossible problems? How many times, for example, do you find yourself saying things like 'I really don't understand this maths problem', or 'I can't get into the school team'?**
Well, maybe it's time to introduce yourself to the power of 'yet'. By adding this simple word, you can change everything. 'I really don't understand this maths problem *yet*.' 'I can't get into the school team *yet*.'
Suddenly, the impossible becomes possible. You can imagine those things happening.

2 I read about a school that has changed the way it marks its students' exams. The school recognised that the old pass/fail system wasn't helping student motivation. If you passed, then great, but those students who didn't pass often felt like failures. So now students who don't get the score they need to pass don't see a big red F for fail on their exam papers; they see a 'Not yet' instead. That way the students feel that they are on a journey. They haven't reached the end, but they know that they are going the right way.

3 This kind of thinking is part of what experts call 'having a growth mindset'. People with a growth mindset don't concentrate on failure. They aren't worried by not getting things right the first time and are happy to keep trying until they do. They enjoy the challenge and believe they can change. In contrast, people who just focus on the failure have what the experts call 'a fixed mindset'. These people are always worried about failure and are happy to give up when things don't go right. They don't think that they are able to change. Clearly, it is better to have a growth mindset than a fixed mindset.

4 But don't worry if you think that you have a fixed mindset. You can train yourself to develop a growth mindset. Remember that it all starts with questioning the things you believe about yourself. Stop believing that you can't or you haven't and realise that you just can't or haven't *yet*. Once you start doing this, you'll wonder why you didn't do it before. It's one small but very powerful word.

2 2.04 **Read and listen to the text and answer the questions.**
1 How does the word yet make a difference?
2 Why did the school change the way it graded exams?
3 How do people with a growth mindset behave?
4 How are people with fixed mindsets different?
5 What's the first step needed to change from a fixed to a growth mindset?

3 SPEAKING **Make a list of three things you would like to be better at. Work with a partner and discuss how you could achieve these things.**

I'd like to be really good at the guitar.
Find time to practise for an hour every day.
Get lessons off the internet.
Learn to play your favourite songs.

Train to TH!NK

Learning about texts

4 **Choose the best description of this text.**
A an adventure story to entertain the reader
B an ad to sell the reader something
C a magazine article to give the reader information
D a letter to persuade the reader to do something

5 **Choose the title that best sums up the content of each paragraph. Write 1–4. There is one extra title.**
A ☐ A real-life example
B ☐ You can change
C ☐ The best advice is always free
D ☐ It's all about 'yet'
E ☐ Two ways of thinking

24

Culture note

The power of 'yet' is the foundation of *growth mindset*, a motivational idea pioneered by Stanford psychologist Carol Dweck. The idea is that a person's intelligence, athletic skill, musicianship, etc. is capable of development through continued learning, perseverance and good mentoring.

TH!NK more

Workbook
Reading p22, Ex.1–5

Emotional Development
Empathy and relationship skills
Shows understanding of other people's perspectives and feelings.

Critical TH!NKing
Understanding and analysing links between ideas
Distinguishes between main and supporting arguments.

6 Does (life) sometimes seem to be full of impossible (problems)?
I read about a school that has changed the way it marks its students' (exams). The school recognised that the old pass/fail system wasn't helping.
The students feel that they are on a journey.
RULE: 1 a 2 an 3 the 4 – (no article)

7 During feedback, refer to the rule box to clarify answers if necessary.
1 –, – 2 The 3 an, the 4 – 5 the, –

8 1 – 2 – 3 a 4 – 5 – 6 A 7 the

Workbook p19

9 Check answers and elicit some sample sentences from students to clarify meaning. This is quite a challenging activity and students may need several examples to clarify the differences between the verbs.

10 1 think 2 believe 3 imagine 4 realised 5 believe 6 recognise 7 guess 8 concentrate 9 wondered 10 suppose

Pronunciation
Word stress

Student's Book p120

11 Before students work in pairs, ask: *What do you think about most? Do you think about different things at different times of day?*

Workbook p20

Homework
Ask students to write five true sentences using the verbs from Exercise 9, e.g., *I remember when I was five, we had a holiday in Italy.*

Activity idea Fast finishers
Ask students to decide which of the verbs can be followed by these words: *who*, *it*, *that*. Tell them that some of the verbs can be followed by more than one of the words. They should use a dictionary to check their ideas. Check answers during feedback on Exercise 9.

GRAMMAR
a, *an*, *the* or no article

6 **Look at the sentences from the magazine article. Underline *a*, *an*, *the* and the nouns that come after these articles. Then go through the sentences again and circle the nouns with no article. Finally, complete the rules with *a*, *an*, *the*, – (no article).**

Does life sometimes seem to be full of impossible problems?
I read about a school that has changed the way it marks its students' exams. The school recognised that the old pass/fail system wasn't helping.
The students feel that they are on a journey.

> RULE: We use [1]______ or [2]______ + a singular countable noun when the listener/reader doesn't know exactly which thing we are talking about.
> *You can have **an apple** or **a banana**.*
> *We've got **a new car**.*
> [3]______ + noun when it is clear which thing(s) or person/people we are talking about.
> ***The apples in this pie** are from our garden.*
> ***The bananas that I bought** yesterday are horrible.*
> [4]______ + plural countable noun or + uncountable noun, when we are talking about things in general.
> ***Bananas** are sweeter than **apples**. **Chocolate** isn't good for you.*

7 **Complete each sentence with *a*, *an*, *the* or – (no article).**

0 She is __*a*__ good student.
1 She eats a lot of ______ fruit and ______ vegetables.
2 ______ book that you gave me was really good.
3 I have ______ idea. Let's watch ______ new Beyoncé video.
4 I never drink ______ coffee – I hate it.
5 I like lots of sports, but ______ sport I like most is ______ tennis.

8 **Complete the text with *a*, *an*, *the* or –.**

[0]__*–*__ People need to drink. Of course [1]______ orange juice and [2]______ apple juice are very popular, but they are not always [3]______ good choice. [4]______ Orange juice has got a lot of sugar in it, so don't drink too much of it. The best drink for your brain is [5]______ water. [6]______ glass of water is the best drink you can get, but [7]______ water that you drink needs to be fresh and clean.

→ workbook page 19

VOCABULARY
Verbs about thinking

9 **Find these verbs in a dictionary and write their definitions in your notebook.**

believe | concentrate | guess | imagine | realise | recognise | remember | suppose | think | wonder

10 **Choose the correct words.**

1 The task was very difficult. I had to *remember / think* about it for a long time.
2 Come on, don't be silly. I don't *believe / realise* in ghosts!
3 Can you *imagine / concentrate* how great it must be to live at the beach?
4 When the teacher asked the question a different way, I *supposed / realised* that I knew the answer!
5 Did they really say they are moving to New York? I don't *suppose / believe* it!
6 I haven't seen her for six years. I don't think I would *realise / recognise* her.
7 I have no idea what the answer is. I'll just have to *recognise / guess*.
8 I was so tired that I found it hard to *think / concentrate* on the test.
9 Have you ever *wondered / believed* why I haven't phoned you for months?
10 If we want to get there faster, I *wonder / suppose* we should take a taxi.

PRONUNCIATION
Word stress Go to page 120.

11 SPEAKING **Work in pairs. Ask and answer the questions.**

1 Are there any places where you can think really well or not well at all?
2 Does music help you to concentrate or make it difficult for you to concentrate? Does it matter what kind of music it is?
3 In what situations can you imagine things really well? Do you find it difficult to use your imagination sometimes?
4 Do you find it difficult to remember things sometimes? What sort of things?
5 Have you ever tried meditation? Do you think meditating is useful?

→ workbook page 20

TH!NK more

Practice Extra
Unit 2 Practise it!

Workbook
Grammar p19, Ex.6–9
Vocabulary p20, Ex.3–5
Pronunciation p118

Worksheets
Grammar Worksheets 2
Grammar presentation: Articles *a*, *an*, *the* or no article
Vocabulary Worksheets 2

Warmer

Write on the board: *on a boat, in a forest, under a motorway bridge, on a train platform, in a cave, in a football stadium.* (These are all locations of real schools around the world.) Ask: *Would you like to go to school in any of these places? What type of school would it be? What would you learn? Can you think of any disadvantages of this type of school?* Listen to their ideas and encourage open class discussion.

▶ 06 TH!NK Schools with a difference

1 Before students read the article, get them to cover it and just look at the photo and title and speculate the answer to the question. Accept all ideas before giving the answer.
The school is on a boat.

2 2.07 Have students underline the names of all three schools in the article before finding the answers.
1 the Train Platform School (1985)
2 the West Philadelphia School of the Future (2006)

3 Monitor to help with any difficulties, but do not interrupt as this is a fluency activity. You might also offer ideas if students have none.

TH!NK Schools with a difference

Culture

1 Look at the photo and the title. What do you think is different about this school?

2 2.07 Read and listen to the article. Which school is the oldest? Which school is the newest?

Schools with a difference

Every year Bangladesh is hit by heavy rains which cause large floods across the country. At these times life becomes difficult for millions of people who have no electricity or clean water. Many schools in these areas are forced to close. Shidhulai Swanirvar Sangstha is a charity which has provided education to more than 70,000 children with their floating schools since 2002. Each morning a school boat picks up children from nearby villages and when every child is on board, lessons can begin. In some of the lessons children learn about climate change and about protecting the environment. The charity has around 100 solar-powered boats and each one is fitted with a small library, a computer and internet access. The teachers also teach adults how to use the computers.

Each year more than 4,000 of India's poorest children get their education on the platforms of the country's railway stations. The idea for the Train Platform School came from a teacher called Inderjit Khurana. She wanted to do something for the children she met begging on the train she took to work each morning. She knew that without education, these children had no hope for their futures, and in 1985, she set up the first school and the school still exists today. Music and drama are among the methods used to teach the children how to read and write. When the children are ready, they can transfer to a full-time school. The schools also provide the children with food and medicine when it is needed.

You won't find any books at the West Philadelphia School of the Future in the US. Instead, all students have their own computers and learn on specially designed apps. Teachers don't use traditional whiteboards – they use hi-tech Smart Boards. When the school opened in 2006, both the teachers and the students found it difficult. They didn't know how to use all the technology. Since then the school has improved and these days students get high marks in Maths and reading, making it a very popular school with parents. The people who started the school hope that other schools will follow their example.

3 SPEAKING What makes your school different? Discuss in pairs. What could you change to make your school more unique?

26

Culture notes

Shidhulai Swanirvar Sangstha was founded in Bangladesh in 1998 by Mohammed Rezwan, who was frustrated by the month-long interruptions during his childhood education. The non-profit organisation centred on mobile, accessible education, the concept being that if children marooned by floods could not attend school, then the school should come to them. Rezwan and the organisation have won many awards, including the Sri Sathya Sai Award for Human Excellence in 2016.

The Train Platform Schools of India was founded by Inderjit Khurana in 1985. Today, there are ten Platform Schools operating at the major railway stations of Odisha, India. Children are taught for four hours every day, with supplementary health-care services. The schools have, so far, reached out to over 4,000 underprivileged children and their families. In 2007, Inderjit Khurana received The World's Children's Honorary Award for her struggle for the most vulnerable children's right to education.

Microsoft School of the Future (commonly referred to as the School of the Future) is a public high school in Philadelphia, United States, for grades 9–12. The school opened on 7th September 2006.

Social Responsibility
Understanding own and others' cultures
Describes basic information about other countries.

4 Ask students to refer to the language in the article that helped them find the answer.
1 India 2 US 3 Bangladesh
4 Bangladesh 5 US 6 US
7 Bangladesh 8 India

5 1 solar 2 improved 3 traditional
4 floods 5 floating 6 methods
7 begging 8 charity

1 Before students do the exercise, tell them they are going to read an email from a girl describing her new school.
1 She's enjoying it.
2 She thinks he's cool and they have lots of fun together.
3 She's spending more time at school and she's getting a lot more homework.
4 Art. She loves the projects.
5 No. She says 'I guess it's not so different for you'.

2 Encourage students to underline the sentences in the email.
a Are you enjoying your new school?
b His mother is working the UK …
c I'm spending more time at school …
d We're also getting a lot more homework.
She uses the present continuous tense.
She uses it for temporary actions or situations happening in and around the present time.

3 Give weaker classes the first (and last) word in each sentence to help them.
1 There's a new kid in my class too.
2 I come home at 5.45 three times a week.
3 But I love the projects we do in this class.
Present simple – for actions or situations which are permanent or happen regularly.

4 Tell students that there is a basic format which should be followed when writing an email and that Ruby's email follows this format.
1 c 2 a 3 d 4 b

5 Tell students they are going to write a response to Ruby's email. Working individually, students make notes on what to include. Monitor and help students with ideas.

6 Encourage students to organise their writing as outlined in Exercise 4 and to use the present continuous.

4 **Read the article again. Complete the sentences with *Bangladesh, India* or *US*.**

1 The children here learn at stations. ____
2 This school uses the most modern technology. ____
3 The weather makes life difficult here sometimes. ____
4 This school uses solar power. ____
5 It's difficult to get a place at this school. ____
6 This school wants other schools to be like them. ____
7 Children here have 'floating' lessons. ____
8 The children get more than just an education. ____

5 VOCABULARY **There are eight highlighted words in the article. Match the words with these meanings. Write the words.**

1 of or from the sun ____
2 got better ____
3 usual, things as they have always been ____
4 when there is too much water on the land ____
5 staying above water ____
6 ways of doing something ____
7 asking people for money in the streets ____
8 an organisation which helps people, animals, the environment etc. ____

WRITING
An email describing your school routine

1 INPUT **Read Ruby's email. Then answer the questions.**

1 How does Ruby feel about her new class?
2 What does Ruby think of Nathan and why?
3 How does her work for school compare to last year?
4 What subject does she get a lot of homework for, and how does she feel about it?
5 Does Ruby think you've got less schoolwork than her?

2 **Find sentences in the email where Ruby writes about these things. What tense does she use in those sentences? Why does she use it?**

a asks how you feel about your new school
b talks about Nathan's mother
c compares school this year to last year
d talks about the amount of homework this year

3 **Put the words in the right order. Write the sentences. What tense are they in and why?**

1 new / too / class / kid / There's / a / my / in
____
2 a week / at / three times / come home / 5.45 / I
____
3 love / projects / I / class / But / the / do / this / in / we
____

4 ANALYSE **Match the four paragraphs of Ruby's email with the content.**

Paragraph 1 a Ruby's new class
Paragraph 2 b a request to write soon
Paragraph 3 c an introduction
Paragraph 4 d work this year compared to last

Ruby
ruby@yourmail.com
Hi!

Hi there!

I hope this finds you well. I haven't heard from you since the beginning of the holidays. Are you enjoying your new school?

I am, big time! I'm in a class with all my friends again – Rosa, Liz, Jacob and all the others. There's a new kid in my class, too. His name's Nathan and he's from Nantes in France. His mother is working in the UK for two years, and the whole family have come over. He's cool. We have lots of fun together.

But of course, it's not all fun. We've got important exams this year so there's a lot of work to do. I'm spending more time at school than last year, and I come home at 5.45 three times a week. We're also getting a lot more homework, especially for Art. But I love the projects we do in this class!

Well, I guess it's not so different for you. If you've got a bit of time, please let me know how things are going. I'd really like to know what life at school is like for you. And remember, please, you've got a friend in Brighton who would really like to get mail from you more often!

Write soon!

Ruby

5 PLAN **Read Ruby's email again. Make notes with your own ideas on how:**

a to answer the question in her introduction
b to describe your new class (new school? classmates?)
c to compare your work this year to last year's
d to say how you feel about your subjects (any subjects you particularly like/don't like? Why?)
e you could finish your email (what do you want to know from Ruby?)

6 PRODUCE **Write an email to Ruby (about 200 words). Look at your notes from Exercise 5 and make sure you include all your ideas. Make sure you use the present simple when necessary.**

27

Homework

Ask students to research another unusual school from around the world. They can upload a picture with a description of the school in English. If students do not have access to the internet, they can create their own ideas. As a follow-up, students can bring the picture to the next lesson and present their school to the class.

Activity idea Mixed ability

Stronger students could attempt Vocabulary Exercise 5 without re-reading the article. With weaker students, give them the first letter of each word to guide them. Check answers and check the pronunciation of new vocabulary.

TH!NK more

Practice Extra
Unit 2 Master it!

Workbook
Developing Writing p23

Tests
Unit, extension and skills test 2

1 In B1 Preliminary for Schools Reading Part 6, candidates have to fill six gaps in a text using only one word in each gap. This part of the exam tests candidates' understanding and knowledge of grammatical structures, phrasal verbs and common phrases.

Encourage your students to do the following when they approach this task:

- Skim the text to find out the topic and general meaning.
- Think of a possible word which makes sense in each gap.
- Check if the word fits the meaning and grammar of the sentence and the whole text.
- Check the spelling is correct.
- Read the completed text again to check that it makes sense.

1 Since 2 or 3 will 4 up
5 sure 6 has

Workbook p115

2 2.08 In B1 Preliminary for Schools Listening Part 1, there are seven short recordings, each with a question and three images. Candidates have to listen to the text, then choose the image which best answers the question. This part of the exam requires candidates to listen for specific information.

Encourage your students to do the following when they approach this task:

- Read the question and look at the images for each question.
- During the first listening, listen for specific information, choosing the best option.
- During the second listening, check that the answer is correct, focusing on the key information in the text.

1 B 2 A 3 A 4 A 5 C
6 B 7 B

Workbook p17

B1 Preliminary for Schools

READING
Part 6: Open cloze

→ workbook page 115

1 For each question, write the correct answer. Write one word for each gap.

The Tan-y-Bryn Outdoor Adventure Centre

The Tan-y-Bryn Outdoor Adventure Centre is on the island of Anglesey in North Wales. [1]______ opening its doors in 1975, it has welcomed thousands of young people from all over the UK to enjoy fun, education and adventure in the beautiful Welsh countryside. Whether they are climbing up Mount Snowdon, swimming in the Menai Straits [2]______ birdwatching in the woodlands, visitors enjoy hands-on experiences they [3]______ never forget.

For school groups, youth clubs and families the Centre offers comfortable accommodation for [4]______ to 50 children and 10 adults. It also provides a full breakfast, lunch and dinner to make [5]______ no one goes hungry. Safety is a top priority – there [6]______ never been a serious accident at the Centre.

LISTENING
Part 1: 3-option multiple choice

→ workbook page 17

2 2.08 For each question, choose the correct answer.

1 What did Sally buy at the shops?

2 What time is it?

3 How did Brian get to work?

4 Which lesson did Fred enjoy most?

5 What month is Tom's brother's birthday?

6 What's the score in the football match?

7 Which man are the police looking for?

28

1 1 formed 2 active 3 lost 4 creative 5 wonder 6 realise 7 guess 8 brave 9 recognise 10 got

2 1 haven't opened 2 bus 3 didn't see 4 didn't open 5 haven't seen 6 the bus

3 1 Can I have a glass of ~~an~~ orange juice, please?
2 I've travelled to ~~already~~ more than twenty capital cities already.
3 We've lived here ~~since~~ for ten months.
4 I~~'ve gone~~ went to the cinema last night.
5 This is my computer. I've had ~~had~~ it for two years.
6 It's important to drink a lot of ~~the~~ water if you want to be healthy.

4 1 A Can B afraid
2 A Let's B idea
3 A thinking B definitely
4 A OK B go

TEST YOURSELF UNITS 1 & 2

VOCABULARY

1 Complete the sentences with the words in the list. There are two extra words.

active | believe | brave | creative | formed | got | guess | lost | realise | recognise | take | wonder

1 I think I ________________ the wrong opinion of her. She's actually really nice.
2 My grandmother's quite old, but she's still very ________________ – she's always doing things!
3 He ________________ the race by less than one second.
4 I didn't like the birthday cards in the shop, so I decided to be ________________ and make one.
5 It's strange that Eve isn't here. I ________________ where she is.
6 It's midday! Wow! I didn't ________________ it was so late.
7 I didn't know the answer, so I had to ________________.
8 She didn't run away when the tiger was running towards her – she was very ________________.
9 I'm sure he saw me, but he didn't say hello. Maybe he didn't ________________ me.
10 I've ________________ a reputation for always being late. I don't think it's fair.

/10

GRAMMAR

2 Complete the sentences with the words in the list. You need to write the correct form of the verbs.

bus | the bus | not open (x2) | not see (x2)

1 My best friend gave me my present this morning, but I ________________ it yet.
2 I'm tired – I don't want to walk. Let's go by ________________.
3 She was at school today? Really? I ________________ her there.
4 There was a sign on the gate that said 'No entry!', so I ________________ it.
5 There's a new film on Netflix, but I ________________ it yet.
6 We were late because ________________ arrived 45 minutes late.

3 Find and correct the mistake in each sentence.

1 Can I have a glass of an orange juice, please?
2 I've travelled to already more than twenty capital cities.
3 We've lived here since ten months.
4 I've gone to the cinema last night.
5 This is my computer. I had it for two years.
6 It's important to drink a lot of the water if you want to be healthy.

/12

FUNCTIONAL LANGUAGE

4 Complete the mini-dialogues with the words in the list.

afraid | Can | definitely | go | idea | Let's | OK | thinking

1 A ________________ I use your pen, please?
B Sorry, I'm ________________ I'm using it right now.
2 A ________________ go and see the new Marvel film tonight.
B That's a great ________________!
3 A I'm ________________ about doing a walk for charity. What do you think?
B Yes, you should ________________ do it.
4 A Is it ________________ if I use your dictionary?
B Yes, of course, ________________ ahead.

/8

MY SCORE /30

22–30 | 10–21 | 0–9

29

The Cambridge Life Competencies Framework

Critical Thinking

Understanding and analysing links between ideas

Watch this video for a tip on developing your students' critical thinking skills.
Scan the QR code here

Warmer

Write the following questions on the board: *How often do you go to the cinema? What is your favourite type of television programme? How often do you play computer games? Do you like going to the theatre?* Students discuss their answers with a partner. Listen to some of their answers with the whole class.

▶ 07 Get TH!NKing

Play the video and discuss the question with your class.

1 Say the words for students to repeat and check pronunciation.
A5 B4 C3 D1 E2 F6

2 Monitor and help with any questions. Ask some of the students to share their opinions with the rest of the class.

3 Give a couple of your own ideas as examples before students work in groups.

4 Before students read the article, get them to cover it and just look at the pictures and the title. Give them two minutes to answer the question.

5 🔊 **3.01** Before you play the audio, tell students not to worry about understanding every word, but to focus on getting a general understanding of the article.
A

6 **Check/clarify:** *director, animation/animator, advantage, plot, produces, exhibitions.* Before students read the article again, get them to read the questions.

3 ON THE SCREEN

OBJECTIVES

FUNCTIONS: comparing things and actions; asking for and offering help

GRAMMAR: comparative and superlative adjectives (review); *(not) as ... as*; making a comparison stronger or weaker; adverbs

VOCABULARY: types of films; types of TV programmes; expressions with *get*

Get TH!NKING ▶07
Watch the video and think: what's your favourite form of entertainment?

READING

1 **Match the words in the list with the photos. Write 1–6 in the boxes.**

1 concert | 2 cinema | 3 play | 4 sports event | 5 TV programme | 6 video game

2 SPEAKING **Which of these kinds of entertainment do you like? Tell your partner.**

3 SPEAKING **Work in small groups. Talk about the things in Exercise 1. Say why people like or don't like them. Use the words in the list to help you.**

crowds | enjoyable | expensive | friends | fun | interesting | relaxing

I think people enjoy going to the cinema because it is relaxing.

4 **Look at the pictures and the title of the article on the next page. What do you think the article is about?**
A a director
B an actor
C a type of film

5 🔊 3.01 **Read and listen to the article and check your ideas.**

6 **Read the article again. Find:**
1 two examples of things that influenced Tim Burton
2 the reason people were upset when Burton chose Michael Keaton for *Batman*
3 two examples of types of film that Burton has made
4 an example of creative work that Burton does apart from directing films

30

1 Horror stories and drawing
2 He was too short.
3 Possible answers include: animation, superhero, horror, children's films
4 He exhibits his drawings and cartoons around the world.

Objectives

Functions and speaking Comparing things and actions; **Developing speaking:** Asking for and offering help
Grammar Comparative and superlative adjectives (review); *(not) as ... as* comparatives; making a comparison stronger or weaker; adverbs and comparative adverbs
Vocabulary Types of films; types of TV programmes; **WordWise:** Expressions with *get*
Values Preconceived ideas
Life Competencies Achieving your goals

Resources for this unit

All available online

Videos
- Get **TH!NK**ing: *What's your favourite form of entertainment?*
- Grammar rap!: Making a comparison stronger or weaker
- Vlog: Achieving your goals

Tests
- Unit, extension and skills test 3
- End of term test 1

Worksheets
- Grammar and vocabulary: Basic, Standard and Extension Worksheets
- Project: What's on TV?
- Communication: That's entertainment
- Literature Worksheets: *Twelve Years a Slave*
- Grammar presentation: Adverbs and comparative adverbs
- Get **TH!NK**ing, Grammar rap! and Life Lessons video Worksheets

Reading; TH!NK Values

Culture notes

Timothy Walter Burton was born in 1958 and is an American filmmaker, artist, writer and animator. He is known for his dark, gothic and eccentric horror and fantasy films such as *Beetlejuice* (1988) and *Edward Scissorhands* (1990), as well as the blockbuster *Batman* films, the sci-fi film *Planet of the Apes* (2001) and the fantasy film *Alice in Wonderland* (2010).

Michael John Douglas (known professionally as Michael Keaton) was born in 1951 and is an American actor, producer and director. He played the title character in Tim Burton's *Batman* (1989) and *Batman Returns* (1992), and since then has appeared in a variety of films such as *RoboCop* (2014) and *Spider-Man: Homecoming* (2017). He has also provided voices for characters in animated films such as *Cars* (2006), *Toy Story 3* (2010) and *Minions* (2015).

7 Read the first sentence in open class and ask students which opinion they agree with. Listen to some of their reasons before students complete the task individually.
Students' own answers

8 Divide the class into small groups and ask students to compare their answers to the other questions. As feedback, listen to some of the students' ideas with the whole class and continue the debate.

Homework

Ask students to research Tim Burton or Michael Keaton. You could then start off the next lesson by asking students to tell the class what they have found out.

Activity ideas Mixed ability

Weaker students: Ask students to work with a partner and read the article again to complete Exercise 6.

Stronger students: Ask students to work with a partner and try to answer the questions from memory before reading the article again to check.

Critical TH!NKing
Evaluating ideas, arguments and options
Gives reasons for an argument's plausibility.

ON THE SCREEN UNIT 3

A new kind of SUPERHERO

Tim Burton is one of the most famous American film directors. His most popular films include: *Batman* (1989), *Edward Scissorhands* (1990), *Batman Returns* (1992) and *Dumbo* (2019). In 1990, he got a Daytime Emmy Award for his cartoon series *Beetlejuice* and in 1991 he got a Hugo Award for *Edward Scissorhands*.

Tim grew up watching horror films and cartoons. He read Edgar Allan Poe's horror stories and he loved drawing. He also made short films in his back garden. After leaving school, Burton studied animation. Then, he got a job at Walt Disney studios. He was a very good animator, but he didn't draw in the Disney style. So he left Disney and started to make his own films.

One of his most successful films is *Batman*. At first, people were upset when Tim Burton chose the comedy actor Michael Keaton to play Batman. Batman is a superhero who is taller and stronger than ordinary men, and Michael Keaton was too short. At 1.75 m, he was in fact the shortest actor ever to play Batman. However, the film was very successful and everybody loved Michael Keaton as Batman.

One of Tim Burton's most interesting characters is Edward Scissorhands. The idea for the character came from a drawing that Burton made in high school. Edward isn't human and he has got scissors instead of hands. In the film, Johnny Depp plays Edward. However, his character in the film is not as scary as Tim Burton's original drawing.

In one of his latest films, *Dumbo*, Dumbo the elephant has got bigger ears than the other elephants and they laugh at him. However, his big ears are an advantage. He can fly. This new film is more exciting than the old Disney film, but the CGI elephant is not as cute as the cartoon elephant in the 1941 film. There are some changes in the plot, but the new film is still as sad as the old one.

Tim Burton has directed many other films, including some of the best-loved children's stories like *Charlie and the Chocolate Factory* and *Alice in Wonderland*. He still produces films today, and sometimes he shows some of his drawings and cartoons at exhibitions around the world.

TH!NK values

Preconceived ideas

7 **Read the sentences. How much do you agree with each one? Write a number: 1 (I agree), 2 (I'm not sure) or 3 (I don't agree).**

1 If there is a film about a real-life famous person, the actor should look as much like that person as possible. ☐
2 I won't go to see a new film if there is an actor in it that I don't like. ☐
3 Cheap things are never worth buying. ☐
4 There are some shops where I would never buy clothes. ☐
5 It's crazy not to like someone because of the way they speak. ☐

8 SPEAKING **Work in groups. Compare your ideas.**

I don't agree with number 1. It's impossible to find actors who look the same.

Do you think so? I agree with it. I think they should wear make-up to make them look very similar.

31

Activity idea Extension

Find trailers of the films mentioned in the article and show them in class. Ask students to discuss the trailers and decide which one makes them want to see the film most.

TH!NK more

Worksheets
Project What's on TV?
Communication That's entertainment
Get TH!NKing *What's your favourite form of entertainment?*

Warmer

Ask two confident students to come to the front of the class. Ask: *Who is taller? Alex or Joe?* Then ask another two students to come up. Ask: *Who is the tallest? Who is the shortest?* Elicit comparisons in height.

1 Ask students to answer the questions from memory before referring back to page 31 to check.
1 taller, stronger 2 the shortest 3 bigger 4 more exciting than

2 Elicit what is being compared in the first example (the character in the film and the original drawing) and in the second (the new film and the old film).
1 original drawing 2 No, the new film is the same amount of sad.
RULE: 3 as 4 as

3 *Students' own answers*

4 *1 isn't as slow as 2 is as tall as 3 aren't as quiet as 4 is as expensive as 5 isn't as difficult as 6 isn't as untidy as*

Workbook p28

Pronunciation
Words ending in /ə/

Student's Book p120

Get it Right!
Comparatives and *than*

Student's Book p122

5 Before students do the task, get them to cover the words and look at the pictures. In pairs, give students two minutes to write as many of the film types as possible.
1 science fiction (sci-fi) 2 action film 3 animated film 4 romantic comedy (rom com) 5 comedy 6 horror film 7 documentary 8 thriller

GRAMMAR
Comparative and superlative adjectives (review)

1 Complete these sentences from the article on page 31 with the correct form of the words in the list.

big | exciting | short | strong | tall

1 Batman is a superhero who is ________ and ________ than ordinary men.
2 At 1.75 m, he was in fact ________ actor to ever play Batman.
3 Dumbo the elephant has got ________ ears than the other elephants.
4 This new film is ________ the old Disney film.

(*not*) *as … as* comparatives

2 Look at the examples of (*not*) *as … as* to compare things. Answer the questions. Then complete the rule.

His character in the film is not as scary as Tim Burton's original drawing.
The new film is still as sad as the old one.
1 Which is scarier: the original drawing or the character in the film?
2 Is the new film sadder than the old film?

RULE: When we want to say that two things are (not) the same, we can use (*not*) [3] ______ + adjective + [4] ______.

3 Complete each sentence with your own ideas.

1 a Football isn't as exciting as *skiing*.
b Football is more exciting than *golf*.
2 a English is easier than ________.
b English isn't as easy as ________.
3 a Watching TV isn't as good as ________.
b Watching TV is better than ________.

4 Complete the second sentence so it has the same meaning as the first. Use the word in brackets.

0 Ben's sister is younger than him. (old)
Ben's sister *isn't as old as* him.
1 Travelling by train is faster than travelling by bus. (slow)
Travelling by train ________ travelling by bus.
2 Tom is 1.65 m. Sue is 1.65 m, too. (tall)
Tom ________ Sue.
3 Dogs are noisier than cats. (quiet)
Dogs ________ cats.
4 This mobile phone costs €225. And the bicycle costs €225, too. (expensive)
The mobile phone ________ the bicycle.
5 Jo thinks Geography is easier than History. (difficult)
Jo thinks Geography ________ History.
6 My room is tidier than yours. (untidy)
My room ________ yours.

PRONUNCIATION
Words ending in /ə/ Go to page 120.

workbook page 28

VOCABULARY
Types of films

5 Write the types of films in the list under the pictures.

action film | animated film | comedy | documentary | horror film | romantic comedy (rom com) | science fiction (sci-fi) | thriller

1 ________

2 ________

3 ________

4 ________

5 ________

6 ________

7 ________

8 ________

workbook page 30

6 SPEAKING **Can you think of an example of each type of film? Are any of your examples more than one type?**

Spies in Disguise is an action film.

32

6 Give a couple of your own ideas as examples before students work in pairs.

Workbook p30

Language notes

Comparative and superlative adjectives (review)

Remind students we use *more … than* in English. It may be useful to remind students of the spelling rules for comparatives and superlatives:

- one-syllable adjectives: add *-er/-est*, e.g., *fast – faster – fastest*
- one-syllable adjectives ending in consonant + vowel + consonant: double the final consonant + *-er/-est*, e.g., *big – bigger – biggest*
- two-syllable adjectives ending in consonant + *-y*: delete the *-y* and add *-ier/-iest*, e.g., *tidy – tidier – tidiest*
- two or more syllable adjectives: add *more/most* in front of the adjective, e.g., *more/most successful*
- irregular adjectives, e.g., *far – further – furthest*

(*not*) *as … as* comparatives

Remind students that we use *as … as* in positive sentences when two things are the same and *more … than* in comparative sentences.

TH!NK more

Workbook
Grammar p28, Ex.1–5
Pronunciation p118
Vocabulary p30, Ex.1–4
Vocabulary Extra p31, Ex.1–2

Worksheets
Grammar Worksheets 3
Vocabulary Worksheets 3

Listening; Grammar; WordWise

7 3.04 Before students listen, explain that they will hear two people – Emma and a radio presenter – talking on a radio show.
She won a prize for making a film.

8 **3.05 Check/clarify:** *director, full-time, animated, script, professional.*
Before listening, ask students to underline the key information to listen for in each question.
1 A 2 C 3 C

▶ 08 Grammar rap!
Making a comparison stronger or weaker

9 1 a lot 2 a little
RULE: 3 a lot 4 much 5 a little

10 1 Sharks are a lot more dangerous than dolphins. 2 My brother is a bit taller than me. 3 My new phone's far better than my old one. 4 Her hair is a little longer than yours. 5 The film's much more exciting than the book.

11 Point out that we use *and* when the second part of the sentence agrees with the first, and we use *but* when the second part contradicts the first, e.g., *I think English is far more difficult than Art, but it's more interesting.*
Students' own answers

Workbook p29

12 1 d 2 b 3 c 4 a

13 Check that students understand what *get* means in each of the phrases (*get home/there* = arrive; *get bored/angry/better* = become; *get a drink* = buy). Go through the first sentence as an example. Remind students to take note of the tenses being used.
1 got bored 2 got there 3 get home 4 got better 5 get angry 6 get a drink

14 1 c 2 a 3 e 4 b 5 d

Workbook p30

LISTENING

7 3.04 **Listen to Part 1 of an interview. Why is Emma Harding a guest on the radio show?**

8 3.05 **Listen to Part 2 of the interview. For each question, choose the correct answer.**

1 Emma says that making a Lego film
  A takes a lot of time.
  B is far easier than you think.
  C requires lots of drawing.
2 When she was making the film, Emma
  A used her own camera.
  B didn't have any lights.
  C had some help from a friend.
3 Emma says that her film is
  A 10 seconds long.
  B 18 seconds long.
  C 20 seconds long.

Grammar rap! ▶08

GRAMMAR
Making a comparison stronger or weaker

9 **Read the sentences. Choose the phrase that has a different meaning from the other two. Then complete the rule.**

0 Eighteen photos look *a lot / much / a little* better than ten photos.
1 Together we made the script *a little / a lot / a bit* better.
2 I'm sure it's *a little / much / far* more difficult than it looks.

RULE: Use [3]______ / [4]______ / *far* to make a comparative stronger.
Use *a bit* / [5]______ to make a comparative weaker.

10 **Rewrite these sentences using the words in brackets.**

1 Sharks are more dangerous than dolphins. (a lot)
2 My brother is taller than me. (a bit)
3 My new phone's better than my old one. (far)
4 Her hair is longer than yours. (a little)
5 The film's more exciting than the book. (much)

11 **Write sentences comparing these things. Use *much / far / a lot* or *a bit / a little.***

0 watching TV / reading a book (interesting / easy)
I think watching TV is a lot more interesting than reading a book – and it's far easier, too.
1 gorillas / snakes (dangerous / beautiful)
2 English / Art (difficult / interesting)
3 my country / US (big / beautiful)

→ workbook page 29

WordWise: Expressions with *get*

12 **Look at the sentences from the unit so far. Choose the correct meaning of *get* in each one.**

1 Then you need to get yourself a camera.
2 He got a Daytime Emmy Award for his cartoon series *Beetlejuice*.
3 I couldn't wait to get home and tell my mum.
4 I still get emotional now when I think about it.

a become
b received
c arrive
d obtain, buy

13 **Use a phrase from the list to complete each sentence.**

get a drink | get angry | get home
got better | got bored | got there

1 The film was terrible – after 20 minutes, I ______ and fell asleep.
2 I was really late for school – when I ______, it was already ten o'clock!
3 There's still a long way to go. I don't think we'll ______ before midnight.
4 He was ill for about a week, but then he ______, I'm happy to say.
5 It was just a joke. Please don't ______ with me!
6 If you want, we can ______ in that café in the town centre.

14 **Match the questions and answers.**

1 Let's go and get a drink. ☐
2 When do you get angry with people? ☐
3 Do you ever get bored watching TV? ☐
4 What time do you get to school? ☐
5 Do you ever get a cold? ☐

a When they say things I don't like.
b Usually about eight o'clock.
c OK. The shop over there sells water.
d Sometimes – in winter, usually.
e Only when it's a programme I don't like.

→ workbook page 30

Activity idea Fast finishers

Ask students to think of some more types of films. Write their ideas on the board and check understanding by asking students for examples of that genre.

Activity idea Extension

Ask students to rank the film types 1–8 according to how often they watch that type of film. Divide the class into small groups so they can compare their lists. As feedback, hold a vote to find out which are the most commonly watched types of films.

Homework

If your students are interested in films, ask them to write a 100-word summary of the plot of a film, without giving the title or names of characters. In the following lesson, they can read them out in open class for other students to guess the title.

TH!NK more

Workbook
Listening p34, Ex.1–2
Grammar p29, Ex.6–7
WordWise p30, Ex.5

Worksheets
Grammar Worksheets 3
Grammar rap! Making a comparison stronger or weaker

Warmer

Write the names of some popular TV programmes on the board. Ask students to talk in pairs and discuss which of the programmes they watch / don't watch and why/why not. Ask students which is the best channel on TV and why. Ask whether they watch more programmes on TV or on the internet.

1 Give students two minutes to read the article and write the titles. Encourage them not to focus on every word for now.
1 A 2 B 3 D 4 C

2 **3.06 Check/clarify:** *significantly, consequently, luxury, broadcasters, sitcom, streaming services, posts.*
Ask students to read and listen to the text again and answer the questions.
Students compare answers with a partner before a whole-class check.
1 Because there was no 'Watch next episode' button.
2 Because people could watch one episode after another.
3 Major sports events
4 It adds up to a lot more screen time.

3 When students have discussed fully, you may like to mix up the groups for them to present their answers to their new group. Encourage students to speak at length without interruption.

4 Ask students to try to complete the sentences from memory before referring back to the article to check. Encourage them to underline the sentences in the article.
1 cheaper 2 patiently
3 long 4 easily

THE HISTORY OF watching TV

READING

1 Read the article quickly. Write the titles in the correct spaces 1–4.
A The rise in screen time
B TV as a family activity
C The changing world of TV
D Non-stop drama

1 ______
Television (TV) has been in people's homes since the 1930s, but our way of watching TV has changed significantly over the years. In the 1950s, families that had TVs, only had one TV set and three channels to choose from. Nowadays, we can watch a TV show on many different devices, anywhere and at any time of the day or night. Consequently, our generation is watching TV more frequently than any other generation before.

2 ______
TVs were luxury items in the 1950s, and the families that did have one had to sit very close to it as the screens were very small.
Then in the 1960s, TVs became cheaper and more families owned one. Most people had a TV in their living room and families sat together and watched their favourite shows. Oh, and there was no 'Watch next episode' button. People had to wait patiently for a week to watch the next part of their favourite soap opera.

3 ______
Then, in the mid-2000s, TV broadcasters started to make programmes available via the internet. It was called on-demand TV and became very popular because people could choose when they wanted to watch a programme. Now, you could watch an episode of a sitcom straight away. Instead of watching one episode, people happily binge-watched six hours of their favourite TV series in one afternoon. Drama series became like one long film. And if you missed a documentary or an episode of your favourite reality show, you could easily watch it online later.
During this decade, far fewer people sat down with their families to watch a TV show. However, people still preferred to watch major sports events (such as the FIFA World Cup) live.

4 ______
In the 2010s, children and young adults began to watch much less broadcast TV than in the past. They watched their entertainment on smartphones, games consoles and via streaming services. This meant they could watch a show more easily at any time. Now, people spend more hours watching TV. In fact, the average person in Britain spends almost ten years of their life watching TV! As well as watching a show, they also need to read all the posts about it quickly, and tweet about it, too. This adds up to a lot more screen time.

2 3.06 Read and listen to the text again. Answer the questions.
1 Why did you sometimes have to wait seven days in the early years of TV to watch a programme?
2 How did 'on-demand' TV change the way people watch TV?
3 In the 2000s, which type of programme did people prefer to watch at the time it was broadcast?
4 What effect do social media have on the amount of time people spend looking at screens?

3 SPEAKING Which statements are true for you? In groups, compare your ideas.
1 I prefer to watch TV alone rather than with other people.
2 I sometimes binge-watch drama series.
3 I sometimes use social media to discuss TV programmes with friends.
4 I spend more time on a tablet or computer than I do in front of a TV.

GRAMMAR
Adverbs and comparative adverbs

4 Look at the sentences from the article. Complete them with the words in the list.

cheaper | easily | long | patiently

1 TVs became ______.
2 People had to wait ______ for a week to watch the next episode.
3 Drama series became like one ______ film.
4 You could ______ watch it online later.

34

TH!NK more

Workbook
Reading p32, Ex.1–2
Grammar p29, Ex.8–9

Worksheets
Grammar Worksheets 3
Grammar presentation: Adverbs and comparative adverbs

5 significantly, consequently, frequently, patiently, happily, easily, quickly
RULE: 1 adjective 2 adverb 3 adverb 4 adjective

6 During feedback, ask students for the responses and check their pronunciation of the adverbs.
1 carefully 2 cleverly 3 happily 4 well 5 badly 6 easily 7 fast

7 To help clarify meaning, ask students to underline examples in the text before completing the rule.
RULE: 3 more

8 1 more clearly 2 more carefully 3 more slowly 4 earlier 5 worse 6 harder 7 better

Workbook p29

9 This could easily be made into a matching activity. Ask the class for the names of their favourite TV programmes and write them on the board. Ask students to match the names to the types of TV programmes. Which are the least/most popular types?
Students' own answers

10 Monitor to help with any difficulties, but do not interrupt as this is a fluency activity. Encourage students to make notes which can be used in the writing activity that follows.

Workbook p30

11 Students should organise their work to follow the same format as the questions in Exercise 10. Remind students to refer back to their answers for that exercise if necessary. They should use words and phrases from Unit 3. When they have finished, ask them to read their paragraph to the class or to a partner.

Homework

Have the students keep a journal for two or three days. In their journal, students have to keep a record of what they watched on TV and write a short description of some of the programmes.

5 Look again at the text on page 34 and find the adverbs. Then complete the rules with *adjective* and *adverb*.

> RULE: Use an ¹______ to talk about a noun:
> *He's a slow runner.*
> Use an ²______ to talk about a verb:
> *He runs slowly.*
> We usually form an ³______ by adding *-ly* (or *-ily*) to the ⁴______, but some adverbs are irregular: *fast* → *fast*, *good* → *well*.

6 Write the adverbs.

0 quick *quickly*
1 careful ______
2 clever ______
3 happy ______
4 good ______
5 bad ______
6 easy ______
7 fast ______

7 Look at the examples of comparative adverbs from the text on page 34. Then complete the rules.

1 This meant they could watch a show **more easily** at any time.
2 Our generation is watching TV **more frequently** than any other generation before.

> RULE: To form the comparative of most regular adverbs, add the word ³______ before the adverb: *easily* → *more easily*.
> If an adverb has one syllable, make the comparative by adding *-er*: *soon* → *sooner*, *hard* → *harder*, *fast* → *faster*.
> - There are some irregular comparative adverbs: *badly* → *worse*, *well* → *better*.
> - Notice that the comparative of *early* is *earlier*.

8 Complete the sentences. Use the comparative adverb forms of the words in brackets.

0 Sue runs (fast) than me. *faster*
1 George writes ______ (clear) than me.
2 You need to do your homework ______ (careful) if you want to get good marks.
3 Sorry, I don't understand. Can you speak ______ (slow), please?
4 The party starts at ten o'clock, but you can come ______ (early) if you want to.
5 I only got 22% in the test, but you did even ______ (bad) than me!
6 Isabella always works ______ (hard) than the other kids.
7 Martina speaks English ______ (good) than I do.

→ workbook page 29

VOCABULARY
Types of TV programmes

9 Look at the different types of TV programmes. Can you think of an example for each one?

10 SPEAKING **Work in pairs. Ask and answer the questions.**

1 What kind(s) of programmes do you really like?
2 What kind(s) of programmes do you really NOT like?
3 What's your favourite programme at the moment? Why?
4 What's your least favourite programme at the moment? Why?
5 How do you watch TV programmes – on TV, on your phone, on a tablet ...?

→ workbook page 30

WRITING
A paragraph about your TV habits

11 Write a paragraph about your TV habits.

- Use your answers to the questions in Exercise 10 to help you.
- Try to use grammar and vocabulary from the unit (comparative adjectives, words for TV programmes, etc.).

Activity ideas Mixed ability

Weaker students: Write on the board: *1 I am nervous before exams. 2 I waited nervously before the exam results arrived.* Ask: *Which sentence contains an adjective?* (1); *Which contains an adverb?* (2). Elicit the formation of regular adverbs (adjective + *-ly*). Follow the procedure for stronger students.

Stronger students: Look at the four words in the box in Exercise 4, and ask students which are adjectives (*cheaper*, *long*) and which are adverbs (*easily*, *patiently*). Ask students what adjectives do (describe nouns) and what adverbs do (describe verbs). Students complete the sentences in Exercise 4. Check answers.

TH!NK more

Practice Extra
Unit 3 Practise it!

Workbook
Grammar p29, Ex.8–9
Vocabulary p30, Ex.3–4
Vocabulary Extra p31, Ex.1–2
Developing Writing p33

Worksheets
Grammar Worksheets 3
Grammar presentation: Adverbs and comparative adverbs
Vocabulary Worksheets 3

Warmer

Elicit reasons for feeling tired or sleeping badly. In pairs, students discuss how well they sleep, what causes them to sleep badly and what helps them to sleep well. Bring the discussion to a close with a group discussion.

1 🔊 **3.07** Tell students to cover the dialogue, look at the photo and discuss the question in pairs before listening and reading to check their answers.
She's tired because she was awake until three o'clock in the morning watching a TV programme.

2 *1 A Maths question*
2 She has watched TV until late at night.
3 Running a long race
4 He tells her to look at a book.

3 At the end of the exercise, listen to some of the students' ideas and encourage open class discussion.

4 Write the underlined expressions on the board. Ask students for an L1 translation before they complete the conversation in English.
1 Guess what 2 Have a look at this 3 In fact 4 come on 5 looks like 6 after all

5 After students have answered the questions, elicit from the class examples of when and why these sentences are used.
1 A 2 O 3 O 4 A

6 After students have completed the dialogues, focus on the pronunciation and pay attention to the intonation. Students should use falling intonation for all the questions.
1 Can you 2 Could you, Is everything OK / all right? 3 Can I

7 Encourage students to use the dialogues in Exercise 6 as a model.

DEVELOPING SPEAKING

1 🔊 3.07 **Look at the photo. Why do you think the girl is tired? Listen and read to check.**

Megan: Hi, Josh. Have you got a moment? I'd like some help with a Maths question.
Josh: Hey, Megan. Sure. How can I help? Is everything OK? Looks like you haven't slept for about a week!
Megan: Well, I didn't sleep much last night. Or the night before. In fact, I haven't slept well for three nights.
Josh: Why not?
Megan: It's that new drama – *The Big Show*. It came out last week. It's fantastic. And last night I watched it until ... well, quite late.
Josh: How late?
Megan: Well, three o'clock in the morning. I watched all 20 episodes in three nights.
Josh: Wow! I'm not surprised you're tired and can't concentrate.
Megan: But it's so good! Last night there were only two more episodes to watch, I had to keep going. It's like running a long race – it starts to hurt but you have to carry on! My parents always tell me not to give up halfway through something.
Josh: But you shouldn't stay up all night.
Megan: I know. But it's brilliant. Anyway – could you help me with the Maths problem? Please?
Josh: Here, have a look at this.
Megan: A book!?
Josh: Yes, it explains everything. Just don't fall asleep while you're reading it, OK?
Megan: Oh come on, Josh! Please help me.
Josh: Sorry, I can't. I've got to go now. So, you'll have to do it yourself after all. Oh, and guess what? You've got ten minutes to do it before the lesson starts!

2 **Read the dialogue again and answer the questions.**
1 What does Megan want Josh's help with?
2 What has Megan done for the last three nights?
3 What does she compare watching the TV series to?
4 What does Josh tell her to do to understand the Maths problem?

3 SPEAKING **Discuss the questions in pairs.**
1 Is it OK for Megan to ask Josh to help her?
2 Is her comparison with running a good one?
3 Was Josh right not to help Megan?

Phrases for fluency

4 **Find the underlined expressions in the dialogue and use them to complete the conversation.**
Jim Hi guys. [1]________ ? I'm in the football team!
Mike You're joking!
Jim No, I'm not. [2]________. It's the team list.
Mike But you're not a good player, Jim. [3]________ , you're terrible!
Alice Oh, [4]________ , Mike! He's not so bad.
Susie That's right. And the school has picked him to play, so [5]________ you're wrong, Mike.
Mike Well, I guess so.
Jim Yes. I'm good enough for the school team [6]________ !

FUNCTIONS
Asking for and offering help

KEY LANGUAGE
Could you ... ? Can you ... ?
Can I ... ? Is everything OK / all right?

5 **Look at these sentences. Are they asking for or offering help? Write A (asking) or O (offering).**
1 Can you lend me a hand? ___
2 Can I help you at all? ___
3 Is everything OK? ___
4 Have you got a few minutes? ___

6 **Complete the mini-dialogues using the expressions from the Key Language box.**
1 **Maisie** ______ help me with my homework please, Mum?
Mum Of course, Maisie, what subject is it?
2 **Pablo** ______ give me a hand, Mr Terrence?
Mr Terrence No problem. ______
3 **Sofia** ______ have some ice cream, Grandma?
Grandma No, Sofia, dinner is almost ready.

7 SPEAKING **Work in pairs. Use the questions in the Key Language box and in Exercise 5 to act out conversations in a shop, at home, at school and in other places.**

36

Activity ideas Disappearing sentences

Write out the conversation in Exercise 4 on the board. Put students in A/B pairs and get them to practise the conversation. Cover a small section of the conversation, beginning from the right-hand side of the screen or board. Students practise the conversation again, including the part which they have to remember.

Students have to try to remember the part they can no longer see. Repeat the activity again and again, covering more and more of the conversation each time. Continue until all the conversation is covered and students are practising it from memory.

Life Competencies

Warmer

Ask students for things they can't do but would like to be able to do. Make a list on the board. For each item, elicit ways to achieve the goal.

▶ 09 Life Lessons: Achieving your goals

1 ▶ 09
One kilometre

2 ▶ 09 **Check/clarify:** *to be proud of someone.*
Step 1: run 10 km
Step 2: crowd calling my name, a medal, feeling great
Step 3: laziness, really old trainers, my phone
Step 4: limit my phone use; get up off the sofa and run

3 Ask students to rank this list from best piece of advice to worst.
Students' own answers

4 *Students' own answers*

5 Allow students six to eight minutes to discuss the best way to achieve their goal before deciding on the final order. Monitor to make sure all students are on task.

6 Monitor to help with any difficulties, but do not interrupt as this is a fluency activity.

Homework

Ask students to make a presentation about how to achieve a goal of their choice, e.g., how to be a good English speaker. Encourage them to make a list of at least five tips. As a follow-up, ask students to read their tips to the class, without saying what the goal is. The rest of the class have to guess the goal.

Activity idea A poster

Students could make posters of their advice for display in the classroom and further discussion.

ON THE SCREEN UNIT 3

LIFE COMPETENCIES

Everybody has got something they find really difficult. But just because it's hard doesn't mean we can't do it – whether it's getting better grades at school, improving at sport or even learning a new language. Commitment and determination can help us achieve our goals, no matter how large or small.

1 ▶ 09 Watch the video. How far did Kieran get in the 10 km race?

2 ▶ 09 Watch again and complete Kieran's notes.

Step 1: Identify goal
Step 2: Best thing about achieving my goal
Step 3: What may stop me
Step 4: How to make sure those things DON'T stop me

3 SPEAKING Work with a partner. What do you think of this advice? Are there any ideas you don't think are good?

How to achieve your goals:

1 Divide your main goal into smaller goals.
2 Make a weekly plan of action for each small goal.
3 Take the first step!
4 Expect some problems and be ready to solve them.
5 Ask friends and family for encouragement.
6 Review how well you're doing and make changes to your plan if necessary.
7 Stay focused!
8 Reward yourself!

4 Alex is shy, so people often think she's unfriendly. As a result, she doesn't have many friends. She'd like to make more friends, so she's going to follow the advice in Exercise 3. Complete her notes with your own ideas. Compare with a partner.

1 ______
2 ______
3 Start on Monday 12th.
4 ______
5 Tell Mum and my friend Katy about the plan. Update them every week.
6 Review the plan with Mum or Katy every Sunday.
7 Set calendar on mobile to remind me of plan every day.
8 ______

Me and my world

5 Choose one of the ideas from the list below that you would like to work on (or choose one of your own). Make notes like Alex's about how you're going to achieve your goal.

- Spend less time looking at screens
- Help more around the house
- Read more
- Eat more healthily

6 SPEAKING Tell your friends about your plans. Listen to each other and give ideas and advice.

TIPS FOR ACHIEVING YOUR GOALS

- Make a plan. It is a good way to ensure you have a clear idea of what you want to achieve.
- Be realistic when setting goals. Changing how you behave takes time.
- Reward yourself when you achieve something, but don't feel too bad and punish yourself if you don't.

37

TH!NK more

Practice Extra
Unit 3 Master it!

Worksheets
Life Lessons: Achieving your goals

Tests
Unit, extension and skills test 3
End of term test 1

Emotional Development
Managing own emotions
Managing stress by employing strategies.

Emotional Development
Managing own emotions
Discusses own emotions (mainly with friends) and chooses the best coping strategy.

Warmer

Ask students: *What do you use social networks for?* If your students have mobile devices, ask them to use them to compare answers. Ask: *Do you all use the same apps and networks?* Listen to some of their ideas in open class and encourage discussion.

▶ 10 Get TH!NKing

Play the video and discuss the question with your class.

1 Look at the logos and check students can name them. Are there any that students use that are missing from the list? In small groups, students discuss the questions. See if the class can agree on what the best social network is.
1 Snapchat 2 Pinterest 3 Facebook 4 Twitter 5 Instagram 6 WhatsApp

2 Give students some silent thinking time to think of their answers to the question before putting them in pairs to discuss.

3 **Check/clarify:** *footprints.*
Before students read the article, get them to cover it and just look at the photos and answer the question.

4 **4.01 Check/clarify:** *digital footprints, retweets, apps, tracked, database, PINs.*
Tell students they are going to read an article giving advice on using the internet.
1 F 2 T 3 T 4 T 5 T 6 T 7 F 8 F

4 ONLINE LIFE

OBJECTIVES

FUNCTIONS: giving advice

GRAMMAR: indefinite pronouns (*everyone, no one, someone*, etc.); *all / some / none / any of them; should(n't), had better, ought to*

VOCABULARY: IT terms; language for giving advice

Get TH!NKING
Watch the video and think:
do you post too many things on social media?

1 2 3 4 5 6

READING

1 SPEAKING **Work in pairs. Answer the questions.**
1 Which of these social networks do you know?
2 What do you think of them?
3 Do you know any other social networks?

2 SPEAKING **Read these statements about using social networks. Which of them are true for you? Discuss them with a partner.**
1 I've got a Facebook account but hardly ever use it.
2 I don't post many comments, but I like to read other people's posts.
3 I constantly check for updates on social media.
4 I sometimes post comments that I regret later.

3 **Look at the photos on the next page. What do you think the article is about? Read the article quickly to check your ideas.**

4 4.01 **Read and listen to the article about online behaviour again. Mark the statements T (true) or F (false).**
1 A digital footprint is like a footprint in sand because it disappears after time. ____
2 People who use the internet create an online history for themselves. ____
3 What you do online can lead to you receiving certain kinds of advertisements. ____
4 What you write online can be misunderstood by other people. ____
5 People should be careful about what personal information they include when they write online. ____
6 You can make life more difficult for thieves by not putting personal information online. ____
7 It's OK to put a credit card number in an email, but not a password. ____
8 It's possible not to leave a digital footprint if you go online. ____

5 SPEAKING **Work in pairs. Correct the false statements in Exercise 4.**

38

5 Ask students to work together with a partner and correct the false statements. Stronger students may be able to do this without looking back at the article.
1 A digital footprint is not like a footprint in sand because it never disappears.
7 You should never put a credit card number or a password in an email.
8 It is impossible not to leave a digital footprint if you go online.

Objectives

Functions and speaking Giving advice
Grammar Indefinite pronouns (*everyone, no one, someone*, etc.); *all / some / none / any of them; should(n't), had better, ought to*
Vocabulary IT terms; language for giving advice
Values Responsible online behaviour
Train to TH!NK Logical sequencing

Resources for this unit

All available online

Videos
- Get **TH!NK**ing: *Do you post too many things on social media?*
- Grammar rap!: *should(n't), had better, ought to*
- Culture: The evolution of writing

Tests
- Unit, extension and skill test 4

Worksheets
- Grammar and vocabulary: Basic, Standard and Extension Worksheets
- Project: Staying safe online
- Communication: Social networking
- Get **TH!NK**ing and Grammar rap! video Worksheets

Culture notes

Snapchat (or 'Snap') is a multimedia messaging app used globally. Pictures and messages are usually only available for a short time before they become inaccessible. Snapchat is popular among people under 16.

Pinterest is a social media company. It lets users share images associated with projects, goods and services, and to discover new interests by browsing images others have posted. People save images they found on the internet (or on Pinterest itself) to different boards (used to categorise their image collections).

Facebook is an online social networking service where users post comments, share photographs, chat live, watch short-form videos or even order food. It is open to anyone in the world over the age of 13 and was the most downloaded app of the decade 2010–19.

Twitter is a microblogging and social networking service on which users post short (280-character maximum) messages known as 'tweets'.

Instagram (or 'Insta') is a photo- and video-sharing social networking service. The app lets users upload photos and videos, which can be edited with filters and organised with tags and location information. Users can like photos and follow other users to add their content to a feed.

WhatsApp Messenger is a messaging service that lets users send text and voice messages, make voice and video calls, and share images, documents, and other media.

Imagine you are walking in the sand on a beach somewhere, or through deep snow on a mountain. As you walk, you leave footprints where you've been. Later, of course, the footprints disappear. But imagine if they didn't – if your footprints stayed there forever. And imagine, too, that you left footprints everywhere you walked, including in your home and in your town – so that someone could see everywhere you've been. How happy would you be about that?

Well, that's what happens when you use technology – computers, mobile phones, tablets. It's your digital footprint – a record of where you've been and what you've seen that you leave when you go online. Your comments on social media, your retweets, the apps you use, the emails you send, everything you've searched for – all of them are part of your digital footprint, and other people can see your footprint, or it can be tracked in a database.

Does this matter? Why would anyone be interested in what you write on Twitter or post on Instagram? Well, companies who sell things are interested, that's for sure – they want to send you adverts for things they want you to buy. But apart from businesses, there are other reasons why your digital footprint should matter to you.

1 HOW PEOPLE SEE YOU

Of course, you have nothing to hide, but if people get information about you, they might pick bits to make you look good – or bad. Perhaps one day you write something silly online. Maybe you make a bad joke. Years later, it's found by the university you're applying to, and they don't think it's funny. Then what? Maybe they decide you're not the 'right' kind of person for them.

2 YOUR PRIVATE INFORMATION

Everyone has information about themselves that they don't want everyone to know (for example, you might share your school reports with your parents but not friends), but the internet doesn't make the same decisions that you would.

3 KEEPING YOUR MONEY SAFE

There are plenty of people looking at information about you, and some of them want to steal from you, but the less information you put out, the harder it is for them. Bank details, card numbers, passwords or PINs – none of them should be written in emails, text messages or anything else.

Overall, the message is: remember that you have a digital footprint, and think carefully before you click 'send' or 'post'. No one can go online and not leave a footprint – but with care, you can control it.

TH!NK values

Responsible online behaviour

6 **Read the statements. Write them in two lists under *Do* and *Don't*.**

1 Say bad things about other people online.
2 Talk to your teacher or another adult if you get bullied on social media.
3 Think carefully before you write a post about yourself or other people.
4 Write a post about someone when you are angry with them.
5 Write posts containing personal information about your family.
6 Think before you post a photo of yourself or someone else.

7 SPEAKING **Work in pairs. Compare your lists. Think of at least two more statements for each list.**

6 **Check/clarify:** *bullied, a post.* Students work individually to complete the exercise. Monitor and help with any difficulties.
Do: 2, 3, 6 Don't: 1, 4, 5

7 Students compare their lists with a partner. Create a dos and don'ts list on the board and ask individuals to add to it.

Homework

Ask students to translate at least five of the text messages they have sent that day into English (if suitable!!). They can bring them to the next lesson for partners to read and respond to them.

Activity idea Extension

If your students are interested in this topic, ask them to work in pairs and recommend a social network for the following: sending photos; doing business; keeping in touch with old friends; looking for a job; making live comments on a sports game.

Social Responsibilities
Understanding and discussing global issues – environmental, financial and social
Understands how personal habits and behaviour have the capacity to affect others and the environment.

Critical TH!NKing
Evaluating ideas, arguments and options
Analyses causes and effects of problems.

Critical TH!NKing
Understanding and analysing links between ideas
Compares points and arguments from different sources.

TH!NK more

Worksheets
Project Staying safe online
Communication Social networking
Get **TH!NK**ing *Do you post too many things on social media?*

Warmer

Recap the dos and don'ts from the last lesson.

1 Ask: *Do the indefinite pronouns refer to people, places or things?* (things: *everywhere, something,* people: *no one*)
1 everywhere 2 something
3 No one
Imagine you are walking in the sand on a beach somewhere so that someone could see everywhere you've been.
Why would anyone be interested in what you write on Twitter or post on Instagram?
Of course, you have nothing to hide.
Everyone has information about themselves that they don't want everyone to know.
none of them should be written in emails, text messages or anything else.

2 Copy the table onto the board and elicit the answers.
1 something 2 nowhere 3 anyone
RULE: 4 every 5 some 6 any 7 no

3 Go through the first sentence as a class, asking students why the correct answer is *everywhere*. Remind students to look carefully at each sentence and decide if the missing word is a person, place or thing first.
1 everywhere 2 Everyone
3 no one 4 Someone 5 something
6 anywhere 7 nowhere
8 somewhere

4 As an alternative, students could write three true sentences and one untrue sentence, all of which must contain an indefinite pronoun. Their partner then guesses which of the sentences is untrue.

Workbook p36

GRAMMAR

Indefinite pronouns (*everyone, no one, someone*, etc.)

1 **Complete these sentences from the article on page 39. Find other examples of indefinite pronouns in the article.**

1 Imagine, too, that you left footprints ______ you walked.
2 Perhaps one day you write ______ silly online.
3 ______ can go online and not leave a footprint.

2 **Complete the table. Use the article on page 39 to help you. Then complete the rules with *some / any / no / every*.**

everything	[1] ______	nothing	anything
everyone	someone	no one	[3] ______
everywhere	somewhere	[2] ______	anywhere

RULE: The words beginning with
- [4] ______ mean 'all' (people / things / places).
- [5] ______ mean that we don't know exactly which (person / thing / place).
- [6] ______ mean that we don't care or it doesn't matter which (person / thing / place).
- [7] ______ mean 'not any' (person / thing / place).

3 **Complete the sentences with words from the table in Exercise 2.**

1 Where's my pen? I've looked ____________, but I can't find it.
2 Using social media can be a real problem. ____________ should know that.
3 The teacher asked a question, but ____________ knew the answer.
4 ____________ has left a message for you at reception.
5 Ouch! There's ____________ in my eye!
6 I've no idea where Sally is. She could be ____________.
7 Do you want a place to relax on your holiday? There's ____________ better than here!
8 It's so noisy. Let's go ____________ quieter.

4 **Complete these sentences so that they are true for you.**

1 Everyone knows that I ____________________.
2 For my next holiday I'd like to go somewhere ____________________.
3 I don't like eating anything that has got ____________________ in it.
4 I think anyone can learn to ____________________.

→ workbook page 36

VOCABULARY

IT terms

5 **Match the phrases with the meanings. Write numbers 1–10.**

1 to key in your password | **2** to install a program
3 to attach a file | **4** to have network coverage
5 to upload a photo | **6** to delete a message
7 ~~to open an attachment~~ | **8** to buy an app
9 to activate flight mode | **10** to download a file

a to click on the icon of a file that comes with an email [7]
b to have a signal that lets you make phone calls, etc. [ ]
c to add a separate element (e.g. a photo, a document, a video) to an email [ ]
d to make an image available on the internet [ ]
e to pay for a program for your mobile or tablet [ ]
f to type a secret word that gives you access to a computer or a website [ ]
g to put a program on a computer [ ]
h to switch on a function on your mobile or tablet so you can't go online [ ]
i to remove a piece of text so it cannot be seen any more [ ]
j to copy information or a program from the internet onto your computer hard disk [ ]

6 SPEAKING **Work in pairs. Ask and answer these questions.**

1 How many different ways do you have to go online?
2 How often do you post something on social media?
3 What kind of things do you usually post?
4 What ways do you know of keeping passwords secure but remembering them?

7 **Draw spider diagrams for these verbs.**

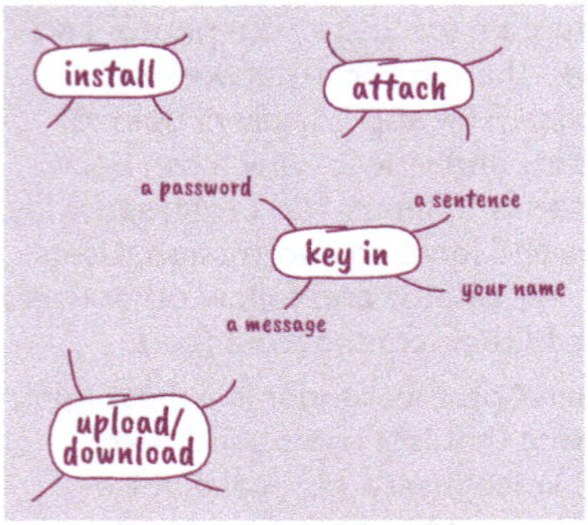

→ workbook page 38

5 A lot of technology vocabulary is international, so students are likely to have seen some of it before.
b 4 c 3 d 5 e 8 f 1 g 2 h 9 i 6 j 10

6 **Check/clarify:** *secure*.
Give students a few minutes to discuss the questions with a partner. Ask each pair to feed back to the class and if there are any interesting points, discuss these as a class.

7 Look at the spider diagram for *key in*. Divide the class into three and ask each group to create a spider diagram for one of the other three verbs. Ask individuals to re-create their group's spider diagram on the board. Elicit further words from the class to add to each spider diagram.

Workbook p38

THINK more

Workbook
Grammar p36, Ex.1–3
Vocabulary p38, Ex.1–3
Vocabulary Extra p39, Ex.1–2

Worksheets
Grammar Worksheets 4
Vocabulary Worksheets 4

Language note Indefinite pronouns (*everyone, no one, someone*, etc.)

Explain that *some-* and *every-* words are used in positive statements and *no-* words are used in negative statements with positive verbs. A typical mistake for many students is to use double negatives (e.g., **I don't know nothing*).

8 a6 b2 c5 d3 e1 f4

9 Ask individuals to share their experiences with the class and find out who has had the most serious problem.

10 4.02 Before students listen, explain that they will hear two people – Mark and his dad – discussing a phishing scam.
1 Because Mark's grandfather has fallen for a scam and lost £5,000.
2 He doesn't want him to fall for any (online) scams.

11 4.02 Before listening again, tell students to read the sentences carefully and to pay particular attention to sentences with negative verbs, as these often cause confusion. Let students compare answers with a partner before playing the audio again.
1 F – almost all the money he had. (£5,000) 2 T 3 F – It's a bigger problem 4 F – It was offering him a tablet 5 T 6 F – Teenagers, adults, grandads – anyone can fall for scams.

12 Make sure students understand why *all of them* is the answer for the example. Stronger students may be able to do this without referring to the article.
1 some of them 2 none of them

13 RULE: 1 none 2 things 3 more

14 1 None 2 any 3 some 4 Any 5 all 6 none 7 any 8 some

15 If you're short on time, set this exercise as homework.
1 none 2 some 3 all / some 4 any 5 none 6 Some

Workbook p36

Get it Right!

Any vs. – (no article)

Student's Book p123

Homework

Ask students to research groups of famous actors. They can upload a photo and write sentences describing them using *none of them / all of them / some of them*, e.g., *All of them have brown eyes. Some of them are wearing ties.* As a follow-up, students can bring the photo to the next lesson. Several photos can be put up on the wall and students present their 'group' to the class. The other students have to guess which group of actors it is.

LISTENING

8 Match the words and phrases with the meanings. Write the numbers 1–6 in the boxes.

1 to fall for a scam | 2 personal data
3 phishing | 4 identity theft
5 a pop-up | 6 a PIN

a a secret number you use with your bank card ☐
b information about you and your life ☐
c a new window or message that appears on your computer screen ☐
d when people try to get you to give information over the internet ☐
e to not understand when someone tries to get money from you with lies ☐
f to steal information about someone, then pretend to be them ☐

9 SPEAKING Work in pairs. Answer the questions.

1 Which of the things in Exercise 8 did you already know about?
2 Do you know anyone who has had problems because they sent personal data to someone else?

10 4.02 Listen to Mark and his dad. Answer the questions.

1 Why is Mark's dad angry?
2 What does he want Mark not to do?

11 4.02 Listen again. Look at the six sentences. Mark them T (true) or F (false). Then correct the false ones.

1 Mark's grandfather didn't lose much money.
2 Mark doesn't think he will fall for a scam.
3 Identity theft is less of a problem now than before.
4 Mark got an email offering him a new laptop.
5 The brother of one of Mark's friends lost money.
6 Mark's dad thinks only teenagers are tricked online.

GRAMMAR

all / some / none / any of them

12 Complete the sentences. Look back at the article on page 39 to check.

The apps you use, the emails you send, everything you've searched for – [0] ___all of them___ are part of your digital footprint
There are plenty of people looking at information about you, and [1] ______________ want to steal from you.
Bank details, card numbers, passwords or PINs – [2] ______________ should be written in emails.

13 Complete the rule with *things / more / none*.

RULE: We use the expressions *all / some /* [1] ______ */ any of them* to refer back to a group (of [2] ______ or people) and say [3] ______ about it.

14 Choose the correct words.

1 My friends had a great time at my birthday party. *All / None* of them wanted to leave!
2 Which of these pens is Carla's? They all look exactly the same, so *any / some* of them could be hers.
3 These bikes all look good, but I'm sure *some / any* of them are better than others.
4 These T-shirts are really cool. *None / Any* of them would be fine for me.
5 These caps weren't expensive. I got *all / none* of them for £12.
6 I tried on lots of different jeans, but *none / some* of them were the right size for me.
7 All the questions were really hard – I couldn't answer *none / any* of them!
8 Her songs are OK – I quite like *some / any* of them.

15 Complete the sentences with *all / some / none / any*. (There may be more than one possible answer.)

1 There are 32 students in Sarah's class. It's amazing that ___all___ of them like music, but ______ of them listen to jazz.
2 I like most American TV shows, but ______ of them are terrible!
3 OK, he scored three goals – but ______ of them were lucky!
4 The cakes that I made were horrible – we couldn't eat ______ of them, so we threw them all away.
5 My three brothers like IT, but ______ of them is as good with computers as my sister.
6 Look at those cameras. ______ of them are very cheap, but others are very expensive.

→ workbook page 36

Language note *all / some / none / any of them*

If we are talking about a group that includes the person speaking (or writing), we use *all / some / none / any of us*. If the group includes the listener (or reader), we use *all / some / none / any of you*.

Activity idea Fast finishers

Ask students to write some sentences about their families using *all / some / none of them / us*.

TH!NK more

Workbook
Listening p42, Ex.1–2
Grammar p36, Ex.4–5

Worksheets
Grammar Worksheets 4

Warmer

Write on the board: *email; text message; social media post*. Divide the class into small groups and ask students how often they use each of the three types of communication. Discuss in open class and find out who sends the most messages.

1 Give students just two minutes to look at the messages. Tell them not to focus on every word for now.
1d 2a 3c 4b 5e

2 🔊 **4.03 Check/clarify:** *apologise, acoustic guitar, condition, afford.* Ask students to read and listen and answer questions 1–6.
1C 2A 3B 4B 5A 6C

3 Ask students to underline words and phrases which helped them make their decisions.
1c 2d 3a 4b 5e

4 At the end of the exercise, listen to some of the students' ideas and encourage open class discussion.

Activity idea Extension

Tell the class they are going to imagine a conversation between the two main characters from the messages. Divide the class into two groups and give each group one of the following characters: Billy or Gemma. Students discuss some of the things their character might say when they first meet and during the guitar practice. When students have some ideas, re-assemble the class into pairs containing one student from each of the groups. Students act out a conversation between the two characters. Monitor and take note of any repeated errors, but do not interrupt, as this is a fluency activity. Listen to some examples in open class as feedback.

READING

1 Look at the messages. Match them with the types of communication in the list. Write a–e in the boxes.

1 email ☐
2 message on a messaging app ☐
3 post on an advertisement website ☐
4 social media post ☐
5 text message ☐

2 🔊 4.03 Read and listen to the messages and choose the correct answers.

1 Why does Billy apologise to his brother Sam?
A He wants to buy another guitar.
B He has dreams that may not come true.
C He won't be home in time to make dinner.

2 What's the purpose of Gemma's message (a)?
A To invite Billy to her house on Sunday
B To tell Billy she's not a good guitarist
C To ask Billy if he can play a song

3 In her post (b), Gemma
A says she learned something new.
B tells people she had a good time with Billy.
C says that Billy's a good guitar player.

4 In her post (c), Gemma says the guitar
A is new and is in OK condition.
B is an acoustic guitar.
C comes in a case which costs extra.

5 Billy writes an email (d)
A to suggest that he and Gemma play guitar together again.
B to say he wants to buy her guitar.
C to say he knows some good videos on YouTube.

6 In his message (e), Billy says that he
A doesn't like Neil Young's music.
B liked the guitar practice, but not the tea.
C hopes they can play together again.

Train to TH!NK

Logical sequencing

3 Read the messages again. Work out a logical order. Write letters a–e in the right order.

☐ 1 ☐ 2 ☐ 3 ☐ 4 ☐ 5

4 SPEAKING Work in pairs. Compare your ideas and discuss any differences.

42

Hi Sam,
You know I want a better guitar. Well, my friend Jake told me that his friend is selling one, so I'm going to check it out this evening. I'm going to be really late back. So sorry – you'd better make your own dinner tonight. When your brother is a big star, he'll buy you dinner every night. ☺
Billy Smith

a
Hey Billy. I'm not doing anything on Sunday. Want to come round? I've been practising a song called *Heart of Gold* – do you know it? Maybe we could play together? To be honest, I'm not very good at the guitar. How about you? Gemma
Gemma Black

b
Gemma Black
Great fun yesterday. A new friend came round and we played guitar together. He's a beginner, but I'm not great, so we had fun. We watched a YouTube lesson for a song called *Heart of Gold* – it's not too difficult to play. We had tea together afterwards, too.

c
Sign in | Post
Hi everyone, I've got an acoustic guitar that I want to sell. It's a two-year-old Yamaha, perfect condition, £250 with the case. Anyone interested? If not, tell your friends please!

d
To: Gemma
From: billy@thinkmail.com
Hi!

Hi Gemma,
I've thought about the guitar. It's really nice but a bit more than I can really afford, so I'm going to stick with my old one for now.
But it was nice to talk. Thanks for the tip about the YouTube lessons – that guy is much better than the one I've been using. You know, we ought to practise together some time. What do you think?
Billy

e
MESSAGES
Contacts
Hi G,
Thanks for last Sunday. It was fun playing the guitar with you and the tea was nice, too. I've listened to some more songs by Neil Young. Old guy, but cool tunes! We should do it again soon.
B
PS Love the photo on Instagram!

TH!NK more

Workbook
Reading p40, Ex.1–3

Critical THINKing
Understanding and analysing links between ideas
Identifies the basic structure of an argument.

Grammar; Vocabulary; Functions

▶ 11 Grammar rap!
should(n't), had better, ought to

5 1 'd better 2 should 3 ought to

Read the rule with students and elicit answers. Give an example of *had better*, e.g., *You had better study hard or you won't pass.*

RULE: 4 advice 5 negative 6 don't

6 1 g, 'd better 2 f, ought to
3 d, ought to 4 e, 'd better
5 a, shouldn't 6 b, should
7 c, better not

7 Give your own example before students do the task.

Workbook p37

Get it Right!
will vs. should

Student's Book p123

8 This is a challenging exercise, so you could explain the difference between the verb *to advise* and the noun *advice* before completing b and c.

Ask: *Who gives you the best advice: a friend, a family member, the internet?* Write on the board: *My mother gives me ___ advice. She advises me ___ work hard. She advises me ___ playing computer games. I ___ her advice.* Elicit words to fill the gaps.

a Advice is a noun; advise is a verb.
b to ignore [someone's] advice, to take / follow [someone's] advice
c Students' own answers

9 During feedback, make sure students are pronouncing *advice* /s/ and *advise* /z/ correctly.

1 ignored, advice 2 advice about
3 advised, follow / take, advice
4 advises against

Workbook p38

10 Read the questions with students and quickly elicit some possible answers.

Language for giving advice

Point out that we say *to advise someone to do something*, but we *advise against doing something*. Tell students that this is because *against* is a preposition and is therefore followed by a noun or the gerund (*-ing*) form of the verb.

GRAMMAR
should(n't), had better, ought to

5 **Complete these sentences from the messages on page 42. Then choose the correct words to complete the rules.**

1 You ______ make your own dinner tonight.
2 We ______ do it again soon.
3 We ______ practise together some time.

> RULE: *Should, had better* and *ought to* are used to give [4]**advice / information**.
> - *Should* and *ought to* mean more or less the same, but we usually don't use *ought to* in questions and negative statements.
> - The meaning of *had better* is often a little stronger. The speaker wants to say that there are [5]**positive / negative** consequences if you ignore the advice.
>
> These verbs [6]**do / don't** use an auxiliary verb in the negative: *shouldn't, oughtn't to, had better not.*

6 **Match the questions to the answers. Write a–g in the boxes. Choose the correct word in each answer.**

1 I've broken my friend's watch. What should I do? ☐
2 I've got toothache. What should I do? ☐
3 I didn't do very well in the test. What should I do? ☐
4 I'd like to go climbing, but I've never done it before. What should I do? ☐
5 I got an email from someone, asking me to send them money. Should I reply to it? ☐
6 I'm angry with my brother. He said something I didn't like. What should I do? ☐
7 This sweater my sister gave me looks terrible. I don't like it at all. What should I do? ☐

a You *should / shouldn't* respond. It could be a scam.
b You *should / shouldn't* tell him. It's best to be honest with him.
c You'd *better / better not* return it to the shop. That would really hurt her feelings.
d You *shouldn't / ought to* go back and study everything again.
e You'd *better / shouldn't* get some training. It can be dangerous.
f You *ought to / shouldn't* see a dentist.
g You'd *better / shouldn't* say sorry the next time you see your friend.

7 **Look at these pictures. Write short dialogues with (serious or funny) answers giving advice.**

1 *What should I do?*
You should run after the man and give him his wallet.

→ workbook page 37

VOCABULARY
Language for giving advice

8 **Look at the phrases below and answer the questions.**

to give (bad / good / practical / useful) advice about [something]
to take / follow [someone's] advice
to ignore [someone's] advice
to advise [someone][to do something]
to advise against [something]
to be advisable

a What's the difference between *advice* and *advise*?
b Which of the phrases mean(s)
– not to listen to somebody's advice?
– do what somebody has advised you to do?
c How do you say 'advisable' in your language?

9 **Complete the sentences with phrases from Exercise 8. Use the correct verb forms.**

1 I've told Peter he shouldn't post photos like that, but he has always ______ my ______.
2 Should I buy a tablet or a laptop? Can you give me some ______ what's better?
3 He wants to become a web designer. His dad has ______ him to take a course. He should ______ that ______.
4 My uncle has a heart problem. This web page ______ fatty foods.

→ workbook page 38

FUNCTIONS
Giving advice

10 SPEAKING **Ask and answer questions with a partner.**

1 Imagine you meet somebody who has never used a computer. What advice would you give them about social networking?
2 Are you good at giving advice? Say why (not) and give examples.
3 When do you find it difficult to follow someone's advice?

Activity idea Extension

Ask students to imagine some problems that they have. You could either put them in pairs and ask them to create dialogues as in Exercise 6, or ask them to walk around asking people for advice for their problems. This encourages them to use the language of advice spontaneously. When students have asked for advice several times, ask individuals to give feedback in open class and decide as a class what the best piece of advice was.

TH!NK more

Practice Extra
Unit 4 Practise it!

Workbook
Grammar p37, Ex.6–7
Vocabulary p38, Ex.4–7

Worksheets
Grammar rap! *should(n't), had better, ought to*
Grammar Worksheets 4
Vocabulary Worksheets 4

Warmer

Write the word *books* on the board. Go round the class, quickly nominating students to name a book by an English-speaking author. Write any answers on the board. Ask: *How long ago were the first books written? Do you know where?*

▶ 12 TH!NK
The evolution of writing

1 Before students do the task, get them to cover the article and just look at the photos. In pairs, give students two minutes to answer the question.
Cave paintings; e-book; printing press; engraved text on stone

2 Read the paragraph headings to check understanding. Tell students not to worry about difficult vocabulary at this stage but to focus on matching the paragraphs with the headings. To make the exercise easier, students could choose from just the four correct headings (b, c, e, and f).

3 4.04
1 e 2 b 3 f 4 c

4 Encourage students to express themselves in English and to use any vocabulary they have learned from the article.

Pronunciation
The short /ʌ/ vowel sound

Student's Book p120

Activity idea Extension

Ask students to imagine the following situation:

You are digging in your garden when you find a 2,000-year-old stone tablet that proves the existence of life on other planets. What would you do with the information? Would it be better not to tell anybody?

Ask students to discuss in pairs, then hold an open class discussion.

TH!NK more

Workbook
Pronunciation p119

TH!NK
The evolution of writing

Culture

1 Look at the photos. What do they show?

FROM CAVES TO KINDLES – HOW READING HAS CHANGED

1 ☐

Cave paintings are the oldest pictures. Some of them, like the beautiful images in the caves of Altamira in the north of Spain, are almost 30,000 years old. Many of these paintings show animals or hunting scenes. The images do not have written words, but when we look at them, we get an idea of the emotions the people felt when drawing them. The paintings tell stories of hopes and fears. They are an early form of communication.

2 ☐

Sometime between 4000 and 3000 BCE, people in Egypt and Mesopotamia developed the skill of writing. They engraved text on stone tablets first. But it was impossible to carry stones from place to place. The invention of papyrus allowed documents to be moved easily. Writing on papyrus made it easier to correct mistakes, too. And do you know how they did that? When a scribe – the person who wrote the documents – made a mistake, they licked the ink off the papyrus before it got dry and made their corrections!

3 ☐

People made the first books from papyrus and from thin animal skins. Paper was invented in China as early as 105 CE. The quality of paper soon became very good. The world's oldest known printed book is from China, too. It was published on May 11, 868 CE. In Europe, books were written manually until the middle of the 15th century, when Johannes Gutenberg invented the printing press in Germany. Since that time, almost 140 million books have been published worldwide. For many people, one of life's greatest pleasures is spending a few hours in a bookshop browsing through the books.

4 ☐

Books will be around for many years, of course. But there are many other ways of reading books and magazines, such as e-books and apps on mobile phones, which allow you to buy and download reading material to carry around with you and read whenever and wherever you want to.

2 **Read the article quickly. Match the paragraph headings with the paragraphs. Write the letters a–f. There are two headings you don't need.**

a The invention of books by Gutenberg
b Early forms of written communication
c Books in their most modern form
d From stone tablets to the printing press
e Communication without reading and writing
f The history of bookmaking

3 4.04 **Read and listen to the article and check your answers in Exercise 2.**

4 SPEAKING **Work in pairs. Discuss the questions.**

1 How important are books for you? Give reasons.
2 What book(s) have you read recently? Did you like it / them?
3 Do you prefer printed books or e-books? Why?

PRONUNCIATION
The short /ʌ/ vowel sound Go to page 120.

44

Culture notes

The Cave of Altamira is in Cantabria, Spain, and is famous for its Upper Palaeolithic cave drawings. The cave was closed in 1977 as the paintings were being damaged by the carbon dioxide in the breath of visitors.

Egypt is a nation state in northeastern Africa. Ancient Egypt saw some of the earliest developments of writing. Their ancient writing system of hieroglyphics has been found on clay tablets dating from the 33rd century BCE.

Mesopotamia is an area of land between the Tigris and Euphrates rivers, in modern-day Iraq, Turkey and Syria. Five thousand years ago, it consisted of the Sumer, Akkadian, Babylonian and Assyrian empires. Sumerian writing is thought to be the main influence on Egyptian hieroglyphics.

Papyrus is a thin paper-like material made from the papyrus plant. It was used in Ancient Egypt and throughout the Mediterranean region as a writing material.

Johannes Gutenberg (c.1398–1468) was a German printer who introduced printing to Europe. He invented mechanical movable-type printing in around 1439. This introduced the era of mass communication.

Social Responsibility
Understanding own and others' cultures
Understands the contributions of different cultures to their own lives.

5 **Check/clarify:** *hunting scenes, scribe, manually.*
1 papyrus 2 browsing 3 emotions 4 published 5 licked 6 engraved 7 printing press

1 Before students answer the questions, get them to focus on the safety tips web page. Ask: *Who would this be important for?* (anyone using a computer in a public place).
1 hostel, library, airport
2 Students' own answers
3 Someone else could access your account.
4 If you haven't logged out, your account information may still be accessible to someone else.

2 2 Don't click 'Yes'.
3 Make sure you do not simply close the browser.
4 You should always log out.
5 Ask them politely to go somewhere else.

3 Before students match the sentences and situations, elicit that all of the sentences in Exercise 2 are used to give advice.
They are used to give advice.
a 2 b 3 c 1 d 5 e 4

4 Get students to underline the language in the web page that helped them choose their answers.
Introduction: d Bullet point 1: e Bullet point 2: b Bullet point 3: a Bullet point 4: c

5 Ask students to read the four ideas and discuss what advice they would give in each situation. Tell them to use the web page as an example and to use words like *should, ought to, make sure*, etc.

6 Encourage students to organise their writing as outlined in Exercise 4. This can be done as a collaborative writing activity in class with pairs of students working together. On completion, you could ask students to exchange their texts with another pair for them to read and correct any grammatical errors.

ONLINE LIFE UNIT 4

5 VOCABULARY **There are eight highlighted words in the article. Match the words with these meanings. Write the words.**

0 a large hole in a cliff or mountain that goes inside ___cave___
1 paper made from plants ______
2 looking through a book or magazine, without reading everything ______
3 happiness, love and anger ______
4 produced (and sold) a book ______
5 moved the tongue across something ______
6 words that are cut into stone ______
7 a machine to make newspapers, books or magazines ______

WRITING
A web page giving advice

1 INPUT **Read this information and decide who it would be important for. Then answer the questions.**

1 Where do people use public computers?
2 What other examples not mentioned in the text can you think of?
3 Why should you never save a password on a public computer?
4 What's the problem with just closing the browser when you want to finish a session?

HOW TO USE A
PUBLIC COMPUTER
– SAFETY TIPS

There are times when you may want to use a public computer, for example in a hostel, a library or at an airport. That's when it's especially important to be smart and safe.

- Don't save! When you want to log into a social networking website or your email, the system will ask you, 'Do you want to save this password?' Don't click 'Yes' when you are working on a public computer.
- Log out! Make sure you do not simply close the browser when you want to leave a site. You should always log out of all sites when you finish your session.
- Close windows! If you need to walk away from the computer for any reason, you should close all the windows on the computer first. Don't leave any information on the screen that other people shouldn't see.
- Watch out! Be careful of people looking at the screen over your shoulder. Ask them politely to go somewhere else so you can use the computer in private.

2 **Rewrite the sentences by putting the words in brackets in the right position.**

1 Read our advice. (carefully)
Read our advice carefully.
2 Click 'Yes.' (don't)
3 Make you do not simply close the browser. (sure)
4 You should log out. (always)
5 Ask them to go somewhere else. (politely)

3 **Are the sentences above used to give advice or to give an opinion? Match each of them with one of the situations below. Write the numbers 1–5.**

a when the system asks you 'Do you want to save the password?' ☐
b when you want to leave a site ☐
c to be smart and safe when using public computers ☐
d if someone looks over your shoulder and watches you ☐
e when you finish your session ☐

4 ANALYSE **Match the content with the five sections of the text.**

Introduction	a	Don't leave important information on the screen.
Bullet point 1	b	Log out properly.
Bullet point 2	c	Don't let people watch you.
Bullet point 3	d	What is the purpose of this text?
Bullet point 4	e	Don't save information.

5 PLAN **What would be important advice for good online behaviour? Make notes.**

Here are some ideas:
what (not) to share on social networks
creating secure passwords and how to keep them safe
what to do when you receive offensive comments on social networking websites
what you should know about uploading photos on social networks

6 PRODUCE **Write your text for a web page giving advice on good online behaviour (about 200 words).**

Use an introduction and bullet points to structure your text.
Use language from Exercises 2 and 3 to give advice, and make sure your readers understand what situations your advice refers to.

45

Homework

Ask students to write a short paragraph containing at least five of the 'computer' words from page 45. In the next lesson, students read out their paragraphs, pausing before computer words for partners to guess the word, e.g., *Yesterday I opened my computer and typed in my … password!*

Activity idea Extension

Students could discuss whether or not they follow the recommended online behaviour. Their partner could give them advice if they don't.

THINK more

Practice Extra
Unit 4 Master it!

Workbook
Developing Writing p41

Tests
Unit, extension and skills test 4

1 In B1 Preliminary for Schools Reading Part 2, candidates have to read five short descriptions of people followed by eight short texts on a particular topic. They have to match each person to one of five of the texts. This part of the exam tests the candidates' detailed comprehension of factual material. Encourage your students to do the following when they approach this task:

- Read the five descriptions of the people.
- Read the eight texts carefully and underline any parts that match anything in the descriptions of the people.
- Compare the description again with any possible matches, checking that the text meets all the requirements of the description.
- Avoid using one or two identical words to choose an answer, but instead focus on the meaning of the whole text before choosing the answer.

1C 2G 3D 4A 5E

Workbook p43

B1 Preliminary for Schools

READING
Part 2: Matching

workbook page 43

1 For each question, choose the correct answer. The young people below are looking for a film to watch. Look at the eight film reviews. Decide which film would be most suitable for the people below.

1 Dawn loves thinking about the future and how human society will be different. She's a fan of films that are set in a time many years from now but doesn't really enjoy films that are too frightening.

2 Paula's job is very boring so when she gets home she likes watching films with special effects, but she's not a fan of sci-fi. She also likes films with fast action.

3 Keith is a romantic guy who enjoys a good love story but it must have a happy ending. He doesn't like serious films very much, and likes to have a laugh, too.

4 Lisa's not really a fan of fiction and only watches films about real life. She's interested in anything from history to nature to science, as long as she learns something from it.

5 Graham likes many different kinds of films, but cartoons are his favourite. He especially likes them when they are based on a true story, especially on historical events.

HOT NEW FILMS

A THE INVISIBLE WORLD
Using the most advanced camera technology in the world, this documentary takes us to places that have never been filmed before. From deep under the sea to inside the human body, this film contains some of the most amazing images you will ever see.

B THE KING WHO NEVER WAS
In 1936 Edward VIII decided to give up being king after less than a year so he could be with the woman he loved. This film revisits one of the most popular 'royal stories' of all time and mixes fact and fiction to create an interesting drama. It will keep audiences entertained.

C IT COULD HAPPEN TO YOU
Imagine waking up in the future in a house that is not the house you went to sleep in. Imagine not recognising your children – even though they all seem to think you are their mum. This fascinating sci-fi takes us to a world where people buy and sell memories.

D WILL THEY? WON'T THEY?
Ever since school, Jack and Jill have been best friends. But now they are in their twenties, and their feelings are changing. Is either of them brave enough to see that they are falling in love? Will they do something about it? Of course, it is all OK in the end in this likeable rom com.

E JOAN OF ARC
The well-known story of the young French woman who fought and died for the freedom of her country, back in the 15th century. Her fantastic story is told in a very emotional way in this animated version, with the voices of many famous film stars. It is also a historically accurate account. Young children might find it disturbing.

F TOMORROW NOW
The year is 2080 and for the last ten years Earth has been in contact with aliens. Today is the day that we finally welcome them to our planet. How will they change our lives and are they really as friendly as they seem? One of the scariest films you will see this year.

G COUNTDOWN TO DISASTER
A speeding train is going to crash into a nuclear power station and no one can stop it. Or can they? Special agent Ryan has got an hour to stop the disaster, but there's a problem – he has a bomb tied around his waist. Car chases, explosions and amazing special effects – this thriller has got it all.

H OLIVER TWIST
This wonderful version of the famous Charles Dickens story will be enjoyed by everyone. An animated cartoon, it takes us back to Victorian London and wonderful characters like Oliver himself, The Artful Dodger and Fagin. There have not been many better animated fiction films in the past twenty years.

WRITING
Part 2: An article or story

workbook page 107

2 Choose one of these questions. Write your answer in about 100 words.

Question 1
- Your English teacher has asked you to write a story.
- Your story must begin with this sentence.
  I had tickets to see my favourite band and I was very excited.
- Write your **story**.

Question 2
- You see this notice in an international English-language magazine.
- Write your **article**.

ARTICLES WANTED!
USING LESS ENERGY
What things in your everyday life do you use energy to do?
What can you do to reduce the amount of energy you use?
Why is it important to save energy?
Tell us what you think.
Write an article about these questions and we will publish the most interesting in our magazine.

46

2 In B1 Preliminary for Schools Writing Part 2, candidates have to write either an article or a story of about 100 words. For the article, they are given a small text with the topic and a couple of questions to respond to. This part of the exam tests the candidates' ability to write well-organised texts with a real communicative purpose.

Encourage your students to do the following when they approach this task:

- Candidates should read both tasks and consider the topic and the language that is needed in each before choosing the task that best suits them.
- When writing the story, pay close attention to any names or pronouns used in the opening sentence and make sure the rest of the story continues in the same way. For example, if the story begins in the third person, it should continue that way.
- When writing the article, read the notice and the questions carefully, to identify what is required and who it is for, and what kind of information is needed.
- Plan the outline of the story/article before writing the final answer. Make sure that it is well organised and has a range of tenses, expressions and vocabulary.
- Read the story again to check that it makes sense and that it has a clear link to the opening sentence. Or read the article again to check that it makes sense and that all the content points have been included. Check the spelling.

Workbook p107

1 1 mode 2 comedy 3 download 4 documentary 5 advice 6 news 7 advise 8 attachment 9 key 10 ignore

2 1 no one 2 best 3 someone 4 none 5 better 6 Everyone

3 1 Grandad looks really tired. I think we ought to go home now.
2 The film isn't as good ~~than~~ as the book.
3 There were four football matches on TV last night, and all of them ~~was~~ were brilliant!
4 It's the ~~most bad~~ worst party I've ever been to.
5 He talks more ~~quiet~~ quietly than his brother.
6 She's really angry. We'd better ~~to~~ go and say sorry.

4 1 everything, should 2 help, would 3 with, against 4 hand, ought

TEST YOURSELF — UNITS 3 & 4

VOCABULARY

1 Complete the sentences with the words in the list. There are two extra words.

advice | advise | attachment | comedy | documentary | download | ignore | key | mode | news | thriller | upload

1 If you're on a plane, don't forget to put your mobile phone in flight __________ .
2 There was a __________ programme on TV last night – I've never laughed so much in my life!
3 You need to fill in a form. You can __________ it from our website.
4 There was an interesting programme last night – a __________ about the history of my country.
5 Let me give you some __________ . Don't go to that new café, it's awful.
6 My father always watches the __________ on TV to see what's happening in the world.
7 I'm sure you think it's a good idea, but I'd __________ against it, to be honest.
8 I got your email but you forgot to send the __________ with it. Can you send it, please?
9 The first thing I do when I switch my computer on is __________ in my password.
10 He doesn't know what he's talking about, so you should just __________ his advice! /10

GRAMMAR

2 Complete the sentences with the words in the list.

best | better | everyone | no one | none | someone

1 I advertised my bike for sale, but __________ wanted it.
2 This place makes the __________ hamburgers I've ever eaten.
3 I've got a problem and I need to talk to __________ , please.
4 I asked all my friends, but __________ of them knew the answer.
5 I think her new film is __________ than her last one.
6 The school trip was wonderful. __________ had a really good time.

3 Find and correct the mistake in each sentence.

1 Grandad looks really tired. I think we ought go home now.
2 The film isn't as good than the book.
3 There were four football matches on TV last night, and all of them was brilliant!
4 It's the most bad party I've ever been to.
5 He talks more quiet than his brother.
6 She's really angry. We'd better to go and say sorry. /12

FUNCTIONAL LANGUAGE

4 Complete the mini-dialogues with the words in the list.

against | everything | hand | help | ought | should | with | would

1 A Is __________ OK?
B Yes, thanks. But perhaps I __________ take an aspirin.
2 A Can I __________ you at all?
B Well, yes, that __________ be great. Thanks!
3 A Could you help me __________ something? I want to send money to someone who wrote me an email.
B Well, you know, that's not a good idea. I'd advise __________ it.
4 A Joe? This is heavy. Can you lend me a __________ ?
B Hmm, it looks too heavy. You __________ to use a machine. /8

MY SCORE /30

22–30 | 10–21 | 0–9

47

The Cambridge Life Competencies Framework

Collaboration

Listening respectfully and responding constructively to others' contributions

Watch the video to discover how you can help your learners work more effectively with their peers and develop their listening skills.

Scan the QR code here

Warmer

Ask the class to stand up. Nominate a student to say the name of a musician or group. Students who like songs by this artist sit down. Keep going until everybody is sitting down.

▶ 13 Get TH!NKing

Play the video and discuss the question with your class.

1 5.01
1 pop 2 rap 3 opera 4 jazz 5 dance music 6 rock

2 Write *types of music* in the centre of the board. In groups, ask students to think of as many genres of music as possible and to create a spider diagram with genres leading to other genres, e.g., *rock* leading to *punk*, *heavy metal*, *rock and roll*, *glam rock*, etc. After three minutes, ask a student to come to the front and draw their mind map. Then, elicit further genres from the rest of the class and add them to the mind map.

3 You might like to write some adjectives on the board for students to use (e.g., *brilliant*, *great*, *terrible*, *awful*).

4 Before students read the article, get them to cover it and just look at the photos. In pairs, give students two minutes to answer the questions. Do not check answers for now.

5 *1 Prince Harry, Meghan Markle, Sheku Kanneh-Mason*
2 Sheku Kanneh-Mason played the cello at the wedding of Harry and Meghan.

5 MUSIC TO MY EARS

OBJECTIVES

FUNCTIONS: asking about feelings; making helpful suggestions

GRAMMAR: present perfect continuous; present perfect simple vs. present perfect continuous

VOCABULARY: making music; musical instruments; phrases with *out*

Get TH!NKING
Watch the video and think: how do you listen to music?

1 ____ 2 ____ 3 ____ 4 ____ 5 ____ 6 ____

READING

1 5.01 **Listen. What type of music do you hear? Write the words under the pictures.**

dance music | jazz | opera | pop | rap | rock

2 **What other types of music can you think of?**

3 SPEAKING **Work in pairs. What kind of music do you like? Ask and answer questions.**

Do you like ... ?
I love/like/can't stand ...
I've never listened to ...

4 **Look at the photos on the next page and answer the questions.**
1 Who are the people?
2 What do you think the connection between the photos is?

5 **Read the article quickly and check your ideas.**

6 5.02 **Read and listen to the article again and answer the questions.**
1 What type of music did Sheku play at the royal wedding?
2 How many people watched him play at the wedding?
3 When and where did Sheku first play in front of the prince?
4 How did Sheku announce he was playing at the wedding?
5 Where did Sheku study music?
6 Who did Sheku perform with on a talent show?
7 Why was he offered a record contract?
8 How successful was *Inspiration*?

48

6 5.02 **Check/clarify:** *chapel, cellist, audience, charity, scholarship, institution.*
1 Classical music 2 600 people in the church and millions around the world 3 a year before / in 2017 at a charity concert in London 4 On Twitter 5 the Royal Academy of Music in London 6 his older sister and brother 7 Because he won the BBC Young Musician of the Year competition. 8 It spent four weeks in the UK top 40 charts.

Objectives

Functions and speaking Role play: Helpful suggestions; **Developing speaking:** Asking about feelings; helpful suggestions
Grammar Present perfect continuous; present perfect simple vs. present perfect continuous
Vocabulary Making music; musical instruments; **WordWise:** Phrasal verbs with *out*
Values Following your dreams
Life Competencies Managing your money

Resources for this unit

All available online

Videos
- Get **TH!NK**ing: *How do you listen to music?*
- Grammar rap!: Present perfect simple vs. present perfect continuous
- Vlog: Managing your money

Tests
- Unit, extension and skills test 5

Worksheets
- Grammar and vocabulary: Basic, Standard and Extension Worksheets
- Project: Music for all
- Communication: My life in music
- Literature Worksheets: *Twelve Years a Slave*
- Get **TH!NK**ing, Grammar rap! and Life Lessons video Worksheets

Culture notes

Harry (born Henry Charles Albert David Windsor on 15 September 1984), Duke of Sussex, is a member of the British royal family. He is the younger son of Charles, Prince of Wales, and Diana, Princess of Wales. He's also the grandson of Queen Elizabeth II.

Meghan (born Rachel Meghan Markle on 4 August 1981), Duchess of Sussex, is an American-born member of the British royal family and former actress. From 2011 to 2018, she played Rachel Zane on the American legal drama *Suits*.

Sheku Kanneh-Mason was born on 4 April 1999 and is a British cellist who won the 2016 BBC Young Musician of the Year award. He was the first black musician to win the award since its launch 38 years earlier. He has six brothers and sisters, all of whom play musical instruments to a high level.

The Royal Academy of Music in London, England, is the oldest conservatoire in the UK, founded in 1822. Famous Academy alumni include Sir Elton John and Annie Lennox.

A BRIGHT STAR

On Saturday May 19th 2018, millions of people around the world watched as Prince Harry married the American actress Meghan Markle at St George's Chapel in Windsor Castle, in front of 600 guests. As they signed the marriage register, a young cellist played three pieces of classical music.

It was a dream come true for 19-year-old Sheku Kanneh-Mason. It was the biggest performance of his short professional career so far, and a sign that he was quickly becoming one of the most admired classical musicians in the world.

This wasn't Sheku's first performance in front of the prince. A year earlier Harry was in the audience for a charity concert in London. Perhaps it was Sheku's performance at this concert that resulted in his royal invitation. The following April an excited Sheku announced on Twitter that Meghan had phoned him to see if he would like to play at the wedding.

Sheku has been playing the cello since he was six. He is one of seven children in an amazingly talented family from Nottingham in England. Sheku and his six brothers and sisters are all extremely talented classical musicians. His eldest sister, Isata, won a scholarship to the famous Royal Academy of Music in London to study the piano. A few years later, Sheku followed her when he gained a place at the same institution to study the cello. He was only nine years old. He has been performing with Isata and his older brother Braimah for many years. In 2015 they decided to enter the talent show *Britain's Got Talent* as the Kanneh-Masons. Their performances on the show were watched by several million people and they reached the semi-finals.

A year later Sheku entered the BBC Young Musician of the Year competition, which he won. He became the first black musician ever to win the award. He was just 17 years old. As a result of this success he also got a contract with the music publishing company Decca to record an album.

In 2018, he released his first album, *Inspiration*. The album spent four weeks in the UK top 40 charts and it contains many famous classical pieces. Sheku also includes classical versions of songs by Bob Marley and Leonard Cohen on the album. It has introduced a younger audience to classical music.

The future is looking bright for Sheku Kanneh-Mason!

TH!NK values

Following your dreams

7 **Match these people with their dreams.**

1. Jessie is a really good artist. ☐
2. Kylie loves acting. ☐
3. David is great at football. ☐
4. Lance has written a book. ☐

a 'I want to get it published.'
b 'I want to be in a play.'
c 'I want to play professionally.'
d 'I'd love to have an exhibition of my work.'

8 **What should the people in Exercise 7 do to realise their dreams? Give advice. Make notes for each one.**

David / join club

9 SPEAKING **Work in pairs. Compare your ideas.**

10 SPEAKING **Discuss these questions in small groups.**

1. What is your dream?
2. What can you do to make it come true?

7 As an alternative, you could ask students to cover a–d and get them to guess what the dreams are.
1d 2b 3c 4a

8 This is an opportunity to review the language of advice from Unit 4.

9 Students can decide which is the best piece of advice for each of the people.

10 You might like to tell students about your ambitions when you were younger. You could put a photo that illustrates your dream on the board, hidden. Gradually reveal it and ask students to guess what your dream was. Ask: *Did the dream come true?*

Encourage students to go into detail about what they want to do and how they plan to make it happen. Their partners should give advice to them.

Homework

Ask students to choose three types of music and write sentences saying why they like / don't like each type. This can be shared in the next lesson.

Activity idea Extension

Show students some clips of videos by Sheku Kanneh-Mason. Ask students to work in pairs and give their opinions on the music and Sheku's talent. This can be done as a speaking or writing exercise.

TH!NK more

Worksheets
Project Music for all
Communication My life in music
Get **TH!NK**ing *How do you listen to music?*

Critical TH!NKing
Participating in creative activities
Actively participates in "what if" (cautionary or wishful thinking) and "if only" (wishful thinking) discussions.

Warmer

Ask students to draw a timeline to represent their life. Students think of something they have been able to do for a long time and mark on the timeline when they started doing it. Ask for some examples, e.g., *I can swim. I started swimming when I was six.*

1 Ask students to try to answer the questions from memory before referring back to page 49 to check.
1 has been playing 2 has been performing

2 With weaker classes, you may like to do this as a whole-class activity.
RULE: 1 b 2 a 3 c

3 **Check/clarify:** *barked/barking*.
1 talking 2 been 3 hasn't 4 been 5 haven't 6 barking

4 You may like to review the use of *for* and *since*. Write *three days*, *1989*, *yesterday*, *a week*, *last Tuesday* and *twenty minutes* on the board. Ask students to decide whether to use *for* or *since* with each.
1 've been running, for 2 've been waiting, for 3 's been watching, since 4 's been lying, since 5 've been walking, for 6 's been working, since

5 You may want to talk about an experience of your own as an example.

Workbook p46

Pronunciation

been: strong /biːn/ and weak /bɪn/

Student's Book p120

GRAMMAR
Present perfect continuous

1 Complete the sentences with the correct form of the words in brackets. Check your answers in the article on page 49.

1 Sheku ________________ (play) the cello since he was six.
2 He ________________ (perform) with Isata and his older brother Braimah for many years.

2 Match the example sentences below with the rules. Write the numbers 1–3.

1 I've been learning the piano for two years.
2 I've been practising the piano since 10 am.
3 I've been playing the piano all day and I'm tired now.

RULE: The present perfect continuous is used for actions happening over a period of time. We use it to:
a emphasise how long an activity has been happening. The activity may or may not be complete. ☐
b talk generally about situations or activities that started in the past and are still continuing now. ☐
c talk about situations or activities that have stopped but have a result in the present. ☐

3 Choose the correct words.

1 He's been *talking* / *talked* on the phone all morning.
2 I've *being* / *been* playing this game for hours now.
3 Jo *hasn't* / *haven't* been feeling well for a few days.
4 They've *been* / *being* studying since ten o'clock.
5 We *haven't* / *hasn't* been living here for very long.
6 The dog's been *barked* / *barking* for half an hour.

4 Complete the sentences. Use the correct form of the words and *for* or *since*.

1 We're tired because we ________________ (run) ____________ hours.
2 I ________________ (wait) for her ____________ 40 minutes!
3 He ________________ (watch) TV ____________ 9 am.
4 She's red because she ________________ (lie) in the sun ____________ this morning.
5 They ________________ (walk) in the rain ____________ an hour and they're really wet.
6 Dad's exhausted because he ________________ (work) in the garden ____________ he got up.

5 SPEAKING Work in pairs. Find out how long your partner has been doing these things.

1 living in their house
2 learning English
3 going to school
4 talking

How long have you been learning English?
For two years.

→ workbook page 46

PRONUNCIATION
been: strong /biːn/ and weak /bɪn/
Go to page 120.

VOCABULARY
Making music

6 Complete the story of Dymonde with the verbs in the list.

enter | entered | going | playing | record | released | start | streaming | won | writing

Alana Bolan started out as a teacher, but she always wanted to be a musician and she always loved [1]______ *music* and *lyrics* for songs. One day she decided to [2]______ *a band*, so she put an advert online. She soon found the band mates she was looking for. They called themselves Dymonde. They practised hard and started [3]______ *local gigs*. A few months ago they decided to [4]______ *a talent show*. They [5]______ *the competition*, and their prize was a day in a recording studio. They used it to [6]______ *a single* called *New Love*. They [7]______ *the single* a week ago, and loads of people have been [8]______ *it*. It's already [9]______ *the charts*. Radio stations have been playing it lots, too. Next month their album is coming out and they are [10]______ *on tour* all over the country. Get your tickets fast! They are running out quickly.

7 SPEAKING Work in pairs. Ask your partner about their favourite band. Use the expressions in Exercise 6.

Who writes the songs?
Have you been to any of their gigs?

→ workbook page 48

WRITING
The story of your favourite band

8 Write the story of your favourite band.

Write about:
- how they started.
- how long they have been together.
- how long you have liked them and why.

6 1 writing 2 start 3 playing 4 enter 5 won 6 record 7 released 8 streaming 9 entered 10 going

7 To maximise speaking, make sure each person in the pair has a different favourite. Make a note of any students who use the vocabulary in Exercise 6 and ask them to repeat their sentence during feedback.

Workbook p48

8 If mobile phone use is permitted, encourage students to search on the internet. In the next lesson, ask students to present their work to the class.

Language note Present perfect continuous

Point out that with the verbs *work* and *live*, the present perfect continuous and simple can both be used with little difference in meaning, e.g., *I've lived here for three years. / I've been living here for three years.*

TH!NK more

Workbook
Grammar p46, Ex.1–6
Pronunciation p119
Vocabulary p48, Ex.1
Vocabulary Extra p49, Ex.1–2
Developing Writing p51

Worksheets
Grammar Worksheets 5
Vocabulary Worksheets 5

9 5.05 Before students listen, explain that they will hear an interview between two people. Tell them not to focus on understanding every word for now, but to just listen for the answer.
How important music is to her

10 5.05 Before listening again, elicit which key information students should listen for in each question and ask them to underline it. If necessary, play the audio and stop it after the answer to the first question and go through this as an example.
1 Very important 2 The guitar 3 Classical music 4 They're not very important to her – she doesn't really listen to them.

11 5.06 Elicit what type of information students will need to complete each sentence.
1 Piano lessons when he was younger 2 Not keen on jazz music 3 Lyrics aren't important

12 Check/clarify: *feeling down, depending on, influences, melody, taste in music.*
Students can do the quiz individually and work out their score before discussing their answers in pairs.

13 Check/clarify: *the major change in meaning of run and out in the phrase run out of.*
Explain that many verbs in English are often followed by a preposition, e.g. *listen to.* Point out that these verbs are not always phrasal verbs – their meaning can be more obvious. Elicit examples of verbs like this that students know already, e.g., *listen to, depend on*, etc.
1 started 2 coming 3 running 4 sort 5 go 6 Find

14 *1 b 2 a 3 c 4 d 5 f 6 e*

15 Point out that students will need to change the tense of the verb in some of the sentences.
1 went out 2 came out 3 've run out 4 find out 5 sorted, out 6 started out

Workbook p48

LISTENING

9 5.05 **Listen to the interview with Dana. What is she talking about?**

10 5.05 **Listen again and answer the questions.**
1 How important is music for Dana?
2 What instrument would Dana like to play?
3 What music does Dana listen to when she's studying?
4 What does Dana think about song lyrics?

11 5.06 **Now listen to Ben answering the same questions. Write three things he has in common with Dana.**
1 ______
2 ______
3 ______

SPEAKING

12 Work in pairs. Do the quiz. Then discuss your answers to these questions.
- What do you agree or disagree with your score? Why?
- What music do you listen to when you are sad?
- What songs have special memories for you?
- What are your favourite song lyrics?
- How do you choose what music to listen to?
- What music do your friends like?

DOES MUSIC ROCK YOUR WORLD?
COULD YOU LIVE WITHOUT IT?

Take our quiz and find out just how important music is in your life.

For each question, choose the sentence that describes you best. Then work out your score and find out just how music mad you are.

1 A I only listen to music when I'm happy. ☐
B Music makes me feel better when I'm feeling down. ☐
C I listen to different music depending on how I feel. ☐

2 A I have loads of memories connected to different songs. ☐
B I never listen to music from when I was younger. ☐
C I get bored with songs quickly. ☐

3 A My musical taste influences the clothes I wear. ☐
B Music has nothing to do with fashion. ☐
C I don't really think about what I wear. ☐

4 A I have the same musical tastes as my best friends. ☐
B I like different music from most of my friends. ☐
C I always know if I'm going to be friends with someone when they tell me their taste in music. ☐

5 A I always listen to the lyrics in songs. ☐
B Melody is more important than lyrics. ☐
C Melody and lyrics are both really important in a song. ☐

GO TO PAGE 127 TO FIND OUT YOUR SCORE!

WordWise: Phrasal verbs with *out*

13 Complete each of these sentences from the unit so far with a word from the list.

coming | find | go | running | sort | started

1 Alana Bolan ______ out as a teacher.
2 Next month their album is ______ out.
3 Hurry up and get your tickets. They are ______ out quickly.
4 When I've got a problem to ______ out, listening to classical music can help.
5 I'd never ______ out and buy any music.
6 ______ out just how music mad you are.

14 Match the phrases and the meanings.

1 to start out ___
2 to find out ___
3 to go out ___
4 to come out ___
5 to run out ___
6 to sort out ___

a to discover
b to begin your working life
c to leave your house
d to become available
e to find an answer or solution to a problem
f to finish, use or sell all of something, so that there is none left

15 Complete the sentences with the correct form of the verbs in Exercise 14.

1 John isn't here. He ______ about 20 minutes ago.
2 It's a really old film. I think it ______ in 2005.
3 We need to go to the supermarket – we ______ of milk.
4 The police are trying to ______ who started the trouble last night.
5 We had some problems with the computer, but we ______ them ______ yesterday.
6 She's a famous singer now, but she ______ as a dancer.

→ workbook page 48

Activity idea Extension

Find some videos of music that was popular when you were the students' age. Play the videos on the interactive whiteboard (IWB). Ask: *Does the music sound good to you?* Discuss whether music was better then than now.

TH!NK more

Workbook
Listening p52, Ex.1
WordWise p48, Ex.4–6

Reading

Warmer

Ask students if they like any music that no one else in the class listens to. Ask: *What about your parents? Do they listen to strange music?* Divide the class into groups. Groups take it in turns to try to name artists that other groups have not heard of. To prove they have heard of an artist, students need to name a song by them.

1 Give a couple of your own ideas as examples before students work in pairs.

2 Give students just two minutes to scan the article quickly to find the answer to the question. Encourage them not to focus on every word for now but just to find the answer.
ABBA

3 🔊 **5.07** Students should read the sentences carefully and decide which key information they need to look out for. Tell them that there will usually be more than one answer that seems to be correct at first reading, so they should not go straight for the first answer that looks right.

As they read, they should underline the information in article the that helped them choose their answer.
1 C 2 A 3 B 4 D

Culture note

ABBA /abə/ are a Swedish pop group formed in Stockholm in 1972 by Agnetha Fältskog, Björn Ulvaeus, Benny Andersson and Anni-Frid Lyngstad. The group's name is an acronym of the first letters of their first names. They became one of the most commercially successful acts in the history of popular music, topping the charts worldwide from 1974 to 1982. ABBA won the Eurovision Song Contest in 1974 at The Dome in Brighton, UK, giving Sweden its first triumph in the contest. They are the most successful group to have taken part in the competition.

TH!NK more

Workbook
Reading p50, Ex.1–4

READING

1 SPEAKING Work in pairs. Make a list of advantages and disadvantages of listening to live music compared to listening to recorded music.

Advantages	*Disadvantages*
More exciting	*It's expensive*

2 Read the article quickly. Which band is thinking of using holograms on stage?

THE FUTURE OF LIVE MUSIC

Technology has always played an important part in the development of pop music – from the instruments that the bands play and the live shows that they perform to the way we listen to music in our homes or on the move. But advances in technology over the next few years are promising to bring even bigger changes.

HOLOGRAMS

For around 50 years, people of all ages have been enjoying ABBA's music. They have played almost 100 international concerts, but since 1982, when the band played their last show, fans have had little hope of ever seeing their favourite group live on stage again. That is now about to change as the band have announced plans for their first shows in nearly forty years. Bands from the 70s and 80s playing together again is nothing new, but it is no surprise that a band as big as ABBA are planning to do things a little bit differently. The four members of the band will not be on the stage together. Instead, they will appear as holograms. The holograms will show the band as they looked back in 1979, when ABBA were the biggest band in the world. And they won't be the only band to have returned to the stage via holograms. In 2018 Freddie Mercury appeared in hologram form alongside Queen in Las Vegas, even though he died more than 25 years ago.

VIRTUAL REALITY (VR)

VR technology has made lots of progress recently. You may soon be able to enjoy watching your favourite band live without even leaving your house. Developers have been making plans to launch a new app that will allow fans to watch live concerts that are being streamed directly to VR headsets. Not only will you be able to watch the band from the crowd, but you will also have the possibility of watching the show on stage with the band. And all of this will cost you about a tenth of the ticket price for the venue.

These advances in technology are very exciting, but do fans really want to watch a show knowing that their musical heroes aren't really there? And can watching through a VR headset ever really match up to the experience of actually being there? Is the latest technology really always the best? Perhaps we should look at the case of vinyl. Who would have thought that a format that was replaced by the CD, then downloading and, finally, streaming, would have made such a big return. Perhaps sometimes the old-fashioned ways of doing things might just be better.

3 🔊 5.07 **Read and listen to the article again. Answer the questions.**

1 Which sentence best describes ABBA's popularity?
   A They are mainly liked by older people.
   B They are more popular now than they were fifty years ago.
   C They have been successful for half a century.
   D They were forgotten for quite a few years.

2 How will ABBA's new shows be different?
   A The band won't be there on stage.
   B They will play mainly new songs.
   C They will all be a lot older.
   D The audiences will be mainly young people.

3 Why might watching a concert using Virtual Reality be considered better than going to a venue?
   A Most people already have the technology in their homes.
   B It allows you to watch from different places in the venue.
   C You can play with the band on stage.
   D It costs 50% less.

4 What is the writer's conclusion about technology and music at the end of the text?
   A Technology can be used to bring people what they want.
   B There's nothing we can do to stop new technology from taking over.
   C We should always be looking for better ways of doing things.
   D It might not always be true to say that new is better.

52

Activity idea Extension

Write on the board: *What would be your ideal concert? Which musicians would you like to see in hologram form? Do you think concerts are too expensive?* Discuss in groups and then as a class.

▶ 14 Grammar rap! Present perfect simple vs. present perfect continuous

4 Another way to explain this rule is to elicit the difference between *how long* and *how much/many*. Ask: *Which sentence answers the question how long?* (1); *Which tense is used?* (present perfect continuous); *Do you ask how many or how long if sentence 2 is the answer?* (how many); *Which tense is used in sentence 2?* (present perfect simple).
1 have been 2 have played
RULE: 3 continuous 1 4 simple 2

5 Encourage students to check their answers against the rules in Exercise 4.
1 's written, 's been writing
2 's been taking, hasn't taken
3 've been playing, 've played
4 've been watching, 've eaten
5 've made, 've been preparing

6 *1 has been collecting, has collected*
2 has been working, has worked
3 has been driving, has driven
4 have been swimming, have swum
5 has taught, has been teaching
6 have been picking, have picked

Workbook p47

Get it Right!
Present simple or present continuous vs. present perfect continuous

Student's Book p123

7 Before students do the task, get them to cover the words in the list and just look at the pictures. In pairs, give students two minutes to write as many of the instruments as possible. During feedback, say the names of the instruments for students to repeat and check pronunciation.
1 guitar 2 drums 3 violin
4 keyboard 5 saxophone 6 piano
7 bass guitar 8 trumpet

8 🔊 5.08
2 trumpet 3 saxophone 4 drums
5 piano 6 keyboard 7 guitar
8 violin

Workbook p48

9 You may want to talk about an experience of your own as an example.

Grammar rap!

GRAMMAR
Present perfect simple vs. present perfect continuous

4 Look at the article on page 52 to complete the sentences. Then complete the rules and match them with the example sentences.

1 For around 50 years, people ______ enjoying ABBA's music.
2 They ______ almost 100 international concerts.

RULE:
- Use the present perfect [3]______ to talk about an action that is not finished. ☐
- Use the present perfect [4]______ to stress the *finished result* of a completed activity and the *amount* completed. ☐

5 Complete the sentences with the phrases in the list.

's been taking | 've been preparing | 've been watching | 've eaten | hasn't taken | 've played | 've been playing | 's been writing | 's written | 've made

1 Sarah ______________ more than 200 poems.
She ______________ poems since she was eight.
2 He ______________ piano lessons for three years.
He ______________ any piano exams yet.
3 I ______________ football since I was five.
I ______________ for three different teams.
4 We ______________ films all evening.
We ______________ three bags of popcorn.
5 I ______________ more than 100 cakes.
I ______________ for the party all day.

6 Complete the sentences using the correct forms of the verbs in brackets.

1 He ______________ autographs since he was ten.
He ______________ over 500. (collect)
2 Jade ______________ at Netflix for five years.
She ______________ there since 2016. (work)
3 Mum ______________ since 6 am.
She ______________ over 400 km. (drive)
4 We ______________ for an hour.
We ______________ more than 2 km! (swim)
5 Tom ______________ more than 2,000 children.
He ______________ since he was 22. (teach)
6 They ______________ apples all day.
They ______________ hundreds! (pick)

→ workbook page 47

VOCABULARY
Musical instruments

7 Write the instruments in the list under the pictures.

bass guitar | drums | guitar | keyboard | piano | saxophone | trumpet | violin

1 
5 
2 
6 
3 
7 
4 
8 

8 🔊 5.08 Listen. Which instrument is playing?
1 *bass guitar*

→ workbook page 48

SPEAKING

9 Work in pairs. Answer the questions.
1 Do you play an instrument? If yes, how long have you been playing it? If no, would you like to learn to play one?
2 Which of the instruments in Exercise 7 do you really like? Which instruments don't you like?
3 What famous musicians can you think of? How long have they been playing music? Have you seen them playing live?

Homework
Ask students to keep a journal for three days and make a note of the music they listen to, what they were doing when they listened to it and whether they enjoyed it.

Activity idea Extension
Give each student a piece of paper and ask them to write their answers to the questions in Exercise 9, e.g., *I have been playing the guitar for three years. I saw U2 play live in London in 2017.* Collect the pieces of paper and read some of them out. The other students have to guess who wrote the sentences.

TH!NK more

Practice Extra
Unit 5 Practise it!

Workbook
Grammar p47, Ex.7–11
Vocabulary p48, Ex.2–3

Worksheets
Grammar rap! Present perfect simple vs. present perfect continuous
Grammar Worksheets 5
Vocabulary Worksheets 5

Warmer

To revise musical instruments, give groups two minutes to think of as many different instruments as they can. After two minutes, play a game of 'vocabulary tennis', with each group taking it in turns to say one instrument until one group runs out of ideas.

1 🔊 5.09 Tell students to cover the dialogue and discuss the questions in pairs before listening and reading to check their answers.
Tom's unhappy because he can't afford to buy the keyboard he wants even though it's 25% off.

2 **Check/clarify:** *scratch.*
Have students underline the answers in the dialogue.
1 £150
2 £90
3 They haven't got any spare money because they've just bought a car.
4 It's got a scratch on it.

3 At the end of the exercise, listen to some of the students' ideas and encourage open class discussion.

4 Write the underlined expressions on the board. Perhaps ask students for an L1 translation before they complete the sentences in English.
1 What's up 2 Tell me about it
3 There's no point in 4 I can't wait
5 No way 6 if you say so

5 Before students complete the task, write the four questions on the board and ask students to suggest possible responses. Write any good answers on the board. During feedback, ask students for the responses and check their pronunciation.
a 3 b 4 c 1 d 2

6 As a follow-up, students could act out a scenario in the class.
ROLE PLAY Monitor to help with any difficulties, but do not interrupt as this is a fluency activity. You might also offer ideas if students have none.

DEVELOPING SPEAKING

1 🔊 5.09 **Look at the photos. Why does the boy look unhappy? Listen and read to check.**

Laura: Tom! Hi! Here you are, looking in the music shop window. Why am I not surprised!?
Tom: Oh, hi Laura. You OK?
Laura: Well, I'm fine. But you don't look very happy. <u>What's up</u>?
Tom: Nothing.
Laura: Oh, come on. What's the matter?
Tom: Well, I'm just a bit upset. Look. There's that keyboard, the one I've always wanted, 25% off. Down to £240. And I still can't afford it.
Laura: Oh, I see. But you've been saving for ages, haven't you?
Tom: Yes, and I've saved £150. But it's not enough, is it? Even with 25% off, I still need another £90.
Laura: Can't you ask your parents to help? Can they lend you some money?
Tom: <u>No way</u>. They've just bought a car. They haven't got any spare money at the moment.
Laura: <u>Tell me about it</u>. I asked my parents to lend me some money the other day. They were nice about it, but they said no. They're saving to go to Canada to see my uncle.
Tom: OK, <u>there's no point in</u> standing here looking in the window. I'll just have to forget about it for now. Let's go.
Laura: Well, <u>if you say so</u>. What a shame.
Man: Hello! Looking at the keyboards? Come in and have a look. You can try one if you want.
Tom: Thanks, but no thanks. I can't afford the one I want. That black one, the Condor.
Man: That one? I've got another one in the shop. It's got a scratch on it, so I'm thinking of taking another £100 off the price. Interested?
Tom: Absolutely! <u>I can't wait</u> to see it!
Laura: Come on, Tom, let's go in!

2 Read the dialogue again and answer the questions.
1 How much money has Tom saved?
2 How much more does he need to buy the keyboard he wants?
3 Why won't Tom's parents be able to lend him any money?
4 Why is the shop-owner going to reduce the price of one keyboard by another £100?

3 SPEAKING **Think of Tom's situation. Look at the statements below and discuss in pairs.**
1 Would you save up for a more expensive keyboard model or buy a cheaper one with the money you have got?
2 Would you buy a damaged product if it is cheaper/reduced in price?

Phrases for fluency

4 Find the underlined expressions in the dialogue and use them to complete the conversations.
1 A Hey Mandy. [1]__________?
B I'm tired! I had problems with the homework last night.
A [2]__________! I took four hours to finish it! And I think I got some things wrong.
B Me, too. Oh well. [3]__________ worrying about it. Let's give it to the teacher and see.

2 A The Cup Final's on TV tonight. [4]__________!
B I know. It's really exciting. Do you want to come and watch it with me at my house?
A [5]__________! Your television's terrible.
B Well, [6]__________. But I think our TV's really good.

FUNCTIONS
Asking about feelings

KEY LANGUAGE
1 What's up? 3 How are you feeling?
2 Is something the matter? 4 Are you OK?

5 Match these answers to the questions in the Key Language box.
a Not great. ___
b Yes, I'm fine. ___
c Nothing. ___
d I'm just a bit upset. ___

6 SPEAKING **When you feel upset, what other things can people do to help you feel better? Discuss in pairs.**

ROLE PLAY **Helpful suggestions**

Work in pairs. Student A: go to page 127. Student B: go to page 128. Look at the role cards and do the role play.

54

Activity idea Weaker students

Weaker students might benefit from some preparation time before the role-play conversation. Divide the class into two groups, As and Bs, and give each group five minutes to prepare ideas for their side of the conversation before pairing up students A with B.

Life Competencies

Warmer

Write *money* on the board and elicit situations when students have wasted money. Encourage them to come up with as many different situations as they can.

▶ 15 Life Lessons: Managing your money

1 ▶ **15** Ask students to write down the sentence and compare with a partner.
Suggested answer: Each person has to find the right balance between spending and saving money.

2 ▶ **15** Ask students to try to answer the questions from memory before watching the video again to check.
1 Money, trees 2 cake, eat 3 fool, money

3 **Check/clarify:** *second-hand.* Before doing the exercise, elicit ideas from students for raising £80.

4 Ask students to discuss who they think made the best choices and why.

5 As feedback, hold a vote to find out how many students found it more difficult.

6 Monitor to help with any difficulties, but do not interrupt as this is a fluency activity.

7 *30%*

8 Encourage students to add colour to their pie chart. Display them on the wall.

Activity idea Extension

Ask students to interview each other on how they spend their money each week. How would their spending habits change if they had £500 a week?

LIFE COMPETENCIES

Learning to manage your money is an important skill to develop. By planning what you spend, you can buy the things you need and not waste your money on things that aren't important.

1 ▶ 15 **Watch the video. Summarise Anna's advice about money in one sentence.**

2 ▶ 15 **Watch again and complete the sayings.**

1 ______ doesn't grow on ______.
2 You can't have your ______ and ______ it, too.
3 A ______ and his ______ are easily parted.

3 **You have £80 for the week. How will you spend it? For each question, choose an option. Add up your answers and make sure you have enough money!**

1 Computer games
- Play the games you have – free
- Buy a second-hand game – £20
- Buy a brand-new game – £50

2 Clothes
- Wear what you have – free
- Buy something second-hand – £20
- Buy something new – £50

3 Food
- Eat at home – free
- Buy some snacks at school – £10
- Go for a meal with your friends – £20

4 Mobile phone
- Don't use any data or make any calls – free
- Get a cheap plan with some data – £5
- Get a plan with unlimited calls and data – £15

5 Saving money
- Don't save any money – £0
- Save £10
- Save £30

4 SPEAKING **Compare your spending choices with a partner. Explain how you made your decisions.**

5 **Complete your choices again, but this time you have £40. Was it more difficult?**

6 SPEAKING **Discuss these questions with your partner.**

1 Are you saving money at the moment? What for?
2 What do you do when you have no money?
3 Do you have a spending plan?
4 If you don't, do you think it might be useful to have one?

Me and my world

7 **Look at the pie chart. What percentage of their money does this person save?**

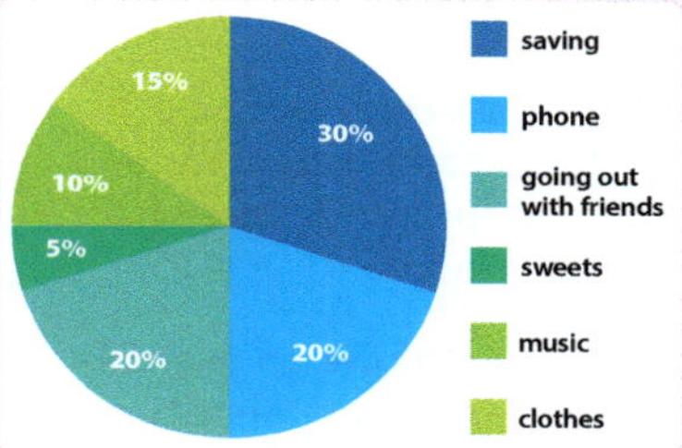

8 SPEAKING **Draw a pie chart for how you spend your money. Then work with a partner and compare your pie charts. Are they similar or very different?**

TIPS FOR MANAGING YOUR MONEY

- Keep a spending diary and write down what you've bought each week. Then you'll be able to see what you spend your money on.
- Try to save a little bit of money each week. And when you receive lots of money at once try to save half of it. That way, you'll always have money when you need it.
- Open a bank account. It's easier to know how much you have saved, and harder to waste money, if you don't have the cash on you.

Language note Proverbs

A proverb is a short sentence, usually known by many people, stating something commonly experienced or giving advice. Anna uses three British proverbs in the video. You may like to discuss their meanings and whether there are any similar ones in the students' L1.

Money doesn't grow on trees: said to warn someone to be careful how much money they spend, because there is only a limited amount.

You can't have your cake and eat it (too): to have or do two good things at the same time that are impossible to have or do at the same time.

A fool and his money are easily parted: said to warn someone that foolish people spend money without thinking.

THINK more

Practice Extra
Unit 5 Master it!

Tests
Unit, extension and skills test 5

Worksheets
Life Lessons: Managing your money

Social Responsibility
Understanding and discussing global issues – environmental, political, financial and social
Understands basic banking products and the responsibilities involved in their use.

Reading

Warmer

Write *tnneemvorin* in the centre of the board. Ask students: *Which word has been mixed up?* Elicit *environment*. Write *saving the environment* on the board. Ask: *How can we save the environment?* Hold a brainstorming session. Write some of their ideas on the board.

▶ 16 Get TH!NKing

Play the video and discuss the question with your class.

1 Ask students to describe what they can see in the photos before looking at the words in the list.
A5 B3 C4 D6 E1 F2

2 During whole-class feedback, listen to some of their ideas and encourage further discussion if students disagree.

3 You may like to give an example from your own experience to get students started.

4 Before students read the article, get them to cover it and just look at the photo. In pairs, give students two minutes to think about the answer to the question. Give students another two minutes to read the article quickly and check ideas. Encourage them not to focus on every word for now.

5 🔊 **6.01 Check/clarify:** *activists, reactions, Conference, generations, governments, a national movement.*
As they read, students should underline the parts of the text which helped them find the answer.
1T 2F 3F 4F 5F 6T

6 NO PLANET B

OBJECTIVES

FUNCTIONS: expressing surprise and enthusiasm

GRAMMAR: *will* (*not*), *may* (*not*), *might* (*not*) for prediction; first conditional; *unless* in first conditional sentences

VOCABULARY: the environment; verbs to talk about energy

Get TH!NKING
Watch the video and think: do you use a lot of plastic?

READING

1 Match the words and phrases in the list with the photos. Write 1–6 in the boxes.

1 a beautiful beach | 2 a dirty beach
3 clean water | 4 an attractive landscape
5 an endangered species | 6 a polluted river

2 SPEAKING Work in pairs. Which of the above are easy / difficult / impossible to find in your town or country? Use the expressions below.

- There is / are lots of … in …
- I think 50 years ago there were more / fewer …
- It would be good to have more …

3 SPEAKING Tell your partner about places you have visited. Which of the things in Exercise 1 did you see?

Years ago I visited …
I was surprised / disappointed to see …
I saw lots of …

4 Look at the photo on the next page. What do you think the article is about? Read the text quickly to check your ideas.

5 🔊 6.01 Read and listen to the article again. Mark the sentences T (true) or F (false).

1 More people came to the meeting than Jackson Hinkle expected. ____
2 Team Zissou want more people to use plastic bottles. ____
3 JUST Water bottles are made of plants. ____
4 Brittany Trilford wrote a letter to world leaders. ____
5 Brittany thinks people her age are happy with world leaders. ____
6 Brittany believes that politicians should do more than they have. ____

6 SPEAKING Work with a partner. Correct the false information in the sentences in Exercise 5.

56

6 2 Team Zissou want people to stop using plastic bottles. 3 JUST Water comes in a paper-based bottle. 4 Brittany spoke at a conference where world leaders were present. 5 Brittany thinks that people her age are angry with world leaders.

Objectives

Functions and speaking Expressing surprise and enthusiasm
Grammar *will* (*not*), *may* (*not*), *might* (*not*) for prediction; first conditional; *unless* in first conditional sentences
Vocabulary The environment; verbs to talk about energy
Values Caring for the world
Train to TH!NK Different perspectives

Resources for this unit

All available online

Videos
- Get **TH!NK**ing: *Do you use a lot of plastic?*
- Grammar rap!: First conditional; *unless* in first conditional sentences
- Culture: Green solutions around the world

Tests
- Unit, extension and skills test 6
- End of term test 2

Worksheets
- Grammar and vocabulary: Basic, Standard and Extension Worksheets
- Project: Alternative energies
- Communication: Making a difference
- Literature Worksheets: *The Lost Stradivarius*
- Get **TH!NK**ing and Grammar rap! video Worksheets

7 Ask students to re-read the article and find reasons for their choices.
1, 4, 5, 6

8 Encourage students to use the sentence stems.

9 At the end of the exercise, listen to some of the students' ideas and encourage open class discussion.

Homework

Ask students to write a short paragraph summarising their discussion in Exercise 9.

Culture notes

The United Nations Conference on Sustainable Development (also known as the Rio Earth Summit 2012) was a major UN conference held from 20th to 22nd June 2012. The summit included participation from 192 UN member states – including 57 Heads of State and 31 Heads of Government, private sector companies, NGOs and other groups. It was intended to be a high-level conference, resulting in a focused political document designed to shape global environmental policy.

JUST Water is an eco-friendly carton water brand, founded in 2015 by Jaden Smith, the son of Hollywood actor Will Smith. The launch came in response to growing consumer concern over minimising plastic pollution. JUST water uses packaging which is made up of 82% renewable resources, mostly paper from managed sources. The container is recyclable in nine out of ten communities in the UK.

Many young people today are very worried about the future of the planet. This week, we look at what two teen activists are doing in their fight to save the Earth. As always, we are curious to get our readers' reactions. So tell us what you think!

Jackson Hinkle, *the US*

American teenager Jackson Hinkle and his friends invited classmates to the first meeting of an adventure club on Instagram. They thought around 30 students might come to the meeting. In fact, 300 students turned up. The group decided to set up Team Zissou Environmental Organization, and it quickly became a national movement. Their main goal is to end single-use plastics in schools and communities. Team Zissou's first campaign took place on World Water Day and they made several important promises:

We will raise money for water fountains across the school district.

We will get local businesses to stop selling single-use plastic water bottles because they cause a lot of pollution.

We will sell JUST Water in our canteens.

Jackson has learned one very important thing from his campaigning: Never give up. You must keep trying.

JUST Water comes in a paper-based bottle and has a plant-based cap. The bottle is made from 82% renewable resources, so it won't damage the environment. If sales go well in the four schools, the district might get rid of plastic water bottles and sell JUST Water in all 64 schools.

Brittany Trilford, *New Zealand*

When she was just 17, Brittany Trilford, from Wellington in New Zealand, was invited to speak to world leaders at the United Nations Conference in Rio de Janeiro, Brazil. She spoke about climate change and the need to stop talking and to act now to make real change. Brittany wants to protect the beautiful environment she lives in – an environment that will be seriously affected by climate change. She wanted world leaders to know that young people feel angry – angry because world leaders are not doing enough to protect the environment for future generations.

Her message to governments around the world is that they need to act now and think of new and better laws that may help the serious situation. Young people don't want more promises, they want action. They want to see results. Promises won't be enough.

One thing we all know now – we ARE destroying our environment. There is no Planet B, so please, let's ALL look after this one. Brittany Trilford and Jackson Hinkle have done amazing things. It's OUR turn now.

TH!NK *values*

Caring for the world

7 Read and tick (✓) the values that are connected to the problems discussed in the article.

1 We have responsibilities towards future generations. ☐
2 People have a right to express their opinions freely. ☐
3 All people have a right to live in peace. ☐
4 Our behaviour can make a difference. ☐
5 Humans have a responsibility to use environmentally-friendly materials. ☐
6 We must change our behaviour towards our planet. ☐

8 SPEAKING **Work in pairs. Say what you think about the values.**

I think number … is an important value.

It says … and I agree that … . Do you agree?

Yes. If we don't … , then future generations will/won't …

9 SPEAKING **Work in pairs. What environmental issues are you worried about? What do you think you could do to help?**

Activity idea Extension

Give students a minute or so to reflect on and rank the values in Exercise 7 in order of importance. Students discuss their rankings with a partner to find how similar they are. Monitor and encourage students to expand on their ideas, and also to challenge their partners, giving praise to those who do. During whole-class feedback, ask for a show of hands to find out which values were ranked highest.

Social Responsibilities
Understanding and discussing global issues – environmental, political, financial and social
Understands how personal habits and behaviour have the capacity to affect others and the environment.

Critical TH!NKing
Understanding and analysing links between ideas
Distinguishes between main and supporting arguments.

Critical TH!NKing
Evaluating ideas, arguments and options
Assesses strengths and weaknesses of possible solutions.

Social Responsibilities
Understanding personal responsibilities as part of a group and in society
Understands the rights and responsibilities of individuals in society at local and national levels.

TH!NK more

Worksheets
Project Alternative energies
Communication Making a difference
Get TH!NKing *Do you use a lot of plastic?*

Warmer

Write *In the next 20 years …* on the board and underneath write *Will we definitely lose thousands of species?* (yes); *Will all the tigers definitely die?* (no, it's possible but not definite). Elicit alternatives for *will* (*might* and *may*). Ask a few students to give you an example of their own for each modal verb.

1 Ask students to try to complete the sentences from memory before referring back to the article to check.
1 might come 2 will sell 3 won't be
RULE: 4 won't 5 may

2 1 will be 2 will live 3 won't like 4 will win 5 will start 6 won't be

3 **Check/clarify:** *sunrise*.
1 will 2 may not 3 might 4 may 5 won't 6 may

4 Give students a few minutes to discuss their weekends. Remind them to use *will* / *won't* and *might* / *may not*. Monitor and note down any errors or pronunciation problems to go through as a class.

Workbook p54

Get it Right!
Future with *will*

Student's Book p123

5 Practise pronunciation of words 1–6 as you check the answers.
a 2 b 4 c 5 d 1 e 6 f 3

6 Encourage students to make a note of their answers and to report back to the class.

7 6.02 After completing the exercise, play the audio again, pausing for students to repeat each word.
A 3 B 4 C 2 D 1

GRAMMAR
will (not), may (not), might (not) for prediction

1 **Complete the examples from the article on page 57. Underline other examples of *will, won't, may (not)* and *might (not)*. Then complete the rule.**

1 They thought around 30 students _____ to the meeting.
2 We _____ JUST Water in our canteens.
3 Promises _____ enough.

RULE: Use *will* or ⁴_____ to express future certainty, and ⁵_____ *(not)* or *might (not)* to express future possibility.

2 **Complete the sentences. Use *will* or *won't* and the verbs in brackets.**

1 I'm not exactly sure, but I think she _________ (be) home by eight o'clock at the latest.
2 I wonder if people _________ (live) on other planets in the future.
3 I'm worried about him coming with us. I'm sure he _________ (like) any of the people at the party.
4 Who do you think _________ (win) the next World Cup?
5 It's getting cloudy. Do you think it _________ (start) raining soon?
6 Oh, don't worry about my parents. I'm sure they _________ (be) angry.

3 **Read the sentences and choose the correct words.**

1 Don't worry, I *will* / *might* pick you up at 7.
2 The weather's a real problem. We *may* / *may not* be able to go for a walk.
3 She's not feeling well at all. She *might* / *might not* have to stay at home.
4 It *may* / *may not* be cold later, so take a jumper with you.
5 It's my dad's birthday tomorrow. My wife and I are going to visit him, so we definitely *won't* / *might not* be here.
6 I'd like to get up and watch the sunrise with you, but I *may* / *won't* just sleep instead.

4 SPEAKING **Work in pairs. Think about next weekend. Talk about:**

- a sport you will / won't do
- someone you may / may not see
- a film you might / might not watch

→ workbook page 54

VOCABULARY
The environment

5 **Match the words with the meanings.**

1 extinct 2 laws 3 waste 4 melt 5 flood 6 pollution

a official rules that say what people are allowed and not allowed to do ☐
b change from solid to liquid (for example, from ice to water) ☐
c a large amount of water covering an area that is usually dry ☐
d not existing any more ☐
e things that make water, air and the ground unclean ☐
f material that people throw away ☐

6 SPEAKING **Work in pairs. Ask and answer questions.**

1 Which animals do you know that are extinct or in danger of extinction?
2 What laws to protect the environment are there in your country?
3 What problems with waste are there where you live?
4 What might happen if the ice around the North and South Poles melts?
5 Are floods common in your country?
6 Are the air and water very polluted in your area? What could your class do to help fight pollution?

7 6.02 **Match the words in the list with the photos. Write 1–4 in the boxes. Then listen, check and repeat.**

A B C D

1 smog | 2 recycling | 3 litter | 4 rubbish

8 **Think about the environment in your country. Write notes.**

some rivers polluted *air pollution from factories*

58

8 Encourage students to think of positive things as well as problems!

Language note *will (not), may (not), might (not)* for prediction

Remind students that the negative form of *will* is *won't* and that it is the same for all persons.

Activity idea Extension

Ask students to work in small groups and make a list of the three environmental issues that they think should concern us most. Ask a group to write their list on the board. Ask them to give reasons for their choices. Ask a different group to replace one of the items in the first list, giving a reason why their choice should concern us more than the original choice. Continue with other groups. Encourage the rest of the class to say whether they agree with the changes, but do not change the list. When several groups have come to the board, hold a vote to decide which are the most serious problems.

TH!NK more

Workbook
Grammar p54, Ex.1–6
Vocabulary p56, Ex.1–2

Worksheets
Grammar Worksheets 6
Vocabulary Worksheets 6

Vocabulary; Listening; Functions

9 Ask a spokesperson from each group to summarise their conversation.

Workbook p56

10 Check/clarify: *radishes, roundabout, eccentric.*
If students have a garden, ask: *What is growing in it? Have you ever planted a vegetable and watched it grow? Were you successful?* If students don't have a garden, ask: *Have you ever grown anything indoors or on a balcony?* Listen to some of their ideas with the whole class.

11 🔊 **6.03** Encourage students to use *might* and *may*.

12 🔊 **6.03**
1 Growing free food locally
2 Everyone 3 Mary Clear and her friend 4 There were many negative things happening in the world, so they decided to do something positive.
5 The idea was popular and the reaction was amazing.

13 Ask students to consider the advantages of the experiment, but also what might go wrong. Ask: *Do you think it would be a success in your neighbourhood?*

Culture notes

Incredible Edible was set up in 2008 by Pamela Warhurst and Mary Clear with the aim of bringing people together through local food. Starting with small herb gardens and community plots, the group has since founded a food knowledge hub and fishery at the local high school, as well as a market garden for young people to grow and sell their own produce. It has also backed successful campaigns such as encouraging the keeping of free-range chickens and bees.

There are now more than 100 groups in the UK and more than 1,000 groups around the world in the Incredible Edible network.

14 🔊 **6.03** During feedback, practise the pronunciation of the phrases.
Wow! ✓ That sounds wonderful! ✓
That's amazing! (wonderful! etc.) ✓
What a brilliant idea! ✓

15 Give students time to practise the dialogue. Students may like to try to do so without the book.
3, 8, 4, 6, 2, 7, 1, 5

NO PLANET B UNIT 6

9 SPEAKING Work in pairs. Look at your notes from Exercise 8. Make predictions for the next 30 years. Which environmental issues concern you the most? Then report to the class.

Some of the rivers in our country are polluted, for example ... We think this will create big problems for the fish, and ...

In some parts of the country, for example in ... , the air is polluted. We think this will change. There will be stricter laws so there won't be ...

→ workbook page 56

LISTENING

10 Read the headlines in the online newspaper story and look at the images. Write down six words you might find in the article.

11 🔊 6.03 Use the information from the newspaper headlines and your imagination to say what you think is special about the town of Todmorden. Then listen to the story and check your ideas.

12 🔊 6.03 Listen again and answer the questions.
1 What's the 'Incredible Edible' project all about?
2 Who takes part in the project?
3 Who had the idea?
4 Why did they decide to do something?
5 What was the reaction to their idea like?

13 Do you think the experiment will last? Why (not)? Would you like to see a similar experiment in your town or neighbourhood?

FUNCTIONS
Expressing surprise and enthusiasm

14 🔊 6.03 Listen to the radio programme again. The phrases below can be used to express enthusiasm. Tick (✓) the ones that the reporter uses.
- ☐ Oh, really?
- ☐ Wow!
- ☐ That sounds wonderful!
- ☐ How exciting!
- ☐ That's amazing! (wonderful! etc.)
- ☐ What a brilliant idea!
- ☐ Incredible! (Cool! Fascinating! etc.)

15 Put the dialogue in order. Read it out with a partner.
- ☐ A He's offered me a role in his next film.
- ☐ A I'm only going to meet Steven Spielberg.
- ☐ A I'm going to California this summer.
- ☐ A Three hours.
- ☐ B Cool!
- ☐ B Oh, really? Only three hours. Why's that?
- ☐ B How exciting! What are you going to talk about?
- ☐ B Wow! That sounds exciting. How long are you going to stay there?

16 SPEAKING Practise dialogues with a partner. A says something surprising, B reacts, using one of the expressions from Exercise 14, and asks a question. A says something surprising again, etc. Use your own ideas, or the ones here.
- go to the moon
- meet Zendaya
- win a big prize
- see an alien
- only eat white food
- stay up all night

59

---

16 Allow students six to eight minutes to prepare their dialogues. Praise students for original ideas.

Homework

Ask students to make a list of possible places in their town where Incredible Edible could plant vegetables. As a follow-up, students can discuss the locations as a class and make a definitive list.

Activity idea Extension

Divide the class into five pairs or small groups and ask each group to imagine they are news reporters. Assign a different question from Exercise 12 to each group. Students write an article about the question to be read out in a news programme at the end of the activity.

TH!NK more

Workbook
Vocabulary p56, Ex.1–2
Listening p60, Ex.1–2

Worksheets
Vocabulary Worksheets 6

Warmer

Write the words *electrical appliances* on the board. Elicit or give the meaning and ask students to brainstorm all the appliances they have in their home. Make a list on the board for later in the lesson.

1 Ask students to underline words and phrases in the texts which helped them make their decisions. You could tell weaker students which two text types are not used (*note* and *adventure story*). Stronger students can cover up the text types and try to guess what they are just from reading the texts 1–4.
1 diary entry 2 text message 3 informative leaflet 4 online article

2 Ask students to circle words and phrases in the texts that helped them decide on their answers.

3 6.04 Ask students to read and listen to the text to find the answers.
Article
Students' own answers

4 **Check/clarify:** *standby, charge, wasting, reuse, suffer, rinse, drip, charity.*
Encourage students not to look back at the text, but allow them to do so if necessary.
Suggested answers: 1 change our behaviour 2 fossil fuels and natural gas (to produce electricity) 3 has increased its use of renewable energy 4 energy-saving light bulbs

5 Give students some time to discuss in small groups and then hold a class vote to decide which they feel is best, has the most effect and would be the easiest to implement.

Train to TH!NK

Different perspectives

1 Read these different texts. Match them with the text types in the list. Write numbers 1–4. Give your reasons. There are two text types you don't need to use.

- ☐ note
- ☐ diary entry
- ☐ text message
- ☐ online article
- ☐ informative leaflet
- ☐ adventure story

2 SPEAKING Work in pairs. Discuss who the texts are for and what their purpose is.

I think text 1 is probably for ... I think somebody wrote it in order to ...

1 This morning we took part in the Incredible Edible project. I was so proud when I saw that all of the students in my class had brought vegetable plants ...

2 Meeting the guys who want to plant vegetables by the football field at 5... Hope to CUL8R S.

3 ... to buy OUR vegetables. They come from local farms. They are organic and fresh – and you don't have to pick them yourself. Prices are reasonable; the quality is high!

4 Our reporter has learned that the council will publish a list of spare land that can be used by the Incredible Edible project. It has been ...

READING

3 6.04 Read and listen to the text. What type of text is it? Choose from the text types in Exercise 1. Who might this text be for?

ENERGY MATTERS

Unless we change our behaviour, our planet won't survive. To produce electricity, we burn coal and oil, known as fossil fuels, but creating energy in this way puts CO_2 into the air and causes air pollution and smog. As a result, we are destroying our Earth. What can we do to solve these problems? If we use renewable energy, it will provide us with cleaner air and water. So what is renewable energy? It is energy that doesn't use up the resource used to make it. Solar power, wind power and hydroelectric power are examples of renewable energy sources.

SOLAR POWER

Using the power of the sun produces very little pollution and it is also much cheaper than using fossil fuels. Morocco is now using solar power in a big way. When we say big, we mean big! They have the largest solar plant on Earth. Its wind and hydroelectric power plants will soon provide half of Morocco's electricity. Morocco might become the world's superpower in solar energy, producing enough electricity for one million homes.

HYDROELECTRIC POWER AND WIND FARMS

In the past, Turkey relied on fossil fuels and natural gas to produce electricity. In recent years, it has increased its use of renewable energy. Private companies have built nine small hydroelectric power plants and they use river water stored in dams to produce electricity. They have also built six wind farms, and they have set up 20 other renewable energy projects. Wind power is another clean alternative to fossil fuels. It is everywhere! Wind farms use very little land and they don't use any water.

A SIMPLE WAY TO REDUCE ENERGY

Something simple that everyone could do to help save the environment: using energy-saving light bulbs. Mexico has given almost 23 million of them to families for free. Now, more than 5.5 million Mexican families use energy-saving light bulbs. If they use energy-saving light bulbs, they may save up to 18% on their electricity bill. This is a simple thing that YOU can do, too. You will use a tenth of the electricity if you use energy-saving light bulbs at home.

4 Work in pairs. Cover up the text and try to complete the sentences.

1 In order to survive, we will need to ...
2 In the past, Turkey relied on ...
3 In recent years, Turkey has ...
4 Mexico has given away 23 million free ...

5 Read the text again. Which of the ideas ...

- do you think is best?
- has the most direct effect on people's lives?
- would be easy or difficult to do in your country?

60

Culture notes

Morocco (population around 36 million) is in North Africa. It overlooks the Mediterranean Sea to the north and the Atlantic Ocean to the west. The capital is Rabat and the largest city is Casablanca.

The Republic of Turkey (population around 82 million) is mainly in Western Asia, with a small portion in Southeast Europe. Much of the border is coastline, with the Black Sea to the north and the Mediterranean Sea to the south. The largest city is Istanbul while Ankara is the capital.

Mexico (population over 129 million) is in the southern portion of North America. Much of its border is coastline, with the Pacific Ocean to the south and west and the Caribbean Sea and the Gulf of Mexico to the east. Mexico is the most populous Spanish-speaking country in the world.

TH!NK more

Workbook
Reading p58, Ex.1–4

Critical TH!NKing
Evaluating ideas, arguments and options
Gives reasons for an argument's plausibility.

Critical TH!NKing
Evaluating ideas, arguments and options
Identifies assumptions and inferences in an argument.

Social Responsibilities
Understanding and discussing global issues – environmental, political, financial and social
Is aware of different global issues (e.g. poverty, migration, global warming, human rights violations, pandemic diseases etc.).

Critical TH!NKing
Evaluating ideas, arguments and options
Examines possible solutions to a given problem and states how effective they are.

Grammar; Vocabulary

▶ 17 Grammar rap! First conditional; *unless* in first conditional sentences

6 To check the first conditional, ask: *Which verb goes in each half of the sentence?*
1 will provide 2 won't survive
3 will use RULE: 4 possible 5 if not

7 1 c 2 a 3 d 4 b

8 1 If I give this phone to charity, they'll find someone who needs it.
2 If this tap doesn't stop dripping, how much water will we waste in a day?
3 The situation will become worse if they don't change their behaviour.
4 Look – battery full! If you don't disconnect the/your charger, you'll waste energy. 5 If she reads this book, she'll understand the situation better. 6 If you don't stop shouting, I won't listen any more.
Unless could be used in sentences 3, 4 and 6.

9 Remind students to look for the *if*/*unless* phrase carefully.
1 don't study, will … get 2 is, 'll go
3 invites, will … buy 4 won't help, asks 5 come, will … show

10 You may like to give an example of your own.

Workbook p55

11 🔊 **6.05** Elicit verbs to talk about energy.
a 8 b 3 c 5 d 2 e 7 f 6
g 1 h 4

12 Encourage students to use the vocabulary from Exercise 11.

Workbook p56

GRAMMAR
First conditional; *unless* in first conditional sentences

6 **Complete the sentences with the correct form of the verbs. Look at the leaflet on page 60 and check your answers. Then choose the right answers to make the rules.**

1 If we use renewable energy, it ______ (provide) us with cleaner air and water.
2 Unless we change our behaviour, our planet ______ (not survive).
3 You ______ (use) a tenth of the electricity if you use energy-saving light bulbs at home.

> RULE: We use the first conditional to talk about the consequences of a [4]**possible / impossible** future action.
> - Condition clause: *if* + present simple
> - Result clause: *will* / *won't* + main verb
>
> The condition clause can come before or after the result clause.
> *Unless* means [5]**only if / if not**.

7 **Match the parts of the sentences.**

1 Unless someone lends me a bit of money, ☐
2 I'll only be able to go to the concert ☐
3 They won't pass the exam ☐
4 Won't she miss the train ☐

a if my dad drives me there.
b if she doesn't leave for the station now?
c I won't be able to take the bus home.
d unless they study hard.

8 **Write first conditional sentences. Then decide in which of them you could use *unless*.**

0 environment / suffer / if / we not recycle more
The environment will suffer if we don't recycle more.
The environment will suffer unless we recycle more.
1 if / I give this phone / charity / they find someone who needs it
2 if / this tap not stop dripping / how much water / we waste in a day?
3 situation / become worse / if they not change behaviour
4 Look – battery full! / if you not disconnect charger / you waste energy
5 if she read this book / she understand situation better
6 if / you not stop shouting / I not listen any more

9 **Complete the questions. Use the correct form of the verbs.**

0 What __*will*__ you __*do*__ if they *don't help* you? (do / not help)
1 If you ______, ______ you ______ good marks in your test? (not study / get)
2 Unless the weather ______ really bad on Sunday, we ______ to the beach. (be / go)
3 If she ______ you to her birthday party, ______ you ______ her a present? (invite / buy)
4 She ______ him unless he ______ her very nicely. (not help / ask)
5 If I ______ to visit you, ______ you ______ me around your town? (come / show)

10 SPEAKING **Work in pairs. Ask and answer questions using the first conditional. Use your own ideas or the ones here.**

1 What will you do if it rains all weekend?
2 What will you buy if you get some extra money this month?
3 What will you do tonight if you don't have any homework?

→ workbook page 55

VOCABULARY
Verbs to talk about energy

11 🔊 6.05 **Match the verbs with their definitions. Write 1–8. Listen and check.**

> **1** to reuse | **2** to throw away | **3** to recycle
> **4** to waste | **5** to charge | **6** to disconnect
> **7** to save | **8** to leave on standby

a to not switch an appliance off completely so it is ready to be used at any time ☐
b to collect and treat rubbish in order to produce useful materials that can be used again ☐
c to fill up an empty battery again ☐
d to get rid of something ☐
e to stop something from being wasted ☐
f to stop the connection between an electrical appliance and the power source ☐
g to use something again ☐
h to use too much of something or use it incorrectly ☐

12 SPEAKING **Work in pairs. Discuss these questions.**

1 Do you waste a lot of energy? What could you do to save energy?
2 What things do you reuse?
3 What things do you recycle? Do you think there is enough recycling done where you live? Why?

→ workbook page 56

Language notes First conditional; *unless* in first conditional sentences

1 Remind students that the *if* phrase can come first or second in the sentence but the present simple tense always goes with the *if* phrase.

2 Remind students that *unless* means *if not*.

3 Students may say *Unless I don't work, I will …* . Remind them that *unless* is always followed by a positive verb.

Activity idea Extension

Write the following on the board:

more cars on the road / more pollution   *ice melt / sea levels rise*

Divide the class into small groups. Each group chooses a prompt and makes a chain of first conditional sentences. For example:

If there are more cars on the road, there will be more pollution.

If there is more pollution, there will be more illness.

If there is more illness, there will be more work for doctors.

Ask some groups to read out their chain sentences to the class.

TH!NK more

Practice Extra
Unit 6 Practise it!

Workbook
Grammar p55, Ex.7–11
Vocabulary p56, Ex.3–4
Vocabulary Extra p57, Ex.1–2

Worksheets
Grammar rap! First conditional: *unless* in first conditional sentences
Grammar Worksheets 6
Vocabulary Worksheets 6

Warmer

Ask students to give you the name of an animal. After a few examples, ask students to name an endangered animal and continue around the class. Write any correct answers on the board. Use the interactive whiteboard (IWB) to search for images of endangered animals and ask students to name the animals. You could also search to find out how endangered individual animals are. Ask: *Are there any endangered animals in your country?* Ask students to name the animals on page 62 (butterflies, leopard).

▶ 18 TH!NK Green solutions around the world

1 Get students to cover the text and just look at the photos. Give them a minute to answer the question.

2 🔊 **6.06 Check/clarify:** *council, pedestrian area, discouraged, expand, rely on, precious, sealed-together, chimney, lung infections, effect, habitat, traps, protected.*
Students' own answers

3 1 The Netherlands 2 Ecuador 3 The Netherlands 4 Ecuador 5 Mexico 6 The Netherlands

4 Ask students to discuss in small groups.

TH!NK
Green solutions around the world

Culture

1 Look at the photos. Where do you think these places might be?

2 🔊 6.06 Read and listen to the article. Check your ideas.

GREEN SOLUTIONS AROUND THE WORLD

THE NETHERLANDS

Can a ban on cars help business?

In the mid-seventies, there was a problem in the city of Groningen, in the Netherlands. Lots of people used the motorway in the city centre and there were too many cars. This caused a lot of traffic jams. The city council decided to replace the motorway with green areas, pedestrian areas, cycleways and bus lanes. They stopped cars from parking in the market square and discouraged cars from entering the city centre.

At first, shop owners said they would lose customers. But they didn't, and soon businesses and shops which were not in the car-free zone wanted the council to expand it.

Today, 61% of trips taken in the city are done by bicycle. The city centre is full of places for bikes to park and most buildings have bicycle garages. As a result, today Groningen has got the cleanest air of any big Dutch city.

ECUADOR

Can a camera trap programme help save a nature park?

The Bigal River nature park is located between the Amazon forest and the Andes. It is a beautiful area, and is home to many different animals and birds. However, human activity has had a negative effect on the wildlife that lives there. Many animals and birds are endangered because of loss of habitat and hunting.

To show people how wonderful the nature park is, the Sumac Muyu Foundation set up camera traps around the park. These traps record a video whenever an animal enters a certain place in the park. It shows where they are in the park, and it studies changes in behaviour caused by humans.

The camera traps have been in the nature park since 2014. They have collected hundreds of hours of film showing wildlife, and the material is being used to help fight new building projects in the protected land.

MEXICO

Can a wood-burning stove really be environmentally friendly and still be efficient?

People in many countries still rely on open fires. Although the fires help people cook and stay warm, the smoke and gas can cause illnesses. They also use precious fuels such as wood or coal. The so-called Patsari stove uses less wood and so it improves both air quality in the home and family health.

The stove was developed in Mexico. It is made of sealed-together brick stones so no gas can come out from the stove. The stones heat up when somebody lights a fire underneath, and the back of the stove is attached to a chimney, which takes the smoke out of the home.

Health studies show that families with a Patsari stove get 30% fewer lung infections and 50% fewer eye infections.

3 SPEAKING Work in pairs. Read these things people say. Are they from the Netherlands, Mexico or Ecuador?

1 'People in our town feel much healthier now.'
2 'I hope those birds don't disappear.'
3 'I still get a lot of customers in my restaurant.'
4 'We're happy that they didn't build there – and the video certainly helped.'
5 'It's much nicer inside my house now.'
6 'I never have a problem – there's always somewhere to leave it.'

4 Do you know of any other towns, cities or countries where there has been an environmental project?

62

Culture notes

The Netherlands is a country in north-western Europe, consisting of 12 provinces that border Germany, Belgium and the North Sea. The three largest cities are Amsterdam, Rotterdam and The Hague. Amsterdam is the country's capital, while The Hague holds the seat of the States General, Cabinet and Supreme Court. The Port of Rotterdam is the busiest port in Europe, and the busiest in any country outside Asia. The country is a founding member of the EU and many intergovernmental organisations and international courts are centred in The Hague.

For notes on Mexico, see page 60.

Ecuador (officially the Republic of Ecuador) is a country in north-western South America bordered by Colombia, Peru and the Pacific Ocean. Ecuador also includes the Galápagos Islands. The capital is Quito, which is also its largest city. Archaeological evidence suggests that the region was first inhabited 16,500–13,000 years ago. It is the most species-diverse country in the world.

Social Responsibility
Understanding own and others' cultures
Makes informed comparisons between their own society and other societies.

5 1 habitat 2 behaviour 3 precious 4 effect 5 discouraged 6 sealed 7 expand

Pronunciation

/f/, /v/, /b/ consonant sounds

Student's Book p120

1 **Check/clarify:** *alarming, politicians, stricter laws, riverbanks.*
Ask: *Where might you see this text? What is the purpose of the text?* Give students two minutes to read the article quickly and think about the answers (in a school magazine, to encourage people to clean up the river).
1 The water is polluted, there are hardly any fish left, it smells terrible and the riverbanks are covered in litter.
2 Factories are polluting the water and people are throwing waste into the river.
3 The river will get worse.
4 Factories should stop polluting, stricter laws should be made by politicians, and people should get together to help clean up the riverbanks.

2 1 The Quiller River was once so beautiful.
2 The situation is alarming.
3 And just look at the riverbanks.
Evidence:
1 There is even a song about it.
2 Newspapers have recently reported that the water in the river is totally polluted. There are hardly any fish left, and the water itself smells terrible.
3 They are covered in litter.

3 1 c – possible consequence
2 a – suggestion 3 e – possible consequence 4 d – suggestion
5 b – prediction

4 a paragraph 4
b paragraph 1
c paragraph 3
d paragraph 2

5 Divide the class into small groups to share ideas before writing individually.

6 Students should organise their work in the same format as the article in Exercise 4. Ask them to read their article to the class or a partner. As an alternative, you could ask students to do this exercise for homework.

---

5 VOCABULARY **There are eight highlighted words in the article. Match the words with these meanings. Write the words.**

0 an organ in the chest that you use to breathe *lung*
1 the place where an animal or plant usually lives ______
2 things that people or animals do, or the way they act ______
3 of great value because of being rare, expensive or important ______
4 the result of an action or other cause ______
5 tried to prevent something from happening ______
6 very tightly closed ______
7 make something bigger ______

PRONUNCIATION
/f/, /v/, /b/ consonant sounds
Go to page 120.

WRITING
An article for the school magazine

1 INPUT **Read this article from a school magazine. Then answer the questions.**

1 How has the river changed?
2 What are the main reasons for the problems?
3 What will happen if the situation doesn't change?
4 What should be done?

Quiller River POLLUTION

The Quiller River was once so beautiful that there is even a song about it. And now?

The situation is alarming. There are lots of factories along the river. Newspapers have recently reported that the water in the river is totally polluted. There are hardly any fish left, and the water itself smells terrible. The situation will be even worse in a few years unless factories stop polluting the water. That is why I really think politicians should do something about it. We need stricter laws to protect our river.

And just look at the riverbanks. They are covered in litter. It seems that there are lots of people who throw their waste into the river. This must stop! We should all get together and help clean up the riverbanks.

In conclusion, if politicians wake up and we all do something, we might once again be able to enjoy the beauty of the river. Let's hope it's not too late.

2 **Put the words in the correct order to make sentences from the article. Then go through it and find the evidence the writer uses to support each of these statements.**

1 so / the / beautiful / once / Quiller River / was
2 situation / alarming / is / the
3 the / riverbanks / and / look at / just

3 **Match the sentence halves. Which of them talk about possible consequences? Which are suggestions? Which are predictions?**

1 If politicians wake up and we all do something, ☐
2 We need stricter laws ☐
3 In a few years' time ☐
4 So I really think politicians ☐
5 The situation will be even worse in a few years ☐

a to protect our river.
b unless factories stop polluting the water.
c we might once again be able to enjoy the beauty of the river.
d should do something about it.
e all the fish may be dead.

4 ANALYSE **The article has four paragraphs. Which of them ...**

a expresses the writer's hope that the situation will be better in the future?
b introduces the topic?
c describes problems and says what should be done?
d describes problems, says what will happen if nothing is done and what should be done?

5 PLAN **Choose a local environmental problem and make notes about what the situation is now, possible consequences and what should be done.**

6 PRODUCE **Write an article for your school magazine raising awareness about the environmental issue you have chosen.**

- Find a good title.
- Write an introduction that catches the reader's interest.
- Describe what the problems are, what you think the consequences might be and what should be done.

Activity idea Extension

Write the words *global warming* on the board. Students have three minutes to make as many other words as they can from it. You can give three points for three-letter words, two for two-letter words, etc. The student with the most points is the winner!

TH!NK more

Practice Extra
Unit 6 Master it!

Workbook
Pronunciation p119
Developing Writing p59

Tests
Unit, extension and skills test 6
End of term test 2

1 In B1 Preliminary for Schools Reading Part 5, candidates have to read a short text with six numbered spaces, then decide which of the four words provided belongs in each gap. This part of the exam tests understanding of words within a context.

Encourage your students to do the following when they approach this task:

- Skim the text to find out the topic and general meaning.
- Work through the six questions, reading the whole sentence to choose the correct word to complete each gap.
- After choosing an answer, check the other three options and decide why they are wrong.
- Read the completed text again to make sure it makes sense.

1A 2B 3D 4B 5C 6A

Workbook p79

2 🔊 6.09 In B1 Preliminary for Schools Listening Part 2, candidates have to listen to six short dialogues and answer six three-option multiple-choice questions. This task tests listening for gist.

Encourage your students to do the following when they approach this task:

- Read and listen to the instructions to understand the context of the conversations.
- On the first listening, try to understand the gist and choose the best option for each question.
- On the second listening, check all the answers carefully.

1B 2C 3C 4C 5C 6A

Workbook p35

B1 Preliminary for Schools

READING

Part 5: 4-option multiple-choice cloze

→ workbook page 79

1 For each question, choose the correct answer.

GLOBAL fishing crisis

A growing concern around the world is how the food production industry is being affected by changes in the environment. For example, millions of people around the world consider fish to be an important part of their [1]______ diet. However, fishing to meet this demand has become a major environmental issue, along with animal extinction, air [2]______ and global warming.

Certain [3]______ of fish are in danger and are no longer found in their usual feeding areas, so fishing boats must travel further out to sea to catch fish. More fishermen are now choosing to catch rarer fish to sell at higher prices, which is affecting populations of less [4]______ fish.

Unfortunately, the problem of overfishing is getting worse and some fish populations could possibly [5]______ out if certain changes aren't put in place. Many people know that we need to [6]______ our oceans and sea life, so they are fighting for stricter fishing laws.

	A	B	C	D
1	regular	frequent	proper	ordinary
2	climate	pollution	condition	damage
3	collections	numbers	descriptions	species
4	ordinary	common	usual	typical
5	blow	carry	run	wear
6	protect	care	prevent	keep

LISTENING

Part 2: 3-option multiple choice

→ workbook page 35

2 🔊 6.09 Listen to six short conversations. For each question, choose the correct answer.

1 You will hear a girl and her brother talking about the girl's night with her two friends.
What does the girl say about the night out?
A Everyone thought the film was incredibly funny.
B The most enjoyable part of her night took place after the film.
C She learned some surprising information about school from her friends.

2 Listen to a man and a woman talking about a tennis match.
What does the man say about the match?
A He disagrees with the coach's decision.
B He thinks the match wasn't very exciting.
C He doesn't understand the actions of the coach.

3 Listen to a boy and a girl talking about the boy's phone.
What does the boy say about the phone?
A Every time he has a conversation, the phone switches off.
B When the battery is running out, the phone always switches off.
C There are two things wrong with the phone.

4 You will hear a boy and a woman in a shop.
Why does the boy want to change the pullover?
A It's the wrong size and the wrong colour.
B It was too expensive.
C He would rather have a T-shirt.

5 Listen to two friends talking.
What has the girl done?
A She has changed the colour of her hair.
B She has had her hair cut and changed the colour.
C She has had her hair cut shorter than it was before.

6 Listen to two friends talking about music at a party.
What did the girl think about the music?
A She didn't enjoy listening to the band.
B She wanted to dance, but the music wasn't great.
C The DJ didn't play good music for dancing.

64

1 1 charge 2 melt 3 waste
4 record / release / stream
5 release 6 enter 7 tour 8 flood
9 extinct 10 standby

2 1 won't 2 have been playing 3 if
4 might not 5 unless
6 have played

3 1 He's ~~being~~ been working here for over five months.
2 If it ~~will rain~~ rains, we'll stay at home.
3 I've ~~been writing~~ written forty invitations for the party next week.
4 We might ~~to~~ go to the game later.
5 You won't do well in the test unless you ~~don't~~ study. / You won't do well in the test ~~unless~~ if you don't study.
6 Ouch! I've ~~been cutting~~ cut my hand.

4 1 matter, bit 2 up, How 3 feeling, not 4 news, sounds

TEST YOURSELF UNITS 5 & 6

VOCABULARY

1 Complete the sentences with the words in the list. There are two extra words.

charge | enter | extinct | flood | melt | record | release | standby | stream | throw away | tour | waste

1 Is it OK if I ____________ my mobile phone in your room?
2 It's getting warm now, so I think the snow will ____________ soon.
3 Don't ____________ water. You shouldn't stay in the shower for more than four minutes!
4 It's really easy to ____________ songs – all you need is an internet connection!
5 They've made a new record, and they're going to ____________ it next week.
6 You can't win the competition if you don't ____________ it!
7 After the band released their new record, they went on ____________ for six months.
8 If it carries on raining like this, there might be a ____________ tonight.
9 There aren't many of these monkeys left in the world. They could be ____________ in a few years.
10 Don't switch it off completely – leave it on ____________, OK?

/10

GRAMMAR

2 Complete the sentences with the words in the list.

have been playing | have played | if | might not | unless | won't

1 I didn't study for the test. I ____________ pass it, I'm sure!
2 Sorry, Mum. My shirt is really dirty. I ____________ football in the park.
3 We won't have a picnic ____________ it rains.
4 I don't feel very well, so I ____________ go to the cinema tonight. I'm not sure.
5 I'll never finish this washing up ____________ you help me. Please!
6 Everyone in the team is really tired. We ____________ three games this week already!

3 Find and correct the mistake in each sentence.

1 He's being working here for over five months.
2 If it will rain, we'll stay at home.
3 I've been writing forty invitations for the party next week.
4 We might to go to the game later.
5 You won't do well in the test unless you don't study.
6 Ouch! I've been cutting my hand.

/12

FUNCTIONAL LANGUAGE

4 Complete the mini-dialogues with the words in the list.

bit | feeling | how | matter | news | not | sounds | up

1 A Hi, Paul. What's the ____________ ?
B Nothing much. I'm just a ____________ upset.
2 A What's ____________, Olivia? Why are you crying?
B I'm crying because I'm happy. I won a competition.
A ____________ exciting! I'm really happy for you.
3 A How are you ____________ ?
B Well, ____________ great. But I'll be OK, I think.
4 A I've got some ____________ . We're going to get a new dog.
B That ____________ great! I'm sure you're really happy.

/8

MY SCORE /30

22–30 10–21 0–9

65

The Cambridge Life Competencies Framework

Social Responsibilities
Understanding and discussing global issues - environmental, political, financial and social
Watch this video for a tip on how to encourage your students' awareness of social responsibilities.
Scan the QR code here

Warmer

Ask: *Can you think of any items you own that would have seemed incredible 100 (or even 20) years ago?* Listen to some of their ideas and encourage open class discussion.

▶ 19 Get TH!NKing

Play the video and discuss the question with your class.

1. You may like to put a copy of the photo up on the board before students open their books.
2. Before students read the newspaper, get them to cover it and just look at the pictures and describe them.
   Spacecraft, a steak/meat, a woman sleeping, a man sending a message by thought
3. Ask students to do an online search to find some stories.
4. With the stories on page 67 covered, give students two minutes to answer the question. Give students another two minutes to read the stories quickly and check ideas. Encourage them not to focus on every word for now.
   It's a newspaper from the future – 2042.
5. 🔊 **7.01 Check/clarify:** *vegetarian, demonstrators, celebrate, charger, handheld device, audience.*
   1 T 2 F 3 F 4 F 5 F
   6 T 7 T 8 T
6. Stronger students may like to try to correct the sentences before re-reading the stories.

7 THE FUTURE IS NOW

OBJECTIVES

FUNCTIONS: checking information; agreeing

GRAMMAR: future forms; question tags; *nor, neither* and *so*

VOCABULARY: future time expressions; arranging a party; phrases with *about*

Get TH!NKING ▶19

Watch the video and think:
how will the world be different 50 years from now?

READING

1 Look at the photo. What can you see? Discuss your ideas.

2 Look at the pictures in the newspaper on the next page. What do they show?
This one shows a spacecraft travelling to another planet.

3 SPEAKING Work in pairs. Talk about a news story for each of the following newspaper sections.

communication | food | science | travel

Can you think of a science story?

Yes, machines to automatically clean everything inside your house.

4 Read the stories on the next page quickly. What is 'different' about this newspaper?

5 🔊 7.01 Read and listen to the stories again. Mark the sentences T (true) or F (false).

1. It will take SS Marstrek more than one Earth day to get to Mars. ____
2. There will only be two passengers on the first SS Marstrek flight. ____
3. The meeting about meat production started last Monday. ____
4. Two groups of people will celebrate outside the building. ____
5. By 2050, people will only need 60 minutes' rest a day. ____
6. A journalist will be the first person to test the new device. ____
7. To send a thought message, you need a handheld device. ____
8. Dr Andrea Gomez says it will always be necessary to have a device for thought messaging. ____

6 SPEAKING Work with a partner. Correct the false sentences in Exercise 5.

66

2 There will be more than two passengers. 3 The meeting starts next Monday. 4 There will be one group there celebrating – consisting of people from animal rights groups. The other group there – the cattle farmers – will be there to ask ministers to think again. 5 They will only need to rest for about 30 minutes a day.

Objectives

Functions and speaking Checking information; **Developing speaking:** Agreeing

Grammar Future forms; question tags; *nor, neither* and so

Vocabulary Future time expressions; arranging a party; **WordWise:** Phrases with *about*

Values Believe in a better future

Life Competencies Being flexible

Resources for this unit

All available online

Videos

- Get **TH!NK**ing: *How will the world be different 50 years from now?*
- Grammar rap!: Question tags
- Vlog: Being flexible

Tests

- Unit, extension and skills test 7

Worksheets

- Grammar and vocabulary: Basic, Standard and Extension Worksheets
- Project: Tomorrow's world
- Communication: Future fun
- Grammar presentation: Question tags
- Get **TH!NK**ing, Grammar rap! and Life Lessons video Worksheets

Culture note

Currently there are over 70 different government and intergovernmental space agencies. Thirteen of these have space launch capabilities, including NASA, the European Space Agency (ESA), the Russian Federal Space Agency (Roscosmos) and the China National Space Administration (CNSA). However, in the last decade, several commercial companies have also begun to develop commercial spacecraft to send private customers into space. These include SpaceX founded by Elon Musk, Blue Origin established by Amazon CEO Jeff Bezos and Richard Branson's Virgin Galactic. These businesses are currently taking reservations for trips into the upper atmosphere, where customers can experience zero-gravity and observe the curvature of the Earth. NASA has also announced plans to allow private individuals to visit the International Space Station, with the first flights scheduled for 2020. It has been estimated that by 2030, the global space market could be worth £400 billion.

TODAY'S WORLD

THE FUTURE IS NOW UNIT 7

22nd July 2042

TRAVEL

FASTER TO MARS

Tomorrow will be another great day in the history of space flight when the SS Marstrek makes its first journey to Mars. The spaceship will carry passengers to the red planet in just 28 hours – three days faster than any other passenger flight! The spacecraft takes off at 10 o'clock in the morning and arrives the next day at 3 o'clock in the afternoon (Mars time). Among the passengers on this exciting first flight will be singer Marion Hyde and actor Karl Costly. To begin with, there will only be one flight a week. But with tickets costing $500,000 each, few of us will be flying on the SS Marstrek just yet!

FOOD

WILL MEAT BE HISTORY SOON?

Government ministers from over 50 countries are meeting on Monday next week to discuss stopping all meat production in their countries. One minister who will be at the meeting said yesterday, 'We know how much people like eating meat. But the fact is that more and more people are becoming vegetarian. We also know that meat production is very bad for the environment. And, of course, we should think about the animals themselves.'

There will be a lot of demonstrators outside the building where the meeting is held. Animal rights groups say they are going there to celebrate, while many cattle farmers also plan to be there, to ask the ministers to think again about the plans.

SCIENCE

SLEEP TO BECOME 'A THING OF THE PAST'

Sleep will become unnecessary by 2050, say scientists. They are working on a device which will make sleep a thing of the past. Instead of going to bed, all a person will have to do is put their hands up against a charger and rest for about half an hour. After that, they will not feel tired any more. Doing this once a day will be enough for most people to stay awake for 24 hours. They are going to start tests next month to make sure that there are no negative side effects. The first human to test the device will be journalist Glenn Martin.

COMMUNICATION

SENDING MESSAGES BY THINKING

Thought messaging! Imagine that you want to send a message to your friend. So, instead of writing a message, all you do is pick up your handheld device, think 'message Jim' and then you think the content of your message ('Hi Jim, how about coffee tomorrow morning?'). The message goes automatically to your handheld device, which writes it and sends it to Jim! At a conference yesterday, Dr Andrea Gomez, Chief Scientist at the Steiger Institute, told the audience that this will be possible in two years' time, but she stressed that it will never be possible to send thoughts directly from one person to another without a device.

TH!NK values

Believe in a better future

7 What kind of future do you think these stories show?

- 😊 a positive future
- 😐 not positive or negative
- ☹ a negative future

- ○ Travel to Mars
- ○ No more meat
- ○ No more sleep
- ○ Thought messages

8 SPEAKING Work in pairs. Compare your ideas with your partner. Give reasons.

I think the story about stopping meat production shows a positive future because then animals won't be killed any more.

9 SPEAKING Think of a positive future. What will it be like? Think about these things.

medicine | poverty | sport
technology | weather | world peace

No one is hungry.

67

7 Ask students to work individually.

8 Encourage further open class discussion.

9 Ask students to decide how positive they are about the future of the world. Ask them to choose a number between 1 and 10, where 10 is extremely positive and 1 is extremely negative. Group the students according to their responses (all the 10s together, all the 9s together, etc.) and ask them to complete the exercise. When they have some ideas for each of the areas, re-group the students so that positive students are grouped with negative students. This should encourage a lot of communication. Students compare their ideas about the future and try to convince the others in their groups that their ideas are right.

Homework

Ask students to use some of the ideas in the stories and write a paragraph describing a negative future, e.g., *More and more people will eat meat and we will lose all the forests.*

Activity idea Extension

Ask students to think about the future of other areas, e.g., education, transport, fashion. In groups, students make a list of how these may change in the future. Give each group a different topic. Challenge groups to come up with as many ideas as possible. Ask all groups to present their ideas to the class and encourage reactions.

Critical TH!NKing
Evaluating ideas, arguments and options
Assesses strengths and weaknesses of possible solutions.

Critical TH!NKing
Evaluating ideas, arguments and options
Analyses causes and effects of problems.

Critical TH!NKing
Synthesising ideas and information
Selects key points from diverse sources to create a new account and/or argument.

TH!NK more

Worksheets
Project Tomorrow's world
Communication Future fun
Get TH!NKing *How will the world be different 50 years from now?*

Warmer

Drill the names of the days of the week, then the months of the year. Display a calendar of the current month on the board. Point to today's date and say *today*. Point to tomorrow and elicit *tomorrow*. Continue with *this week*, *next week*, etc. Ask students if they can name any other time expressions and write any correct answers on the board.

1 Ask students to complete the sentences with different future forms before referring back to page 67 to check.
a takes b meeting c will d start
RULE: 1 a 2 d 3 c 4 b

2 Point out the use of a 24-hour clock at the airport.
1 opens at 7 am 2 arrives at 15.30 3 starts at 10 pm 4 leaves at 10 am

3 You may like to elicit the answer for the first statement as an example. Tell students to look at the rule if they have any difficulties.
1 P 2 I 3 F 4 A 5 F 6 P 7 I 8 A

4 During feedback, encourage students to explain why each option is correct. If you're short on time, set this exercise as homework.
1 'm working 2 do you finish 3 won't 4 'm having 5 are coming 6 won't be 7 will be

Workbook p64

5 Use the calendar from the Warmer to clarify the meaning of the expressions.
1 next 2 long 3 time 4 next 5 after 6 later 7 from 8 near

6 Students' own answers

Workbook p66

GRAMMAR
Future forms

1 Complete the example sentences with the verbs in the list. Check your answers with the stories on page 67. Then match the sentences with the rules. Write a–d.

meeting | start | takes | will

a The spacecraft ______ off at 10 o'clock in the morning.
b Government ministers from over 50 countries are ______ on Monday next week.
c Sleep ______ become unnecessary by 2050.
d They are going to ______ tests next month.

RULE: We often use
- the present simple tense to talk about fixed future events. [1]______
- *be going to* to talk about future plans and intentions. [2]______
- *will/won't* to make predictions about the future. [3]______
- the present continuous to talk about future arrangements. [4]______

2 Complete the sentences. Use the present simple form of the verbs in the list.

arrive | ~~finish~~ | leave | open | start

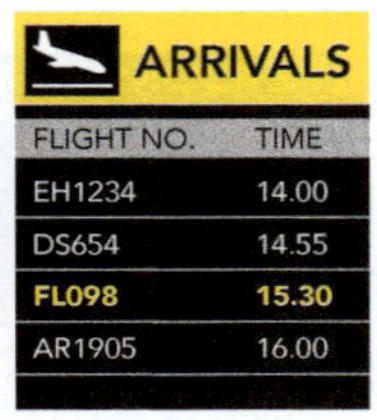

0 The sale *finishes on Friday*.
1 The shop ______.
2 Flight FL098 ______.
3 The concert ______.
4 The train ______.

3 Read the sentences. Mark them P (prediction), I (intention), A (arrangement) or F (fixed event).

1 She won't do very well in her exams. ______
2 They're going to buy a new car soon. ______
3 The match starts at 3 pm. ______
4 He's meeting his mother for lunch on Friday. ______
5 The new zoo opens on Friday. ______
6 One day we'll all live under the sea. ______
7 I'm going to write a novel one day. ______
8 They're having a party on Tuesday. ______

4 Choose the best future form to complete the dialogue.

A [0]*Are you doing* / *Do you do* anything on Friday evening?
B Yes, I [1]*'m working* / *'ll work* at the restaurant.
A Oh, what time [2]*are you finishing* / *do you finish*?
B The restaurant usually closes at 9 pm and I work until then, but there's a party this Friday so I [3]*won't* / *don't* finish until at least 10 pm. Why?
A Well, I [4]*'m having* / *'ll have* a party. Lots of people [5]*come* / *are coming* and I wanted to invite you, too.
B I'd love to come.
A You [6]*won't be* / *aren't being* too tired?
B No way. It [7]*is being* / *will be* the perfect way to start the weekend.

→ workbook page 64

VOCABULARY
Future time expressions

5 Complete the time expressions with the words in the list.

after | from | later | long | near | next (x2) | time

1 the week after ______
2 before too ______
3 in two weeks' ______
4 ______ weekend
5 the day ______ tomorrow
6 ______ today
7 four years ______ now
8 in the ______ future

6 Complete these sentences with your own ideas. Think about your family, friends, school, town and country.

Predictions
1 I think ______ in the near future.
2 I think ______ 40 years from now.
3 I think ______ in 20 years' time.

Intentions
4 I ______ the week after next.
5 I ______ next Friday.
6 I ______ before too long.

Arrangements
7 I ______ this weekend.
8 I ______ later today.
9 I ______ tomorrow morning.

→ workbook page 66

68

Get it Right!
Future forms and time phrases

Student's Book p124

Language note Future forms

1 Students may produce statements like: *I will go to Brazil on holiday.* Remind them that if something is already arranged, we use the present continuous: *I'm going to Brazil on holiday.*
2 Students may find it useful to translate some of the examples in Exercise 3 into their own language to compare them.

THINK more

Workbook
Grammar p64, Ex.1–4
Vocabulary p66, Ex.1–3

Worksheets
Grammar Worksheets 7
Vocabulary Worksheets 7

Listening; WordWise

7 Students should do this individually. You may like to elicit a model question for each person as an example.

8 Encourage students to share their ideas in open class.

9 🔊 **7.02** Encourage students not to focus on understanding every word for now, but just to listen to see if their questions are asked.
Marion:
How are you feeling?
Is this your first time away from Earth?
What are your plans for the trip?
And when are you coming back?
Won't you get bored?
Glenn:
How do you feel about the tests that start next week?
Do you know how long the tests are going to last?
Do you have any worries before you start?
And how about your work?
But won't you get lonely?

10 🔊 **7.02 Check/clarify:** *helicopter, pilot's licence.*
Ask students to underline the key words in the questions and to make sure they understand what is happening in each picture.
1 C 2 B 3 B 4 C

11 Write the word *about* in the middle of the board. Ask students to think of any words that could go before or after *about*. Write any correct answers on the board.
1 think about 2 about half an hour
3 how about 4 about to
5 Sorry about

12 1 b 2 e 3 d 4 a 5 c

13 As an alternative, students could write one false sentence for their partner to guess.

Workbook p66

Homework

Ask students to plan and present a holiday that they will go on with other classmates. They should answer the following questions:
Where are you going? When do you leave? What are you going to do? What do you think you will enjoy most?

LISTENING

7 You are going to listen to two interviews with people from the news stories on page 67: singer Marion Hyde and journalist Glenn Martin. Work in pairs. Write three questions to ask Marion or Glenn.
- Student A: Write three questions to ask Marion.
- Student B: Write three questions to ask Glenn.

8 SPEAKING Compare your questions with your partner.

9 🔊 7.02 Listen to the interviews. Do they ask your questions? What questions do they ask?

10 🔊 7.02 Listen again. Choose the correct answer A, B or C.

1 What is one of Marion's plans for her time on Mars?

2 What else might she do?

3 What is Glenn going to take with him when he does the tests?

4 What kind of work is he going to do?

WordWise: Phrases with *about*

11 Complete the sentences from the unit so far with a phrase from the list.

sorry about	about half an hour	how about	think about	about to

1 We should ______________ the animals themselves.
2 All a person will have to do is put their hands up against a charger and rest for ______________.
3 Hi Jim, ______________ coffee tomorrow morning?
4 We're talking to Marion Hyde as she's ______________ board the SS Marstrek.
5 Oh dear! ______________ that! You won't get bored?

12 Match the questions and answers.
1 How tall is Jack? ☐
2 You haven't tidied up! ☐
3 I'm tired. How about a rest? ☐
4 Has your sister left school now? ☐
5 John had an accident yesterday. ☐

a Yes. She's about to go to university.
b About 1 metre 65, I think.
c Yes, I heard about it. Is he OK?
d Yes, OK.
e Oh, sorry about that.

13 SPEAKING Complete these sentences so they are true for you. Then compare with a partner.
1 I usually get up at about …
2 When I think about the future, I …
3 I've got a friend who is about to …

→ workbook page 66

Activity idea Fast finishers

Ask students to write some sentences explaining what they are going to do next weekend, using the four future forms as appropriate.

Activity idea Fast finishers

Ask students to write down some more future time expressions which follow similar patterns to those in the lesson, e.g. *the day after next, in twenty minutes' time, last weekend*, etc.

TH!NK more

Workbook
Listening p70, Ex.1–2
WordWise p66, Ex.5

Warmer

Tell students to discuss in pairs how they celebrated their last birthday. Write on the board: *Did you have a party? Did you celebrate with friends? How many people were there? Did you have a cake? Did you listen to music and play party games?*

1 **Check/clarify:** *decorations, invitations.*

2 Ask students to explain why they ranked things in the way that they did. During whole-class feedback, encourage students to explain why they think certain things are more important than others. Have a class vote on the most important thing.

3 Give students two minutes to read through the messages quickly and answer the questions. There is some quite difficult language in the messages, so tell students to focus on the questions and not to worry about unknown words or phrases. Encourage students to underline the parts of the messages that helped them answer the questions.
A surprise birthday party for Paula
Students' own answers

4 7.03 **Check/clarify:** *hired the hall, anxious, taken care of.* During feedback, refer to the parts of the messages that helped them decide on their answers.
food – Simon's parents (pizzas), Joanna and her mum (desserts)
music – No one
venue – Simon
decorations – Becky
invitations – Becky

READING

1 Imagine you are organising a party. Put these things in order of importance.

- ☐ food
- ☐ music
- ☐ venue (where you are going to have the party)
- ☐ decorations
- ☐ invitations

2 SPEAKING Work in pairs. Compare your answers to Exercise 1.

A special venue's not very important. I'll just use my house.

Music's very important. You can't have a party without good music.

3 Read the messages quickly. What kind of party are they arranging? Do you think Becky is a good organiser?

4 7.03 Read and listen to the messages again. Who is responsible for each of the things in Exercise 1?

Messages

Becky: Hi everyone. Just want to check some things for the big surprise party next week.
Mark: Hey everyone! I'm looking forward to the party!!
Joanna: So am I. Anyone heard from Simon? He's never around, is he?
Mark: He'll reply later, I'm sure. But good news – he's hired the hall for the party.
Becky: Well, that is good news, isn't it? By the way, you haven't said anything to Paula, have you?
Joanna: No, I haven't said anything.
Mark: Nor have I. I'm not a fool, Becky.
Becky: Sorry. I'm just a bit anxious, that's all. It's not easy to keep something a secret when you have to talk to about 30 people about it! By the way, I've sent out the invitations.
Simon: Hi guys, just reading messages now! No signal on the train – sorry about that. I didn't miss anything important, did I?
Mark: No, not really.
Becky: Now, is the food organised? Simon?
Simon: Yes, my parents are going to make pizzas. We've got permission to be there from 4 pm. That should be OK, shouldn't it?
Joanna: Yes! My mum and I are making desserts. It's all taken care of.
Becky: Brilliant. What about decorations, Mark?
Mark: That's not me, that's you, Becky.
Becky: Are you sure? How could I have forgotten?
Mark: Didn't you write it down?
Becky: Yes. I always write things down. But then I forgot to look at my notes!
Simon: Don't worry, I can help decorate the hall.
Joanna: So can I. Quick question, how are we going to get Paula to go to the hall on the day? We need a plan, don't we?
Becky: Argh! I haven't thought about that yet.
Simon: Neither have we. Don't worry, Becky, you can't do everything.
Mark: Here's an idea. I'll say I'm taking her to the cinema and we'll stop at the hall on the way.
Joanna: She isn't going to believe that, is she? We need a better idea than that.
Simon: Just thought of something else – what about the music? Has anyone booked a DJ?
Becky: Oh, no!

70

TH!NK more

Workbook
Reading p68, Ex.1–3

Grammar; Pronunciation; Vocabulary; Writing

▶ 20 Grammar rap! Question tags

5 1 is 2 have 3 did 4 shouldn't 5 don't 6 is

6 RULE: 1 positive 2 do 3 doesn't 4 did

7 During feedback, practise the intonation of question tags.
1 will you 2 did she 3 can't you 4 isn't he 5 wasn't it 6 do they 7 haven't you 8 are you

8 Before students complete the task, ask them to think of three things they like and three things they don't like, e.g., *I like football. I don't like going to the dentist*. Say a sentence and ask students to agree with it. Elicit *so/neither/nor do I*. Repeat with things the students can/can't do and elicit *so/neither/nor can I*. Point out that we repeat the auxiliary verbs when agreeing with statements in this way.
1 am 2 can 3 have 4 have
RULE: 5 so 6 nor/neither

9 1 Nor did I. / Neither did I.
2 Nor can I. / Neither can I.
3 So should I.
4 So am I.
5 Nor do I. / Neither do I.
6 Nor will I. / Neither will I.
7 So was I.

Workbook p65

Get it Right!
Question tags

Student's Book p124

Pronunciation
Intonation of question tags

Student's Book p121

10 Tell students they may need to add an article (*a* or *the*) to the nouns.
book a DJ, decorate the room, get permission, hire the room, organise food and drinks / the invitations / a DJ, send out the invitations

11 Tell students to use question tags in their discussion.

Workbook p66

12 Encourage students to use images and colours to make the invitation look interesting. Hold a class vote to choose the best party.

GRAMMAR
Question tags

5 **Complete the sentences. Look at the messages on page 70 and check your answers.**

1 He's never around, ______ he?
2 You haven't said anything to Paula, ______ you?
3 I didn't miss anything important, ______ I?
4 That should be OK, ______ it?
5 We need a plan, ______ we?
6 She isn't going to believe that, ______ she?

6 **Use the sentences in Exercise 5 to complete the rules.**

RULE: Question tags are short questions which we use to check facts or make conversation.
- With positive statements, use a [0] <u>*negative*</u> question tag.
- With negative statements, use a [1] ________ question tag. (sentence 2)
- When *be* is used in the statement, repeat it in the question tag. (sentences 1, 6)
- With present or past simple verbs, use [2] ________, *don't*, *does*, [3] ________ (present simple) or [4] ________, *didn't* (past simple). (sentences 3, 5)
- With modal verbs (*can*, *might*, etc.) and most other verb forms, repeat the modal or the auxiliary verb in the question tag. (sentence 4)

7 **Complete the questions with tags.**

0 She sings beautifully, <u>*doesn't she*</u> ?
1 You won't say anything, ____________ ?
2 Claudia didn't phone, ____________ ?
3 You can come to my party, ____________ ?
4 He's Jamie's brother, ____________ ?
5 That meal was delicious, ____________ ?
6 They don't live with you, ____________ ?
7 You've met Leon, ____________ ?
8 You aren't going to university, ____________ ?

Nor, *neither* and *so*

8 **Complete the sentences. Then complete the rules.**

Mark I'm looking forward to the party.
Joanna So [1] ______ I.
Simon I can help with the decorations.
Joanna So [2] ______ I.
Joanna No. I haven't said anything.
Mark Nor [3] ______ I.
Becky I haven't thought about that yet.
Simon Neither [4] ______ we.

RULE: We can use *so* and *nor/neither* to agree with statements.
- We use [5] ______ to agree with positive statements.
- We use [6] ______ to agree with negative statements.

After *so* and *nor/neither* we repeat the verb used in the statement. If the statement is in the present or past simple, we use *do/did* to agree with it. (See rules on question tags.)

9 **Write replies to agree with the statements.**

0 I love school. <u>*So do I.*</u>
1 I didn't watch any TV last night. ____________
2 I can't go to the party. ____________
3 I should do my homework. ____________
4 I'm going to bed early tonight. ____________
5 I don't eat meat. ____________
6 I won't be late. ____________
7 I was very upset with Tim. ____________

→ workbook page 65

PRONUNCIATION
Intonation of question tags Go to page 121.

VOCABULARY
Arranging a party

10 **Match the verbs with the nouns to create a 'to do' list. Use the posts on page 70 to help you. Use one of the nouns twice.**

Verbs	Nouns
book | decorate | get | hire | organise | send out	DJ | food and drinks | invitations | permission | room

Get permission for the party.

11 SPEAKING **Work in pairs. In what order should you do the things on your to do list?**

You should get permission first, shouldn't you?

→ workbook page 66

WRITING
An invitation to a party

12 **You are having a party. Write the invitations. Be sure to mention the date, time and place of the party and also what your guests should bring (or not bring).**

Language notes Question tags

Students may find this difficult because of how their own language works. They may produce incorrect statements like: *He's Carlos, is he?* Remind them that in English the question tag is generally the opposite of the verb.

nor, *neither* and *so*

Point out to students that to disagree with a statement we use the auxiliary verb in the negative, e.g., *A: I love going to concerts. B: I don't.*

TH!NK more

Practice Extra
Unit 7 Practise it!

Workbook
Grammar p65, Ex.5–7
Vocabulary p66, Ex.4
Vocabulary Extra p67, Ex.1–2
Pronunciation p120
Developing Writing p69

Worksheets
Grammar rap! Question tags
Grammar Worksheets 7
Grammar presentation: Question tags
Vocabulary Worksheets 7

Warmer

Ask students to write a list of five ways they like spending time at the weekends. In small groups, students share their ideas and respond with *So do I, Neither do I.*

1 7.06 Tell students to cover the dialogue and discuss the questions in pairs before listening to check their answers.
They're trying to arrange a time for a picnic over the weekend.

2 1 She had a lot of homework.
2 Have a picnic
3 The weather forecast isn't good.
4 She's taking her gran out.

3 Encourage students to use the language from the dialogue when giving their answers.

4 During feedback, say the sentences for students to repeat. Drill sentences to ensure correct pronunciation.
1 Lucky you 2 that's a shame
3 Thank goodness 4 In other words
5 What do you reckon 6 There's nothing wrong with

5 As an alternative, you could ask students to cover a–d and get them to guess what the responses are.
1 b 2 c 3 d 4 a

6 If space allows, encourage students to walk around the classroom to find someone who agrees with their statements. Ask students to report their findings back to the class and encourage them to use the phrase *So does he/she/[student's name].*

DEVELOPING SPEAKING

1 7.06 **Look at the photos. It's Friday evening. What do you think they are talking about? Listen and read to check.**

Hannah: So, Friday evening, it's finally the weekend. Thank goodness! I've had a really hard week.
Tracey: So have I. There's nothing wrong with Mr Gordon but he gives so much homework! I've never had so much work to do in my life! But next week we've got two days off at my school!
Hannah: Lucky you! But listen, let's do something together at the weekend.
Tracey: Yes, let's. Got any ideas about what we could do?
Hannah: How about a picnic? I haven't had a picnic … well, in a long time!
Tracey: Neither have I. That's a great idea. But the weather forecast isn't good for Saturday, and I'm busy on Sunday morning …
Hannah: Oh, that's a shame. Well, what about Sunday afternoon? What do you reckon?
Tracey: Sunday afternoon sounds fine. Let's hope the weather's nice. Picnics are always better on sunny days. Oh! Hang on! On Sunday afternoon I'm taking my gran out. Mum and Dad usually take her somewhere, but it's my turn this Sunday.
Hannah: Can't you take her out in the morning?
Tracey: Not really. We always take her out in the afternoon. It's important for her to have a routine – I don't want to change that.
Hannah: OK, ask your brother to take her.
Tracey: Well, he's got football and, anyway, he took her out last week. Sorry.
Hannah: In other words, we can't have our picnic. I was looking forward to it!
Tracey: So was I, Hannah. I'd love to have a picnic, but, you know. I hope we can do it next weekend.
Hannah: So do I. I'll call you. And I'll try to be a bit more flexible than you. Bye, Tracey!
Tracey: Oh Hannah, don't be …

2 **Read the dialogue again and answer the questions.**
1 Why was last week hard for Tracey?
2 What does Hannah suggest they do this weekend?
3 Why can't they do it on Saturday?
4 What is Tracey doing on Sunday afternoon?

3 SPEAKING **Discuss the statements in pairs. What do you think?**
1 Tracey could talk to her grandmother and change her plans.
2 Tracey isn't very flexible.
3 Hannah could be more understanding.

Phrases for fluency

4 **Find the underlined expressions in the dialogue and use them to complete the conversations.**
1 A My parents just won a holiday in a competition.
B Wow! [1]__________!
A The holiday is for two people, so I can't go.
B Oh, [2]__________.
2 A How's Ben? Any news?
B Yes. He's OK. His arm's not broken. [3]__________.
A [4]__________, it's not as serious as we thought.
3 A Look at that guy's clothes. They're horrible! [5]__________?
B Well, I don't like them much. But I don't think you should be so critical.
A Hey! [6]__________ saying what you think!

FUNCTIONS
Agreeing

KEY LANGUAGE
a So do I. c Neither have I.
b So have I. d So was I.

5 **Match the sentences to the replies in the Key Language box.**
1 I've had a really hard week. ☐
2 I haven't had a picnic for a long time. ☐
3 I was looking forward to it. ☐
4 I hope we can do it next weekend. ☐

6 SPEAKING **Complete these sentences with true information about you. Then find people who agree with you and write their names.**
Tonight I'm going to __________
and so is __________.
I'm not going to __________
nor is __________.
Yesterday I __________
and so did __________.
Yesterday I didn't __________
nor did __________.

72

Life Competencies

Warmer

Write *flexible* on the board and elicit the meaning in this context (able to change easily according to the situation). Ask students to give themselves a mark for flexibility between 0 and 10. Does their level of flexibility change depending on who they are interacting with?

▶ 21 Life Lessons: Being flexible

1 ▶ 21
He wanted to do a vlog about money but Anna had already filmed her one.

2 ▶ 21
1 Because if they weren't, they would fall over in a strong wind.
2 He wanted to go to his friend's house.
3 She said he should think about his dad and sister too.
4 He thought she was right.

3 Play a video game (Urban Quest) with Nicole

4 Students' own answers

5 Give students three or four minutes to think about their answers before discussing.

6 You may want to talk about an experience of your own as an example.

Homework

Ask students to write ten sentences describing similarities between themselves and their family using *So do I* and *Neither do I*.

Activity idea Extension

Students write five sentences describing the most and/or least flexible people that they know.

LIFE COMPETENCIES

Being flexible means being willing to change your plans or ideas if a situation changes. We can't always do what we want, often because friends or family have different ideas or plans. But sometimes, being flexible helps to create a positive result.

1 ▶ 21 **Watch the video. What did Kieran want to talk about and why couldn't he?**

2 ▶ 21 **Watch again and answer the questions.**
1 Why do buildings need to be flexible?
2 Why did Kieran want to eat earlier one Saturday?
3 Why did his mother say no to his request one day?
4 What did Kieran think about her decision?

3 **Read the phone conversation. What does Jade want to do?**

Jade I've just bought Urban Quest!
Nicole Wow! I've heard it's amazing.
Jade Me, too. So I thought that maybe …
Nicole Sorry, I can't. I'm going to see Steve.
Jade Come on! This is Urban Quest!
Nicole No, he's been really bored since he broke his leg playing basketball. I promised I'd go and see him.
Jade Nicole, listen. I've been excited about this for weeks and weeks. You, me, the big TV in the living room and the best computer game of the year.
Nicole Really sorry, Jade. I promised.
Jade Mum said we can order pizzas if you come.
Nicole I'd like to, but I can't. Why don't you come to Steve's, too? I'm sure we can play it there.
Jade But Steve's a terrible player! It'll be boring. And he doesn't have a big TV. Please! I'm going crazy! Playing alone isn't as much fun.
Nicole I know, but why don't you come anyway? We can play at your house next weekend.
Jade I don't know …

4 SPEAKING **Work in pairs. Discuss these questions with your partner.**
1 How does Jade feel?
2 How do you think Jade will feel if she stays at home?
3 How do you think Nicole feels after speaking with Jade?
4 What do you think will happen if Jade goes to Steve's house?
5 What should Jade and Nicole do?

Me and my world

5 SPEAKING **Work in pairs. What would you do in these situations?**
1 It's Saturday morning and you want to go shopping for trainers. Your friend wants to come, too, but he's busy. He's free this afternoon.
2 Your friend wants to start a band. You've always wanted to be a singer, but your friend has already asked somebody else. She has asked you to play the drums.
3 You spend a long time writing a story for homework. Your teacher says that it's very good, but then suggests changing the ending.
4 You want to celebrate your birthday at the new pizza place in town. When you call to book a table, they tell you that it's full on that day. They offer you a table for the weekend after.

6 SPEAKING **Work in pairs. Talk about a situation in which you had to be flexible.**

TIPS FOR BEING FLEXIBLE

- If you're not sure what to do, ask for some time to think before making a decision.
- How will you feel if you aren't flexible? Being inflexible can leave us feeling sad, lonely and angry.
- Don't cause an argument. If you or your family and friends want to do something else, that's OK.

Emotional Development
Empathy and relationship skills
Showing understanding of other people's perspectives and feelings.

Emotional Development
Empathy and relationship skills
Negotiating conflict constructively.

TH!NK more

Practice Extra
Unit 7 Master it!

Worksheets
Life Lessons: Being flexible
Unit, extension and skills test 7

Warmer

Read out the unit title. Ask students what they think it means. Elicit ideas and encourage discussion.

▶ 22 Get TH!NKing

Play the video and discuss the question with your class.

1 *1 a fire 2 a wheel 3 electricity 4 a mobile phone 5 a car 6 paper 7 a (steam) train*

2 Encourage students to think of at least three reasons for question 1 and three ideas for question 2.

3 For extended speaking practice, re-group the students and ask them to compare their answers.
1 A discovery is recognising something that already exists for the first time, that nobody has found before. An invention is creating something totally new with one's own ideas and development.

4 Before students read the article, get them to cover it and just look at the pictures and think about the connection between them. Write some of the students' ideas on the board to refer back to after the next exercise. Do not give the answer just yet.

5 🔊 8.01
Students' own answers

6 **Check/clarify:** *have in common, observe, investigate, discover, kettle, boil, curious, steam, spout, lid, milkmaids, disease, vaccine.*
1 The steam made the lid jump up and down. 2 That steam was very powerful 3 He thought about how fewer people in the country got smallpox. 4 Because he allowed Jenner to give him a potentially life-threatening disease. 5 Because vaccines stop the spread of dangerous diseases and have saved millions of lives.

8 SCIENCE AND US

OBJECTIVES

FUNCTIONS: talking about past habits; talking about imaginary situations; talking about scientific discoveries

GRAMMAR: past simple vs. past continuous (review); *used to*; second conditional; *I wish*

VOCABULARY: direction and movement; science

Get TH!NKING
Watch the video and think: what scientific discoveries are you grateful for?

1 
2 
3 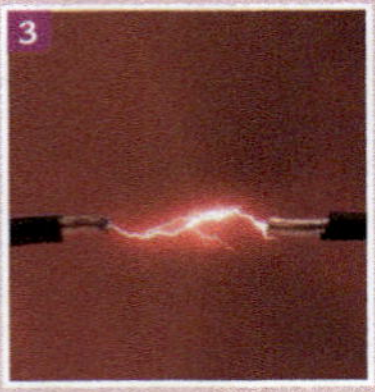
4 
5 
6 
7 

READING

1 Look at the photos. Say what each one shows.

Picture 3 is electricity.

2 SPEAKING Work in pairs. Answer the questions.
1 Why are the things in the photos important?
2 What was life like for people before they had these things?

Before people had fire, they couldn't cook meat. And they were cold in winter.

3 SPEAKING Work in pairs or small groups. Discuss the questions.
1 Electricity and fire are *discoveries*. The other things are *inventions*. What's the difference?
2 Which of the things in the photos do you think is the most important? Why?
3 Can you think of other discoveries or inventions that changed how people live?

4 Look at the pictures on the next page. What do you think the connection between them is?

5 🔊 8.01 Read and listen to the article. Check your ideas about the pictures.

6 Read the article again and answer the questions.
1 What did Watt notice while he watched the kettle?
2 What did he discover?
3 How did observing the milkmaids influence Jenner's ideas?
4 Why was James Phipps brave?
5 How did Jenner's discovery change the world?

74

Objectives

Functions and speaking Talking about past habits; talking about imaginary situations; talking about scientific discoveries
Grammar Past simple vs. past continuous (review); *used to*; second conditional; *I wish*
Vocabulary Direction and movement; science
Values How science helps people
Train to TH!NK Using criteria

Resources for this unit

All available online

Videos
- Get **TH!NK**ing: *What scientific discoveries are you grateful for?*
- Grammar rap!: Past simple vs. past continuous (review)
- Culture: Simple inventions

Tests
- Unit, extension and skills test 8

Worksheets
- Grammar and vocabulary: Basic, Standard and Extension Worksheets
- Project: Inventions
- Communication: Science counts
- Literature Worksheets: *The Strange Case of Dr Jekyll and Mr Hyde; The Nothing Equation*
- Get **TH!NK**ing and Grammar rap! video Worksheets

Culture notes

Sir Isaac Newton was born in England in 1643. He became famous for his work on gravity and his three laws of motion as well as his work on light, colour and calculus. The famous story of an apple falling from a tree illustrates how Newton's work on gravity was inspired by things he observed in the world around him.

Archimedes (c.287–212 BCE) was a Greek mathematician, physicist, engineer, inventor and astronomer. He is most famous for discovering the law of hydrostatics, sometimes known as 'Archimedes' principle', which explains why an object sinks or floats. Archimedes is supposed to have made this discovery in his bath, exclaiming 'Eureka!'

James Watt, born in Scotland in 1736, was an inventor, engineer and scientist during the industrial revolution. While repairing a model steam engine in 1764, he made such improvements that his new steam engine used 75% less fuel. His work was so important that the unit of power was named after him: the watt.

Edward Jenner was an English scientist, born in 1749. He discovered the smallpox vaccine; in 1980, the World Health Organisation declared it an 'eliminated disease'. Vaccination now prevents an estimated 2–3 million deaths every single year. Jenner's work is said to have saved more lives than the work of any other human.

7 Students' own answers (Careful observations can lead to great discoveries.)

8 Encourage students to refer to the sentences in the article which support their answer.

9 As an alternative, you could ask students to think of examples of their own and get their partner to say why it's important.

Curious minds

What makes a great scientist? Maybe it's hard work or an interest in understanding how the world works? Yes, these things are important. But one thing that many scientists have in common is that they like to observe – watch – the world carefully. Whether it was Newton watching the apple fall from the tree, or Archimedes watching the water spill out from his bath, scientists like to watch things happen and then start thinking 'why?' Then they investigate a little bit more and what they discover tells us more about the world we live in. Two of the 18th century's greatest discoveries started in exactly this way.

One day in 1748, 12-year-old **James Watt** was sitting in the kitchen, when his aunt started to heat water in a kettle. He was watching the kettle boil, when the lid began to jump up and down. He was curious about it and decided to experiment. He held the lid of the kettle down and noticed that the steam came out of the spout. When he took his hand away, the lid started moving again. James realised that the steam had great power. It was an experiment he never forgot, and years later, he used the ideas to improve the design of the first steam engine.

Another scientist whose observations changed the world was **Edward Jenner**. Back in the late 1700s, there was a terrible disease called smallpox. It killed many people and left many others with horrible injuries. It was an awful disease and there was no cure.

Jenner wanted to do something to help fight the disease. One day he was watching some women working on a farm. The women were getting milk from the cows. While he was watching the women, Jenner had an idea. He knew that fewer people caught smallpox in the countryside than in the city. He also knew that people who worked with cows often caught a disease called cowpox. Cowpox was a less serious disease than smallpox. It made people ill, but didn't kill anybody.

Jenner started to wonder if getting cowpox stopped people from getting smallpox. He decided to test his ideas with the help of a very brave boy called James Phipps. He took some cowpox disease and gave it to James. James caught cowpox and was ill, but got better soon afterwards. Then, Jenner gave James smallpox. Thankfully, James never developed the disease. Jenner's discovery was very important for two reasons. First, because Jenner discovered a way of stopping the spread of smallpox, and second, because he created the world's first vaccine.

Since Jenner's discovery, vaccines have been used around the world and have saved millions of lives.

TH!NK values

How science helps people

7 **Choose the sentence that you think best summarises what the article is about.**

1 Careful observations can lead to great discoveries.
2 You shouldn't believe everything you read about science.
3 Scientists should be more famous than they are.
4 It's important to know something about science.

8 SPEAKING **Compare your ideas with others in the class.**

9 SPEAKING **Here are four things that we have, thanks to science. Write down some more. In pairs, discuss how these things help us every day.**

the internet   the telephone   medicine   the fridge

__________   __________
__________   __________

Homework

Write on the board: *internet*, *telephone*, *medicine*, *fridge*. Ask students to choose one of the four items and to research and write about the history of the item.

Activity idea Extension

In pairs, give students four minutes to brainstorm other important scientific discoveries/inventions. Write their ideas on the board. Give students another few minutes to rank the items in order of importance in everyday life. At the end, listen to some of the students' ideas, encourage open class discussion and try to create a definitive order.

TH!NK more

Worksheets
Project Inventions
Communication Science counts
Get THINKing *What scientific discoveries are you grateful for?*

Critical THINKing
Understanding and analysing links between ideas
Distinguishes between main and supporting arguments.

Critical THINKing
Understanding and analysing links between ideas
Compares points and arguments from different sources.

Warmer

To revise past simple verb forms, play 'past forms tennis'. In pairs, one student says an infinitive verb and the other student must reply with the correct past form as quickly as possible.

▶ 23 Grammar rap! Past simple vs. past continuous (review)

1 Use sentence 1 to elicit which tense shows the first action was in progress (past continuous) and which tense tells us it was interrupted by the second action (past simple).
1 was watching, began
2 was watching, had
RULE: 3 past simple 4 when
5 past continuous 6 while

2 Go through the example and ask: *Which action began first?* (watching a thunderstorm); *What interrupted it?* (he got some ideas).
1 were doing, started 2 didn't stop, didn't have 3 went, was doing 4 discovered, was surfing 5 were … talking, saw 6 found, became

3 1 were walking / were standing 2 doing 3 were walking / were standing 4 saw 5 was riding 6 was going / was riding / was cycling 7 cycled / rode 8 hit 9 knocked 10 didn't stop

Workbook p72

Grammar rap!

GRAMMAR
Past simple vs. past continuous (review)

1 Complete the sentences from the text on page 75 with the verbs in the correct form. Then complete the rules with *past simple, past continuous, when* and *while*.

watch x 2 | have | begin

1 He ______ the kettle boil, when the lid ______ to jump up and down.
2 While he ______ the women, Jenner ______ an idea.

RULE: We use
- the [3]______ for an action that happened at a particular moment in the past. We often use [4]______ with this tense.
- the [5]______ for a background action or to describe a situation over a period of time in the past. We often use [6]______ with this tense.

Remember that some verbs can't be used in the continuous form.

2 Complete the sentences with the correct past tense form of the verbs.

0 While Benjamin Franklin ___*was watching*___ a thunderstorm, he ___*got*___ some ideas about electricity. (watch / get)
1 We ______ an experiment at school when a fire ______. (do / start)
2 They ______ for lunch because they ______ enough time. (not stop / not have)
3 The electricity ______ off at home while I ______ my homework. (go / do)
4 I ______ a great science site while I ______ the net. (discover / surf)
5 Who ______ you ______ to when I ______ you in town yesterday? (talk / see)
6 When the scientist ______ the answer to the problem, she ______ very famous. (find / become)

3 Sally saw an incident in her town centre. Complete her statement to the police with the past simple or past continuous form of the verbs in the list. Sometimes more than one verb is possible.

~~buy~~ | cycle | do | go | hit | knock
not stop | ride | ~~sit~~ | see | stand | walk

Last Saturday morning I [0]*bought* a magazine, and I [0]___*sat*___ down on a bench in the town centre to read it. People [1]______ around and [2]______ their shopping. There was a group of four people near me – they [3]______ together and laughing. Then I [4]______ a boy, about 16 years old. He [5]______ his bike down the street. He [6]______ very fast. Suddenly, he had to change direction because there was an old lady in front of him, and he [7]______ right into the group of people. His bike [8]______ a man and [9]______ him over. And the boy [10]______. He just cycled away!

→ workbook page 72

VOCABULARY
Direction and movement

4 Complete the sentence. Then check your answer in the text on page 75.

The lid began to jump ______ and ______.

5 Match the phrases with the pictures.

1 It's coming **towards** her.
2 It's running **away from** her.
3 They're running **around** the tree.
4 She's leaning **backwards**.
5 She's leaning **forwards**.
6 He's walking **up and down** the room.

Look
Forwards and *backwards* are the only words here that are never followed by an object.
The words *towards* and *away from* always have an object after them.

6 Which way(s) can these things move?

1 a car
2 a plane
3 a helicopter
4 a lion in a cage

→ workbook page 74

4 *up, down*

5 **Check/clarify:** *up and down – to walk in one direction and then the other, usually when feeling nervous.*
Demonstrate with hand gestures if necessary.
A 1 B 6 C 3 D 5 E 2 F 4

6 Students' own answers

Workbook p74

Activity idea Extension

Ask students if they can think of any more words describing movement (e.g., *over, through*). Ask them to think of situations where they might use these, e.g., *You can go over a bridge, through a tunnel.*

TH!NK more

Workbook
Grammar p72, Ex.1–3
Vocabulary p74, Ex.1–2

Worksheets
Grammar rap! Past simple vs. past continuous (review)
Grammar Worksheets 8
Vocabulary Worksheets 8

Listening; Grammar; Pronunciation; Functions

7 Check/clarify: *alchemist, metal, gold.*
A That Earth was the centre of the universe
B That the world was flat (and you could fall off the edge)

8 🔊 **8.02**
That other metals could be turned into gold

9 🔊 **8.02**
1 How the world works
2 They discovered that the sun was the centre of the universe, not the Earth.
3 He sailed around the world and didn't fall off.
4 That metal could be turned into gold
5 Because it's possible to turn sand into glass.
6 That in the future people will laugh at some of the things we believe in now

10 Ask: *Do the people in sentence 1 believe these things now?* (no); *Did they believe them in the past?* (yes); *Did they do the things in 1, 2 and 3 once in the past or many times?* (many times); *In 4, do people have scientific equipment now?* (yes).
1 believe/think 2 believe/think 3 be 4 have
RULE: 5 used to 6 use to 7 use to

11 1 used to be, don't live 2 didn't use to listen, don't listen 3 don't like, used to be 4 used to go, prefer 5 used to believe 6 didn't use to care, think 7 did … use to have

Workbook p72

Get it Right!
used to vs. *usually*

Student's Book p124

Pronunciation
The /juː/ sound

Student's Book p121

12 Give your own example to demonstrate.

13 Point out the use of *used to* to describe a repeated past action.

Homework
Students can do a mini-project about their school and how it has changed. They can illustrate it or add photos and write a short paragraph about the changes.

LISTENING

7 Look at the pictures. What ancient beliefs about the world do they show?

A

B

8 🔊 8.02 Listen to the science lesson and check your ideas. What other idea do they talk about?

9 🔊 8.02 Listen again. Answer the questions.
1 What can science help us understand?
2 What belief did Copernicus, Galileo and Kepler change?
3 How did Christopher Columbus prove the Earth isn't flat?
4 What did alchemists believe?
5 Why did they think this was possible?
6 What does Mrs Roberts think about the future?

GRAMMAR
used to

10 Complete these sentences with the words in the list. Then choose the correct words to complete the rules.

be | believe | have | think

1 Many people used to ______ that our planet was the centre of the universe.
2 Did people use to______ that the Earth was flat, too?
3 Sailors used to ______ afraid of sailing out too far into the sea.
4 People didn't use to ______ all the scientific equipment we have these days.

RULE: We can use *used to* + verb to talk about things that happened regularly in the past but not any more.
In the positive, we say [5]**used to / use to** + verb.
In the negative, we say *didn't* [6]**used to / use to** + verb.
For questions, we say *Did [you]* [7]**used to / use to** + verb.

11 Complete the sentences. Use the correct form of *used to* and the present simple.
0 That shop ___*used to be*___ (be) a book shop, but now it ___*sells*___ (sell) clothes.
1 He ______________ (be) my friend, but we ______________ (not live) near each other any more.
2 When we were younger, we ______________ (not listen) to country music, but now we ______________ (not listen) to anything else.
3 I really ______________ (not like) pizza now, but it ______________ (be) my favourite food.
4 We ______________ (go) to Greece on holiday, but now we ______________ (prefer) Spain.
5 My sister ______________ (believe) there were monsters under her bed.
6 I ______________ (not care) about science, but now I ______________ (think) it's really interesting.
7 When you were small, ______________ you ______________ (have) an imaginary friend?

→ workbook page 72

PRONUNCIATION
The /juː/ sound Go to page 121.

FUNCTIONS
Talking about past habits

12 Think about life when you were little. Write some things that you or others used to do or believe.

____
____
____
____

13 SPEAKING Work in small groups. Talk about the things you wrote. Who has the funniest story?

When I was little I used to think that there was a person inside the post box who took the letters.

My brother and I used to hide in my sister's wardrobe and then jump out and scare her when she opened the door.

Language note *used to*

1 Students may produce incorrect questions like: *Did he used to like punk music?* Remind them that the question form is *did* + *use to*.
2 They may also produce incorrect statements like: *Did she used to going to university?* Remind them that we use *used to* + infinitive without *to*.

Activity idea Extension

In small groups, students think about their own town or city and how it has changed. They must produce a sentence using *used to* to describe the change, e.g., *There used to be a vegetable shop near the square. There's a supermarket there now.* Ask groups to feedback to the class.

TH!NK more

Workbook
Listening p78, Ex.1–2
Grammar p72, Ex.4
Pronunciation p120

Worksheets
Grammar Worksheets 8

Warmer

Write on the board: *a pair of flying shoes, an invisible winter jacket, an extremely fast bicycle, a memory chip for your brain.* Ask: *Would you like to have these things? Why/Why not?* Ask students to discuss in pairs.

1 Ask students to work individually and think of further examples of things that haven't been invented yet.

2 Before students read the web forum, get them to cover it and just look at the pictures and answer the question. Write their ideas on the board.

3 **Check/clarify:** *clone, laboratory.* Give students just two minutes to scan the forum quickly to find the answer to the question. Encourage them not to focus on every word for now but just to find the ideas that are mentioned.
A clone, a way to stop feeling tired, a super-quick travel machine, a huge laboratory

4 **8.05**
1 Eve 2 Aimee 3 Oliver 4 Matthew

5 Students rank the ideas individually.

6 Ask students to try to come to agreement on the best ranking.

7 Possible answers: expensive, safe

8 Students rank individually before comparing with a partner. At the end of the exercise, listen to some of the students' ideas and encourage open class discussion.

READING

1 SPEAKING What would you like to invent? Why? Compare your ideas with a partner.

I'd like to have a flying skateboard.

2 A web forum asked readers what invention would make their life better. Look at the pictures. What things do you think the forum readers suggested?

3 Read the forum. Check your answers to Exercise 2. What other idea is there?

4 8.05 Read and listen to the forum again. Then write the names of the people described in these statements.

1 This person needs more rest. ______
2 This person wants to improve life for everyone. ______
3 This person wants to avoid doing the unpleasant things in life. ______
4 This person wants to go places. ______

Train to TH!NK

Using criteria

5 Here are the four ideas from the forum. Put them in order 1–4 (1 = the most useful, 4 = the least useful).

- ☐ a a clone of yourself
- ☐ b a treatment for tiredness
- ☐ c a super-quick travel machine
- ☐ d a secret laboratory

6 SPEAKING Compare your ideas with a partner.

7 In Exercise 5, you evaluated the ideas on how useful they were. Below are two different criteria. Think of two others.

- How ___possible___ is it?
- How ___important___ is it?
- How ______ is it?
- How ______ is it?

8 SPEAKING Choose one of the criteria in Exercise 7 and order the things in Exercise 5 again. Then compare your ideas with other students.

78

Home | Forum | News | Sign in

Q We asked you, our readers, 'What invention or discovery would make your life better?' Here are some of your answers.

A clone. If I had a clone of myself, I would have so much more time. I'd send my clone to do all the boring stuff I don't like doing. He would take all my exams and he would wait in all those long boring queues for me. That would leave me more time to do the things I really want to do.
Oliver

I wish someone would find a way to stop me feeling tired in the mornings. It doesn't matter what time I go to bed, I never want to get out of bed the next morning, even at the weekends when I don't have to get up early for school. I'd stay in bed until the afternoon if I could. Life without an alarm clock – that would be perfect!
Eve

I wish I had a super-quick travel machine like they have in the *Star Trek* films. You know what I mean, a machine that could transport me anywhere in the world in seconds. So, imagine you're in one place. You enter some coordinates into the machine and two seconds later you're there. For example, you could have breakfast in Italy, visit the Amazon in the morning and spend the afternoon at the South Pole. If there was a machine like that, I'd visit the whole world.
Matthew

I want to be a scientist when I grow up, so the thing that I would like most is a huge laboratory underneath my house. A secret one that only I knew about. Down there I'd do lots of research and experiments. Then I would invent lots of different things that would make peoples' lives better, like cures for diseases. If anyone can help make my dream come true, please get in touch.
Aimee

TH!NK more

Workbook
Reading p76, Ex.1–3

Critical TH!NKing
Evaluating ideas, arguments and options
Examines possible solutions to a given problem and states how effective they are.

Critical TH!NKing
Evaluating ideas, arguments and options
Gives reasons for an argument's plausibility.

Critical TH!NKing
Evaluating ideas, arguments and options
Assesses strengths and weaknesses of possible solutions.

9 1 had, would 2 there was, visit 3 stay, could do
imagined situations

10 RULE: 1 an improbable 2 past 3 would

It might be useful to compare the rules for the first conditional and the second conditional. Write a first conditional sentence on the board and ask students to give you an example of a second conditional sentence, e.g. *If I win the lottery, I'll buy a new car. If I had lots of money, I'd buy a new car.*

11 Remind students to look carefully at the verbs and to see where the *if*-clause is.
1 would learn, listened 2 was, would have 3 would lend, asked 4 was, would stay 5 would give, knew

12 1 would … talk, had 2 would like, were 3 didn't make, wouldn't do 4 could, would … choose

13 Point out that this use of the past tense is similar to its use in the second conditional.
Both ideas are impossible / unreal.

14 1 were 2 could 3 wasn't 4 weren't making / wouldn't make

15 Students' own answers

Workbook p73

Get it Right!
Second conditional tenses

Student's Book p124

16 1 d 2 e 3 f 4 g 5 c 6 h 7 a 8 b

17–18 Check students are using the second conditional and *wish* correctly.

Workbook p74

Homework
Ask students to write a short paragraph about one of the following questions for homework:

What would you do if …

… you went to a park and a dog started chasing you?

… (a famous person) invited you to dinner?

… you had £20 million?

GRAMMAR
Second conditional

9 **Complete these sentences with the phrases in the list. Are the sentences about real or imagined situations?**

would | could do | had | stay | there was | visit

1 If I ______ a clone of myself, I ______ have so much more time.
2 If ______ a machine like that, I'd ______ the whole world.
3 I'd ______ in bed until the afternoon if I ______.

10 **Complete the rules.**

RULE: We use the second conditional to talk about the consequences of an unreal present action or [1]a probable / an improbable future action.
- Condition clause: *if* + [2]______ simple.
- Result clause: [3]______ / *wouldn't (would not)* + verb.

The condition clause can come before or after the result clause.

11 **Choose the correct words.**

0 If I *had* / *would have* a bit more time, I *went* / *would go* and see my friends tonight.
1 They *would learn* / *learned* more if they *would listen* / *listened* more carefully.
2 If my school *would be* / *was* a long way from home, I *would have* / *had* to take a bus.
3 He *lent* / *would lend* you his tablet if you *asked* / *would ask* him nicely.
4 If he *was* / *would be* really ill, he *stay* / *would stay* in bed.
5 I *gave* / *would give* you her address if I *knew* / *would know* it myself.

12 **Complete the sentences with the correct form of the verbs.**

0 I think it *'d be* (be) a great party if the food *was* (be) better.
1 Who ______ you ______ (talk) to if you ______ (have) a really serious problem?
2 She ______ (like) you if you ______ (be) nicer to her.
3 If his father ______ (not make) him tidy his room, he ______ (not do) it.
4 If you ______ (can) have any present you want, what ______ you ______ (choose)?

I wish

13 **Read the sentences. How are they alike?**

1 I wish someone would find a way to stop me feeling tired.
2 I wish I had a super-quick travel machine.

14 **Complete the sentences with the correct form of the underlined verbs.**

0 The bus isn't here. I wish the bus *was* here.
1 We aren't a good team. I wish we ______ a better team.
2 I can't go home. I wish I ______ go home.
3 It's raining. I wish it ______ raining.
4 They are making so much noise! I wish they ______ so much noise!

15 SPEAKING **Work in pairs. Which person in the pictures is thinking which thing from Exercise 14? (More than one answer is possible.)**

→ workbook page 73

VOCABULARY
Science

16 **Match the words with the definitions.**

1 ☐ a cure
2 ☐ to discover
3 ☐ an experiment
4 ☐ to invent
5 ☐ a laboratory
6 ☐ a machine
7 ☐ to do research
8 ☐ a scientist

a to study something
b someone who works in an area of science
c a room for scientific work
d something that makes a sick person well again
e to find something new
f a test to see if something works or is true
g to make something new
h a piece of equipment that does a specific kind of work

17 SPEAKING **Work in pairs. What invention or discovery would make your life better? What invention or discovery would make the lives of all people better?**

18 SPEAKING **In class, compare everyone's ideas and vote for the best ones.**

→ workbook page 74

Language notes Second conditional
Explain that after *if I* in the second conditional we can use *was* or *were*, e.g., *If I were you, I'd …* or *If I was you, I'd …* Explain that *were* can also be used with third person singular in the second conditional.

I wish
It is common to use *were* instead of *was* after *I wish / If only*, e.g., *I wish I was/were rich* or *If only he was/were here now* are all correct.

THINK more

Practice Extra
Unit 8 Practise it!

Workbook
Grammar p73, Ex.5–8
Vocabulary p74, Ex.3–4
Vocabulary Extra p75, Ex.1–2

Worksheets
Grammar Worksheets 8
Vocabulary Worksheets 8

Warmer

Elicit any ancient civilisations that students can remember and write them on the board, e.g., Mayan, Inca, Roman, Egyptian, etc.

▶ 24 TH!NK
Simple inventions

1 Before students read the article, get them to cover it and just look at the images and answer the question. Write their ideas on the board.

2 🔊 **8.06** Tell students not to worry about difficult vocabulary at this stage as this will come up later. Ask students to explain the reason for their choices.
A4 B1 C2 D3

Culture

TH!NK Simple inventions

1 Look at the images. What can you see in each one?

2 🔊 8.06 Read and listen to the article about four inventions. Match the images with the inventions. Write 1–4 in the boxes.

AMAZING INVENTIONS FROM ANCIENT CIVILIZATIONS

Throughout history, humankind has progressed thanks to amazing inventions and discoveries. Some of the inventions we use in our everyday life are a lot older than you might think. Here are four of them.

1 Nanotechnology – *Ancient Italy*

The Lycurgus Cup is a beautifully decorated glass cup that was made in Italy in the fourth century.

For years, it confused scientists because it seems to change colour. When light shines through it from the front, it looks green, but when it shines from the back, it appears red. In the 1990s, scientists looked at the glass under a microscope. They discovered something amazing. Whoever had made the glass had used tiny pieces of gold and silver. Some of these pieces measured 50 nanometres across – about one-thousandth the size of a piece of salt. It is these tiny pieces that make the cup change colour. The Lycurgus Cup shows that the ancient Romans were using nanotechnology more than 1,600 years ago.

2 Earthquake detector – *Ancient China*

More than 2,000 years ago, an inventor called Zhang Heng built the world's first earthquake detector. The machine was a large metal vase on which there were eight dragon heads. The dragons marked the eight points of a compass, and each one had a metal ball in its mouth. Below each dragon head, there was a metal frog. When the machine detected tremors in the earth, one of the dragons (facing in the direction of the tremor) would drop its ball into the mouth of the frog that sat below it. This made a loud noise that warned people of the earthquake. The machine could detect earthquakes hundreds of kilometres away.

3 Electricity – *Iraq*

In 1936, during some excavations in an ancient village near Baghdad, an archaeologist found some unusual clay pots. The pots were more than 2,000 years old.

Hanging inside each pot was a copper cylinder and inside this cylinder was a piece of iron. Nobody knew why somebody had made these pots with metal inside, but the archaeologist thought that they could be some sort of early battery. A few years later American scientists made copies of the pots. They discovered that the original theory was right: they could make electricity. But why? What did people use this electricity for? That is the great mystery of this discovery.

4 The calendar – *Ancient Scotland*

Very early calendars from ancient civilizations have been found in many countries around the world. But archaeologists believe that they have discovered a calendar in Scotland that is 10,000 years old. It was made by Stone Age Britons, who used it from 8000 BCE to 4000 BCE. The calendar was made of 12 pits dug into the ground. The pits represented the months of the year and were laid out in a long line that was 50 metres long. The Ancient Britons would measure time using the sun and the moon. This ancient calendar used both to keep track of the days, weeks and months of the year.

A

B

C

D

80

Culture notes

The Lycurgus Cup is a 4th-century Roman glass cage cup measuring 15.8 cm high. The cup was probably designed for drinking from at feasts. Alternatively, it may have been a suspended oil lamp. It is the only complete Roman glass object made from this type of glass.

Zhang Heng (78–139 CE) was a Chinese astronomer and inventor. He correctly recognised that the moon reflected the light of the sun rather than being a light source. As well as inventing the first seismoscope (which could sense distant earthquakes and show in which direction they were happening), he was the first person in China to apply a grid system to maps. He also invented the odometer – an instrument for measuring the distance travelled by a wheeled vehicle.

The 'Baghdad Battery' was found in 1938 in Khujut Rabu, Iraq. It is thought to be from between 150 BCE and 650 CE and consists of a ceramic pot, a tube of copper and a rod of iron. If filled with a weak acid, like vinegar, the combination produces around one volt. Its true origin and purpose remains unclear.

Warren Field near Crathes Castle, in the Aberdeenshire region of Scotland, is the location of a mesolithic calendar monument built about 8,000 BCE. It is considered to be the oldest lunar calendar yet found and predates other Mesopotamian calendars by nearly 5,000 years.

Social Responsibility
Understanding and describing own and others' cultures
Understands the contributions of different cultures to their own lives.

3 Give students just a few minutes to scan the article quickly to find the answers to the questions. Encourage them not to focus on every word for now but just to find the countries.
1 Iraq, Scotland 2 China 3 China 4 Scotland 5 Scotland 6 Italy 7 Italy 8 Iraq

4 **Check/clarify:** *nanometre, earthquake, dragon, detect, excavations, copper, iron, battery.*
1 microscope 2 detected 3 pits 4 cylinder 5 tremors 6 theory 7 nanotechnology 8 archaeologist

5 Hold a class vote for the most important invention.

1 Ask students how often they read blogs. Ask: *What sort of things do you read about?* Let students check their answers with a partner before whole-class feedback.
1 Read, listen to the radio, sing songs together, tell each other stories
2 She doesn't think life would be very good without it.

2 If there are any problems with the use of *used to* and the second conditional, use this as an opportunity to review the grammar.
used to: First paragraph – to say how life was different in the past
Second conditional: second paragraph – to theorise how life might be different

3 Ask students to explain why they chose the paragraph headings.
A paragraph 2 B paragraph 1

4 Encourage students to underline parts of the blog which support their answer.
Her personal opinion

5 Encourage students to think carefully about their choice and to make sure they will have something to write about!

6 This could be set for homework.

SCIENCE AND US UNIT 8

3 **Read the article again and write the names of the countries next to the information.**

1 The item was discovered under the ground here. ______
2 The item found here was decorated with animals. ______
3 The invention let them know about a danger here. ______
4 The invention was used for 4,000 years here. ______
5 They used the moon here to mark the passing of the year. ______
6 The item discovered here kept its secret for a long time. ______
7 The item discovered here contained valuable metals. ______
8 We're not sure what the people here used the invention for. ______

4 VOCABULARY **There are eight highlighted words in the article. Match the words with these meanings.**

1 an instrument for looking closely at very small things ______
2 noticed or discovered, using special equipment ______
3 large holes in the earth ______
4 tube ______
5 movements of the earth ______
6 an idea (often about science) ______
7 science involving very very small things ______
8 someone who digs the earth to find objects from the past ______

5 SPEAKING **Which of the inventions do you think is the most important? Why? Share your ideas with the class.**

WRITING
A blog entry

1 INPUT **Ellen wrote a blog entry with the title 'A world without television'. Read what she wrote and answer the questions.**

1 What did people do before they had television?
2 What does Ellen think life would be like without TV?

2 ANALYSE **Look at Ellen's blog entry again.**

1 In which paragraph does Ellen use *used to*? In which does she use the second conditional? Why does she use them?

3 **Match the paragraphs with these headings.**

A Imagine life without television ☐
B Life before television ☐

4 **What type of text is Ellen's blog? Give reasons.**

- her personal opinion
- a fictional story
- a factual article
- an article for the school magazine

Ellen's blog

A WORLD WITHOUT TELEVISION

1 It isn't easy to imagine life without television, but people only started to have television at home about 60 years ago. So a lot of people who are alive today lived without it in the past. Before television, people used to read in the evening or listen to the radio. I read once that families used to get together and sing songs or tell each other stories. I think it was probably a bit boring but perhaps people enjoyed it.

2 If we didn't have television these days, I think things would be OK. I mean, we would still have films and the internet that we could watch on laptops, wouldn't we? We would get all the information and entertainment we need there, and in fact many people already do. I know a lot of people who don't watch television at all; they watch sport and things by streaming them. But of course, they're using TV programmes when they do that – so maybe a world without TV wouldn't be such a good idea!

5 PLAN **You are going to write a blog entry like Ellen's. Choose one of these pieces of technology, or use your own idea. Write a plan and make notes.**

mobile phones tablets
the internet calculators

6 PRODUCE **Write your blog entry. Write 120–180 words. Use your notes to help you.**

81

Activity idea Extension

In groups, students discuss how they would spend their time if they didn't have TV or other screens.

Homework

Ask students to research an invention from their country and write a few sentences. As follow-up, students could present it to the class.

TH!NK more

Practice Extra
Unit 8 Master it!

Workbook
Developing Writing p77

Tests
Unit, extension and skills test 8

1 In B1 Preliminary for Schools Reading Part 1, candidates read five short texts. These could be emails, notices, signs or text messages. Candidates will also find three sentences next to each text. Students have to choose one of three options, A, B or C, that best matches the meaning of the text. This part of the exam tests the candidates' understanding of different types of short text.

Encourage your students to do the following when they approach this task:

- Look at the visual information to help identify what type of text it is.
- Read the text to find out more about the context.
- After looking at the text, read the three possible options.
- Compare each option with the text before choosing an answer.
- Read the texts again to confirm the correct answer.

1 C 2 B 3 A 4 B 5 A

Workbook p71

2 In B1 Preliminary for Schools Writing Part 1, candidates have to write an email of about 100 words using an email they have read and four prompts. This part of the exam tests the candidates' ability to write well-organised texts with a real communicative purpose.

Encourage your students to do the following when they approach this task:

- Read the email and the four prompts carefully, to identify what is required and who it is for, and what kind of information is needed.
- Plan the answers and respond to all four prompts.
- Write a rough draft of the email before writing the final answer. Make sure that it is well organised and has a range of tenses, expressions and vocabulary.
- Read your email again to check that it makes sense and that all the content points have been included.

Workbook p61

B1 Preliminary for Schools

READING

Part 1: 3-option multiple choice

→ workbook page 71

1 For each question, choose the correct answer.

1 The recent rain has made the school fields very wet and we might need to move the school sports day from Saturday to Sunday. Please see this notice board for further information.

1 What does the notice say?
A The sports day will now take place on Sunday.
B The weather will be bad this weekend.
C There is a chance the sports day will still take place on Saturday.

2 Hi Claudia – I want to start French lessons. You said John Gray teaches French. Have you got his email address so I can write to him? Best, Anna

2 Why has Anna sent this message?
A She wants Claudia to talk to John Gray.
B She would like to contact the French teacher.
C She wishes she could start French lessons.

3 Jemma – would it be OK if you didn't use any of the eggs? I need them to make a cake when I get back from work. By the way, try the soup – it's delicious. Thanks, Jim

3 What is Jim doing in this message?
A He's telling Jemma she can eat the soup but not the eggs.
B He's asking that Jemma avoid eating any eggs.
C He's saying Jemma can eat the cake.

4 PHOTOGRAPHY FOR BEGINNERS
5-week course starts Tuesday 5th Oct.
There are still a few places.
BOOK WITH STEVE

4 What's true about the photography course?
A The course is already full.
B Contact Steve if you are interested in learning more about the course.
C The course finishes at the end of October.

5 Hi Ashley, Really sorry to miss your party. Hope it's a lot of fun. Work is no fun at all! So boring and I'll finish late tonight. Fin

5 What is Fin telling Ashley?
A Fin wishes he could go to Ashley's party.
B Fin is going to be late for the party.
C Fin thinks that work is as fun as the party.

WRITING

Part 1: An email

2 Read this email from your English-speaking friend Sam and the notes you have made.

Write your email to Sam using all the notes. Write about 100 words.

→ workbook page 61

Science fair

Hi
Do you remember that we talked about going to the science fair? Our teacher suggested we should go.
Well, guess what! I've got two free tickets. Would you like to come with me? (← *accept*)
It's on all weekend. We can go Saturday or Sunday. I'm free on both days. As usual I've got nothing planned. What's best for you? (← *say which day*)
It's not far and there are transport options. (← *suggest a transport option*)
I'm free in the evening, too. Would you like to do anything after? (← *suggest*)
Let me know!
Sam

1 1 next 2 towards 3 experiment 4 invitations 5 later 6 hire 7 cure 8 research 9 up and down 10 near

2 1 will take / should take 2 isn't it 3 was walking 4 Neither / Nor 5 hasn't she 6 So

3 1 When I was a kid, I used to ~~playing~~ play with dolls.
2 If you ~~would work~~ worked harder, you would do better in your tests.
3 When you phoned me, I ~~watched~~ was watching TV.
4 The world ~~was~~ would be a happier place if people laughed more.
5 Dan never watches football, and ~~so~~ nor / neither do I.
6 I wish this question ~~isn't~~ wasn't so difficult!

4 1 wait, Neither 2 used, did 3 wish, So 4 was, do

TEST YOURSELF UNITS 7 & 8

VOCABULARY

1 **Complete the sentences with the words in the list. There are two extra words.**

away | cure | experiment | hire | invitations | later | long | near | next | research | towards | up and down

1 Sorry, I can't come and see you this weekend – but how about the week after ________________ ?
2 I got scared when the dog started running ________________ me.
3 I'm going to do an ________________ to see if my idea works.
4 I think we should send out ________________ to everyone who we want to come.
5 I can't talk to you right now. Could you please phone me back ________________ today?
6 It's my sister's 16th birthday next month, and we're going to ________________ a DJ to play at the party.
7 He's got a serious disease, and the doctor says there's no ________________ for it.
8 I'm going to do some ________________ on the internet before I write my essay.
9 He was very late! I got a bit nervous and started walking ________________ outside the school.
10 We're hoping to buy a bigger car in the ________________ future.

/10

GRAMMAR

2 **Complete the sentences. Put the verbs in brackets into the correct form or write the missing word(s).**

1 I missed the train, so I ________________ (take) a taxi home.
2 This lesson's really boring, ________________ ?
3 I saw Sue while I ________________ (walk) in town yesterday.
4 A I really don't like Kevin.
B ________________ do I.
5 Your sister's got lots of clothes, ________________ ?
6 A I hate Mondays.
B ________________ do I.

3 **Find and correct the mistake in each sentence.**

1 When I was a kid, I used to playing with dolls.
2 If you would work harder, you would do better in your tests.
3 When you phoned me, I watched TV.
4 The world was a happier place if people laughed more.
5 Dan never watches football, and so do I.
6 I wish this question isn't so difficult!

/12

FUNCTIONAL LANGUAGE

4 **Complete the mini-dialogues with the words in the list.**

do | did | neither | so | used | wait | was | wish

1 A I can't ________________ for the Ed Sheeran concert.
B ________________ can I! It's going to be great.
2 A I ________________ to love that film when I was a kid.
B So ________________ I. I thought it was the best.
3 A I ________________ it wasn't so windy.
B ________________ do I. I want to go for a bike ride!
4 A Where's Paul? I wish he ________________ here.
B So ________________ I. Parties are always better with Paul.

/8

MY SCORE /30

22–30 | 10–21 | 0–9

83

The Cambridge Life Competencies Framework

Communication
Managing conversations
Watch this video for a tip on helping your students develop their communication skills and strategies.
Scan the QR code here

Warmer

Ask: *What's my job?* (teacher) *What does a teacher do? When do teachers work? How much holiday do teachers get?*, etc. Ask students to describe their parents' (or another family member's) jobs in pairs.

▶ 25 Get TH!NKing

Play the video and discuss the question with your class.

1 Elicit more jobs, write them on the board and mark the main stress. Say them for students to repeat.
1 police officer 2 dentist 3 waiter 4 doctor 5 pilot 6 musician 7 chef

2 Ask students to think of at least two jobs for each question. Add these jobs to the list on the board.

3 During feedback, ask students to come to the board and underline the answers to each question in a different colour.

4 Before students read the article, get them to cover it and just look at the photos.

5 🔊 9.01 **Check/clarify:** *madness, Netflix, binge-watch, platform, tag, tagger, daredevils, skyscrapers, abseil, cradle, psychologist, veterinary science, zoology.*
1 T 2 T 3 F 4 T 5 F 6 F 7 T 8 F 9 T

6 Ask students to write sentences.
3 You also need to have worked in the film or TV industry for five years. You also need to specialise in a film category, for example, comedy, horror or teen movies. Then there is a very difficult interview for the job.
5 They don't work when it's too windy.
6 They use soap and water.
8 Pet psychologists talk to the owner to find out about the problem with the pet.

9 WORKING WEEK

OBJECTIVES

FUNCTIONS: accepting and refusing offers and invitations; inviting friends to join you

GRAMMAR: the passive (present simple, past simple, present continuous, present perfect)

VOCABULARY: jobs; *work as / in / for; work vs. job;* time expressions with *in*

Get TH!NKING

Watch the video and think: what kind of job do you want to have?

1

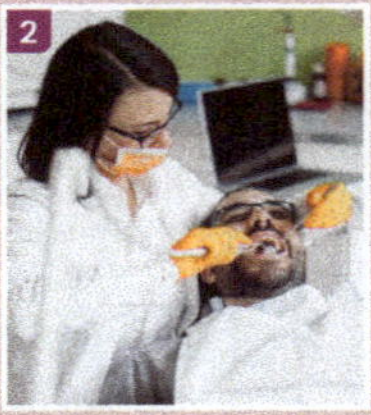
2

3

4

5

6

7

READING

1 **What jobs can you see in the photos? What other jobs can you name in English? With a partner, write down as many as you can.**

2 **Which of the jobs you thought of in Exercise 1 …**
1 sometimes involves work in the evening or at night?
2 needs a lot of training?
3 involves work at weekends?
4 is well paid?
5 gets a lot of holidays?
6 can be dangerous?

3 SPEAKING **Compare your ideas from Exercises 1 and 2 with others in the class.**

4 **Look at the photos on the next page. What jobs do you think the people have? Read the article quickly to check your ideas.**

5 🔊 9.01 **Read and listen to the article again and mark the sentences T (true) or F (false).**
1 Netflix employ about 30 professional film watchers. ____
2 A 'tag' consists of a small number of words describing a film. ____
3 Anyone who loves film can become a Netflix tagger. ____
4 The window-cleaners of the Gherkin use ropes to get to the top windows. ____
5 The window-cleaners work in all kinds of weather. ____
6 The cleaners use a special chemical to clean the windows. ____
7 You need to study at university to become a pet psychologist. ____
8 Pet psychologists can talk to animals. ____
9 A pet psychologist can help owners understand why their dog barks too loudly. ____

6 SPEAKING **Work in pairs. Correct the false sentences in Exercise 5.**

84

Objectives

Functions and speaking Developing speaking: Accepting and refusing offers and invitations; **Role play:** Inviting friends to join you
Grammar The passive (present simple, past simple, present continuous, present perfect)
Vocabulary Jobs; *work as / in / for; work* vs. *job*; **WordWise** Time expressions with *in*
Values What's important in a job?
Life Competencies Taking responsibility for your actions

Resources for this unit

All available online

Videos
- Get **TH!NK**ing: *What kind of job do you want to have?*
- Grammar rap!: The passive: present simple and past simple
- Vlog: Taking responsibility for your actions

Tests
- Unit, extension and skills test 9
- End of term test 3

Worksheets
- Grammar and vocabulary: Basic, Standard and Extension Worksheets
- Project: The world of work
- Communication: What a job!
- Get **TH!NK**ing, Grammar rap! and Life Lessons video Worksheets

Reading; TH!NK Values

Culture notes

Netflix, Inc. is an American media-services provider and production company headquartered in Los Gatos, California. It was founded in 1997 by Reed Hastings and Marc Randolph. The company's primary business is its subscription-based streaming service. As of April 2019, Netflix had over 148 million paid subscriptions worldwide.

30 St Mary Axe, informally known as The Gherkin, is a commercial skyscraper in London's primary financial district, the City of London, designed by Sir Norman Foster. It was opened in April 2004. At 180 metres tall and with 40 floors, it is currently the 18th tallest building in the city. The building has become an instantly recognisable landmark of London and it is one of the city's most widely recognised examples of contemporary architecture.

7 Tell students they should look back at the article to find any evidence to support their answers.

8 At the end of the exercise, listen to some of the students' ideas and encourage open class discussion.

9 You may like to give an example of your own to get students started on this exercise.

10 If space allows, encourage students to walk around the classroom to find someone who has similar ideas. Ask students to report their findings back to the class and encourage them to use the phrase *So does he/she/[student's name]*.

Homework

Ask students to choose five of the jobs from the lesson and write a sentence or two for each, saying why they would like to do that job (or not).

WORKING WEEK UNIT 9

THE PERFECT JOB?

What would you choose as the perfect job? Here are three that could be on your list!

MOVIE MADNESS

For all big film fans out there, this is THE dream job. Most people pay to watch films, but in this job, YOU are paid to watch TV series and films. Around 30 people are employed by Netflix to watch Netflix content. They are required to binge-watch the latest films and TV series on the platform and 'tag' them with a few words. So, how does that work and why is it done? Words to describe each film or TV series are entered into the system. This is done so that Netflix users can search for content more easily. For example, in the sci-fi category, the tags include *future* and *planets*. The release date of the film, the language, the director and actors in the film are also included.

How do you become a Netflix tagger? Well, first you need to have worked in the film or TV industry for five years. You also need to specialise in a film category, for example, comedy, horror or teen movies. Then there is a very difficult interview for the job. All Netflix taggers must have an excellent knowledge of film and TV.

ONLY DAREDEVILS NEED APPLY

window-cleaners abseiling a skyscraper

Are you scared of heights? Then this is not the job for you. But if you are very brave and love rock climbing, then cleaning the windows of really tall skyscrapers is the perfect job for you. There is some on-the-job training to clean the windows: the cleaners are taught to abseil down from the top of the buildings. That means they move down the outside of the windows held by a rope around their bodies.

Imagine cleaning the windows of the famous London Gherkin! It's 180 metres tall and 40 storeys high. It was designed by a very famous English architect and it was built in the 2000s. Cleaners abseil down to the 35th floor. Below the 35th floor, the cleaners can work in a traditional cradle.

It takes nine of them ten days to clean the whole building. Cleaners don't work on days when the winds are too strong. And guess what? The Gherkin is cleaned with soap and water.

Where do the cleaners go for lunch? Well, lunch breaks aren't taken in a café. They are taken sitting at the top of the 40-storey building. Imagine that amazing view every day.

PET PSYCHOLOGIST

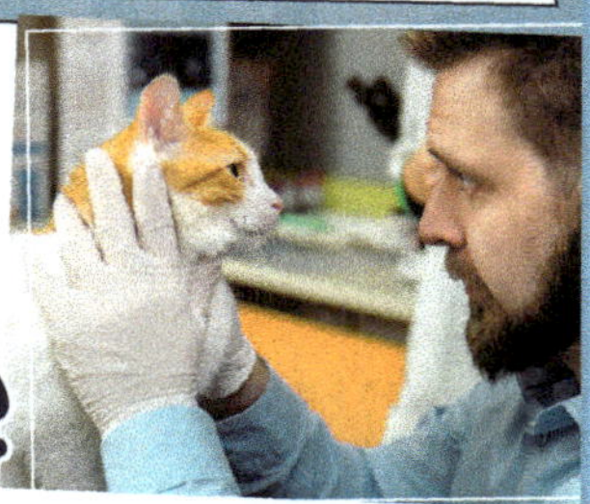

If you love animals, this could be the dream job for you. The pay is good, too. You can earn between £25,000 and £50,000 per year.

The job is to study animal behaviour and help owners discover the causes of their pets' problems. To work as a pet psychologist, you need to have a degree in veterinary science or zoology. You also need experience of working with animals, for example at a vet's or at a zoo.

So, how is the job done? First, they talk to the owner to find out about the problem with the pet. For example, it may run after cars or bark too loudly. Then the animal is observed by the psychologist, and afterwards, once the pet psychologist discovers the causes of the pet's problems, the owners are given advice about how to help their pets.

TH!NK values

What's important in a job?

7 **What do you think about the jobs in the text? Tick (✓) the boxes.**

	Netflix tagger	Extreme window-cleaner	Pet psychologist
1 This job is a waste of time.	☐	☐	☐
2 This job sounds fun.	☐	☐	☐
3 This job didn't exist in the past.	☐	☐	☐
4 This job is dangerous.	☐	☐	☐
5 I would like to have this job.	☐	☐	☐

8 SPEAKING **Compare your ideas with others in the class.**

9 **Think of a job you might like to do in the future and write it down. Look at values a–f below. Rank each one 1–6 (1 = low, 6 = high) for your job.**

Job:

Value	Score
a You can make a lot of money.	
b You might become famous.	
c It helps people.	
d It's fun to do.	
e It gives you lots of free time.	
f It's creative.	

10 SPEAKING **Talk to others in your class. Compare your job and values with theirs.**

85

Activity idea Extension

For further speaking practice, ask students to work in pairs and describe one of the jobs from the lesson, without naming it. Their partner has to guess which job is being described.

Activity idea Extension

Divide the class into small groups. One student chooses a job and mimes it to the rest of the group. The others must guess what the job is. The person miming can only nod or shake their head as an answer. Set a time limit of 20 seconds for the others to guess. The student who guesses correctly mimes a different job. Alternatively, this can be done as a whole-class activity.

Critical TH!NKing
Evaluating ideas, arguments and options
Assesses strengths and weaknesses of possible solutions.

Critical TH!NKing
Understanding and analysing links between ideas
Compares points and arguments from different sources.

TH!NK more

Worksheets
Project The world of work
Communication What a job!
Get TH!NKing *What kind of job do you want to have?*

Warmer

Ask students to brainstorm as many jobs as they can think of.

▶ 26 Grammar rap!

The passive: present simple and past simple

1 For sentences 3 and 4, ask if we know who is doing the action (no).
1 are employed 2 was designed 3 was built 4 aren't taken 5 is observed 6 are given

Refer to the sentences in Exercise 1 for examples of each of the three different uses of the passive. To check understanding, ask students to think of an example sentence in the present simple passive about something in their own country.
RULE: 7 to be 8 isn't 9 want 10 don't know

2 *1 wasn't paid 2 aren't found 3 was written 4 are designed 5 was … painted 6 is chosen 7 Were … asked 8 wasn't … given*

Pronunciation

/tʃ/ and /dʒ/ consonant sounds

Student's Book p121

Get it Right!

Present simple passive vs. past simple passive

Student's Book p125

3 In teams, give students three minutes to write as many sentences as possible. After three minutes, students pass their sentences to another team to be checked. The winner is the team with the most grammatically correct sentences.

Workbook p82

GRAMMAR

The passive: present simple and past simple

1 Complete these sentences from the article on page 85. Then choose the correct options to complete the rules about the passive.

1 Around 30 people ______ (employ) by Netflix to watch Netflix content.
2 The Gherkin ______ (design) by a very famous English architect.
3 It ______ (build) in the 2000s.
4 Lunch breaks ______ (not take) in a café.
5 The animal ______ (observe) by the psychologist.
6 The owners ______ (give) advice about how to help their pets.

> RULE: Form the passive with the verb [7]to be / to have + the past participle of the main verb.
> We use the passive when
> - it [8]is / isn't important who does or did the action.
> - we [9]want / don't want to focus on the action itself and not the person doing it.
> - we [10]know / don't know who does or did the action.

2 Complete the sentences with the present simple passive or past simple passive form of the verbs.

0 Every year, hundreds of films *are made* (make) in Hollywood.
1 It was interesting work, but she ____________ (not pay) very much money.
2 Tigers ____________ (not find) in Africa.
3 This novel ____________ (write) a hundred years ago.
4 Lots of new websites ____________ (design) especially for small children.
5 When ____________ the Mona Lisa ____________ (paint)?
6 In the US, the president ____________ (choose) every four years.
7 ____________ you ____________ (ask) to help with the party?
8 Why ____________ permission ____________ (not give) for the party?

PRONUNCIATION
/tʃ/ and /dʒ/ consonant sounds Go to page 121.

3 How many passive sentences can you make? (Your sentences can be positive or negative.)

Millions of pizzas	build	fifty years ago
The World Cup	buy	every day
How many emails	eat	last night
Our house	discover	in 1492
America	make	in China
This email	play	to me by mistake
How many songs	send	every four years
This book	write	two years ago

→ workbook page 82

VOCABULARY

Jobs

4 Read the essay. Which jobs does the writer talk about?

My first job was as a waiter. I did it when I first left school, just **to earn** money. It was fun, but it was very hard work. I had **to work long hours** and I was always on my feet! It wasn't very **challenging** – I had to remember the customers' orders, but that was all. And I didn't **get paid holidays**.

So, in the end I got bored and I **gave in my notice** and got a job as a shop assistant in a bookshop. I really enjoyed that because I like books and I like talking to people about them. After a few months I was **promoted** to shop manager. That was great! I got **on-the-job training** about management, and I was happy because I was **starting a career** – well, I thought I was. After two years, the bookstore closed because there wasn't enough business.

Now I've got a few more years' experience, and I work as a management consultant. **The pay** is fantastic and the work is quite interesting. I guess you can say I'm **successful**. Will I still be here five years from now? Who knows? Anything could happen in the next few years.

5 Match the bold expressions in Exercise 4 with their definitions. Write the words.

0 the money you get for doing a job *the pay*
1 to get money for doing a job ______
2 given a higher position ______
3 beginning a job (or series of jobs) that you might do for life ______
4 achieving a lot, and/or making a lot of money ______
5 be paid for the days that you don't work ______
6 said you didn't want a job any more ______
7 to work many hours every day ______
8 a way of learning to do a job at the same time that you do it ______
9 difficult in a way that tests your abilities ______

86

4 *waiter, shop assistant, manager, management consultant*

5 *1 to earn 2 promoted 3 starting a career 4 successful 5 get paid holidays 6 gave in my notice 7 to work long hours 8 on-the-job training 9 challenging*

Language note The passive: present simple and past simple

Students may have a different verb in their own language for this structure and they may have problems using it correctly. Monitor them carefully when they use it, making sure they are using the correct form.

TH!NK more

Workbook
Grammar p82, Ex.1–4
Pronunciation p120
Vocabulary p84, Ex.1
Vocabulary Extra p85, Ex.1–2

Worksheets
Grammar Worksheets 9
Grammar rap! The passive: present simple and past simple
Vocabulary Worksheets 9

Vocabulary; Listening; WordWise

6 Check students know what the jobs are before doing the exercise (A architect B hairdresser C lawyer D engineer E fashion model F vet).
Possible answers
A 3, 4 B 8 C 1, 2, 4 D 3, 4
E 2, 5, 7 F 1, 2

Workbook p84

7 Before doing the exercise, elicit the five senses (use the correct terminology: *sight*, *taste*, *touch*, *smell* and *hearing*) and ask students to think of an animal with an exceptional ability in each area. Divide the class into pairs and ask students to discuss which are their strongest and weakest senses.
A 3 B 2 C 1

8 Encourage students to think of reasons for their answers.

9 🔊 **9.04** Tell students that it is not necessary to understand every word for now, but to focus on listening for the answers.
1 B 2 C

10 🔊 **9.04 Check/clarify:** *get rid of the problems*.
1 She had an operation that went wrong. She was left completely blind.
2 They weren't very supportive.
3 She felt she had no other options.
4 A director of a group of disabled actors
5 One of them
6 Because she didn't let being blind stop her from doing things.

11 Before doing the exercise, write on the board *in the end*, *in the past*, *in the next few years*. Ask students which expression means finally (*in the end*), which means before now (*in the past*) and which means in the future (*in the next few years*).
1 in the past 2 In the end 3 in the next few years

12 During feedback, work on pronunciation and intonation of the sentences.
1 b 2 a 3 c 4 e 5 d

13 You may like to give an example from your own experience to get students started on this exercise.

Workbook p84

6 Look at these jobs. Which sentences can be used to describe each job? (There's often more than one possibility.) Compare your ideas with others in your class.

A 
B 
C 
D 
E 
F 

1 You have to work long hours.
2 The pay can be excellent.
3 If you're good at the job, you might be promoted.
4 It's a very good career.
5 It's not challenging at all.
6 The only reason to do this job is to earn money.
7 If you're successful in this job, you could be famous.
8 You can do this job with on-the-job training.

→ workbook page 84

LISTENING

7 Look at the pictures of these people. Match the words to the pictures.

A

B

C

1 blind 2 deaf 3 in a wheelchair

8 SPEAKING Here are some jobs. Do you think that the people in Exercise 7 could do all of these jobs?

1 teacher 3 musician 5 shop assistant
2 actor 4 pilot 6 taxi driver

I think a person in a wheelchair can be a teacher or an actor.

9 🔊 9.04 Listen to a programme with a woman called Marina Stuart. Choose the correct answers.

1 Marina is …
A deaf.
B blind.
C in a wheelchair.

2 Marina works as …
A an actor.
B a piano teacher.
C an actor and a piano teacher.

10 🔊 9.04 Listen again and answer the questions.

1 What happened to Marina when she was 18?
2 What were the teachers like at her college?
3 Why didn't she leave the job that she hated?
4 Who did Marina meet by accident?
5 How many of the films she was in won an award?
6 Why does Marina think she has been successful?

WordWise: Time expressions with *in*

11 Complete the sentences from the unit so far with a phrase from the list.

in the end | in the next few years | in the past

1 This job didn't exist ______________.
2 ______________ I got bored and gave in my notice.
3 Anything could happen ______________.

12 Match the questions and answers.

1 When's your birthday? ☐
2 Can we go out tomorrow? ☐
3 When will you see your grandparents? ☐
4 Is it hot in your country? ☐
5 When's your next exam? ☐

a Yes, let's meet up *in* the evening.
b It's *in* two weeks' time. I'll be 15.
c *In* the summer holidays, I hope.
d I'm not really sure but I think it's *in* June.
e Yes, *in* the summer.

13 SPEAKING Work with a partner. Answer the questions in Exercise 12 so that they are true for you.

→ workbook page 84

Homework

Write on the board: *How would your life be different if you were deaf? How would your life be different if you were blind? How would your life be different if you were in a wheelchair? Can you think of anything that is done to help people with disabilities?* Ask students to write a paragraph answering the questions.

Activity idea Fast finishers

Ask students to write passive sentences using the verbs *invent*, *discover* and *win*.

TH!NK more

Workbook
Vocabulary p84, Ex.1
Vocabulary Extra p85, Ex.1–2
Listening p88, Ex.1–2
WordWise p84, Ex.5–6

Worksheets
Vocabulary Worksheets 9

Warmer

Ask: *Do you know what jobs your grandparents or great-grandparents did? Did they do any unusual jobs?* You might like to give an example of your own to get them started. Write any interesting vocabulary on the board. Ask: *Can you think of any jobs that people did in the past that no longer exist?*

Culture note

Dubai is the most populous city in the United Arab Emirates and the capital of the Emirate of Dubai. It is located on the southeast coast of the Persian Gulf and is the business hub of the Middle East. Dubai has one of the world's lowest crime rates and in 2018 was ranked the eighth-safest city in the world. The Dubai Police Force was the first to use many new law enforcement techniques, including electronic finger printing, DNA testing and GPS systems to locate stolen vehicles. The Dubai Police Force are known for their use of luxury and high-performance vehicles as police cars. These include Aston Martin, Lamborghini, Maserati and Rolls-Royce among others.

1 Before students do the exercise, give them one minute to match the photos with the job headings in the text (1 trailer maker, 2 journalist, 3 chef, 4 police officer).
1 1 2 4 3 3 4 2

2 9.05
1 Short sports articles 2 100
3 In 24 hours 4 That they're not ready yet to work as a chef
5 By using a touchscreen; shaking their hands

3 Give an example of your own to get them started (vet: robots won't be able to understand animals and vets need a lot of experience to understand pets because they all behave differently).

READING

1 Look at the photos. Which of these people work in …
1 the entertainment industry?
2 law enforcement?
3 the catering industry?
4 journalism?

2 9.05 Read and listen to the article. Answer the questions.
1 What types of articles are computers able to write?
2 How many film trailers did IBM's supercomputer Watson study?
3 How quickly did Watson make a film trailer?
4 What does the cheese and chocolate panini suggest about computers in the kitchen?
5 How can the public interact with the robocop?

3 SPEAKING Think of two jobs that you believe will exist in 30 years. They could be jobs that don't exist yet today, or jobs that will always be necessary. Tell others in the class and explain why.

I think composers will still be needed in 30 years. Robots won't have the creativity to write original music.

WRITING
A short essay

4 Write a short essay about your ideas from Exercise 3. Describe the jobs and explain why you believe they will exist in the future.

1

2

3

4

TECHNOLOGY in the workplace

The world is being taken over by computers. They are doing jobs in seconds that once took us hours to do and they are helping us to do things we once only ever dreamed of doing. Advances in AI (artificial intelligence) and robotics mean that computers have become better at doing difficult tasks and can even teach themselves how to do them. As more and more jobs are being done by computers maybe it's time to start asking – are any of our jobs safe in the future? Here are four which might be in danger.

JOURNALISTS

Are you planning to work in journalism one day? If the answer is yes, you need to be aware that journalists who write articles based on numbers and data, such as business or sports journalists, may lose their jobs to robots in the future. Some short sports articles have already been written by a computer program. However, robots are not good at being creative. They need numbers and data that they can then describe and aren't able to write descriptive articles. So, while some types of journalism jobs may go, those who write more creative articles should be safe from computers taking over their jobs.

TRAILER MAKERS

The first AI film trailer, for a horror film, has been made by a computer. The supercomputer, IBM's Watson, learned how to make one by looking at 100 trailers from other horror films. These were analysed by the supercomputer and it learned how to produce a film trailer. It then watched 20th Century Fox's film, *Morgan*, to find the right moments to include in the trailer. Instead of taking 10 to 30 days to make the trailer, it only took 24 hours.

CHEFS

Can robots cook? The answer to this question is: not yet. Robots cannot prepare, cook or serve full meals, but an AI machine has been trained to create recipes. If you give it information about the ingredients and style of cooking you want, it will give you some ideas for different meals. This could be very useful. Especially when you only have a few things in the cupboard. However, it's not perfect yet. A journalist asked it for a 'Chinese-style' dish with Parmesan cheese and dark chocolate. It suggested a cheese and chocolate panini. Maybe it needs a bit more development before it can work as a chef!

POLICE OFFICERS

Have you seen the sci-fi film *RoboCop*? In one country, fiction may become reality as people may soon see these robot police officers on the streets. A robocop has been developed in the United Arab Emirates and there are robocops working for the police force in Dubai.

These officers cannot solve crimes. However, people can report crimes to them. They have a touchscreen on their chests. People can pay their traffic fines to them, too. They have been designed to be friendly, so they will shake hands with people.

Dubai wants 25% of their police officers to be robots by 2030. They also want to have a smart police station, which will not employ any humans.

88

4 Ask students to make some notes on their answers to Exercise 3. If you're short on time, set the writing as homework.

TH!NK more

Workbook
Reading p86, Ex.1–4
Developing Writing p87

Grammar; Vocabulary

5 Ask students to try to complete the sentences from memory before referring back to the article to check. Encourage them to underline the sentences in the article.
1 is being 2 are being
3 have … been 4 has been
RULE: 5 to be 6 1 7 2 8 3 9 4

6 Ask students to say which phrases in the sentences helped them decide which tense to use.
1 are being designed 2 are being taken over / have been taken over
3 have been developed 4 are being built 5 have been made 6 has been tested

7 Make a note of any repeated errors with the formation of the passive to deal with during feedback.

Workbook p83

8 Point out the three different prepositions that follow *work*.
1 c 2 a 3 b

9 Tell students to check which type of word follows each gap to help them decide on their answers.
1 as 2 for 3 in 4 as 5 in
6 as 7 in 8 as 9 for

10 Read through the *Look* box and check understanding. The difference between the nouns *work* and *job* is difficult for some nationalities due to L1 interference.
1 work 2 job 3 job 4 job, work
5 jobs 6 work 7 work 8 job

Workbook p84

Homework

Ask students to write sentences about their family or friends using *work as / in / for*, e.g., *My father works as a builder. He works in the building industry. He works for Brown and Sons.*

Language note The passive: present continuous and present perfect

Students may have a different verb in their own language for this structure, so they may have problems using it correctly. Monitor students carefully, making sure they are using the the correct form.

GRAMMAR
The passive: present continuous and present perfect

5 **Complete the sentences from the article on page 88 with the words in the list. Then complete the rules.**

are being | has been | have been | is being

1 The world ______ taken over by computers.
2 More and more jobs ______ done by computers.
3 Some short sports articles ______ already ______ written by a computer program.
4 The first AI film trailer, for a horror film, ______ made by a computer.

RULE: The passive is formed using the verb [5]______ + the past participle of the main verb.
- Form the present continuous passive (like sentences [6]______ and [7]______ above) using *is/are being* + past participle.
- Form the present perfect passive (like sentences [8]______ and [9]______ above) using *has/have been* + past participle.

6 **Complete the sentences with the present continuous passive or present perfect passive form of the verbs.**

0 For the last 30 years, the internet *has been used* (use) by people all over the world.
1 New machines ______________ (design) all the time.
2 Some jobs ______________ (take over) by computers.
3 A lot of new medicines ______________ (develop) in the last 50 years.
4 At the moment, thousands of new cars ______________ (build) around the world.
5 From January 1st until now, billions of mobile phone calls ______________ (make).
6 This new plane ______________ (test) over 200 times.

7 **Look at the pictures and make sentences about what is being done and what has been done.**

New doors have been added.

→ workbook page 83

VOCABULARY
work as / in / for

8 **Read the sentences. Then match the verbs with the objects.**

Are you planning to work in journalism one day?
It needs a bit more development before it can work as a chef.
There are robocops working for the police force in Dubai.

1 work in a a person in a job
2 work as b a company, person or organisation
3 work for c an industry

9 **Complete the sentences with *as*, *in* or *for*.**

When my mother was young, she worked [1]______ a waitress to earn some money. After that, she was a secretary. She worked [2]______ some lawyers. Now she works [3]______ the computer industry.
My friend left school two years ago and got a job. She worked [4]______ a tour guide for about six months and really liked it. So she decided she wanted to work [5]______ the travel industry. Now she works [6]______ a travel agent in Australia.
My father works [7]______ television now. He works [8]______ a cameraman. He works [9]______ the biggest television company in the country.

Look
job is a countable noun – we can use it in the plural.
*She did four **jobs** before she became a travel agent.*
work is an uncountable noun – we don't use it in the plural.
*I have a lot of **work** to do tonight.*

work vs. job

10 **Complete the sentences with *work* or *job(s)*.**

0 She left school and got a *job*.
1 Sorry, I can't talk right now, I've got a lot of ______ to do on this project.
2 When the factory closed, my uncle lost his ______ as a manager.
3 I've got a new ______ in a bank.
4 My mother is the manager of a shop. She loves her ______ because it's very interesting ______.
5 There aren't enough ______ in this town.
6 Being a street cleaner is very hard ______.
7 Sometimes I have to take ______ home at the weekend.
8 Cleaning out the garage is a big ______ for one person.

→ workbook page 84

Activity idea Extension

Tell students to do a role play. Student A is the manager of a company and Student B is an employee. Student A has to tell Student B that his job is now obsolete, e.g., *We have electricity now, so we don't need any lamplighters.* Student B has to try to keep his job and say that it is useful, or that he could do different jobs. Ask students to write their dialogue before practising it. Monitor and help with vocabulary. Listen to some of their ideas in open class.

TH!NK more

Practice Extra	Workbook	Worksheets
Unit 9 Practise it!	Grammar p83, Ex.5–8	Grammar Worksheets 9
	Vocabulary p84, Ex.2–4	Vocabulary Worksheets 9

Developing Speaking; Phrases for fluency; Functions

Warmer

Elicit some common jobs for under-16s in your country. Write some ideas on the board and ask students to discuss whether they have done or would like to do any of them.

1 9.06 Before students listen, get them to cover the dialogue and just look at the photo and answer the question. Write their ideas on the board.
Sorting out a garage

2 Have students underline the answers in the text.
1 He wants to earn some extra pocket money (to buy a new skateboard). 2 Some of them are heavy 3 a vase 4 Because he was honest and told her he'd broken the vase.

3 *Students' own answers*

4 Write the underlined expressions on the board. Ask students for an L1 translation before they complete the sentences in English.
1 for a while 2 That sounds great 3 Surely 4 as long as 5 By the way 6 That's not the point

5 During feedback, say the sentences for students to repeat all together and individually. Check pronunciation and intonation.
1 Yes, I'd love to.
2 Yes, I'll [come along / join you / be there].
3 Sorry, no. But thanks for asking me.
4 I'm [really] sorry, I'm afraid I can't.

6 **ROLE PLAY** Allow students six to eight minutes to prepare their role plays. Monitor to make sure all students are on task and to help with any difficulties, but do not interrupt as this is a fluency activity. You might also offer ideas if students have none.

DEVELOPING SPEAKING

1 9.06 **Look at the photo. What do you think the dialogue will be about? Listen and read to check.**

Mrs Ashton: Hello, Andy. Your father was telling me that you want to earn some extra pocket money.
Andy: Hi, Mrs Ashton. That's right. I want to buy a new skateboard.
Mrs Ashton: Well, would you like to sort out my garage? It hasn't been tidied for years. I'll pay you £20 for two hours' work, as long as you do a good job.
Andy: Yes, that sounds great! Thank you. I'll start right away!
Mrs Ashton: OK, you'll find everything you need in the shed. I'm going out for a while, so you'll be on your own. By the way, some of those boxes are a bit heavy!
Andy: Don't worry, Mrs Ashton, I'll be careful.
Mrs Ashton: All right then. I'll see you soon. Have fun!
Two hours later ...
Mrs Ashton: Hello, Andy. My goodness! The garage looks fantastic now. You've done a great job. Thank you.
Andy: I'm glad you like it. But I have to tell you something. I broke a vase.
Mrs Ashton: Oh no! Andy! Surely you haven't broken it! I loved that vase. It was worth a lot of money!
Andy: I'm really sorry, Mrs Ashton. It was an accident. I didn't mean to break it.
Mrs Ashton: That's not the point, Andy. My vase is broken! But anyway – here's your £20, and here's another £2 for being honest.
Andy: I don't understand! I broke your vase and you're going to pay me extra?
Mrs Ashton: You worked hard and you told me what happened. So, you've got your money and I've got a nice, tidy garage!

2 **Read the dialogue again and answer the questions.**
1 Why does Andy want to do some work?
2 What does Mrs Ashton say about the boxes?
3 What did Andy break?
4 Why does Mrs Ashton pay Andy £22 and not £20?

3 SPEAKING **Discuss the statements in pairs.**
1 Andy did the right thing to tell her about the vase.
2 Andy told her about the vase because he knew she'd give him more money.
3 Mrs Ashton shouldn't give Andy money for being honest.

Phrases for fluency

4 **Find the underlined expressions in the dialogue and use them to complete the conversation.**
A Hey. Let's have a party on Saturday. We haven't had a party [1]__________, have we?
B [2]__________! Where?
A Well, I thought perhaps … my place.
B Really? I thought your parents were really strict.
A Yes, they are, usually.
B [3]__________ they'll be OK with a small party.
A Well, I think so, [4]__________ it really *is* a small party. [5]__________, I'm not going to invite Alison. We had a *big* argument yesterday.
B You can tell your parents that the party won't go on late.
A [6]__________. My parents just don't like a lot of noise.

FUNCTIONS
Accepting and refusing offers and invitations

KEY LANGUAGE
Yes, I'd love to.
Sorry, no. But thanks for asking me.
I'm [really] sorry, I'm afraid I can't.
Yes, I'll [come along / join you / be there].

5 **Put the expressions from the Key Language box inthe correct columns.**

Accepting (saying yes)	Refusing (saying no)
Yes, that sounds great.	No, sorry, not this time.
1 __________	3 __________
2 __________	4 __________

6 SPEAKING **Work in pairs. Tell your partner about the last time you accepted or refused an invitation.**

ROLE PLAY Inviting friends to join you

Work in pairs. Student A: Go to page 127. Student B: Go to page 128. Role play the conversations. Invent more short dialogues to practise.

90

Activity idea Self-correction

If students have access to a recording facility (using their mobile phones, for example), they could record their conversation and play it back to check their own pronunciation and intonation. They can then repeat the exercise and listen for improvements.

Warmer

Give students an example of a mistake you made recently. Write *take responsibility* on the board, and elicit what it might mean and how you could take responsibility for your mistake. Encourage students to try and clarify its meaning through examples or explanations in their own words, rather than through a translation. Ask students to read the introductory paragraph to check their ideas.

▶ 27 Life Lessons: Taking responsibility for your actions

1 ▶27
She knew that she was not perfect.

2 ▶27 Ask students to try to answer the questions from memory before watching the video again to check.
1 Anna's friend 2 Anna's teacher 3 Anna's friend 4 Anna 5 Anna

3 *It was her birthday. On Saturday she had a party and spent all day organising it. On Sunday she was answering messages all day. She watched TV. She was too tired.*

4 Monitor to help with any difficulties, but do not interrupt as this is a fluency activity.

5 Give a couple of your own ideas as examples before students work in pairs.

6 Students could write a role play to include the phrases from Exercise 5.

Homework

Ask students to make a presentation about an incident in a TV show or film where a character makes a mistake and either apologises and makes the situation better, or doesn't apologise and makes the situation worse.

LIFE COMPETENCIES

It isn't easy to tell other people when we've made a mistake. We might worry about what they will do or say. But taking responsibility for our actions often means that other people will know to respect and trust us.

1 ▶ 27 **Watch the video. What did Anna's mum already know about her daughter?**

2 ▶ 27 **Watch again. Who said (or thought about saying) these things and why?**

1 Can I copy your homework? ______
2 Why haven't you done your homework? ______
3 The hamster ate it. ______
4 You never had a plate. ______
5 Sorry, but I've had a little accident. ______

3 **Amy is telling her friend about an exam she has failed. What excuses does she give for not studying?**

'Mum and Dad are going to be really angry with me. You know what? They'll probably say I can't visit my cousins in the holidays, and they'll make me study instead. It isn't fair. Mr Jones never gives me good marks. He just doesn't like me.

I didn't have time to study either. It was my birthday at the weekend. I had a party on Saturday evening and I spent all day organising it. I had to tell people what time to meet at the cinema, and I had to call the pizza place to get a table. Then on Sunday, people were messaging me all day to wish me a happy birthday. You can't just turn your phone off when people are being nice enough to message you, can you?

And then it was the first episode of *Lost Kings* on Sunday night, and I was too tired to study after that. Then this morning, I was late for school. Mum forgot to leave me money for the bus so I had to walk to school.'

4 SPEAKING **Work in pairs. Discuss these questions with your partner.**

1 Do you think any of Amy's excuses are good reasons for not studying?
2 Do you think it would be fair if Amy's parents punished her?
3 What should Amy say to her parents when they ask why she didn't study?
4 Do you sometimes blame other people when things go wrong? Do you think you're always right when you do?

Me and my world

5 **Here are some common excuses. Can you think of a time when you have said any of these things? Tell your partner about what happened.**

I didn't see it.	The teacher never told me.
Homework? What homework!?	She was doing it, so I did it, too.
It just broke.	I can't find it.
He started it.	They made me do it.

6 SPEAKING **Think about your answers to Exercise 5. What might be a more responsible thing to say if you're in a similar situation again? Share your ideas with a partner.**

TIPS FOR TAKING RESPONSIBILITY FOR YOUR ACTIONS

- Try to speak directly to someone when telling them what you've done. If you can't do that, write a letter or an email.
- Don't be surprised if the person you need to talk to is angry or upset at first. Stay calm. They will calm down and will respect you for being honest.
- Be sincere. Don't make excuses – just say what happened.

Activity idea Extension

Ask students to write five different invitations. They can work in small groups and make and respond to the invitations.

THINK more

Practice Extra
Unit 9 Master it!

Worksheets
Life Lessons: Taking responsibility for your actions

Tests
Unit, extension and skills test 9
End of term test 3

Social Responsibilities
Understanding personal responsibilities as part of a group and in society – including citizenship
Is aware of positive behaviour in different groups (e.g. class, home, with friends).

Social Responsibilities
Understanding personal responsibilities as part of a group and in society – including citizenship
Understands the rights and responsibilities of individuals in society at local and national levels.

Warmer

On the board, create a pie chart of your free-time activities with rough percentages. Describe it to students and give details of when you do the activities. Ask students to draw their own pie charts, but not to label the activities. Students work in pairs and share their pie charts with their partners, who have one minute to guess the activities.

▶ 28 Get TH!NKing

Play the video and discuss the question with your class.

1 Give students three minutes to think of as many other free-time activities as they can.
1 gaming 2 playing the piano 3 bird watching 4 baking

2 Ask students to rank the activities according to which is best for their health. If students do not think the activities are healthy, ask: *Can you think of a way to make them healthier?*

3 At the end of the exercise, listen to some of the students' ideas and encourage open class discussion.

4 Give students two minutes to cover the text on page 93 and just look at the photos and think about the answer. Give students another two minutes to read the text quickly and check. Encourage them not to focus on every word for now.

5 **Check/clarify:** *cancer, paradises, bird-spotter, touching human document.*
Students underline key information in the sentences before reading, checking whether sentences are positive or negative.

6 🔊 **10.01**
A 4 B 7 C 1 D 3 E 5

10 MIND AND BODY

OBJECTIVES

FUNCTIONS: talking about your health

GRAMMAR: past perfect simple; past perfect continuous; past perfect simple vs. past perfect continuous

VOCABULARY: time linkers; illness: collocations

Get TH!NKING
Watch the video and think: how healthy is your lifestyle?

1

3

2

4

READING

1 SPEAKING Work in pairs. Look at the photos and name the free-time activities. What other activities can you think of?

2 Think about the activities you discussed in Exercise 1. Answer the question and take notes.
How might each of these free-time activities be good for someone's health?

3 SPEAKING Discuss your answers with your partner.

Cooking your own food can be good for your health. You can choose fresh ingredients so the food is better for you.

4 Look at the photos on the next page. What do you think the text is about? Read the text quickly to check your ideas.

5 Read the sentences. Five of them were taken out of the text. Write the numbers 1–7 in the boxes. There are two sentences you don't need.

1 By now she was becoming internationally famous in the birdwatching world.
2 It's not a very beautiful bird and it's not easy to find.
3 Snetsinger had become a legend.
4 She had less than a year to live.
5 She was there enjoying the hobby that had probably saved her life.
6 There were very few countries she hadn't visited.
7 This helped her remain healthy for another ten years.

6 🔊 10.01 Read and listen to the article again to check your answers.

92

Objectives

Functions and speaking Talking about your health
Grammar Past perfect simple; past perfect continuous; past perfect simple vs past perfect continuous
Vocabulary Time linkers; illness: collocations
Values Never give up
Train to TH!NK Logical conclusion

Resources for this unit

All available online

Videos

- Get **TH!NK**ing: *How healthy is your lifestyle?*
- Grammar rap!: Past perfect continuous
- Culture: A different sport?

Tests

- Unit, extension and skills test 10

Worksheets

- Grammar and vocabulary: Basic, Standard and Extension Worksheets
- Project: Healthy lifestyles
- Communication: Keep healthy
- Grammar presentation: Past perfect and past perfect continuous
- Get **TH!NK**ing and Grammar rap! video Worksheets

Culture notes

Phoebe Snetsinger (1931–1999) was a birdwatcher famous for spotting more birds than anyone else in history. When her father died, she inherited a large amount of money and spent the rest of her life travelling the world spotting birds. Three of her four children now work as bird researchers.

Guinness Book of Records (known as *Guinness World Records* since 2000) is a reference book which has been published every year since 1955. It includes records of human achievements and records in the natural world. Over the years, the book has developed into a worldwide business which, as well as checking new world records, now includes TV programmes and museums in many countries.

Missouri (population c.6 million) is a state in midwestern USA. It has a highly varied geography, with the Ozark Mountains in the south and plains to the north, and the Missouri river separating them. The area is home to hundreds of different bird species.

The Mississippi River is one of the longest rivers in the USA. It is 3,726 km long and stretches from close to Canada in the north to the Gulf of Mexico in the south.

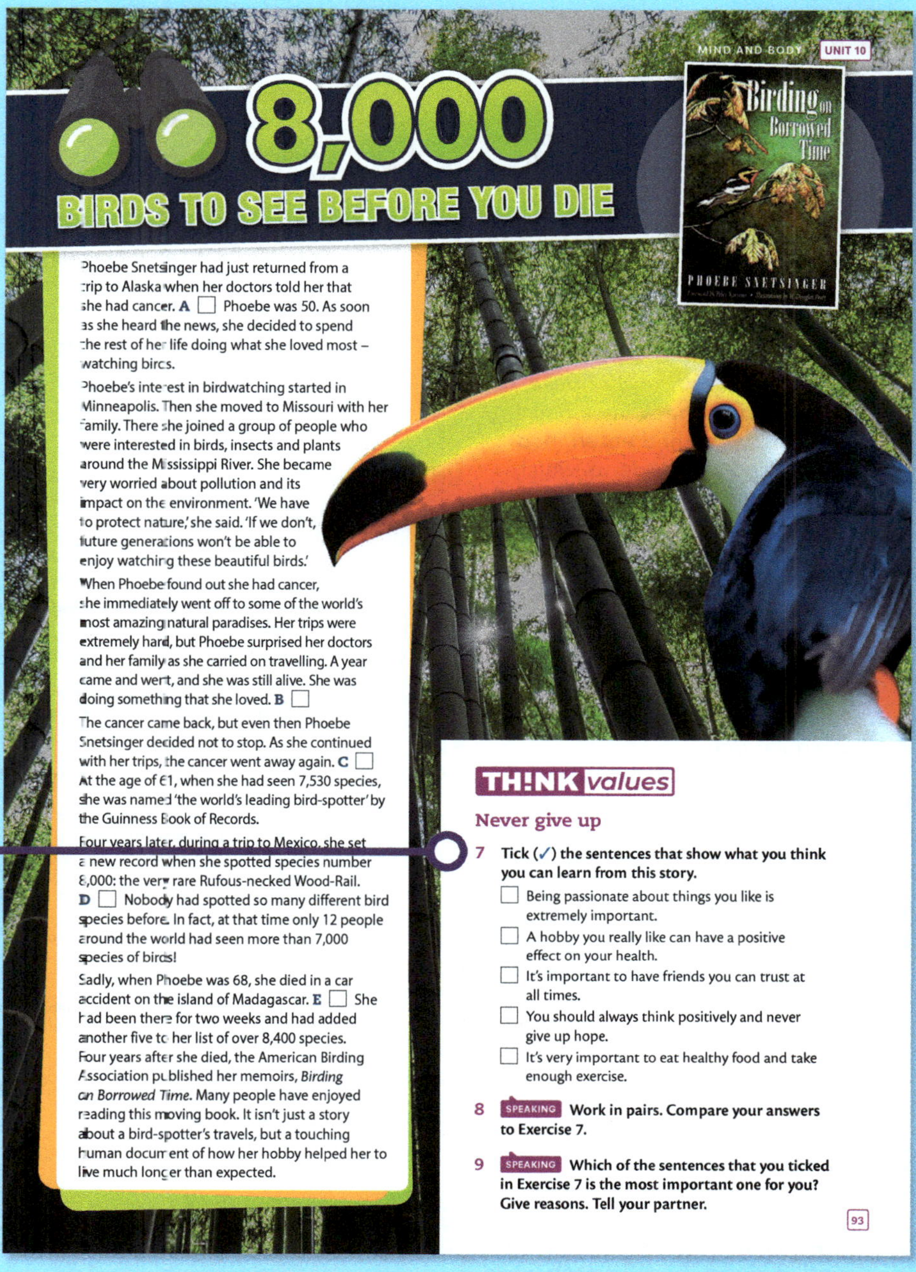

MIND AND BODY UNIT 10

8,000 BIRDS TO SEE BEFORE YOU DIE

Phoebe Snetsinger had just returned from a trip to Alaska when her doctors told her that she had cancer. **A** ☐ Phoebe was 50. As soon as she heard the news, she decided to spend the rest of her life doing what she loved most – watching birds.

Phoebe's interest in birdwatching started in Minneapolis. Then she moved to Missouri with her family. There she joined a group of people who were interested in birds, insects and plants around the Mississippi River. She became very worried about pollution and its impact on the environment. 'We have to protect nature,' she said. 'If we don't, future generations won't be able to enjoy watching these beautiful birds.'

When Phoebe found out she had cancer, she immediately went off to some of the world's most amazing natural paradises. Her trips were extremely hard, but Phoebe surprised her doctors and her family as she carried on travelling. A year came and went, and she was still alive. She was doing something that she loved. **B** ☐

The cancer came back, but even then Phoebe Snetsinger decided not to stop. As she continued with her trips, the cancer went away again. **C** ☐ At the age of 61, when she had seen 7,530 species, she was named 'the world's leading bird-spotter' by the Guinness Book of Records.

Four years later, during a trip to Mexico, she set a new record when she spotted species number 8,000: the very rare Rufous-necked Wood-Rail. **D** ☐ Nobody had spotted so many different bird species before. In fact, at that time only 12 people around the world had seen more than 7,000 species of birds!

Sadly, when Phoebe was 68, she died in a car accident on the island of Madagascar. **E** ☐ She had been there for two weeks and had added another five to her list of over 8,400 species. Four years after she died, the American Birding Association published her memoirs, *Birding on Borrowed Time*. Many people have enjoyed reading this moving book. It isn't just a story about a bird-spotter's travels, but a touching human document of how her hobby helped her to live much longer than expected.

TH!NK values

Never give up

7 **Tick (✓) the sentences that show what you think you can learn from this story.**

☐ Being passionate about things you like is extremely important.
☐ A hobby you really like can have a positive effect on your health.
☐ It's important to have friends you can trust at all times.
☐ You should always think positively and never give up hope.
☐ It's very important to eat healthy food and take enough exercise.

8 SPEAKING **Work in pairs. Compare your answers to Exercise 7.**

9 SPEAKING **Which of the sentences that you ticked in Exercise 7 is the most important one for you? Give reasons. Tell your partner.**

93

7 **Check/clarify:** *passionate, trust, give up hope.* Ask students to underline the parts of the text which support their answers.

8 You may like to give an example to encourage students to give detailed reasons for their answer.

9 At the end of the exercise, listen to some of the students' ideas and encourage open class discussion.

Homework

Write on the board: *Do you have the same hobbies now as you did when you were younger? Do you think you will have the same hobbies when you are older?* Ask students to write some sentences to answer the questions.

Activity idea Extension

Students could role-play an interview with Phoebe Snetsinger. Divide the class into two groups: A (Phoebe) and B (reporter). Ask Group B to look at the text and write five questions for Phoebe. Ask Group A to look at the text and find key information about Phoebe in preparation for an interview. Put the students in A/B pairs and give them time to act out the role play.

Critical TH!NKing
Evaluating ideas, arguments and options
Identifies assumptions and inferences in an argument.

Critical TH!NKing
Understanding and analysing links between ideas
Compares points and arguments from different sources.

Critical TH!NKing
Evaluating ideas, arguments and options
Assesses strengths and weaknesses of possible solutions.

TH!NK more

Worksheets
Project Healthy lifestyles
Communication Keep healthy
Get TH!NKing *How healthy is your lifestyle?*

Warmer

Ask students to make a list of irregular past participles. Then students test each other in pairs – one says the infinitive of the verb and the other says the participle.

1 Dictate for students to write: *I was very angry when I got home yesterday. My brother ___ my chocolate. And he ___ my iPad to his friend's house, so I couldn't check my emails!* Elicit answers (had eaten, had taken) and ask students which actions came first. If necessary, draw a timeline.
1 Her returning from the trip
2 Spotting the birds
RULE: 3 past participle

2 Remind students to think carefully about the past participle they need and if it is a regular or an irregular one.
1 had … gone 2 had changed
3 had lost 4 had stolen
5 had forgotten 6 had … left
7 hadn't given 8 Had … returned

3 Remind students to use the past perfect.

Workbook p90

Get it Right!
Past perfect vs. past simple
Student's Book p125

4 Write on the board: *1 I started studying as soon as I got home. 2 When I got hungry, I had a sandwich. 3 I studied for hours. Then I had a coffee. 4 I studied until 2.30 am. 5 I fell asleep while I was studying.*

GRAMMAR
Past perfect simple

1 **Read the example sentences and answer the questions. Then complete the rules.**

*Phoebe Snetsinger **had** just **returned** from a trip to Alaska when her doctors **told** her that she had cancer.*
1 Which of the two actions came first: her returning from a trip or the doctors telling her she had cancer?

*Four years later she **set** a new record. Nobody **had spotted** so many different bird species.*
2 Which action came first?

> RULE: When we tell a story, we often use the past perfect to talk about one event that happened before another event in the past.
> *She died in a car accident on the island of Madagascar.*
> *She had been there for two weeks.*
> (She was there for two weeks before she died.)
>
> had been there — died
> PAST — (two weeks) — NOW
>
> Form the past perfect with *had* (or *'d*) + the [3] ________ of the verb.

2 **Complete the sentences. Use the past perfect form of the verbs.**

1 When I tried to phone them, nobody answered. They ______ all ______ (go) swimming.
2 He ______ (change) so much that I almost didn't recognise him when I saw him last night.
3 She couldn't phone me because she ______ (lose) her mobile.
4 Somebody ______ (steal) John's car, so he was very angry.
5 Claire had no idea I was coming to see her. Her mum ______ (forget) to tell her.
6 You arrived too late. They ______ already ______ (leave).
7 Her mother ______ (not give) her any money so she couldn't buy the tickets.
8 ______ they already ______ (return) from their holiday when you got to their house?

3 **Think about times in the past when you experienced a strong emotion. Then complete these sentences with your own words. Use the past perfect.**

1 I was really sad because …
2 I was absolutely delighted when I found out that …
3 I was angry when …
4 I was very tired after …

→ workbook page 90

VOCABULARY
Time linkers

4 **Read the story. Complete it with the words in the list.**

as soon as | then | until | when | while

When I was a child, I was never really very interested in nature. [1]______ one day my aunt gave me a book for my birthday. It was called *Birding on Borrowed Time* by a woman called Phoebe Snetsinger. [2]______ she gave it to me I was a little disappointed. It didn't seem very interesting, and I wanted a new game for my games console. My aunt made me promise to read it. So I did, and I loved it. It was so interesting. [3]______ I was reading the book, I completely forgot about time. In fact, I didn't do anything else [4]______ I'd finished it – no TV, no gaming, nothing. [5]______ I had finished the book, I went out and bought myself a pair of binoculars. And that's how my interest in birdwatching started.

5 **Match the parts of the sentence.**

1 I never really liked Annie *until* ☐
2 *As soon as* I saw John's face ☐
3 *When* we got home after school ☐
4 *While* I was riding my bike ☐
5 I read the whole letter. *Then* ☐

a we did our homework immediately.
b I saw it wasn't for me.
c I realised we have a lot in common.
d I noticed something was wrong with it.
e I knew he was really worried.

6 **Complete the sentences so that they are true for you.**

1 While I was walking to school this morning …
2 The first thing I did when I arrived at home yesterday …
3 I had never eaten any … until …
4 As soon as I learned how to (swim / play the violin / write my name …), …
5 I heard my favourite singer for the first time in … . Then …

→ workbook page 92

In pairs, students discuss the meaning of the underlined words (*as soon as* = at exactly the same moment; *when* = at the same moment or soon after; *then* = after that; *until* = up to a point in time; *while* = at the same time as).
1 Then 2 When 3 While 4 until 5 As soon as

5 1 c 2 e 3 a 4 d 5 b

6 As an alternative, students could imagine they are a cartoon character and complete the sentences.

Workbook p92

THINK more

Workbook
Grammar p90, Ex.1–4
Vocabulary p92, Ex.1–2

Worksheets
Grammar Worksheets 10
Grammar presentation: Past perfect and past perfect continuous
Vocabulary Worksheets 10

Language note Past perfect simple

1 Students may confuse the past perfect with the present perfect and produce incorrect statements like: *I have finished my homework when the phone rang.* Remind them of the use of the past perfect in English.

2 Remind them that we don't repeat the main verb in short answers. We don't say: *Had you played tennis before your game last week?* ~~*Yes, I had played.*~~ → *Yes, I had.*

Listening; Train to TH!NK

7 10.02 Write on the board: *How much exercise do you do? Why do you exercise? Do you do more exercise than your parents/ grandparents?* Discuss.

Explain that students will hear two people – Lucas and Jackie – discussing going to the gym.

1 F 2 T 3 F

8 10.02 Give students time to read the notes and imagine possible answers before listening again.

1 heart and legs 2 stairs 3 eat 4 walk 5 doesn't do 6 invisible chair

9 Make sure students know what is happening in each picture first.

B

10 You may want to give your own answers as an example first.

11 Write on the board: *I have no money, ___ I can't go out at the weekend.* Ask: *Which word could complete the sentence?* Students may offer *so*.

Write on the board: *I have no money! ___ , I can't go out at the weekend.* Ask: *Which word could complete the sentence?* Point out that we would not start a sentence with *so*, but that another word with a similar meaning can be used instead. Elicit *therefore*. Explain that we use *so* and *therefore* to make a conclusion. Ask students to give you advice and elicit sentences with *should*.

a so – draws a conclusion b should – makes a suggestion

12 To show the difference between a valid and invalid conclusion, write on the board: *I can speak French. Therefore, I am French.* (invalid)

He has the same date of birth as his brother. Therefore, they are twins. (valid)

A invalid B valid C valid D invalid

MIND AND BODY UNIT 10

LISTENING

7 10.02 **Listen to Lucas and Jackie talking. Jackie is going to the gym. Mark the sentences T (true) or F (false).**

1 Lucas has never been to a gym. ___
2 Jackie and Lucas go into the shopping centre together. ___
3 Lucas goes into the gym with Jackie. ___

8 10.02 **Listen again. At home Lucas tries to remember what Jackie said. He writes some things down but can't remember everything. Complete his notes for him.**

What Jackie said:

- Walking fast is good for your [1] ___ .
- Dancing is good exercise.
- It's better to use the [2] ___ than the escalator.
- One really bad thing is to [3] ___ and [4] ___ at the same time because then the food [5] ___ you so much good.
- A good exercise to do every day is the [6] ___ .

9 **Which of these pictures shows the exercise Jackie mentions?**

10 SPEAKING **Work in pairs. What's your opinion of the things Jackie says about exercise?**

Train to TH!NK

Logical conclusions

11 **Complete the sentences from the conversation with *so* and *should*. Then decide in which of the sentences the speaker makes a suggestion and in which the speaker draws a conclusion.**

a I feel much better afterwards, ___ I go to the gym every week.
b You ___ walk as much as you can, and sometimes walk quite fast.

Look
A conclusion is only valid if it follows logically from the information given. If we need to make assumptions about facts that are not part of the information, then the conclusion is invalid.

12 SPEAKING **Which of these conclusions are valid? Which are invalid? Give reasons.**

A Most kinds of sports are good for your health.
Car racing is a sport.
Therefore car racing is good for your health.
valid ☐ invalid ☐

B Spending time outdoors in the fresh air is good for your health.
Birdwatching is done outdoors in the fresh air.
Therefore, birdwatching is a healthy free-time activity.
valid ☐ invalid ☐

C Vitamins are good for the immune system.
Fruit has got vitamins in it.
Therefore eating fruit is good for the immune system.
valid ☐ invalid ☐

D Positive thinking can be good for your health.
John is a positive thinker.
John will never fall ill.
valid ☐ invalid ☐

The conclusion in A is invalid. It's true that most kinds of sports are good for your health. It's also true that car racing is a sport. But it's not true that all sports are good for your health. The first sentence talks about most kinds of sports, not all sports.

95

Homework

Ask students to write a description of their typical morning routine using the time linkers in this lesson.

Activity idea Extension

If you have access to the internet, do an online search for lateral thinking problems. There are several good websites which offer problems with hints and solutions. Choose one or more of the problems and ask students to work in small groups and try to solve it. If students are allowed to use mobile devices in the classroom, ask them to search for problems themselves and try them out on other students. Students should practise using *so* and *therefore* in their answers.

Critical THINKing
Evaluating ideas, arguments and options
Identifies evidence and its reliability.

TH!NK more
Workbook
Listening p96, Ex.1

Reading

Warmer

Revise body vocabulary. Divide the class into four teams. Point to a part of your body and give a point to the first team to name it. Alternatively, say a part of the body and students have to point to their own.

1 **Check/clarify:** *3D, prosthetics.* Ask students to cover the article, look at the pictures and answer the question. Ask students to read the first paragraph to check. *They both have artificial limbs.*

2 **Check/clarify (Text A):** *greyhound, paw, architect.* **Check/clarify (Text B):** *limbs.* Divide the class into A and B pairs. Tell the pairs that they are each going to read a different story. Monitor to help with any vocabulary difficulties.

Ask students to work with someone from the other group to compare stories.

3 **10.03**
1 B 2 A 3 A and B 4 A
5 B 6 B

Culture note

Team UnLimbited is a charity providing 3D printed prosthetic limbs free of charge for children in the UK and internationally. It was founded in 2015 after Steve Davies and Drew Murray were teamed together via the global partnership programme, e-Nable, to manufacture a 3D-printed left hand. Their 3D printing designs can be openly accessed online and have been downloaded by users across the world over 5,000 times. In 2015, a viral video of Isabella Jennings receiving her device got over three million views on YouTube; it made global news headlines and appeared on Rio Paralympics TV ads in the UK.

READING

1 Look at the photos in the article. What do the dog and the girl have in common?

2 SPEAKING Work in pairs. Student A reads Story A; Student B reads Story B. Then tell your partner about the story you have read.

3D PRINTING
IT CAN CHANGE LIVES

Prosthetics are artificial body parts. They're used by doctors to replace limbs (arms or legs) that are missing or have been damaged. For years, scientists had been making the prosthetics out of metal – steel at first, then lighter materials later. Recently, people have been using 3D printers to make prosthetics. Here are two stories of how lives were changed by 3D-printed prosthetics.

A

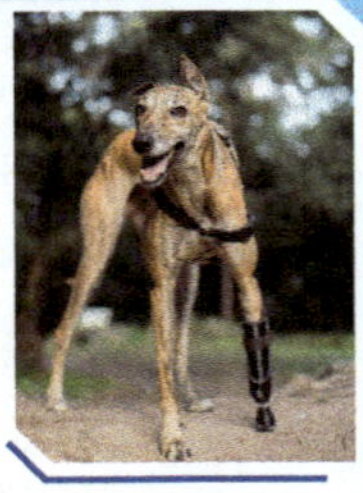

When Millie the greyhound was a puppy, she was in an accident and she lost her left front paw. Her first owner left her at a rescue centre, where Ed and Nora Dieppe found her and took her home. So that Millie could walk, her new owners put a prosthetic on her leg, but Millie soon wore it down and they had to replace it. Ed and Nora bought another prosthetic, but they soon had to replace that one, too. After a few years, they had spent over $10,000 on prosthetics. They wanted to help Millie, but they had to find a different way to do it.

Ed works as an architect. He had been working for some time with 3D modelling, and he had an idea. He talked to a company that helped him design a paw that would fit Millie perfectly. They then printed the leg using a 3D printer. They had to make two or three before the leg fitted perfectly, but soon they had a leg for Millie to wear. Now Millie can run around like other dogs, and if her leg wears out, Ed and Nora can just print a new one for her.

B

Stephen Davies was born without the lower part of his left arm. When he was at school, he wore a prosthetic, which he hated, so for many years he didn't wear a prosthetic at all. One day, he looked at what prosthetic arms were available. He saw that they hadn't changed much from when he was a boy. You could buy better ones, but they were extremely expensive.

That's OK for adults as they can use the same prosthetic arm for years. Children, though, need to change their prosthetic arm every few months because they grow so quickly. Stephen decided to do something. He had been creating lots of inventions in his garden shed. He had read that it was possible to print light, 3D prosthetics and he wondered if he could make them himself. He experimented with simple but very colourful arms and legs. He discovered that he could make good prosthetic limbs quite cheaply.

Now he and his business partner produce 'cool' limbs. Their company is called Team UnLimbited, and they give prosthetics away to children who need them (they ask for money on the internet to help with the costs of making the limbs). One of the first kids to get a 'cool' limb was nine-year-old Isabella Jennings. She had been waiting all her life for something like this. A video of her using the prosthetic arm for the first time was put on YouTube. It was watched by more than 2 million people.

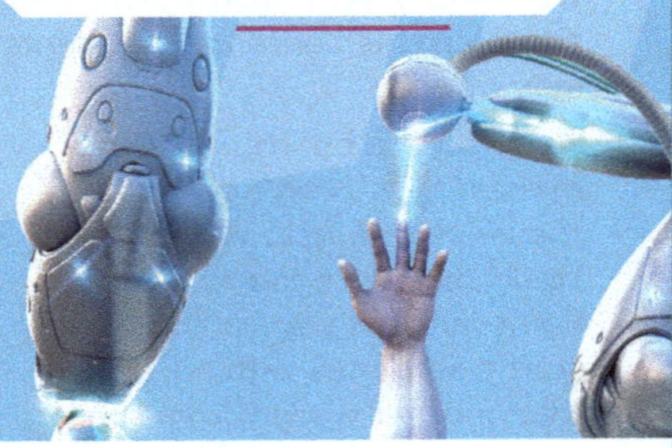

3 10.03 Read and listen to both stories. Mark the sentences A (Story A) or B (Story B).

1 He didn't like his prosthetic at all. ____
2 The artificial limb had to be replaced several times. ____
3 They found a solution with 3D printing. ____
4 She can run and play now. ____
5 They make simple prosthetics that are free. ____
6 It was what she had always wanted. ____

96

Activity idea Extension

Write on the board: *How would a prosthetic limb change your life?* Ask students to work in pairs and think of five examples. At the end of the exercise, listen to some of the students' ideas and encourage open class discussion.

TH!NK more

Workbook
Reading p94, Ex.1–3

▶ 29 Grammar rap!
Past perfect continuous

4 Ask students to try to answer the questions from memory before referring back to page 96 to check. You could ask students to match the three points in the rule with the example sentences.
1 had been working 2 had been creating 3 had been waiting
RULE: 4 past 5 past 6 how long

5 1 had been waiting 2 had been walking 3 hadn't been paying 4 had been trying 5 had … been climbing

6 Write on the board: *1 I'd been looking forward to the holiday for months! 2 I had an ice cream every day. 3 By the end of the holiday, I'd eaten 14 ice creams!* Elicit the names of the tenses in each sentence.
1 had … been playing 2 had been raining 3 had broken 4 had been studying 5 had been

Workbook p91

7 1 f – <u>had an operation</u> 2 a – <u>got better</u> 3 c – <u>make an appointment</u> 4 b – <u>see a doctor</u> 5 e – <u>feeling sick</u>

8 1 had been feeling sick 2 have an operation 3 make an appointment 4 see a doctor 5 take … exercise 6 get better

Workbook p92

Pronunciation
/tʃ/ and /ʃ/ consonant sounds

Student's Book p121

9 Give weaker students time to think and write down their answers first.

Homework
Have the students keep a journal for two or three days. In their journal, students have to keep a record of exercise they did, where they did it and how long they spent doing it.

GRAMMAR
Past perfect continuous

4 **Complete these sentences from the stories on page 96. Choose the correct words to complete the rules.**

1 He ______ (work) for some time with 3D modelling.
2 Stephen ______ (create) lots of inventions in his garden shed.
3 She ______ (wait) all her life for something like this.

RULE: The past perfect continuous is used for actions happening over a period of time. We can use it
- to talk about things that started in the [4]present / past and continued until another time in the past.
- to talk about things that have stopped and had a result in the [5]present / past.
- to focus on [6]how long / how often an activity had been happening.

5 **Complete the sentences with the past perfect continuous form of the verbs in the list.**

climb | not pay | try | wait | walk

1 I arrived late. They ______ for two hours.
2 They ______ for half an hour before they realised they'd left the picnic at the hotel.
3 Our teacher got very impatient with Thomas because he ______ attention at all that day.
4 We ______ to get tickets all afternoon, but the match was sold out by noon.
5 They looked exhausted when I saw them at the top. How long ______ they ______ ?

Past perfect simple vs. past perfect continuous

6 **Complete the sentences with the past perfect simple or continuous form of the verbs.**

1 I got to my friend's house at three o'clock. They ______ already ______ football for hours. (play)
2 Before the match started, it ______ for a long time. (rain)
3 I looked at my laptop and saw that somebody ______ it. (break)
4 She ______ Spanish for years when she went to university. (study)
5 My dad got home late. He told me that there ______ an accident on the motorway. (be)

→ workbook page 91

VOCABULARY
Illness: collocations

7 **Match the sentence halves. Then underline the illness collocation in each sentence.**

0 My dad hasn't <u>taken</u> any [d]
1 Our neighbour is in hospital. He had an [ ]
2 Her doctor gave her medication and she got [ ]
3 If you have a problem with your eyes, make an [ ]
4 Are you sure it's a cold? Maybe you should see [ ]
5 I ate seafood for dinner. I've been feeling [ ]

a better immediately.
b a doctor.
c appointment with a specialist soon!
d <u>exercise</u> for years now. He's not very healthy.
e sick all night.
f operation two days ago.

8 **Complete the sentences with illness collocations from Exercise 7. Use the correct forms of the verbs.**

1 I was really happy I could go to your party on Sunday. I ______ for almost a week.
2 Her knee hurts badly, and the medication she takes doesn't help. The doctors say she needs to ______ .
3 'Hello, this is Jake Miller. Can I ______ with Dr Thacker, please?'
4 I've got an earache, but I don't think it's too serious. If it's not gone in a few days I'll ______ .
5 The doctor says I'm a bit overweight and I should ______ some ______ every day.
6 Sorry to hear you're not feeling well. Hope you ______ soon.

→ workbook page 92

PRONUNCIATION
/tʃ/ and /ʃ/ consonant sounds Go to page 121.

FUNCTIONS
Talking about your health

9 SPEAKING **Work in pairs. Ask and answer questions.**

1 Have you ever felt sick after eating something? What happened?
2 When you have a cold, what do you do to get better?
3 Do you believe that taking exercise is good for you personally? Give reasons.
4 Where you live, is it easy or difficult to make an appointment with a doctor?
5 When you have a slight temperature, do you immediately see a doctor, or do you wait a few days?

Activity idea Extension
Give students the following sentence starters:
John didn't go to school because …
John couldn't hear very well because …
John couldn't walk because …
Students complete the sentences with the past perfect.

TH!NK more

Practice Extra
Unit 10 Practise it

Workbook
Grammar p91, Ex.5
Vocabulary p92, Ex.3–6
Vocabulary Extra p93, Ex.1–2
Pronunciation p121

Worksheets
Grammar Worksheets 10
Grammar presentation: Past perfect and past perfect continuous
Grammar rap! Past perfect continuous
Vocabulary Worksheets 10

Warmer

Elicit some sports that students do and write them on the board: *run, swim, do martial arts.* Underneath, write: *How often do you … ? Where do you … ? Why do you … ?* Ask students to discuss.

▶ 30 TH!NK
A different sport?

1 Before students read the article, get them to cover it and just look at the photos and answer the question. Write their ideas on the board. When they read to check, set a three-minute time limit to encourage them to skim the article quickly and not to focus on every word.
Students' own answers

2 **10.06 Check/clarify:** *membership, register, promoting, aerobics, muscles, slaves, rhythm, demanding.*
Before students read the article again, get them to read the questions.
Tell students not to worry about other difficult vocabulary as this will come up later.
1 5 km, every Saturday
2 Promote good health and a sense of community
3 Aerobics and dancing
4 There is an app that lets you take part wherever you are.
5 Because it was a way for African slaves to practise a martial art.
6 Because it needs strength and balance

3 Encourage students to express themselves in English and to use any vocabulary they have learned from the article.

TH!NK A different sport?

Culture

1 Look at the photos. Where do you think these activities take place?

KEEP IN SHAPE
… WITHOUT GOING TO THE GYM!

Most people would like to be in good shape, but maybe without having to buy membership to a gym or go out cycling in all kinds of weather. There are so many different options these days to keep fit, while doing something you enjoy. Here are three of our favourites.

1 PARKRUN

Running is, of course, great exercise. Back in 2004, a group of 13 runners near London decided to meet up in their local park on Saturday mornings, every week, and run five kilometres. This has grown into an organisation known as ParkRun – and now there are ParkRun events in over twenty countries. In 2018, there were on average about 250,000 people running five kilometres in 1,500 events worldwide every Saturday.

Anyone can register to run: you do it online, and then turn up. Everyone's position and time is recorded, but even though it's a race, a ParkRun event is more about promoting good health and a sense of community. ParkRun is about everyone running 5 km, every week, for free, and forever.

2 ZUMBA

In the mid-1990s, a Colombian dancer called Beto Perez devised a workout programme that was a mixture of aerobics and dancing. He called it Zumba, and it has become an enormous worldwide success. It is said that more than 15 million people in over 180 countries do Zumba regularly.

There are several different forms of Zumba. These can be very easy to do or very strenuous indeed! Because of this, almost anyone of any age can do Zumba. It's an excellent way to keep fit and lose weight. Zumba helps to make muscles stronger, to improve posture – and it's a great way to make new friends, too. And if you can't get to a class, there is, of course, an app that lets you take part in Zumba wherever you are.

3 CAPOEIRA

Another activity that mixes dance and exercise is capoeira. It is an Afro-Brazilian martial art that has become increasingly popular around the world. Capoeira was developed in Brazil in the 16th century. African slaves who had been brought to Brazil used it as a way to practise a martial art in secret. Because it is always performed to music, slave owners thought it was a dance.

To the steady rhythm of the music from a berimbau (a type of string instrument played with a bow), two people perform a series of kicks and flips, but without ever actually touching each other – at least, not intentionally! It is a demanding form of fitness activity that needs strength and balance and can be done by people of all ages.

2 10.06 **Read and listen to the article. Answer the questions.**
1 How long are ParkRun races and when do they happen?
2 What are the ParkRun events intended to do?
3 What two activities did Zumba bring together?
4 Why is it not absolutely necessary to go to a class to do Zumba?
5 Why was capoeira originally a secret activity?
6 How is capoeira a challenging exercise?

3 SPEAKING **Have you ever tried any of these activities? Would you like to? Why? Discuss with a partner.**

I haven't tried capoeira, but I would like to!

98

Social Responsibility
Understanding and describing own and others' cultures
Accepts others and shows respect for cultural difference, challenging prejudice and discriminatory views.

4 1 demanding 2 intentionally 3 devised 4 martial art 5 steady 6 posture 7 strenuous

5 Encourage students to use any vocabulary they have learned from the unit.

1 Ask: *Have you ever been camping or stayed at a holiday camp?*
1 It was raining and they couldn't go up the mountain.
2 Students' own answers
3 Students' own answers

2 During whole-class feedback, elicit further examples of words to add to each group.
1 Last year, On the last day, lunchtime, all morning 2 already, At first, Then, Five minutes later 3 Suddenly, Luckily

3 Tell students that there is a basic format which can be followed when writing a story.
1 past continuous (ongoing/ background action in the past), past simple (shorter action or state in the past), past perfect continuous (situation or action in the past continuing until another point in the past)
2 Paragraph 1 sets the scene; Paragraph 2 explains the problem; Paragraph 3 talks about a dramatic situation; Paragraph 4 talks about the solution to the problem

4 Ask students to make notes on what to include in their story. This can be done as a collaborative writing activity in class, with pairs of students working together to complete the exercise.

5 Encourage students to organise their story as outlined in Exercise 3 and to use a variety of past tenses. On completion, you could ask students to exchange their texts with another pair for them to read and correct any grammatical errors.

4 VOCABULARY **There are eight highlighted words in the article. Match the words with these meanings. Write the words.**

0 encouraging people to support something *promoting*
1 needing a lot of energy ______
2 meaning to ______
3 invented (a system, plan etc.) ______
4 a sport that is a form of defending yourself ______
5 not changing very much ______
6 the way in which someone stands or sits ______
7 needing a lot of physical effort ______

5 SPEAKING **Discuss these questions with a partner.**

- Which of the three activities would be the most popular at your school? Why?
- What other fun activities have you heard of? Can you do any of them at your school?
- What do you do to stay fit and healthy?
- What do you think you should do more of?
- Do you think it's important for schools to encourage young people to stay fit? Why?

WRITING
A story

1 INPUT **Read Jessica's story. Then answer the questions.**

1 Why weren't Jessica and her friends happy at lunchtime on the last day of their holiday?
2 Why do you think Robbie said they couldn't go up the mountain?
3 What do you think Jessica and her friends learned from the experience?

2 **Which of the words in bold in the story are used to:**

1 talk about the time when things happened?
2 talk about the order in which things happened?
3 make the story more interesting?

3 ANALYSE **Read the story again and answer the questions.**

1 Which past tenses does the writer use in the first paragraph and why?
2 The story has four paragraphs. Which of them …
– sets the scene? (who? where? when?)
– explains the problem?
– talks about a dramatic situation?
– tells us about the solution to the problem?

A BIG MISTAKE

Last year I was staying at a holiday camp with some friends. **On the last day**, we wanted to go up a mountain near the camp. But it was **already lunchtime**, and it had been raining **all morning**. So Robbie, our guide, said, 'Sorry, guys, the weather is just too bad. We can't go.' We had all been looking forward to this mountain trip for days.

At first, we were really disappointed. **Then** one of my friends had an idea. 'Why don't we go anyway?' he said. 'Robbie won't notice, and we'll be back before it gets dark'. **Five minutes later** we were ready to leave.

We made good progress. 'We'll be at the top of the mountain in an hour,' we thought. But then the weather changed. It became foggy, and the rain became much heavier. **Suddenly**, we realised that we had lost our way.

Luckily, I had my mobile phone on me. We phoned Robbie at the camp. He told us to stay where we were. When he found us, it was already dark. We were really sorry. We had made a big mistake.

4 PLAN **Choose an activity and think of a real or imagined story. Make a plan that helps you to tell the story in four paragraphs. Make notes about ideas for each of them.**

5 PRODUCE **Write your story in about 200 words. Use Jessica's story to help you.**

- Make sure your story is well structured.
- When you have finished, check the tenses you have used.
- Find a title that you think will make people want to read your story.

Activity idea A poster

Give students time to memorise their story. Allow them to make brief notes if necessary. Write the sequencers on the board. Ask students to tell their story to their partner without reading the original. Encourage them to use the words and phrases on the board.

Homework

Ask students to research and write about an interesting fitness technique. As a follow-up, they can present it to the class.

TH!NK more

Practice Extra
Unit 10 Master it!

Workbook
Developing Writing p95

Tests
Unit, extension and skills test 10

1 In B1 Preliminary for Schools Reading Part 3, candidates have to read a longer text which expresses an opinion or attitude, and choose the correct option, A, B, C or D, in five multiple-choice questions about the text. This part of the exam tests understanding of the writer's attitude or opinion and both the detailed and global meaning of the text.

Encourage your students to do the following when they approach this task:

- Skim the text to have a sense of the topic and general meaning.
- Read the text more carefully.
- Compare each question, one by one, with the text and choose the best option.
- Check the chosen answer carefully against the text. Check the other options and decide why they are wrong.
- Note that questions follow the order of information in the text and the final question focuses on the global meaning.

1 A 2 B 3 A 4 D 5 C

Workbook p97

2 10.07 In B1 Preliminary for Schools Listening Part 3, candidates have to listen to a monologue, identify and write down specific information (e.g., numbers, places, dates, prices or times) in a text. This part of the exam tests candidates' ability to listen for specific and detailed information. It also checks the spelling of common words.

Encourage your students to do the following when they approach this task:

- Read and listen to the instructions carefully.
- Read the text, think about the context and predict the language and information.
- During the first listening, find and write down single words, numbers or short noun phrases to complete the information. Use the order of the information on the page to follow the recording.
- During the second listening, check that the answers are correct and make sense. If the word was spelled in the recording, the answer must also be spelled correctly.

1 journalism 2 photographers 3 Fridays 4 28th July 5 website 6 Robin

Workbook p53

B1 Preliminary for Schools

READING

Part 3: 4-option multiple choice

→ workbook page 97

1 Read the text and questions below. For each question, choose the correct answer.

17-year-old Nadia Clarke talks about her African experience.

Last summer I got the chance to spend a month helping out in a hospital in Rwanda with my parents, who work for a charity. I had one year left at school, and I was interested in studying medicine at university. I thought it was the perfect chance to get some experience and to see if I really wanted to be a doctor.

It was a month that changed my life. I was introduced to a world that is very different to mine in so many ways, and I soon discovered how difficult people's lives can be. But I was also amazed at how positively people go about their everyday lives. The way they come together and help each other is a real inspiration, and something I think a lot of us here in the UK have forgotten. I think many of us don't realise how lucky we are.

My work in the hospital was hard. I spent a lot of time cleaning floors and changing bed sheets, but I also got to spend some time looking after the patients. And I got the chance to talk to some doctors and ask them about the profession. All of them told me how difficult being a doctor in that hospital was sometimes – hard work and long hours, and so many emotional challenges. But all of them also said that they didn't want to practise their profession anywhere else, because having seen the effect they were having on that community, they just wanted to go on. At times, it was a difficult experience, but it didn't change my mind about being a doctor. In fact, it only made me more determined to do medicine and to be like the doctors and nurses I worked with there.

When I finish, I know exactly what I'm going to do: I want to work for an international organisation like the Red Cross or Médecins sans Frontières, so I can spend my life helping people overseas who really need it. I can't wait to get started.

1 Why did Nadia want to go to Rwanda with her parents?
- A She wanted to learn more about being a doctor before deciding on what to study at university.
- B She wanted to help her parents and work for a charity in Rwanda.
- C She wanted to go on a month-long holiday with her parents before going to university.
- D She wanted to make an important decision about her final year at school.

2 What surprised Nadia the most about the experience?
- A She missed the UK more than she imagined and wanted to go home.
- B She was surprised at the kindness and attitude of the people despite the daily challenges.
- C There was no difference in her opinion before or after the experience.
- D She found it difficult to understand the differences between life in Rwanda and her own life.

3 What did the doctors Nadia worked with tell her?
- A They did not want to be doctors anywhere else.
- B It was hard work and long hours, with little satisfaction.
- C They hoped to go on to work in other communities and have a similar effect.
- D They liked the positive and negative feelings that they experienced while working in the hospital.

4 In paragraph 4, Nadia mentions that …
- A she would prefer to have a job as a doctor in her hometown.
- B she doesn't think helping people is a good career choice.
- C she is still thinking about working for a charity like her parents.
- D she is completely sure of her future professional career plans.

5 What might Nadia write home to her friends?
- A The doctors have been really kind here, but I'm not so sure it's what I want to do anymore.
- B The people are very friendly, and I've made some really good friends.
- C It's been difficult, but I really want to work somewhere like this when I'm older.
- D Sweeping floors and cleaning beds! I want to spend more time with the patients.

LISTENING

Part 3: Gap fill

→ workbook page 53

2 10.07 **You will hear a man talking about summer jobs at the local newspaper. For each question, write one or two words or a number or a date or a time.**

The Daily Post – Summer Jobs

The jobs are for people looking for experience in [1] ______ .
The newspaper is looking for two [2] ______ .
The weekly timetable is Mondays and [3] ______ – 1 pm to 6 pm.
Job is for four weeks starting on [4] ______ .
Application forms on the [5] ______ or in the newspaper – this week only!
Contact [6] ______ for more information.

100

1 1 take 2 as 3 career 4 challenging 5 training 6 in 7 notice 8 until 9 make 10 as soon as

2 1 worked 2 was built 3 have been invited / are invited 4 had been working 5 is invited 6 built

3 1 Millions of hamburgers ~~eat~~ are eaten every day.
2 When we got to Moscow, we had ~~being~~ been travelling for 12 hours.
3 Hundreds of buildings have been damaged by the earthquake.
4 The boy was very ill, so they were ~~taken~~ taking him to hospital.
5 Last week, I was hurt in a football match.
6 When he left college, he ~~was~~ had been a student there for four years.

4 1 hurts, see 2 about, sounds 3 feeling, better 4 together, afraid

TEST YOURSELF UNITS 9 & 10

VOCABULARY

1 **Complete the sentences with the words in the list. There are two extra words.**

as | as soon as | career | challenging | feel | in | make | notice | take | then | training | until

1 If you aren't sleeping very well, perhaps you should ________________ more exercise.
2 My brother's working ________________ a postman for the summer.
3 Have you ever thought about a ________________ in marketing?
4 The job's OK, but it isn't very ________________ , so sometimes I don't enjoy it much.
5 At the beginning, we got lots of on-the-job ________________ so we could do it properly.
6 My mum used to be a teacher, but now she works ________________ the travel industry.
7 He didn't like his job much, so after a month, he gave in his ________________ .
8 I'm going to keep trying ________________ I find the answer!
9 I don't feel well. I'm going to phone the doctor and ________________ an appointment.
10 I'll call you ________________ the train arrives.

/10

GRAMMAR

2 **Complete the sentences with the words in the list. You need to write the correct form of the verbs.**

build (x2) | invite (x2) | work (x2)

1 After I left school, I ________________ in a shop.
2 Our school ________________ in 1965.
3 We ________________ to a party next weekend, but I don't know if we can go.
4 My dad ________________ at the school for 20 years when he left his job there.
5 Every year, my sister ________________ to talk at a conference, and she always says yes.
6 They ________________ their house in only six months!

3 **Find and correct the mistake in each sentence.**

1 Millions of hamburgers eat every day.
2 When we got to Moscow, we had being travelling for 12 hours.
3 Hundreds of buildings have damaged by the earthquake.
4 The boy was very ill, so they were taken him to hospital.
5 Last week I hurt in a football match.
6 When he left college, he was a student there for four years.

/12

FUNCTIONAL LANGUAGE

4 **Complete the mini-dialogues with the words in the list.**

about | afraid | better | feeling | hurts | see | sounds | together

1 **A** My leg ________________ really badly.
B Oh, really? Perhaps you should go and ________________ a doctor.
2 **A** Nadia, how ________________ coming shopping with me on Saturday?
B Well, yes, that ________________ fun. Thanks.
3 **A** I haven't been ________________ well this morning.
B Oh, I'm sorry to hear that. I'm sure you'll feel ________________ soon.
4 **A** I thought we could do something ________________ tonight.
B I'm really sorry, but I'm ________________ I can't.

/8

MY SCORE /30

22–30 | 10–21 | 0–9

101

The Cambridge Life Competencies Framework

Social Responsibilities

Understanding personal responsibilities as part of a group and in society – including citizenship

Watch this video for a tip on how to encourage your students' awareness of social responsibilities.

Scan the QR code here

Warmer

If you have an interactive whiteboard (IWB), do an internet search for an online newspaper. Alternatively, bring in a suitable English newspaper. Look through the different sections. Write any interesting vocabulary on the board. Ask: *What do we call a person who writes for a newspaper?* Elicit *journalist*. With the whole class, discuss what a journalist does in their job.

▶ 31 Get TH!NKing

Play the video and discuss the question with your class.

1 Before students answer the question, elicit the different types of news media in the photos (print newspaper, TV news, online news, radio news).

2 See if students can think of some more qualities to add to the list.

3 You may like to give an example from your own experience to get students started on this exercise.

4 You may have to give students some prompts to get them thinking. Write their ideas on the board under the headings *Good* and *Bad*. Discuss whether the students think the internet has ultimately changed the news for the better or for the worse.

5 🔊 **11.01** Encourage students not to focus on every word for now. Ask them to explain the reason for their choices.
1 C, 1917 2 A, 1934 3 B, 1938

6 **Check/clarify:** *fake, interrupted, aliens, panic, invasion.*
Give students time to read the article and answer the questions. Encourage them to justify their answers.
1 3 2 1 3 2

11 BREAKING NEWS

OBJECTIVES

FUNCTIONS: reporting what someone has said; expressing feelings: anger

GRAMMAR: reported statements; verb patterns: object + infinitive

VOCABULARY: fun; more verbs with object + infinitive; expressions with *make*

Get TH!NKING Watch the video and think: would you want to be a journalist?

1

3

2

4

READING

1 Look at the photos. Do you follow the news? How? Do you use any of these sources?

2 SPEAKING Work in pairs. Think about the news on TV, in newspapers or on the internet. What should a news story be?
(0 – not important – 3 very important)
☐ truthful ☐ funny ☐ educational
☐ entertaining ☐ serious ☐ up-to-date

3 Think of stories you have heard recently for each of the categories in Exercise 2.

4 SPEAKING Discuss in pairs. How do you think the internet has changed the news? Give examples of how this can be good and how it can be bad.

5 🔊 11.01 Read and listen to the article. Match the photos with the stories. Write the dates of the stories under the photos.

6 Read the article again. Which story are these people talking about?
1 'I heard about that. They got a famous actor to read out the story.'
2 'How could she keep that secret for so long?'
3 'People probably believed him because of his profession.'

102

Objectives

Functions and speaking Reporting what someone has said; **Developing speaking:** Expressing feelings: anger
Grammar Reported statements; verb patterns: object + infinitive
Vocabulary Fun; more verbs with object + infinitive; **WordWise:** Expressions with *make*
Values Reacting to jokes
Life Competencies Being assertive

Resources for this unit

All available online

Videos
- Get **TH!NK**ing: *Would you want to be a journalist?*
- Grammar rap!: Verb patterns: object + infinitive
- Vlog: Being assertive

Tests
- Unit, extension and skills test 11

Worksheets
- Grammar and vocabulary: Basic, Standard and Extension Worksheets
- Project: Fake or real?
- Communication: Making the news
- Get **TH!NK**ing, Grammar rap! and Life Lessons video Worksheets

Culture notes

The Cottingley Fairies appear in a series of five photographs taken in Cottingley, UK, around 1917 by Elsie Wright and Frances Griffiths, two young cousins. Some people accepted the images as genuine, others believed they were fake. In the 1980s, Elsie and Frances admitted they were faked using cardboard cut-outs of fairies copied from a book, but Frances maintained that the fifth photograph was genuine.

Sir Arthur Conan Doyle (1859–1930) was a British writer who created the character Sherlock Holmes. As a spiritualist, Conan Doyle was enthusiastic about the photographs and interpreted them as clear evidence of psychic phenomena.

The Loch Ness Monster, or 'Nessie', is said to be a creature that lives in Loch Ness in the Scottish Highlands. It is often described as large in size with a long neck and one or more humps protruding from the water. Evidence of its existence is anecdotal.

The War of the Worlds is a science fiction novel by English author H. G. Wells, written in 1897. On 30th October 1938, the 23-year-old actor Orson Welles performed a radio adaptation of it, converting the 40-year-old novel into fake news bulletins describing a Martian invasion of New Jersey. The live recording was quite chaotic, adding to the authenticity of the situation.

BREAKING NEWS UNIT 11

IT'S ALL FAKE NEWS

With the increase of fake news, it can be hard at times to know whether the news we read is true or not. What started as people spreading funny stories over the internet has become something much more serious. At its very worst, fake news is used to make up stories that try to change people's opinions. It is also used to cover or 'hide' uncomfortable stories that some people might not want to answer questions about. These days, fake news can make a big difference to the world. It is, perhaps, the most serious problem facing the world's media.

But fake news is nothing new. It has always been with us. In the past it wasn't such a big problem, though. People used it more for a bit of fun, as these famous examples show.

1 In 1917 two young cousins, Elsie Wright and Frances Griffiths, were having fun taking photos in the garden with Elsie's father's camera. When Mr Wright developed the photos, he saw that they showed the girls playing with fairies. The girls insisted the fairies were real. Elsie's father said he thought the girls were playing a joke on him, but Elsie's mother believed they were real. The photos were shown to the famous author of the Sherlock Holmes stories, Sir Arthur Conan Doyle, who also decided they were real. For years many people were fooled. The truth was only discovered in the 1980s when Elsie finally admitted that the fairies were just made out of paper.

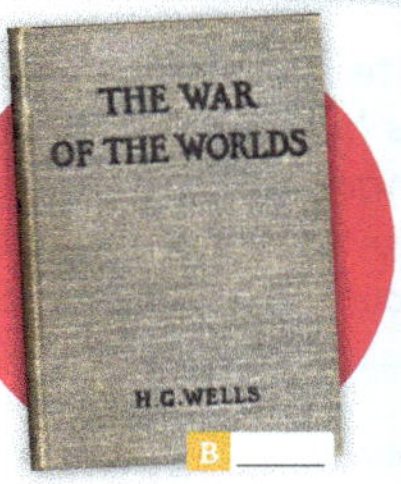

2 For many years people thought that Loch Ness, a large lake in Scotland was home to a giant creature. In 1934, a doctor, Colonel Robert Wilson, announced that he had proof that it existed. He said that while he had been driving past the lake, he had seen the monster in the water. Luckily, he had had his camera with him and had been able to take some photos. The photo fooled many people until 1984, when it was proved to be fake.

3 On the day before Halloween, in 1938, many Americans were listening to the radio when suddenly the programme was interrupted. The announcer said that aliens had invaded the world. Lots of people started to panic. They left their homes and they were going to look for somewhere safe to hide. In fact, what they had heard was the beginning of a radio play of a famous novel by HG Wells, *War of the Worlds*, which is all about an alien invasion.

TH!NK values

Reacting to jokes

7 SPEAKING **Look at the reactions of four people who believed the Loch Ness story and then found out it was just a joke. In pairs, discuss each reaction. Whose reaction do you like most? Why?**

1 'How could I believe that? I feel really stupid and embarrassed.'
2 'It's a really great story. I think it's funny that I believed it.'
3 'It is funny, but I do feel a bit silly for believing it.'
4 'Why would someone want to play such a stupid joke? It makes me angry.'

Number 1 is too serious. It was just a silly joke. It's not important …

8 SPEAKING **Work in pairs. Think of a time when you were the target of a joke. How did you feel? Do you feel differently about it now?**

I remember once my friend …
At the time I felt / I didn't think …
Now I …

9 SPEAKING **Discuss these questions in small groups.**

1 Think of a time when a joke went wrong. What was it and why did it go wrong?
2 Why do you need to be careful when thinking about playing a joke?

103

7 **Check/clarify:** *embarrassed.*

8 Give an example of your own, or a fictional example, first. Encourage students to explain the jokes and their reactions. Nominate an individual from each pair to describe the funniest story to the class.

9 Give students time to think about their answers first.

Homework

Ask students to watch a news programme and make notes on an interesting story. As a follow-up, students report back on it.

Activity idea Extension

Students think up a practical joke and share their ideas in small groups. Discuss which idea would be most believable. Alternatively, if appropriate for your class, they could research something on YouTube and then each group describes/shows it to the rest of the class. The class could vote for the best practical joke.

Critical TH!NKing
Understanding and analysing links between ideas
Compares points and arguments from different sources.

Communication
Participating with appropriate confidence and clarity
Develops a clear description or narrative with a logical sequence of points.

Communication
Managing conversations
Uses appropriate strategies to develop a conversation (e.g. showing interest; giving non-minimal responses; or asking follow-up questions).

TH!NK more

Worksheets
Project Fake or real?
Communication Making the news
Get TH!NKing *Would you want to be a journalist?*

Warmer

Read sentences using different tenses to the class and ask them to name the tenses. Then ask students to make a sentence using the tense.

1 1 believed, were 2 were 3 had been driving, had seen 4 had invaded 5 were going to

2 RULE: 2 past continuous 3 past perfect 4 past perfect continuous 5 past perfect 6 was/were going to 7 could/couldn't 8 would/wouldn't

3 Write on the board: *He said he was hungry. He told me he was hungry.* Elicit the difference (*tell* is followed by an object pronoun).
1 told 2 said 3 said 4 told 5 said 6 said 7 told 8 said, told

4 1 She told me (that) she had flown back from Africa on Friday. 2 They said (that) they had met lots of interesting people. 3 He told me (that) he was going to write a book one day. 4 You said (that) you could work for two days without sleeping. 5 They told me (that) they would call me from the airport. 6 She said (that) she was working on a really interesting story. 7 He told me [or other object] (that) he needed a holiday. 8 She told him (that) she had been writing in her diary when his text arrived.

Workbook p100

Get it Right!

say vs. *tell*

Student's Book p125

5 Elicit or explain the meaning of the words in italics.

6 1 d 2 f 3 a 4 h 5 g 6 b 7 c 8 e

7 Listen to the students' ideas and encourage open class discussion.

Workbook p102

THINK more

Workbook
Grammar p100, Ex.1–3
Vocabulary p102, Ex.1
Vocabulary Extra p103, Ex.1–2

Worksheets
Grammar Worksheets 11
Vocabulary Worksheets 11

GRAMMAR
Reported statements

1 Look at the article on page 103 again. How are these statements reported? Write down how the underlined words change.

0 I think the girls are playing a joke on me.
thought *were playing*
1 I believe the fairies are real.
______
2 The fairies are just made out of paper.
______
3 While I was driving past the lake, I saw the monster in the water.
______
4 Aliens have invaded the world.
______
5 They are going to look for somewhere safe to hide.
______

2 Use the example sentences in Exercise 1 to complete the rules.

RULE: When we report what people say, we often change the verb tenses:
- present simple → [1] *past simple*
- present continuous → [2] ______
- past simple → [3] ______
- past continuous → [4] ______
- present perfect → [5] ______
- *am/is/are going to* → [6] ______
- *can/can't* → [7] ______
- *will/won't* → [8] ______

We often use the verbs *say* and *tell* to report.
After *tell*, use an object (*me, her, them*, etc.). After *say*, don't use an object.

3 Complete the sentences with the correct form of *say* or *tell*.

0 My dad *told* me that he wanted me to tidy my room.
1 The teacher ______ us that we could go home early.
2 I ______ that I was going to phone you when I got home.
3 The weatherman ______ that it would be sunny later.
4 She ______ him that she hadn't forgotten his birthday.
5 They ______ that they were visiting their grandparents on Saturday.
6 He ______ that he had left the books on the desk for me.
7 Dad ______ us we could stay at the party until eleven.
8 He ______ that someone was following him, but I ______ him he was imagining it.

4 Rewrite these quotes as reported speech.

0 'I work really hard.' (He said ...)
He said that he worked really hard.
1 'I flew back from Africa on Friday.' (She told ...)
2 'We've met lots of interesting people.' (They said ...)
3 'I'm going to write a book one day.' (He told ...)
4 'I can work for two days without sleeping.' (You said ...)
5 'We'll call you from the airport.' (They told me ...)
6 'I'm working on a really interesting story.' (She said ...)
7 'I need a holiday.' (He told ...)
8 'I was writing in my diary when your text arrived.' (She told him ...)

→ workbook page 100

VOCABULARY
Fun

5 Read the sentences and think of a sentence to follow each one to explain the meaning of the word in italics.

1 The English summer course was *fun*. ☐
2 I love Steve. He's *hilarious*. ☐
3 Why is everyone *laughing at* me? ☐
4 I don't *get* that *joke*. ☐
5 We *played* a *joke* on him. ☐
6 I'm rubbish at *telling jokes*. ☐
7 I'm not sure she liked you *making fun* of her. ☐
8 That's not *funny* at all. ☐

6 Match sentences a–h with sentences 1–8 from Exercise 5.

a Did I say something silly?
b I always forget the endings.
c She seems quite upset.
d I made loads of new friends there.
e Please don't do it again.
f I mean he's really, really funny.
g But I'm not sure he thought it was funny.
h Can someone explain it to me?

7 SPEAKING **Discuss these questions in pairs.**

1 Who's the funniest person you know?
2 Are you good at telling jokes? Why or why not?
3 Do you always get jokes? What do you do when you don't understand?
4 Have you ever played a good joke on someone? What was it?
5 What's the funniest thing you have ever done?

→ workbook page 102

104

Language note Reported statements

1 Point out that the past perfect doesn't change in reported speech.

2 Remind students that pronouns may also need to be changed in reported speech, e.g., *these – those, this – that, here – there*, as well as some time phrases, e.g., *last night – the night before, tonight – that night, next week – the following week.*

Activity idea Extension

Tell students the following jokes or different ones of your choice: Joke 1 – A man walks into a library, goes up to the librarian and says, 'I'll have a cheeseburger and chips, please.' The librarian responds, 'Sir, this is a library.' The man says, 'Oh, sorry. [in a whisper] I'll have a cheeseburger and chips, please.' Joke 2 – What did one eye say to the other eye? – Don't look now but something between us smells. Hold a class vote to decide which joke students thought was the funniest.

Writing; Listening; WordWise

8 Remind students to use reported speech and to think carefully about how each tense changes.

9 Elicit weather vocabulary. Say the words for students to repeat and check pronunciation. Tell students that *tornado*, *blizzard*, *flood* and *hailstorm* are examples of extreme weather.
1 wind 2 snow 3 rain 4 ice

10 🔊 **11.02**
All photos ticked. A weather journalist reports when the weather is extreme enough to be a news story. A weatherman studies and predicts the weather.

11 🔊 **11.02** Give students two minutes to look at the pictures and to think about which key information they will need to listen for to answer the questions.
1 B 2 A 3 A 4 C

12 Ask students to think of any words that could go after *make*. Write any correct answers on the board.
1 up 2 difference 3 angry 4 fun 5 friends

13 1 make … difference 2 make friends 3 make fun 4 make … up 5 make … angry

Workbook p102

Homework

Ask students to write six true sentences using the expressions with *make* from the lesson.

WRITING
A news report

8 **Choose one of the headlines below and write a short news report for it. Try to include two examples of reported speech.**

FOUND – THE WORLD'S FUNNIEST JOKE

GOOD JOKE GOES WRONG

LISTENING

9 **Which of these words do you associate with the extreme weather conditions in the photos?**

ice | rain | snow | wind

1 tornado

2 blizzard

3 flood

4 hailstorm

10 🔊 11.02 **Warren Faidley is an extreme weather journalist. Listen and say the types of weather in Exercise 9 that he reports on. Then answer the question.**

What is the difference between a weatherman and a weather journalist?

11 🔊 11.02 **Listen again. For each question, choose the correct answer.**

1 How did he escape from the river when he was 12?

2 What danger did he escape from with his father when he was a child?

3 Which of these photos gave Faidley his lucky break?

4 Which of these is the charity that Faidley has started?

WordWise: Expressions with *make*

12 **Complete the expressions from the unit so far with a word from the list.**

angry | difference | friends | fun | up

1 Fake news is used to make ______ stories that try to change what we believe.
2 These days fake news can make a big ______ to the world.
3 Why would someone want to play such a stupid joke? It makes me ______.
4 I'm not sure she liked you making ______ of her.
5 I made loads of new ______ there.

13 **Complete the sentences with *make* + another word.**

1 Doing a lot of exercise can ______ a ______ to your health.
2 When you move to a new school, it can be difficult to ____________ with people.
3 It isn't very nice to ____________ of other people.
4 Is that story really true? Or did you ______ it ______?
5 Those newspaper stories are not accurate. They really ______ me ______.

→ workbook page 102

Activity idea Extension

If your students need a little more support with reported speech, read out these statements (or others of your choice): *My brother is going on holiday next week. I play football every Tuesday. My sister can speak six languages.*

Write *My teacher said …* three times on the board and ask students to work with a partner and complete the sentences with the information you gave them. Monitor to see how students are getting on and to remind them to think carefully about the tense. Elicit: *My teacher said his/her brother was going on holiday next week. My teacher said he/she played football every Tuesday. My teacher said his/her sister could speak six languages.*

Activity idea Extension

Ask students to write a short joke in English. Ask individual students to read their jokes to the class. Take a vote on whose joke is the funniest.

THINK more

Workbook
Developing Writing p105
Listening p106, Ex.1–3
WordWise p102, Ex.4–6

Warmer

Tell students they are going to interview you about your specialist subject: English! Give them two minutes to work in pairs and think of questions to ask you. Answer their questions.

1. Give students time to prepare. Students can invent something if they have no particular specialist subject.
2. Tell students that they should talk for at least two minutes without being interrupted.
3. 11.03 Give students a time limit of two minutes and tell them not to try to understand every word, but to focus only on finding the three names.
   1 a 2 c 3 b
4. Before reading, ask students to underline the key information in the sentences that they need to find in the text.
   The interviewer asks Professor Kelly a question about Korean politics.
   Professor Kelly's daughter comes into the room.
   The interviewer mentions the professor's child.
   Professor Kelly tries to keep his daughter away from the camera.
   Professor Kelly's baby son comes into the room.
   Professor Kelly tries to keep calm and answer the question.
   The professor's wife comes into the room.
   The professor's wife closes the door.
   Professor Kelly says sorry for the interruption.

READING

1 **Imagine you are going to be interviewed by a journalist on a TV programme about a subject you knew a lot about. Read and answer the questions. Make notes.**

1 What is your specialist subject?
Arsenal
2 What do you know about it?
all the players, the history of the club

2 SPEAKING **Work in pairs. Tell your partner about your specialist subject and what you can say about it.**

My specialist subject is Arsenal. I can tell you about all the players. I can tell you where they are from, how old they are …

3 11.03 **Read and listen to the article. Match the people with the descriptions.**

1	☐ Robert E Kelly	a	an expert
2	☐ James Menendez	b	a wife
3	☐ Jung-a Kim	c	a journalist

4 **Read the article again. Put the events in the order they happened. Write 1–9 in the boxes.**

☐ The interviewer mentions the professor's child.
☐ Professor Kelly's daughter comes into the room.
☐ Professor Kelly's baby son comes into the room.
☐ Professor Kelly says sorry for the interruption.
☐ The professor's wife closes the door.
☐ Professor Kelly tries to keep his daughter away from the camera.
☐ The interviewer asks Professor Kelly a question about Korean politics.
☐ Professor Kelly tries to keep calm and answer the question.
☐ The professor's wife comes into the room.

THE DANGER OF LIVE TV

Live interviews can be a dangerous thing. Over the years, many live news reports have been interrupted by people who want to get their faces on TV. Sometimes the journalists stop their reports and tell the people to go away, but most of the time they just carry on professionally and pay no attention to what's happening behind them.

As technology gets better, more and more TV interviews are done using communication software such as Skype©. An interviewer in the TV studio can interview someone who is sitting at their computer in their own home. It's a lot safer, you might think. Problems are rare and the interviews often go well. But things don't always go quite as planned. Just ask Professor Robert E. Kelly, an American politics professor at a South Korean university.

One day, Professor Kelly was being interviewed live on the BBC. He was speaking from his home in Busan, South Korea, where he had set up his computer in his home office.

The interviewer, James Menendez, was asking him to explain recent political events in the region. Suddenly the door behind him opened and Dr Kelly's young daughter, Marion, came in and danced her way over to her father. The interviewer mentioned that they had been joined by one of the professor's children, and as Dr Kelly put his arm out to try and stop his daughter from coming any closer, they were joined by another of his children. This time it was his baby son, James, who entered the room in a baby walker and rolled across the floor behind the professor. Dr Kelly tried to keep calm and carry on talking. He wanted his children to leave the room, but he couldn't stop the interview. Seconds later, Dr Kelly's wife, Jung-a Kim, came running into the room to his rescue. She grabbed one child in each hand and dragged them out of the room while the professor continued to offer his apologies. Finally, his wife reappeared on her hands and knees – trying to avoid being seen by the webcamera – to close the door behind her. Very embarrassed, Dr Kelly apologised and the interview continued.

Of course, this 40 seconds of live action was soon uploaded on to the internet and watched by millions all over the world, and immediately the professor, his wife and children became very famous. Indeed, the next time Professor Kelly was on the BBC, they wanted to interview Jung-a Kim, Marion and James, too.

106

Activity idea Extension

In pairs, get students to discuss funny things they've seen go wrong on live TV or on the internet. You may like to give an example from your own experience to get students started on this exercise. At the end, listen to some of the students' ideas and encourage open class discussion.

TH!NK more

Workbook
Reading p104, Ex.1–3

Grammar; Vocabulary; Speaking; Pronunciation

▶ 32 Grammar rap!
Verb patterns: object + infinitive

5 During feedback, pay attention to the word order and the use of the object pronoun and base form.
1 The journalists tell the people to go away. 2 The interviewer was asking him to explain recent political events. 3 He wanted his children to leave the room.
RULE: 4 pronoun 5 infinitive

6 2 Can you pick the paper up, please? / Please pick the paper up.
3 Can you switch off the lights, please? / Please switch off the lights.
4 Can you be quiet, please? / Please be quiet.

7 Students' own answers

8 1 warn 2 remind 3 allow 4 encourage 5 persuade 6 want 7 invite

9 1 (You/She/He/They) warned (me/her/him/us) to slow down. 2 (You) reminded (me) to watch the programme. 3 (You) allowed (me) to go to the party. 4 (You) encouraged (me) to enter the talent show. 5 (You) persuaded (me) to take (you) to the concert. 6 (You) wanted (me) to play in the school tennis team. 7 (You) invited (me) to go to the cinema.

Workbook p102

10 Give students some examples from your own experience if necessary.

11 Encourage students to go into detail and give examples.

12 During feedback, listen to some of the students' examples and decide who wants the most from their parents.

Pronunciation
Intonation: rude or polite?

Student's Book p121

Homework
Ask students to write five sentences reporting some of the things their parents say to them at home, e.g., *My dad persuaded me to take the dog for a walk.* They can share these in the next lesson.

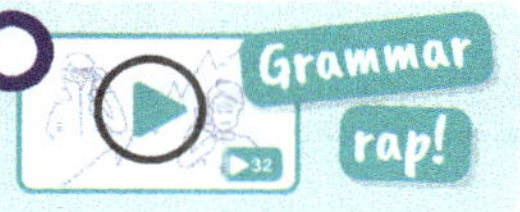

GRAMMAR
Verb patterns: object + infinitive

5 Put the words in order to make sentences from the text. Then complete the rule.

1 tell / the / away / people / the journalists / to / go
2 asking / was / him / recent political / explain / the interviewer / events / to
3 the / he / leave / his / children / to / wanted / room

RULE: Some verbs (*ask, want, tell*) are followed by an object (noun or personal [4]______) and the [5]______ form of the verb.
Mum asked me to tidy my room.

6 Look at pictures 1–4. What does the teacher ask the students to do? Write sentences.

1 *Can you hand out the books, please?*
2 ______
3 ______
4 ______

7 Work in pairs. Take turns to report the sentences in Exercise 6. Use *tell* and *ask*.

He asked her to hand out the books.

→ workbook page 101

VOCABULARY
More verbs with object + infinitive

8 Read what the people say. Match each one with a verb from the list.

allow | encourage | ~~expect~~ | invite
persuade | remind | want | warn

0 'We think you should spend more time on your homework.' *expect*
1 'Slow down. You're going to crash.' ______
2 'Don't forget to watch the programme.' ______
3 'OK, you can go to the party.' ______
4 'You should definitely enter the talent show. You're a really good singer.' ______
5 'Take me to the Ed Sheeran concert – please. I'll be really good. I promise. You will? Oh, thank you!' ______
6 'I've chosen you to play in the school tennis team.' ______
7 'Would you like to go to the cinema?' ______

9 Rewrite the sentences in Exercise 8 with the verbs you matched to each one.

They expected me to spend more time on my homework.

→ workbook page 102

SPEAKING

10 Think about these things. Make notes about them.
1 Two things your parents allow you to do.
2 Two things your parents expect you to do.
3 Two things your parents warn you not to do.

11 Work in pairs. Talk about your notes from Exercise 10.

12 Now discuss these things with your partner.
1 Two things you expect your parents to do for you.
2 Two things you don't expect your parents to do for you any more.
3 Two things you expect your parents to do your whole life – even if you don't want them to.

PRONUNCIATION
Intonation: rude or polite? Go to page 121.

Language note
Tell students that we use many other verbs to report speech, as the information they give makes sentences sound more interesting than always using *say* and *tell*.
Tell students to decide which is the main verb in each sentence that they need to report. Point out that *him* in the answers could be replaced by *her/me/us*.

Activity idea Extension
Student A makes a statement which Student B reports to Student C using reported speech. Student B then makes a statement for C to report to A.

TH!NK more

Practice Extra	Workbook	Worksheets
Unit 11 Practise it!	Grammar p101, Ex.4–7 Vocabulary p102, Ex.2–3 Pronunciation p121	Grammar Worksheets 11 Grammar rap! Verb patterns: object and infinitive Vocabulary Worksheets 11

Developing Speaking; Phrases for fluency; Functions

Warmer

Ask students how often they post on social media. Find out who posts the most every day and elicit different reasons for posting. Ask: *Has anyone seen a post recently that made you angry?*

1 🔊 **11.06** Tell students to cover the dialogue and discuss the question in pairs before reading to check their answers.
They're looking at a tweet about a school football match yesterday.

2 *1 Because Sam Johnson was rude about her brother.*
2 He doesn't think he's good enough to be in the school team.
3 That she's really cross and that Sam tweeted something untrue about her brother
4 Tony persuades her to stick to the facts rather than get emotional.

3 At the end of the exercise, listen to some of the students' ideas and encourage open class discussion.

4 Write the underlined expressions on the board. Ask students for an L1 translation before they complete the dialogue in English. Students could act out the dialogue in pairs.
1 check this out 2 he was like 3 have a word 4 I'm just saying 5 we're talking about 6 It's not worth it

5 As an alternative, you could ask students to cover the Key Language box and try to guess what key words complete the sentences.
1 makes me really cross/angry 2 I hate 3 got so angry

6 Give a couple of your own ideas as examples before students write their lists.

7 Encourage students to use the phrases in Exercise 5 as a model.

DEVELOPING SPEAKING

1 🔊 11.06 **Look at the photo. What do you think they are looking at? Listen and read to check.**

Tony: Hey, Sandra. Check this out. It's a tweet from Sam Johnson, and it's about your brother, Mark.
Sandra: Really? Let me see. 'Our match against Charlton school yesterday finished 1–1. We didn't win because Mark Smith missed an easy goal. Don't even know why he's in the team.' What! That's unfair. And I know for a fact that Mark scored our only goal. I'm going to have a word with Sam.
Tony: No, don't do that. It's not worth it.
Sandra: But it makes me so angry! Sam can't just post whatever he wants to post. Look, he's over there. I'm going to talk to him. Hey, Sam.
Sam: What's up? Oh, I think I know. My tweet about your brother, I guess.
Sandra: Well, yes. Why did you write that? And why didn't you say that he actually scored a goal?
Sam: I can write what I want. And anyway, I don't think your brother's a good player.
Tony: But we're talking about being truthful. He scored the goal. I think that's probably more important than his miss.
Sam: I'm just saying he isn't a good footballer. That's the truth. Get over it.
Tony: And he walks away! Incredible.
Sandra: OK, I'm going to write a tweet now. Here we go. 'I'm really cross! Sam Johnson tweeted something completely untrue about my brother. I think it's because he's jealous.'
Tony: No, Sandra. Don't say you're angry. Just tell people what he said.
Sandra: You're right. I'll change it. 'I asked Sam Johnson why he tweeted something untrue and unfair about my brother. He was like, "It just came into my head and I wrote it." Any thoughts, guys? Let me know!'
Tony: That's it. Let's see what your friends think. Look – someone's already replied.

2 **Read the dialogue again and answer the questions.**
1 Why is Sandra upset about Sam's tweet?
2 What does Sam think about Mark?
3 What does Sandra want to say in her first tweet?
4 Why does she change her mind about what to write?

3 SPEAKING **Discuss the questions in pairs.**
1 Is Sandra right to be angry?
2 Is Sam's reason for his tweet a good reason?
3 Which of Sandra's tweets is best, and why?
4 Should people always be truthful in their messages?

Phrases for fluency

4 **Find the underlined expressions in the dialogue and use them to complete the conversation.**
A Hi, [1]__________! It's my new basketball kit.
B Oh, nice. I wish I could play in the next match.
A Did you talk to Alex about it?
B Yes. But [2]__________, 'No way, you can't play and that's that.'
A Really? That's bad. Should I [3]__________ with him?
B No, it's OK, thanks.
A [4]__________, he shouldn't treat people like that.
B Hmm, but [5]__________ a guy who thinks he is better than everyone else.
A Well, you never know.
B [6]__________. He won't listen to you.

FUNCTIONS
Expressing feelings: anger

KEY LANGUAGE
I get so angry … I hate it …
It makes me really cross / angry …

5 **Complete the mini-dialogues using the phrases from the Key Language box. Use the correct form of the verbs.**
1 **Jorge** What's wrong Emily?
Emily My sister has been reading my texts. It ______ when she does that!
2 **Haruto** ______ it when people don't listen to what I'm saying!
Ethan Me, too! It's so annoying.
3 **Lena** What's up, Isabel?
Isabel My mum said I can't go to the party tomorrow. I ______ when she told me, but now I feel bad.

6 **Make a list of the top three things that make you angry. Write sentences using the phrases in Exercise 5.**
I get so angry when my brother takes my things.

7 SPEAKING **Work in pairs. Tell each other about the things on your lists.**

108

Activity idea Extension

In pairs, ask students to use their ideas from Exercise 6 to create a mini-dialogue. Allow students six to eight minutes to prepare their role plays. Monitor to make sure all students are on task. Encourage them to use the key language. If students have access to a recording facility (using their mobile phones, for example), they could record their conversation and play it back to check their own pronunciation and intonation. They can then repeat the exercise and listen for improvements.

Life Competencies

Warmer

Draw a line on the board. Write *Passive* at one end and *Aggressive* at the other. Discuss the meanings of the words and ask if they are positive or negative. Try to elicit *Assertive* and ask where they would put it on the line. Ask students to decide where they would be on the line and compare with a partner.

▶ 33 Life Lessons: Being assertive

1 ▶33
The soup was cold.

2 ▶33 Ask students to try to answer the questions from memory before watching the video again to check.
1 Kieran's mum
2 Her dad said it wasn't good enough.
3 He apologised to Kieran's mum and took the soup back to the kitchen.
4 The difference between being assertive, passive and aggressive.

3 Do the first question with the whole class as an example.
1 a aggressive, b passive, c assertive
2 a passive, b assertive, c aggressive
3 a passive, b aggressive, c assertive
4 a aggressive, b passive , c assertive
5 a aggressive, b assertive, c passive

4 If you are short of time, each pair could act out the situations being either passive, aggressive or assertive rather than all three. Remind them that it's both the language and the way it's spoken that will determine how they come across. Monitor to make sure all students are on task.

5 You may like to give an example of your own to get students started on this exercise.

6 As a follow-up, have a class discussion. Try to agree on who is the best at being assertive. The class could think of some more tips to help less assertive students.

LIFE COMPETENCIES

Being assertive is making sure you say clearly what you want or think but respect what other people think, too. Being passive or aggressive hurts either you or the people around you, but being assertive means you let people know what's important to you, which is more likely to have positive results for everyone.

1 ▶33 **Watch the video. What was the problem with the meal?**

2 ▶33 **Watch again and answer the questions.**
1 Who wanted to talk to the waiter?
2 Why was Kieran's sister embarrassed?
3 How did the waiter react?
4 What did Kieran learn from the experience?

3 **Read the following situations. Decide which answer is passive, which is aggressive and which is assertive.**
1 A classmate wants to copy your homework.
a Say no, and, in front of the whole class, shout, 'Somebody's not clever enough to do the homework!'
b Give the classmate your homework. They might say bad things about you if you don't.
c Say no, and explain why you don't think it's right to let them copy your work.
2 Your best friend promises to call you but doesn't.
a Feel hurt, but don't say anything about it.
b Call your friend and say, 'You said you were going to call me. Is everything OK?'
c Be angry with your friend without saying why and stop talking to them.
3 You are in class and you don't understand what the teacher has asked you to do.
a Sit and wait to see what the others do.
b Start talking to your friends.
c Put your hand up and say, 'Sorry, I didn't understand. Can you please explain again?'
4 You need to ask permission from your parents to stay out late.
a Just stay out late and tell your parents that you didn't see the time.
b Don't ask. They never give you permission to do anything, so why ask?
c Tell your parents what time the film you want to see finishes, and ask to go.
5 You're in a bookshop looking for a book you want, but you can't find it.
a Say, 'I can't find anything here! I'm going to a better shop.'
b Ask the shop assistant to help you find the book.
c Look on all the shelves again. You don't want to ask for help and look silly.

Me and my world

4 SPEAKING **Work in pairs. Act out one of these situations three times – once being passive, once being aggressive and once being assertive.**
- You're working on a group project, but you are doing much more work than the other members of the group.
- You need your parents to sign a permission form for a school trip, but they haven't signed it yet.
- You're leaving a shop and notice that you have paid twice for something.

5 SPEAKING **Act out your situation for another pair, but don't tell them if you are being passive, aggressive or assertive. After you finish, the other pair guesses which one you are acting.**

6 SPEAKING **Work in small groups. Talk about a situation in your life when you should have been more assertive.**

TIPS FOR BEING ASSERTIVE

- **Remember that having a different point of view doesn't mean you are right and the other person is wrong.**
- **Be honest and tell others how you feel or what you want.**
- **Look at the other person and speak in a normal voice.**

Homework

Ask students to keep a note of when they have been passive, aggressive or assertive between now and the next class. Ask them to write a sentence for each situation and, if they were aggressive or passive, say what they could have done differently.

Emotional Development
Managing own emotions
Dealing with praise, setback and criticism.

Emotional Development
Empathy and relationship skills
Stating opposing opinions in a respectful way.

TH!NK more

Practice Extra
Unit 11 Master it!

Worksheets
Life Lessons: Being assertive

Tests
Unit, extension and skills test 11

Warmer

Write the word *freedom* on the board. Nominate individuals to describe what they understand by *freedom*. Write *Are you free to do anything you want?* on the board and discuss some ideas.

▶ 34 Get TH!NKing

Play the video and discuss the question with your class.

1 Check/clarify: *hang out with.* You may like to give your own example from the list to get students started on this exercise.

2–3 In pairs, ask students to think of five examples for each (at home and at school) and to rank the school rules in order of strictness. At the end of the exercise, listen to some of the students' ideas, encourage open class discussion and come up with a definitive list.

4 At the end of the exercise, listen to some of the students' ideas and encourage open class discussion. Who has the strictest rules in their life?

5 Ask students to cover the article on page 111 and just look at the pictures. In pairs, give students two minutes to think about the answer to the question. Give students another two minutes to read the article quickly and check ideas. Encourage them not to focus on every word for now.

6 🔊 **12.01**
A Greek B both C both D Aztec

12 RULES AND REGULATIONS

OBJECTIVES

FUNCTIONS: talking about permission; following and giving simple instructions

GRAMMAR: *be allowed to / let*; third conditional

VOCABULARY: discipline; consequences and reasons

Get TH!NKING
Watch the video and think: what rules in life are the most important?

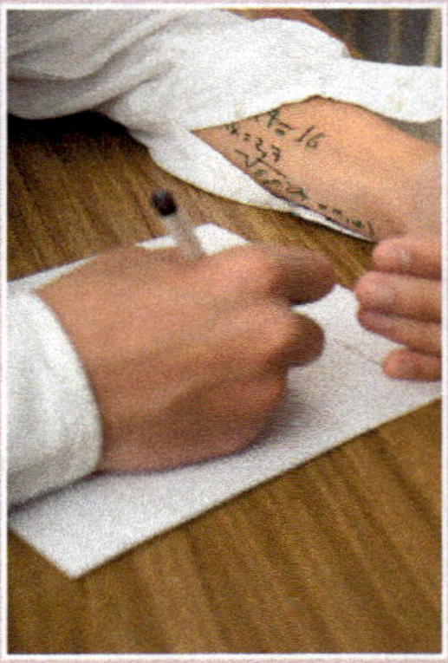

READING

1 **Look at this list. Put a tick (✓) if it's something you can do. Put a cross (✗) if it's something you can't do.**

- ☐ stay up late at weekends
- ☐ invite friends to your home
- ☐ watch any TV programme you want
- ☐ wear any clothes you want at home
- ☐ wear any clothes you want to school
- ☐ use your mobile phone at school
- ☐ listen to music in your bedroom
- ☐ hang out with your friends in town

2 **Now look at the photos. What are the rules like at your school about the things you can see?**

3 **What other things can you think of that you can or can't do at home or at school?**

4 SPEAKING **Discuss with a partner. Who has stricter rules in their life?**

5 **Look at the pictures with the article on the next page. In what way did these children have a hard life?**

6 🔊 12.01 **Read and listen to the article to check your ideas. Under each picture write *Greek, Aztec* or *both*.**

7 **Read the article again and complete the sentences. Use between one and three words.**

1 Ancient Greek parents had ________ to decide if they wanted to keep their babies.
2 Unwanted babies often became ________ .
3 Unlike Greek girls, Greek boys ________ .
4 At military school Greek boys often didn't have ________ to eat.
5 Aztec children who broke the rules received ________ .
6 Ancient Aztecs thought education ________ .
7 Aztec boys and girls ________ to the same school.
8 *Calmecac* schools were for children from ________ .

110

7 Check/clarify: *to get rid of, slave, punishments, unwanted.*
Before reading again, ask students to think about the type of word (noun, verb, etc.) that could go in each gap.
1 five days 2 slaves 3 went to school 4 much food / enough 5 nasty punishments 6 was important 7 didn't go 8 important families

Objectives

Functions and speaking Talking about permission; following and giving simple instructions
Grammar *be allowed to / let*; third conditional
Vocabulary Discipline; consequences and reasons
Values The importance of rules
Train to TH!NK Being creative

Resources for this unit

All available online

Videos
- Get **TH!NK**ing: *What rules in life are the most important?*
- Grammar rap: Third conditional
- Culture: Laws from around the world

Tests
- Unit, extension and skill test 12
- Final test

Worksheets
- Grammar and vocabulary: Basic, Standard and Extension Worksheets
- Project: Making the rules
- Communication: Playing by the rules
- Literature Worksheets: *Much Ado About Nothing*
- Grammar presentation: Third conditional
- Get **TH!NK**ing and Grammar rap! video worksheets

Reading; TH!NK Values

Culture notes

Ancient Greece is the name given to a period of Greek history from 800 BCE to AD 600 [or 600 CE]. In this period, Greece made huge advances in politics, philosophy, architecture, education and science. Greek culture and philosophy had a powerful influence on Roman culture and formed the basis for western civilisation.

The Aztecs were ethnic groups of central and southern Mexico. The Aztec Empire was an efficient social, political, religious and commercial organisation which dominated Central America from the 14th to 16th centuries. The Aztecs built magnificent temples and palaces, some of which are still standing today.

Telpochcalli were Aztec schools attended by teenagers (from age 15 onwards) from the lower classes. Students were taught to serve their community or to become a soldier. The school day started with a cold bath and was largely spent memorising songs or learning how to use weapons. Naughty students were punished with beatings or told to sweep the streets at night, which was considered worse than a beating.

Calmecac were Aztec schools for the upper classes. Students were trained to be priests, judges and teachers.

8 If necessary, elicit or explain that *not allowed to* means *to not have permission* and *let* means *to give permission*. Tell them these words will be covered later in this unit.

1 d 2 b 3 a 4 c

9 Before this exercise, you may need to teach some vocabulary for punishments, e.g., *to be suspended from school* (told to stay at home for a period of time), *to be expelled from school* (told to leave permanently), *to be given a fine*, *to be put in prison*, etc.

HARD TIMES TO BE A KID

'I'm not allowed to stay out late.'
'Why do I have to do my homework before I can watch TV?'
'My parents never let me go to parties.'
'Why is it just Mum and Dad who make the rules? Life's just not fair.'

Do these complaints sound familiar? Well, if you think your life is hard, you might like to think about kids in ancient times. For some of them, life was really hard.

If you were born in Ancient Greece, you weren't even thought to be a real person until you'd been alive for five days. That's right – for five days after you were born, your parents were allowed to get rid of you. If they decided they didn't want you, they'd just leave you outside somewhere to die. Of course, you might get lucky and someone else might pick you up, but then you'd spend the rest of your life as their slave. However, if your parents decided that they wanted you as part of the family, then there was a special ceremony to welcome you.

Only the boys were allowed to go to school. Greek girls stayed at home, where their mothers taught them skills like cooking and weaving – things that would help them find a husband.

At the age of seven, some boys were sent away to very strict military schools, where they were taught how to become soldiers. Life was pretty hard at these schools. For example, the kids were often hungry. The teachers didn't let them have much food – for a reason. They wanted the boys to learn how to survive for themselves by stealing food. But if they got caught, they were punished.

Aztec children in Mesoamerica also had a difficult life in ancient times. If they broke any rules, they could expect some pretty nasty punishments.

On the plus side, Aztecs really believed in the importance of schooling. In the home, children learned practical skills: fathers taught their sons how to fish and farm while mothers taught their daughters home-making skills. Girls and boys also went to school (although the adults didn't let them go to the same schools).

Kids went to schools called *telpochcalli*. They had lessons about history, religion and music. The boys also had lessons in how to fight. If the children were from a more important family, they went to a *calmecac*, where they learned how to read and write, too.

At both schools children had to be on their best behaviour. They knew all about the punishments for behaving badly, and life was hard enough anyway.

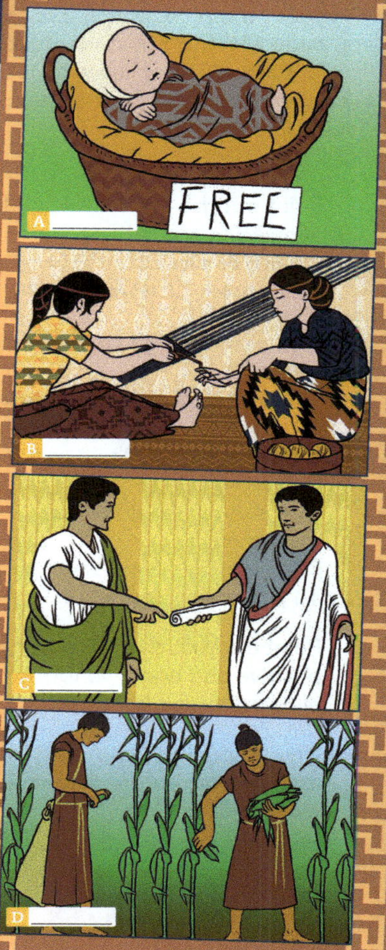

TH!NK values

The importance of rules

8 Read the statements 1–4 and say what type of rule they are.

1 You're not allowed to ride bikes on the pavements.
2 Our parents don't let us leave the dinner table before everyone has finished.
3 I make sure that I tidy my room every weekend.
4 You can't ask a question unless you put your hand up.

a a personal rule
b a family rule
c a school rule
d a rule of society

9 SPEAKING **Work in pairs. Think of more rules (at least one each) for the four types (personal, family, school, society). What is the punishment for breaking these rules?**

111

Homework

Ask students to research jobs that children used to do and write a few sentences for discussion. Which was the worst job?

Activity idea Extension

Separate the class into Greeks and Aztecs and ask students to imagine they meet in a time machine and discuss their lives. Students should compete to prove they have the worst life!

TH!NK more

Worksheets
Project Making the rules
Communication Playing by the rules
Get **TH!NK**ing *What rules in life are the most important?*

Social Responsibilities
Understanding personal responsibilities as part of a group and in society – including citizenship
Is aware of positive behaviour in different groups (e.g. class, home and with friends).

Warmer

Read out the phrases in Exercise 1 on page 110 and ask students to complete the sentences with *You can/can't*, e.g., *You can't listen to … music in your bedroom.*

1 Point out the words which follow *allowed to* and *let*.
RULE: 5 be allowed to 6 be 7 verb 8 let/not let 9 let/not let

2 1 My parents didn't let me go to the party.
2 I wasn't allowed to walk to school on my own until I was 12.
3 The teacher doesn't let us text in class.
4 I'm allowed to play my dad's electric guitar.
5 Dad lets my sister stay up until 11 pm on Saturday nights.

3 Point out that they can use both positive and negative forms of *allowed to* and *let*.

4 Give a couple of your own ideas as examples before students work in pairs.

Workbook p108

Get it Right!
let vs. make

Student's Book p126

5 Tell a story about a naughty thing you did as a child and the punishment.
1 d 2 a 3 f 4 b 5 c 6 e

6 **Check/clarify:** *rebel* /'reb əl/.
1 punished / told off / into trouble
2 behaves well / does what he's told
3 did what she was told / behaved well
4 punished / into trouble / told off
5 to break the rules 6 punished / into trouble / told off

GRAMMAR
be allowed to / let

1 **Look at the example sentences. Then complete the rules with *be allowed to* and *let*.**

1 I'm not allowed to stay out late.
2 My parents never let me go to parties.
3 For five days after you were born, your parents were allowed to get rid of you.
4 The teachers didn't let them have much food.

> RULE: To talk about permission we can use ***be allowed to*** and ***let***.
> We use [5]______ when there's no need to identify who gives (or doesn't give) the permission. The subject of the sentence is the person who receives (or doesn't receive) the permission.
> Form this with subject + [6]______ (*not*) + ***allowed to*** + [7]______. It is a passive construction.
> We use [8]______ when the subject of the sentence is (or isn't) giving the permission.
> Form this with subject + [9]______ + [person] + verb.

2 **Rewrite the sentence using the words in brackets.**

0 My parents don't let me go out on school nights. (I / allowed)
I'm not allowed to go out on school nights.
1 I wasn't allowed to go to the party. (My parents / let)
2 My mum didn't let me walk to school on my own until I was 12. (/ allowed)
3 We aren't allowed to text in class. (The teacher / let)
4 My dad lets me play his electric guitar. (I / allowed)
5 My sister is allowed to stay up until 11 pm on Saturday nights. (Dad / let)

3 **Choose three of the things in the list and write two true sentences and one false sentence about yourself.**

- play video games every day for as long as I want
- watch TV before school
- use my mobile during dinner
- go to the cinema by myself
- buy my own clothes
- meet my friends on a school night

4 SPEAKING **Work in pairs. Read out your sentences. Can your partner guess which sentence isn't true?**

My parents let me go out on a school night.
That isn't true.

→ workbook page 108

VOCABULARY
Discipline

5 **Match the phrases 1–6 with the definitions a–f.**

1 to do what you're told ☐
2 to behave well ☐
3 to get punished ☐
4 to break the rules ☐
5 to get into trouble ☐
6 to get told off ☐

a to be good by acting in the correct way
b to do something you shouldn't do
c to have problems because you did something wrong
d to follow the rules that others make
e to be told that what you did was wrong
f to be made to do something you don't want to do because you did something wrong

6 **Complete the sentences with phrases from Exercise 5. Sometimes there is more than one possible answer.**

1 My sister Claire breaks all the school rules, so she always gets ______.
2 Kenny always ______ in class. The teacher thinks he's perfect.
3 Ana doesn't often listen to her parents. Her mum and dad would be a lot happier if sometimes she ______.
4 My little brother Stan is really naughty. He's always getting ______.
5 Julia's a rebel. She likes ______.
6 If I don't behave well, I usually get ______.

7 **Which of the children in Exercise 6 do you think these pictures show?**

8 SPEAKING **Which sentences are true for you? Compare with your partner.**

- I always do what I'm told.
- I often get told off by my parents and teachers.
- I'm always getting into trouble.
- I never break the rules. I think rules are important!
- I think people should get punished for bad behaviour.
- If you behave well all the time, it's boring!

→ workbook page 110

112

7 A 2 B 3, 4, 6 C 5

8 Encourage students to use language from the exercise.

Workbook p110

Language note *be allowed to / let*

Students may produce incorrect statements like *My dad lets me to stay out late.* Remind them that in English we don't use *to* after the expression *let someone*. Students may also produce incorrect statements like *I'm allowed stay out late.* The expression *allow someone* is always followed by the infinitive with *to*.

TH!NK more

Workbook
Grammar p108, Ex.1–5
Vocabulary p110, Ex.1–3
Vocabulary Extra p111, Ex.1–2

Worksheets
Grammar Worksheets 12
Vocabulary Worksheets 12

9 Check/clarify: *strategy, board, pawns, rooks, knights, bishops, king, queen, diagonally, sideways, checkmate.*
Ask students if they know which game the words are all common to.

10 12.02 Tell students just to try and get a general understanding of the game.
Students' own answers King, queen, knight, bishop, rook, pawn

11 12.02
1 take the other player's pieces and take their king 2 They can move forwards two squares. 3 They can move over other pieces. 4 It's the end of the game. 5 white 6 You can make it into a queen, a rook, a knight or a bishop.

12 Elicit the names of simple games that students can play. Write some on the board and choose four that a lot of students know. Divide the class into four groups and assign a different game to each group (A–D). Students work with a partner from the same group A/A, B/B, etc. and decide on the best way to answer the questions and make notes.

13 Divide the class into pairs. Students take it in turns to describe their games – this gives students a chance to speak at length without interruption.

14 Elicit some names for the chess pieces and hold a class vote.

15 To make the exercise easier, revise some prepositions of movement, e.g., *forwards, sideways, up and down.*

16 Allow students to use colour to make their pieces differ from a traditional set.

17 Listen to the students' ideas and encourage open class discussion.

LISTENING

9 SPEAKING **What do you know about the game of chess? Discuss with a partner.**

10 12.02 **Listen to Lucia talking about chess and look at the chessboard. What are the different pieces called?**

11 12.02 **Listen again and answer the questions.**

1 What is the aim of the game?
2 What can pawns do on their first move?
3 What can the knights do that other pieces can't?
4 What happens if a king is in 'checkmate'?
5 Which colour starts the game?
6 What happens if the pawn reaches the other side of the board?

FUNCTIONS
Following and giving simple instructions

12 **Think of a simple game you like to play that needs two or more people. Answer the questions and make notes.**

- What do you need to play? Dice? Cards?
- How many players are needed to play the game?
- How do the players know when it is their turn to play?
- Do the players score points? If yes, how?
- What are the players *not* allowed to do?

13 SPEAKING **Work in pairs. Describe to each other how to play your game.**

Before you start, ...	Then ...
So how do you play/win?	Finally, ...
The player who ...	First ...

Train to TH!NK
Being creative

14 **Look at the chess pieces. What do you think they could be called?**

I think number one could be a dragon.

15 **In pairs, talk about the pieces.**
1 What moves can they make?
2 What 'special' powers do they have?

16 **Now think of three different chess pieces. Make notes and design them. Think about what they look like and how they can move.**

17 SPEAKING **Show your pieces to your classmates and discuss your ideas.**

Mine moves around other pieces.

Homework
Ask students to write sentences describing the different rules that they have to adhere to with their parents and their grandparents, e.g., *My parents don't let me eat chocolate after dinner. My grandparents let me eat chocolate at any time.*

Activity idea Extension
In small groups, ask students to discuss favourite games that they played as a child. They could be board games, tabletop games, card games or outdoor games. Ask them to come up with a list of their top five. Then hold a class discussion and vote to decide which they feel were the best games.

Creative TH!NKing
Participating in creative activities
Actively participates in "what if" (cautionary or wishful thinking) and "if only" (wishful thinking) discussions.

Creative TH!NKing
Creating new content from own ideas or other resources
Creates personal adaptations of others' songs, poems or stories to reflect personal interests, emotions or identity.

Critical TH!NKing
Evaluating ideas, arguments and options
Assesses strengths and weaknesses of possible solutions.

TH!NK more
Workbook
Listening p114, Ex.1–3

Warmer

Ask: *How many words are there in the English language?* (There is no fixed number. Estimates vary from around 500,000 in 'common' usage to over a million. A Google survey of electronic books found that the English language is growing by around 25,000 words a year.) Ask: *Could you write a story with about 50 words in it?* (of course); *Could you write a story with exactly 50 words in it?* (This is more difficult!)

1 **12.03** Tell students they are going to read five 50-word stories and that each story has a picture. They need to match a picture to each story. Before students complete the exercise, set a three-minute time limit to encourage them to skim the text quickly and not to focus on every word.
1C 2B 3E 4A 5D

2 Encourage students to underline the parts of the text that helped them choose their answers.
a4 c1 d5 e2 f3

3 1 Girls can't play in the ~~school~~ team! Everyone can play in the ~~school~~ team.
2 … and he ate the ~~last~~ biscuit. If I had listened to his rules ~~more~~ carefully, maybe the biscuit would have been mine.
3 When I was a small boy, my father made me eat it ~~at lunch~~.
4 When he went to bed later ~~that evening~~, Kevin felt sad. or When he went to bed ~~later~~ that evening, Kevin felt sad. Playing ball on his own hadn't been ~~much~~ fun.
5 William Webb Ellis was playing football ~~in his PE lesson~~.

4 Discuss which of the statements students agree with and encourage them to say why/why not.
a3 b1 c5 d2 e4

READING

1 12.03 **Read and listen to the results of a contest carried out by a fiction-writing website. Match the pictures with the stories.**

Home | About | Join in | New stories

A

Small is beautiful. So every week we invite our readers to send us their (very) short stories. Each story must be exactly 50 words, not a word more, not a word less – just like this introduction. (Words like 'didn't' count as one word.) And then we publish all our favourites!

B

C

Here are the best from last week's topic:

Changing the Rules

1 'Want to play in the school football team?' the sign said. 'Come along at four o'clock!' So I went. 'But you're a girl!' a boy said. 'Girls can't play in the school team!' 'There's no rule,' I said. And I played. Now there's a rule – everyone can play in the school team.

2 It was the last biscuit. Both of us wanted it. 'Let's toss a coin,' my brother said. 'Heads I win, tails you lose.' He tossed the coin. 'Tails – you lose' and he ate the last biscuit. If I had listened to his rules more carefully, maybe the biscuit would have been mine.

3 I hate cabbage. When I was a small boy, my father made me eat it at lunch. 'The rule is: eat everything on your plate,' he said. I ate it and then I was sick. When I'm a father, my rule will be: 'If you don't like it, you can leave it.'

4 'They're my rules,' Kevin said. 'If you don't like them, find someone else to play with.' When he went to bed later that evening, Kevin felt sad. Playing ball on his own hadn't been much fun. If his rules hadn't been so unpopular, he wouldn't have spent the afternoon on his own.

5 In 1823, William Webb Ellis was playing football in his PE lesson. He picked up the ball and ran towards the goal. Everyone was shocked. 'You can't do that!' they shouted. 'I can,' he said as he put the ball in the goal. 'I've invented a new game. It's called rugby.'

D

E

2 **Match the stories (1–5) to the titles. Write the numbers. There is one title you don't need.**
a No one wanted to play ☐
b A long wait ☐
c Game for all ☐
d How a new sport was invented ☐
e An unfair game ☐
f Parents don't always know best ☐

3 **Each of the stories actually has 52 words. Find two words that you can take out in each one. (There may be more than one pair of words you can delete.)**

4 **Which of the stories are these people talking about? Do you agree with them?**
a 'Children should always eat what they are given by their parents.' ☐
b 'There shouldn't be different teams for boys and girls.' ☐
c 'Things never change if you don't break the rules.' ☐
d 'Brothers and sisters always try to trick each other.' ☐
e 'It's important to be flexible when you make the rules.' ☐

5 WRITING **Choose one of the situations, make a rule for it and use it as a topic for your own 50-word short story.**
- Anyone who wants to come into my bedroom
- Using your phone at the dinner table
- Doing homework
- Taking food from the fridge
- Bedtime on a Friday night

114

5 Tell students that a good way to do this activity is to write a short story to begin with and then reduce the number of words until they get down to 50. When students have completed their story, ask them to exchange with another pair and read each other's stories. Hold a class vote on which is the best story.

Culture note

50-Word Stories is a website set up in 2009 by Tim Sevenhuysen, originally with the aim of him posting one of his own new, original 50-word stories every day for a year. Between 2009 and 2011, he managed to do this and, by the third year, he started sharing more and more stories from reader submissions. The site now posts two reader-submitted stories every weekday. He offers a $10 prize for the best submission each month.

THINK more

Workbook
Reading p112, Ex.1–3

▶ 35 Grammar rap!
Third conditional

6 For each example, ask: *Is the situation in the past or the present?* (past). Elicit or explain that the sentences are showing the person imagining how things might have been different in the past and this is when we use the third conditional.
1 No, she didn't listen to him. No, she didn't get the biscuit. 2 No, they weren't popular. Yes, he spent the afternoon on his own.
RULE: 3 past perfect 4 past

7 During feedback, point out that the *if*-clause and *would*-clause can be reversed, e.g., *The test would have been a lot easier for me if I had studied harder.*
1 d 2 a 3 b 4 f 5 c 6 e

8 1 hadn't invited, would have been
2 had entered, would have won
3 would have gone, hadn't forgotten
4 wouldn't have won, hadn't scored

9 Write the statement on the board. Elicit third conditional sentences to imagine a different past, e.g., *If they hadn't met, they wouldn't have had children.* Check students are using the third conditional correctly.

Workbook p109

10 Write on the board: *He went home because it was raining. He went home because of the rain.* Elicit the difference in how we form phrases with *because* and *because of* (*because* + subject + verb; *because of* + noun).
A 3 B 4 C 2 D 1

11 Nominate some pairs to share a dialogue as feedback.

Workbook p110

Pronunciation
Silent consonants

Student's Book p121

Homework
Ask students to write up the chain of conditional sentences they created in the extension activity.

Grammar rap!

GRAMMAR
Third conditional

6 Read these sentences from the stories on page 114 and answer the questions. Then complete the rules.

*If I **had listened** to his rules more carefully, maybe the biscuit **would have been** mine.*

1 Did she listen to her brother? Did she get the biscuit?

*If his rules **hadn't been** so unpopular, he **wouldn't have spent** the afternoon on his own.*

2 Were his rules popular? Did he spend the afternoon on his own?

> RULE: To talk about unreal situations in the past and their imagined results, we use the third conditional.
> - Condition clause: *If* + [3]______ .
> - Result clause: *would (not) have* + [4]______ participle.
>
> The condition clause can come before or after the result clause.

7 Match the parts of the sentences.

1 If I had studied harder, ☐
2 If I hadn't studied so much, ☐
3 Would she have been late for school ☐
4 If she hadn't got up when her alarm rang, ☐
5 If we hadn't spent all our money, ☐
6 We wouldn't have had enough money to go to the cinema ☐

a I wouldn't have passed the test.
b if she had got up when her alarm rang?
c we would have bought him a present.
d the test would have been a lot easier for me.
e if we had spent it all on food.
f she wouldn't have had time for breakfast.

8 Put the verbs into the correct form to make third conditional sentences.

0 If she ___*hadn't been*___ (not be) so rude, I _*would have helped*_ (help) her.
1 If Paul ______________ (not invite) me to his party, I ______________ (be) really upset.
2 If she ______________ (enter) the competition, I'm sure she ______________ (win) it.
3 They ______________ (go) in the sea if they ______________ (not forget) their swimsuits.
4 We ______________ (not win) the game if he ______________ (not score) that goal.

9 Read the statement. Imagine a different past and write as many third conditional sentences as you can. Compare your ideas with a partner.

My grandparents met each other on holiday.

→ workbook page 109

VOCABULARY
Talking about consequences and reasons

10 Match the conversations with the pictures. Write the numbers 1–4.

1 **A** Why did you stop playing?
B *Because* it started raining, Mum!
2 **A** So, your parents are angry with you again?
B Yes. It's *because of* my bad marks at school.
3 **A** I was really hungry when I got home from school.
B *That explains why* there aren't any biscuits left.
4 **A** I forgot to invite Jim to my party.
B *So that's the reason* he looks so upset.

11 Complete the sentences with your own ideas.

1 **A** My football team lost again yesterday.
B *That explains why …*
2 **A** I've just come back from a two-week holiday.
B *That's why …*
3 **A** It's my best friend's birthday today.
B *So that's the reason …*
4 **A** Is this your favourite computer game?
B *That's right. It's because of …*

→ workbook page 110

PRONUNCIATION
Silent consonants Go to page 121.

Language note Third conditional
Students may produce incorrect statements like *If I looked at my watch, I'd have been OK.* Remind them how to form the third conditional if necessary. Remind them that the *if-clause* can go at the beginning or the end.

Activity idea Extension
Students create a chain of third conditional sentences starting with something that went wrong, e.g., *If I hadn't forgotten my phone, I would have been able to call you. If I had been able to call you, you could have given me a lift home …*

TH!NK more

Practice Extra
Unit 12 Practise it!

Workbook
Grammar p109, Ex.6–9
Vocabulary p110, Ex.4–5
Pronunciation p121

Worksheets
Grammar Worksheets 12
Grammar presentation: Third conditional
Grammar rap! Third conditional
Vocabulary Worksheets 12

Warmer

Ask students to make a list of laws in their country. Give groups three minutes to write down as many as possible. Encourage them to use *be allowed to* where necessary. Write any interesting vocabulary on the board. Ask students if they can think of any strange laws.

▶ 36 TH!NK
Laws from around the world

1 Before students read the article, get them to cover it and just look at the pictures and think what each strange law is.
1 You mustn't climb trees; you have to pay a parking fee to tie an elephant to the parking meter; you can't jump the queue in the ticket hall of the metro system; you must walk your dog at least three times a day.
2 Picture A

2 🔊 **12.06 Check/clarify:** *parking meter, bathtub.*
Tell students to cover the quiz (at the bottom of the page).
1C 2B 3B 4A 5C
6C 7C 8A

3 Ask stronger students to answer any of the questions they can from memory before they read again. Encourage students to underline the key information in the questions that they will be looking for in the article. Suggest that they underline the parts of the article that helped them find their answers.
1T 2F 3F 4T 5F 6T

TH!NK Laws from around the world

Culture

1 Look at the pictures and answer the questions.
1 Each picture is about a strange law. What do you think the law is for each picture?
2 In one picture, someone is breaking a law. Can you guess which one?

2 🔊 12.06 **Read and listen to the article to check your ideas from Exercise 1 and then do the quiz.**

3 Read the laws again and mark the sentences T (true) or F (false).
1 You mustn't climb trees. ____
2 You can take a lion to the cinema but not any other wild animal. ____
3 It is free to tie an elephant to a parking meter. ____
4 Donkeys mustn't be put in a bathtub. ____
5 You mustn't go to the toilet after 10 pm. ____
6 Taxi drivers have to pay money to listen to music in their cars. ____

STRANGE laws from around the world

Laws are important – they help us to live together in a friendly, happy and peaceful way. However, there are a number of laws from various countries around the world that seem really strange. Many of them are rather old, but have never been changed. We've selected some of the strangest for you here.

1 It is against the law to jump the queue in the ticket hall in the underground metro system in ______.
A New York, US B Paris, France C London, UK

2 If you climb a tree in ______, you are breaking the law.
A Beijing, China B Oshawa, Canada C Tokyo, Japan

3 You can't take a pet lion to the cinema in ______ – if you have one!
A Amsterdam, the Netherlands B Baltimore, US C Madrid, Spain

4 If you don't walk your dog at least three times a day in ______, you will get a fine.
A Turin, Italy B Berlin, Germany C Geneva, Switzerland

5 If you tie an elephant to a parking meter in ______, you have to pay a parking fee.
A Amsterdam, the Netherlands B Madrid, Spain C Florida, US

6 If you go to the toilet at night in ______, you must remember that it is illegal to flush the toilet after 10 pm.
A Thailand B The Netherlands C Switzerland

7 If you are a taxi driver in ______, and you play the radio while driving a customer, you have to pay royalties to the musicians you listen to during the journey.
A Italy B Greece C Finland

8 If you own a donkey in ______, you must not keep it in the bathtub.
A Georgia, US B Istanbul, Turkey C London, UK

116

Social Responsibility
Understanding and describing own and others' cultures
Makes informed comparisons between their own society and other societies.

4 Do not correct errors unless they hinder comprehension.

5 1 breaking the law 2 fee 3 own 4 royalties 5 jump the queue 6 fine 7 illegal 8 peaceful

4 SPEAKING Which of the laws do you think is the strangest? Compare with others in the class.

5 VOCABULARY There are eight highlighted words in the article. Match the words with these meanings. Write the words.

1 doing something that is not allowed ______
2 money you pay to allow you to do something ______
3 have something that is yours ______
4 money given to the writer of a song each time it is played ______
5 move in front of people who were there before you ______
6 money you pay for doing something wrong ______
7 against the law ______
8 without violence ______

WRITING
A set of rules

1 INPUT Jemma wrote a set of rules for her house and her family for weekends. What does she say about:

1 food? 5 her sister?
2 sleep? 6 school and teachers?
3 her room? 7 TV?
4 homework? 8 herself?

2 Put the words in the correct order to make sentences from Jemma's rules. What do the sentences tell you about how she feels about homework, her sister and football?

1 allowed / ask / no one / me / is / homework / about / to
______
2 all / isn't / she / at / room / come / allowed / into / to / my
______
3 watch / no one / programme / time / at / other / can / any / that
______

3 ANALYSE Find the phrases and sentences in Jemma's rules that show she isn't 100% serious.

4 PLAN Choose one of the sets of rules below to write about. Make notes about what you want to include in the rules. (You don't have to be serious, but don't be unkind!)

- A set of rules for your family for the weekend.
- A set of rules for your family for the school holidays.
- A set of rules for you and your family when you go out together (e.g. to the cinema or to a restaurant).
- A set of rules for you and your family when you go somewhere on holiday together.
- A set of rules for … anything you like!

Rules for the weekend at home

1. After school finishes on Friday, Mum and Dad are not allowed to talk to me about school or teachers.
2. Between seven o'clock on Friday evening and nine o'clock on Sunday evening, no one is allowed to ask me about homework. (At other times, they can help me if they want.)
3. No noise before 10 am on Saturday. Saturday is my morning for sleeping.
4. For breakfast on Sunday, I can eat anything I want. Anything at all!!! (And that includes ice-cream!)
5. My sister Juliana is not allowed to use my computer – in fact, she isn't allowed to come into my room at all. (Well, only if she brings chocolate.)
6. My room – I will tidy it late on Sunday, but before then: keep out!
7. If there is a football match on TV with my team, no one can watch any other programme at that time.
8. And lastly – I am not allowed to be boring about rules 1–7!

JEMMA (the boss!)

5 PRODUCE Write the set of rules you chose in Exercise 4. Write about 150–180 words. Give them a title. Add some drawings if you want to.

1 1 She can eat anything for breakfast on Sundays.
2 She sleeps until 10 am on Saturdays.
3 She will only tidy it late on Sundays.
4 Between seven o'clock on Friday evening and nine o'clock on Sunday evening, no one is allowed to ask her about homework. At other times, they can help her if they want.
5 Her sister Juliana is not allowed to use her computer, and she isn't allowed to come into her room at all unless she brings chocolate.
6 After school finishes on Friday, her mum and dad are not allowed to talk to her about school or teachers.
7 If there is a football match on TV with her team, no one can watch any other programme at that time.
8 She is not allowed to be boring about rules 1–7.

2 Ask students to cover the set of rules while they do the exercise. During whole-class feedback, point out the use of *not allowed to* in two of the sentences.
1 No one is allowed to ask me about homework.
2 She isn't allowed to come into my room at all.
3 No one can watch any other programme at that time.

3 Ask students to underline the phrases that are not completely serious.
(At other times, they can help me if they want.)
Anything at all!!! (And that includes ice-cream!)
(Well, only if she brings chocolate.)
… but before then: keep out!
I am not allowed to be boring about rules 1–7!
… (the boss!)

4 You may like to give some examples of your own to get students started. Ask them to brainstorm ideas for their set of rules.

5 Encourage them to use similar structures to those in Jemma's set of rules.

Homework

Ask students to make a set of rules for teachers. As a follow-up, they can share them with the class and decide on a definitive list.

Activity idea Extension

Divide the class into pairs. Ask students to draw signs to depict rules. Tell them that they should use a red circle to show that something is not permitted, e.g., a picture of a dog inside a red circle would mean 'No dogs allowed'. When students have finished, ask individuals to come to the interactive whiteboard (IWB) and draw their signs. The class have to guess the meaning of the signs and the first student to guess correctly can score one point.

TH!NK more

Practice Extra
Unit 12 Master it!

Workbook
Developing Writing p113

Tests
Unit, extension and skills test 12
Final test

1 In B1 Preliminary for Schools Reading Part 4, candidates have to read a longer text with five numbered spaces, then decide which of the eight sentences provided belongs in each gap.

This part of the exam tests whether candidates can follow the narrative of a text and understand how a well-structured text is formed.

Encourage your students to do the following when they approach this task:

- Read the whole text to understand the narrative.
- Look at each numbered space and choose one of the sentences to complete each gap.
- After choosing a sentence, check the other seven options and decide why they are wrong.
- Read the completed text again to make sure it makes sense.

1 g 2 b 3 h 4 f 5 d

Workbook p25

2 12.07 In B1 Preliminary for Schools Listening Part 4, candidates have to listen to a longer interview and answer six 3-option multiple-choice questions. This part of the exam tests understanding of the detailed meaning of the text, attitudes and opinions.

Encourage your students to do the following when they approach this task:

- Read and listen to the instructions carefully.
- Read all the questions and options and think about the context.
- On the first listening, try to understand the gist and choose the best option.
- On the second listening, check that the answers are correct and focus on detailed understanding of the attitudes or opinions.

1 B 2 C 3 B 4 C 5 A 6 A

Workbook p89

B1 Preliminary for Schools

READING
Part 4: Gapped text

→ workbook page 25

1 **Five sentences have been removed from the text below. For each question, choose the correct answer. There are three extra sentences which you do not need to use.**

An exhibition at the Science Museum

It was fantastic to go to the Science Museum to see an exhibition about driverless vehicles.

Before my visit to the museum, I didn't know much about vehicles that drive themselves using computer controls. [1]______. One way the exhibition did this was that it pushed me to ask questions about how much control we should let driverless cars have.

Driverless cars might seem like something from science fiction, but they've been around longer than we think. [2]______. It was a car called the Citroen DS19, which was around back in 1960. It drove itself by following a network of cables buried underground. Driverless vehicles have developed a lot since then. Newer ones are used for different purposes, like helping farmers by picking crops, or scientists by exploring under the ice in the Arctic Ocean.

The exhibition was organised into three different zones. [3]______. The first was called 'Land'. I was able to look at how driverless vehicles are already being used on land, and possible developments that will happen in the future.

The issue of safety is a big one. How can a driverless car make the choices a human makes? [4]______. I understood more about how difficult it is when I was playing with the interactive displays. Doing this lets you see the world through the 'eyes' of a driverless car. It's very hard to program a computer to make the decisions a driver usually makes.

In the zone called 'Air', I learned about the flying drones that are being developed to deliver products, but not just for shoppers. [5]______. And in the final zone, 'Water', driverless vehicles are being used to make maps of the sea floor and to understand how climate change is affecting the oceans. The whole exhibition was incredibly interesting and made a great day out!

a Despite this, the vehicles used to be more popular.
b I learned that the first of them appeared years ago.
c If the technology improved, there'd be more like that.
d They're also important for things like medical emergencies.
e In fact, I wish I knew more about how it's made.
f Scientists are working on ways to solve this problem.
g Nor had I thought about them, so going there challenged me.
h Each one of these sections dealt with a different subject.

LISTENING
Part 4: Multiple choice

→ workbook page 89

2 12.07 **You will hear a girl called Lucy talking on a TV programme about a competition she won. For each question, choose the correct answer.**

1 To enter the competition, Lucy had to
A upload a video of herself and then phone someone.
B write to the studio and record a video.
C explain why she wanted to win in a letter and send it with a video of herself.

2 How did Lucy find out that she was the winner of the competition?
A They called her into the studio and told her.
B She got a letter in the post.
C The TV company phoned her.

3 Why did Lucy read the weather multiple times?
A She was enjoying it.
B To become familiar with the equipment.
C She was making mistakes.

4 How did Lucy feel when she did the forecast?
A very nervous
B very worried
C very excited

5 What was the weather like in the forecast Lucy gave?
A There was a variety of types of weather.
B The weather was mainly the same across the country.
C Some areas had unusually freezing cold weather.

6 How have Lucy's future plans changed?
A She'd like to be on TV.
B She'd like to be a weather presenter.
C She'd like to be a teacher.

118

1 1 told 2 because 3 funny 4 encouraged 5 explains 6 warned 7 trouble 8 expected 9 fun 10 because of

2 1 would have gone 2 let 3 hadn't eaten 4 allowed 5 wouldn't have eaten 6 had gone

3 1 They ~~said~~ told me to stay at home.
2 Why didn't they let me ~~to~~ go out?
3 They wanted me to answer some questions.
4 I reminded her to ~~giving~~ give me back my magazine.
5 If I ~~would have~~ had known, I wouldn't have told anyone.
6 They ~~hadn't~~ wouldn't have won the game if Matt hadn't played.

4 1 let, Because 2 makes, why 3 allowed, reason 4 hate, have

TEST YOURSELF — UNITS 11 & 12

VOCABULARY

1 Complete the sentences with the words in the list. There are two extra words.

because | because of | behaved | encouraged | expected | explains | fun | funny | reason | told | trouble | warned

1 I broke a plate and I got ________ off by my parents.
2 We couldn't go out ________ it was snowing.
3 I really didn't like that joke – it just wasn't ________.
4 I didn't want to do karate lessons, but my parents ________ me to give them a try, so I did.
5 Oh, your alarm clock didn't ring. That ________ why you were late.
6 I'm not surprised you feel ill. I ________ you not to eat that old cheese!
7 He has lots of problems at school, and he's always getting into ________.
8 I was surprised when England won. I ________ them to lose.
9 It rained almost the whole time, so our walk really wasn't a lot of ________.
10 We couldn't hear the teacher ________ the noise outside.

/10

GRAMMAR

2 Complete the sentences with the words in the list. You need to write the correct form of the verbs.

allow | go (x2) | let | not eat (x2)

1 I ________ to the concert if I'd had a ticket.
2 We wanted to go, but my mum didn't ________ us.
3 He would have been OK if he ________ a second cheeseburger.
4 When I was a little girl, I wasn't ________ to watch TV after nine o'clock.
5 If I'd known there was meat in it, I ________ it.
6 If everyone ________ to the party, we'd have had a lot more fun.

3 Find and correct the mistake in each sentence.

1 They said me to stay at home.
2 Why didn't they let me to go out?
3 They wanted me answer some questions.
4 I reminded her to giving me back my magazine.
5 If I would have known, I wouldn't have told anyone.
6 They hadn't won the game if Matt hadn't played.

/12

FUNCTIONAL LANGUAGE

4 Complete the mini-dialogues with the words in the list.

allowed | because | hate | have | let | makes | reason | why

1 A I don't understand. Why won't you ________ me read my book?
B ________ it's nearly midnight, and you have to go to sleep!
2 A It ________ me really angry when people don't tell the truth.
B I see. So that explains ________ you were cross with Jim.
3 A We aren't ________ to take our mobile phones into class.
B Oh. So that's the ________ why you didn't phone me.
4 A I ________ it when people shout at me. It's horrible!
B Well, I wouldn't ________ shouted if you had listened to me the first time!

/8

MY SCORE /30

22–30 | 10–21 | 0–9

119

The Cambridge Life Competencies Framework

Creative Thinking

Creating new content from own ideas or other resources

Watch this video for a tip on developing your students' creative thinking skills.
Scan the QR code here

Unit 1
Present perfect vs. past simple
1 Yes I have. I saw it yesterday.
2 Yes, I have. I've been to France twice.
3 Yes, I visited them a few days ago.
4 Yes, I saw him five minutes ago.
5 Yes, I changed it for a better one.
6 Yes, I earned over £100 last week.

Unit 2
Present perfect with *for* or *since*
1 We have been friends since we were ten.
2 I have not seen her since I was five.
3 I have worked in the newsagent's for two years.
4 You have lived in Madrid for six months.
5 My family have not travelled abroad since 2014.
6 I have earned £100 over the last week.

Unit 3
Comparatives and *than*
1 I am much happier than before.
2 If you go to Europe, the weather will be better in July than in February.
3 Which is older, football or rugby?
4 The beaches are cleaner in the countryside than in the city.
5 It will make you fitter and healthier.

Unit 4
Any vs. – (no article)
1 In the countryside there aren't any discos.
2 I didn't take any notice of it and deleted it again.
3 I have been doing homework.
4 We need time to work on this.
5 I have been here for four months and I can't live here any longer.
6 Do you have any money I can borrow?

will vs. *should*
1 In my opinion, you should not move schools.
2 If you like the seaside, you should go to the south coast.
3 If we do it that way, it will be a disaster.
4 On this diet, you must eat healthy food, and you shouldn't drink fizzy drinks.
5 I'll meet you there if you like.
6 Should we study everything for the test or just this unit?

Unit 5
Present simple or present continuous vs. present perfect continuous
1 I have been trying to do that for ages, but I can't manage it.
2 How long has Michael been learning English?
3 I always go to work by train, because I live far away.
4 His friends laugh every time he tells that joke – I don't know why.
5 I need to fill in your address – where do you live?
6 Since last Wednesday I have been going to karate lessons.

Unit 6
Future with *will*
1 We normally go there every Wednesday.
2 I think I know what you mean.
3 So I will see you on the 15th.
4 I'm sure you will want to go there when you see these pictures.
5 When I get home, I'll send you a text.
6 Who will win the next football match?

Unit 7
Future forms and time phrases
1 He will look at my project this week.
2 I can't help you straight away, but I will as soon as I can.
3 I'll do what you've suggested immediately.
4 Will you have it finished by Friday?
5 I will talk to him now.
6 I bet he won't do it like that next time.

Question tags
1 He is working on his project, isn't he?
2 We have always wanted to travel, haven't we?
3 That doesn't sound very interesting, does it?
4 You don't finish work at 6 p.m., do you?
5 It would probably be too far to walk there, wouldn't it?
6 He's driving much too fast on these wet roads, isn't he?

Unit 8
used to vs. *usually*
1 If I have time, I usually play computer games in the evening.
2 When I was younger I used to listen to pop music all the time.
3 They usually hang out every Saturday night so that's when I see them.
4 We used to buy clothes twice a year, but now that we have extra money we go shopping more often.
5 Now that I go to the tennis club, I usually get home late.
6 I used to go on camping holidays, but that was a long time ago.

Second conditional tenses
1 If you answered my email, I would be very pleased.
2 It would be fantastic if you came to visit me.
3 If I found your mobile, I would bring it on Monday.
4 I would be very grateful if you could meet me at 11 on Sunday.
5 If I broke this vase, my parents would be angry.
6 I would love it if you could visit me in the holidays.

Unit 9
Present simple passive vs. past simple passive
1 I always keep shopping until the mall is closed.
2 I was born in Britain and have lived here since then.
3 I'm proud that my town was chosen as City of Culture.
4 The hotel is located in front of the beach, so that will be very convenient.
5 Ten minutes later my tent was flooded and I had to leave it because everything was wet.
6 I was given a puppy for my last birthday.

Unit 10
Past perfect vs. past simple
1 Our PE teacher taught us the rules of tennis and we started to play.
2 I had come home from school when it happened.
3 I didn't give the teacher my homework yesterday because I'd left my bag at home.
4 When we had finished eating and drinking we went for a walk in the town centre.
5 Do you like these jeans? I bought them yesterday.
6 The letter was from Brown University – they accepted me!

Unit 11
say vs. *tell*
1 My parents said that you can come along.
2 (correct).
3 As they said, it is a very big sports centre with a lot of facilities.
4 I want to tell you about this great new computer game.
5 I don't know who I can tell about this problem.
6 (correct).
7 Did you tell her on what day and at what time she has to be here?
8 The customer has made a complaint – he says that his order hasn't arrived yet.

Unit 12
let vs. *make*
1 You can go ahead – I won't make you wait for me.
2 Let me ask you something – do you have any plans for Saturday?
3 Could you let her know I'll be late?
4 That document really makes you think about the problems caused by pollution.
5 They can't make us stay late if we don't want to.
6 If you help me tidy the house and prepare the food, I'll let you invite your friends to the party, too.

Unit 1
Intonation and sentence stress

🔊 **1.06 & 1.07** Students learn to re-create engaged intonation and stress within a sentence. Ask students to read the dialogue and listen to the recording, focusing on the stress of the words in blue. Ask students to say which words show that Lucy likes Harry's idea (*great, course, fun, definitely*). Then ask students to listen and repeat the dialogue.

Unit 2
Word stress

🔊 **2.05 & 2.06** Students learn to identify syllables and stress within a word. Ask students to read the dialogue and listen to the recording. Then ask them to count how many syllables each of the coloured words has (*blue – one syllable, red – two syllables, green – three syllables*). Then encourage them to say these verbs and stress the correct syllable. Finally, ask them to listen again to the dialogue and repeat. Ask students to try and repeat the stress of each of the coloured verbs.

Unit 3
Words ending in /ə/

🔊 **3.02 & 3.03** Students learn to identify and produce words ending in a schwa sound (/ə/), in words with a variety of spellings. Ask students to read the dialogue and listen to the recording. Then ask them to read the dialogue out loud and identify the words ending in the short /ə/ sound (*Monster, Computer, Baker, River, Adventure, Webster, doctor, actor, longer, shorter, dinner, after, funnier, Super, Burger, dinner*). Finally, ask them to listen and repeat the whole dialogue.

Unit 4
The short /ʌ/ vowel sound

🔊 **4.05 & 4.06** Students learn to identify and produce the short /ʌ/ vowel sound. Ask students to listen to the recording. Then ask them to focus on the /ʌ/ sound and repeat the words from the poem that contain this sound (*cousin, London, coming, Monday, young, lovely, funny, loves, sun, running, jumping, doesn't, studying, money*).

Unit 5
been: strong /biːn/ and weak /bɪn/

🔊 **5.03 & 5.04** Students learn to identify and produce the strong and weak forms of *been*, as well as practising distinguishing between the two. Ask students to listen to the dialogue and explain that the same word can have a different form of pronunciation, depending on where it comes in the sentence. Ask them to think of other examples of words that sound like the weak form /bɪn/ (*chin, begin, win*).

Unit 6
/f/, /v/ and /b/ consonant sounds

🔊 **6.07 & 6.08** Students learn to identify and produce the consonant sounds /f/, /v/ and /b/. Ask students to listen to the recording and read the dialogue. Ask them to say the words with /f/ sounds (*beautiful, forests, farms, fantastic, for, fishing, from, Friday, forget*), /v/ sounds (*of, Visit, village, Victoria, river, souvenirs, very, never*) and /b/ sounds (*beautiful, by, buy, buildings, buses, beach*).

Unit 7
Intonation of question tags

🔊 **7.04 & 7.05** Students learn to identify and produce correct intonation when using question tags. Ask students to listen to the recording and read the dialogue. Then, ask students to look at the blue question tags in the dialogue and choose the correct options (*Sam doesn't know the answer to her questions. Her voice goes up*). Then ask students to look at the red question tags in the dialogue and choose the correct options (*Max does know the answer to his questions. His voice goes down*).

Unit 8
The /juː/ sound

🔊 **8.03 & 8.04** Students learn to identify and produce the /juː/ sound.

Ask students to listen to the recording and read the dialogue. They then listen again and say the words with the /juː/ sound (*Stewart, you, used, students, music, computing, university, unusual, future, new*). Then ask them to listen and repeat the dialogue, focusing on the sound.

Unit 9
/tʃ/ and /dʒ/ consonant sounds

🔊 **9.02 & 9.03** Students learn to discriminate between the /tʃ/ and /dʒ/ consonant sounds. Ask students to listen to the recording and read the dialogue. They then listen again and say the words with the /tʃ/ (*choose, Charlie, chess, changed, coach, chance, champion*) and /dʒ/ sounds (*journalist, Jane, journalism, dangerous, job, changed, geography, just, joined*), focusing on the difference between the two. Students then listen and repeat the whole dialogue.

Unit 10
/tʃ/ and /ʃ/ consonant sounds

🔊 **10.04 & 10.05** Students learn to identify and produce the /tʃ/ and /ʃ/ consonant sounds, as well as distinguishing between the two. Ask students to listen to the recording and read the dialogue. They then listen again and say the words with the /tʃ/ (*kitchen, Mitchell, watch, picture, temperature, chop, cherries, much*) and /ʃ/ (*show, chef, demonstration, special, Russian, dish, Patricia, sugar, shouldn't, finished, delicious*) consonant sounds. Students then listen and repeat the whole dialogue.

Unit 11
Intonation: rude or polite?

🔊 **11.04 & 11.05** Students learn how intonation can change whether a sentence sounds rude or polite. Ask students to listen to the recording and read the dialogue. They should listen and say which sentences sound rude (*Could you put your bag down over there, please. Yes, could you put that bag down over there! I mean, could you repeat that politely? I'm terribly sorry*) and which sentences sound polite (*Excuse me. Could you repeat that? Could you put your bag down over there, please?*).

Unit 12
Silent consonants

🔊 **12.04 & 12.05** Students learn to identify silent consonants in words, as well as practising not pronouncing them. Ask students to listen to the recording and read the dialogue. They should then listen and repeat the words with silent consonants (*Listen, talking, hour, castle, should, empty, write, answer, know, mustn't*). Students then listen and repeat the whole dialogue.

Welcome Unit

W.01

It will be a cold day in the north of the country with temperatures around 8 degrees Celsius in Manchester. It gets better the further south we go. In Birmingham it will feel quite warm with maximum temperatures of 16 degrees Celsius, and in London it could get up to 20 degrees Celsius, which is very hot for this time of year. The skies over London will be clear and sunny with very few clouds. It might even feel a little humid. It will also be dry in Birmingham, but it will be a little cloudy at times, too. But back up north, I'm afraid it's not going to be a very nice day. It will be very windy in Manchester, and those winds will bring a lot of rain. So if you have to go out on this rainy day, don't forget your raincoat and umbrella. It will be very wet.

W.02

Patricia So tell me more about your family. I know you have two little brothers.

Alex Yes, Peter and Lawrence. They're twins.

Patricia Twins!

Alex Yes, they're lots of fun.

Patricia And you live with your mum.

Alex Yes, she's called Lynne. She's really cool.

Patricia What about your dad?

Alex My parents are divorced, and my dad doesn't live near us.

Patricia Ah, I see.

Alex But it's no problem. I've got loads of other relatives close by. My mum's got two brothers, Steve and Tony. My uncle Tony's not married but uncle Steve is. His wife's called Mary. They're really nice. And they've got three children – all girls. Hemi, Claire and Becca. They live just down the road so we see them all the time.

Patricia That's nice.

Alex And then there's my grandad, Harry. He's fun. He's like a second dad to me. And he only lives about five minutes away. But anyway, what about your family? Tell me all about your brothers and sisters.

Patricia My family? Have you got a few hours?!

W.03

A Have you ever met a famous person?

B Yes, I have. Millie Bobby Brown.

A Really! Where? When?

B It was last summer. We were on holiday in LA. We were walking out of a restaurant when she walked in.

A Did you say anything to her?

B Yes, I did. I asked her for a selfie.

A Did she give you one?

B Well, I realised that I didn't have my phone with me, so she signed a book that I was carrying.

A What book was it?

B It was my English course book, believe it or not. I had it with me to help me with my English.

W.05

Waiter Good evening! Welcome to Luigi's.

Customer 1 Hello. A table for two, please.

Waiter A table for two? This way, please.

Customer 2 Can we see the menu, please?

Waiter Of course. Here you are.

Waiter Are you ready to order?

Customer 2 Just one question. What soup have you got today?

Waiter Today's soup is our special vegetable soup.

Customer 1 Great, so we'd like the soup to start and then the chicken, please.

Waiter Thank you.

Waiter Is everything OK?

Customer 2 Hmmm, no, not really. This soup is too cold!

Waiter I'm so sorry, I'll change it for you.

Customer 1 Wow, it's very noisy here. There are too many people.

Customer 2 I know, it's awful. And the food … ugh! Let's go!

Customer 1 Excuse me! Can we have the bill, please?

Waiter No coffee or dessert?

Customer 1 No, thanks. We're leaving!

W.06

Conversation 1

Boy Hello. How much are these jeans, please?

Woman 1 49.99. And we've got them in five different styles.

Boy Cool. Can I try some on, please?

Woman 1 Of course, which style do you want to try first?

Conversation 2

Postal clerk Can I help you?

Girl Yes, I want to send this letter to Canada, please – as quickly as possible.

Postal clerk OK. That's express, then. So you have to fill in this form, OK?

Girl OK.

Conversation 3

Boy Can I have these two, please?

Woman 2 Of course. Oh! Did you know that there's a special offer? If you buy three books, you don't have to pay for the third one. Buy three, pay for two. Do you want to get another one?

Boy Oh, right. I'll go and have a look. Thank you!

Conversation 4

Girl Can I try these trainers, please? I'm running in a half-marathon soon!

Man OK. They're 65 pounds. Please remember that you have to wear them two or three times before you run a race, OK?

Girl Yes, I know that, thanks.

Conversation 5

Girl Hi. Just a cup of black coffee, please. No milk.

Woman 3 Sure.

Girl There are a lot of people here today! It was a really long queue.

Woman 3 Yes, that's right. But did you know there's a machine over there? You don't have to wait in a queue. You can use the machine to pay.

Girl Oh, I didn't know that. Is it new?

Unit 1

1.01

Who do you admire the most?

Girl 1 My cousin Renata is an amazing person. She's 26 and she's got a little girl, Bruna, aged 4. Her husband died three years ago, so she is bringing Bruna up on her own. Renata lives in São Paulo, where she works as a teacher. It's hard work but she's always happy and smiling. Renata's a keen athlete too – she's a very good runner and she trains a lot. She's already run two half-marathons, but she hasn't won a race yet. She hopes to run a marathon one day. Her life isn't easy, but she always stays positive about everything. Juliana, 17

Boy 1 There's an elderly man who lives near us called Mr Ronay. He's very charming and I think he's just incredible. He's 85 and he has difficulty walking now, but that doesn't stop him being active and doing the thing he loves most: playing the piano. He has always been a very talented performer. When he was younger, he played concerts all over the world, but he can't do that any more. Now, he teaches the piano. He gives lessons at home, and he's just started to give free lessons to neighbourhood kids. Urgun, 16

Girl 2 There's a boy at my school called Deming. He's 15 years old and he can be quiet and shy, but he's very interesting when you talk to him. He's also a wonderful artist with an amazing memory – he looks at a building for just a few minutes, then goes away and paints it exactly as it is in real life.

He also paints things from his imagination. He's very creative. He has never studied art; he just knows how to draw and paint. He's already sold a lot of paintings, and he's just won a place at an art school in Beijing. But he's very laid-back about the success he's had. Li Ju, 16

Boy 2 My best friend's sister, Anna, is amazing. She's 13 and she was born with a serious heart problem. She's already had about ten operations, but she is incredibly brave. She knows that there will be more operations, but she doesn't complain and always seems so cheerful. The problem makes her very weak so she spends a lot of time in bed or in a wheelchair. But she goes to school when she can, and when she can't go to school, she studies in hospital or at home. She's just had another operation, but she's also just passed all her exams! Luigi, 15

1.03

Sarah Why don't you start, Jack?

Jack Sure, just give me a moment. Right, here we go. "I've never flown in an aeroplane." What about you?

Sarah Ahhh, I have, when we went to Italy.

Ella No, I've never flown in a plane. So you lose, Jack!

Jack Just a minute, Ella! You and your family went to Spain last year!

Ella Yes, but we went by ferry ... not by plane!

Jack Oh, no! OK, your turn now, Ella.

Ella Right. Ummm ... got it! I've never worn a red shirt.

Sarah Hmm, I've got a red shirt that I wear all the time. So, yes.

Jack And I've worn a red shirt, too, so one point to you, Ella. And your turn again.

Ella One point to me. OK, another one. Ummm ... I've never eaten Japanese food. What about you?

Sarah Yes, I have.

Jack Me too.

Ella Yes!! Another point to me.

Sarah But hang on! You have eaten Japanese food!

Ella No I haven't!

Sarah Yes you have! Remember? The other day at school. You had spring rolls for lunch.

Ella Spring rolls? That's Chinese food, not Japanese food!

Sarah Really?

Jack Yes, Sarah, I'm afraid she's right.

Ella Thank you!! So, two points to me and it's my turn again. Let's see. I've never lost a game of 'I've never'.

Sarah Well, nor have I. Because I've never played it before.

Jack Hah! Same here. So you lose, Ella. That wasn't a great idea, was it?

Ella No, it wasn't. OK, let's stop, I'm bored with this game!

Jack and Sarah No / What / Hang on!

Unit 2

2.03

Tom Hey Mum. Is it OK if I borrow your alarm clock?

Mum Yeah, you can, but please make sure you give it back to me when you don't need it any more.

Tom Thanks, Mum, you're the best.

Mum Um. Tom. Can I just ask? Why do you need an alarm clock? Tomorrow's Saturday.

Tom I know but I want to wake up and watch the sun rise.

Mum What? Do you have any idea how early that is?

Tom Yes, it's 5.32 tomorrow. I checked online.

Mum Tom – are you feeling OK? Getting up early on a Saturday – this is very unlike you.

Tom Don't worry, Mum. It's part of a challenge.

Mum What challenge?

Tom I've got this list – ten things to do this summer. It's already July. So I don't have that much time left. I need to start doing some stuff.

Mum And watching the sun rise is one of them?

Tom Yes, it's one of the easiest.

Mum Interesting. Can I have a look at this list?

Tom Sure. I'll send you the link.

Mum So what other things are on it? Learn to help your mum in the kitchen?

Tom Very funny, Mum. No, it's more about stuff you can do outside. Things like eat an apple straight off a tree and feed a bird from your hand.

Mum I like the idea of this list. Anything that gets you off your computer and out into the real world, well, it must be good.

Tom That's the idea, I think. Anyway, a few of my friends and I have decided to do it. We're having a competition to see who can finish first.

Mum So is there anything I can help you with?

Tom Well, yeah, there is. Could you give me a lift to the Malvern hills tomorrow?

Mum The Malvern hills?

Tom Yeah, I need to climb a huge hill. I think they are big enough.

Mum And you want to do this after you've got up at 5.30.

Tom 5.32 – yes. Well, I might go back to bed for a few hours first but then we could go a bit later.

Mum And take a picnic with us. Sounds like a really good idea.

Tom Thanks, Mum.

Mum You get to tick things off your list and I get to spend some time with you!

Tom Careful, Mum. Don't spoil it!

Mum Sorry. Forget I ever said that. Now let's go and get that alarm clock ...

2.08

For each question, choose the correct answer.

One. What did Sally buy at the shops?

Man So, did you get everything on the shopping list, Sally?

Woman 1 Um, well, everything except for the eggs. They didn't have any in the shop today.

Man Oh no! But did you get the milk and the bread?

Woman 1 Yes, and I got some apples, too. I wanted to get some biscuits but I didn't have enough money.

Man Oh well, maybe next time!

Two. What time is it?

Girl Oh no! Are we late for the film?

Boy 1 I don't think so. It starts at quarter past seven. There's enough time.

Girl Are you sure? I think it starts at seven o'clock.

Boy 1 Let me see. Oh, yes! You're right. And it's quarter to seven already! We are late.

Girl So, come on! Let's hurry up and go.

Three. How did Brian get to work?

Woman 2 You're half an hour late, Brian. What happened? Is everything OK?

Man I know, I'm so sorry. I had a problem with my car.

Woman 2 Oh, dear. Did you get the bus?

Man I wanted to, but I just missed it, so I decided to walk to work today.

Woman 2 Really? But you live on the other side of town.

Man I know and I'm exhausted.

Four. Which lesson did Fred enjoy most?

Woman 1 Did you have a good day at school, Fred?

Boy 2 It was OK, apart from History. That was boring as usual. But luckily that was in the morning and the rest of the day was fine.

Woman 1 So what did you do after lunch?

Boy 2 We had Science. That was lots of fun, and then we had Music, which was alright.

Five. What month is Tom's brother's birthday?

Boy 1 It's my brother's 18th birthday soon.

Girl Really? I thought his birthday is in December.

Boy 1 No, that's when my mum's birthday is, on the 17th.

Girl Oh. I see! So it's his birthday before your birthday in July.

Boy 1 Yes, that's right – his is in May.

Girl Great! I'm sure he's really excited.

Boy 1 All I need now is to find him a present.

Girl Good luck!

Six. What's the score in the football match?

Owen shoots and he … misses. That was an excellent chance for the Summertown United striker. It's his second chance in the last five minutes of the match. You just feel that United are getting closer and closer to scoring a second goal to draw. But for now, Castle City are still winning thanks to both goals from Love and Cahill. But can they hang on? And here come United again on the attack …

Seven. Which man are the police looking for?

Following a number of robberies in the last two weeks, the police are looking for a man in his early 20s. He is of average height but a little overweight. He has short dark hair, and a scar on his left cheek. He also sometimes wears glasses. If you see a man of this description, do not talk to him. Phone the police immediately.

Unit 3

3.04

Host Most of you will know what Lego is – the small coloured building bricks for children. Well, today we're with local girl Emma Harding, who's just won a prize for her Lego film. So, Emma, well done, how does it feel?

Emma Well, very cool. I was at school when I heard that I'd won. I couldn't wait to get home and tell my Mum and Dad. I was so happy! And I still get emotional now when I think about it.

Host What was the prize?

Emma Quite a lot of money!

3.05

Emma I'm going to use it to make my next film, I hope.

Host Next film? So you're planning to do another one?

Emma Sure. And maybe one day, I'll be a film director full-time. I'd like to work on animated films.

Host Really, you're an artist as well?

Emma Kind of – I love drawing and I like writing too.

Host Great. Tell me, how do you go about making a Lego film? I'm sure it's far more difficult than it looks.

Emma Erm, it's not difficult but it takes a lot more time than most people think it does. First though, before you start, you should watch some Lego films. They'll give you some ideas. And then, of course, you need some Lego.

Host OK, so what did you do first?

Emma Well, first I built the set! There was a Lego castle and a lake and two Lego mountains. I built everything with Lego. Then of course you need to get yourself a camera. Or you need to find a friend with a camera!

Host So which did you do: get yourself a camera or find a friend with a camera?

Emma A friend with a camera. Her name's Lily and she helped me make the film. She took the photos and I moved the characters.

Host And what about lighting?

Emma That was easy. We used two desk lamps.

Host Then I suppose you also needed a good story.

Emma Yeah, I already had the script. Lily read it and she had some ideas, too. And together we made the script a little better. We had to make it much shorter too.

Host And then …? Were you ready to film?

Emma No … we practised moving the characters first and we had some fun doing that.

Host So what came next?

Emma We took a lot of photos.

Host How many?

Emma Let's see. For every second of film there were more than 10 photos. Sometimes a second took 18 photos. Eighteen photos look a lot better than 10 photos. It looks a lot more professional.

Host So how many photos did you take?

Emma The film is 20 seconds long and we took 360 photos.

Host Wow. So just one more question. When can we see your next film?

Emma Well, I only have a script – oh, and it's not a Lego film.

Host Oh, right. So what is the new film about?

Unit 4

4.02

Mark Hey, Dad. What's up?

Dad I've just come from your grandfather's house. He told me he fell for a scam in an email.

Mark Oh, no. Really? What happened?

Dad Oh, somebody sent him an email pretending to be from his bank. He sent them all of his personal data. But it was a phishing email and they used it to take money from his account.

Mark How much did they take?

Dad £5,000. All the money he had, almost. I'm so angry.

Mark Hmm, it's not his fault but he's not very careful, is he?

Dad No – but I hope you are. All that time you spend on the internet and social media. I hope you haven't fallen for any scams.

Mark Hey, I read my emails a bit more carefully than grandad.

Dad I know, but I also know that a lot of scams are aimed at teenagers because they're …

Mark What? Stupid?

Dad No, I don't mean that. They're just … well, a bit less experienced. I bet a lot of them don't know about identity theft.

Mark People trying to get your information so they can pretend to be you. I know. And you're right, for sure some of the kids at my school don't know about it.

Dad It's a big problem these days, and getting bigger.

Mark You have to be sooo careful about information you give out, don't you?

Dad That's right. Those emails or pop-ups, offering you something fantastic, you should never believe them. If it looks too good to be true …

Mark … then it probably is too good to be true. Yeah, I got an email the other day saying they would give me a new tablet for when I go to university.

Dad See? Someone knows you're planning to go to university. It's in your digital footprint. You didn't do anything, did you?

Mark No, Dad, of course not. I knew it was phishing – you know, they ask for your name, bank account number and PIN 'just to check'.

Dad And these people, sometimes they ask you for money right away – <sarcastically> 'just pay us five pounds and we'll send you £1,000,000'! Huh!

Mark Yeah, my friend's older brother got one of those. Can you believe he sent the money? Never saw the money again, of course.

Dad See? Teenagers, adults, grandads – anyone can fall for scams. You just can't be too careful.

Mark It's sad, huh?

Dad Yes, it is. Come on, let's get something to eat.

Unit 5

5.05

Boy Hi, there. I'm doing some research for the new school magazine about how important music is. Have you got time for a few questions?

Dana Sure, OK. I'm Dana, by the way.

Boy Great. Thanks, Dana. OK. Between 1 and 5 how important would you say music is to you?

Dana Five. Definitely. I don't think I could live without it. It's probably more important to me than fashion. I think I would only put friendship and family above it.

Boy Wow. And is that listening to music or playing it or both?

Dana Just listening, unfortunately. I mean, I'd love to play an instrument, but I can't. I had piano lessons when I was younger, but I gave up. I keep promising myself to start guitar lessons. One day I will.

Boy You should. I play the drums and I just love it. So what kind of music do you like?

Dana I like loads of different stuff. I love dancing, so I like a lot of the dance music. And I like a lot of old stuff. My dad was always playing music when I was little, so I like a lot of bands from the 1990s. I even like classical music, too, especially when I'm doing homework. It helps me concentrate, and sometimes when I've got a problem to sort out, listening to classical music can help.

Boy And is there any music you don't like?

Dana Well, I'm not keen on heavy metal or anything that's too loud, but the music I really don't like is jazz.

Boy And why's that?

Dana I just find it difficult to listen to. It's not relaxing at all. I get really irritated by it. My brother's a big jazz fan and when he plays it, I just have to leave the room; otherwise we'll start fighting.

Boy Oh dear. So just one more question. How important are lyrics for you?

Dana They're not very important. I don't really listen to them. As I said before, I like music to dance to or to relax to. It's not very important what they're singing about.

5.06

Boy Hi Ben. Can I ask you a few questions about music? It's for the school magazine.

Ben OK, what do you want to know?

Boy Well, from one to five, how important is music for you?

Ben Two, maybe. I mean I sometimes put the radio on, but I'd never go out and buy any music.

Boy OK. Um … So I guess you don't play any instrument?

Ben I had piano lessons when I was about 10. I did them for two years, then my mum let me give them up. I hated them.

Boy So, what kind of music do you like?

Ben Just the stuff that's on the radio, I suppose. But don't ask me to name any of the bands. I just don't know any.

Boy So, is there any music that you really don't like?

Ben Um, not really. I mean, I'm not too keen on classical music and jazz but otherwise I'll listen to anything.

Boy So, last question. How important are lyrics for you?

Ben Not at all. I never listen to lyrics.

Unit 6

6.03

Radio host And now over to our reporter Vicky Sandhurst who's currently in Todmorden in West Yorkshire, a little town with a great idea. And that idea is all about carrots and cucumbers, apples and apricots. I'll say no more … Vicky!

Reporter Yes, good morning, Brendan. I'm here in Todmorden, or 'Tod', as the people here call it. What's happening here is amazing. But I want you to hear it from one of the young people who live here. What's your name?

Boy Simon.

Reporter And how old are you?

Boy 15.

Reporter Simon, tell our listeners, please, what's so special about Tod.

Boy That's easy! Incredible Edible.

Reporter And what's Incredible Edible, Simon? Tell us more.

Boy Well, it's the name of a project that we're all involved in. Some people in Tod had the idea some time ago that Todmorden should become the first town in the country that's self-sufficient in food. The idea was that all the free spaces in the town should be used to grow vegetables. People liked the idea, I guess, and started to plant vegetables. Where we had flowers before, you know, now we've got vegetables and fruit trees, and every … everybody can take what they want, and nobody has to pay for it.

Reporter Wow! Well, thanks for talking to us, Simon. That sounds wonderful. Excuse me, you've just taken some broccoli from this flower bed here, which is actually right next to the police station. And they aren't arresting you for doing that?

Man No, not at all. We don't buy our vegetables from the supermarket, we get them free.

Reporter That's amazing! But who plants all those vegetables?

Man We all do, and that's the idea. If we all work together, we do good things for others, and others do good things for us.

Reporter What a brilliant idea! Enjoy your lunch!

Man Thank you.

Reporter And I'm now joined by the woman who started it all – Mary Clear. Mary, I heard that you came up with this wonderful idea when you were drinking coffee with a friend. Is that right?

Mrs Clear Yes, we were talking and found we were both pretty unhappy about the state of things. There are so many negative things happening in the world … so we thought, let's just do something positive.

Reporter Wow. And how did people react?

Mrs Clear At our first public meeting 60 people showed up. And the reaction was amazing. Incredible Edible …

6.09

Listen to six short conversations. For each question, choose the correct answer.

Reader One. You will hear a girl and her brother talking about the girl's night with her two friends. What does the girl say about the night out?

Brother Hey Ali, so what was the film like last night?

Ali Not bad. It was funny, but not very funny if you know what I mean.

Brother And what did the others think?

Ali Julie loved it but Nadia was like me, she laughed a bit but not so much.

Brother But overall you had a good time, right?

Ali Oh yes. It's always good fun to be with Nadia and Julie. We had ice cream afterwards – that was when I really had a good laugh! Julie's so funny when she talks about school and stuff.

Two. Listen to a man and a woman talking about a tennis match. What does the man say about the match?

Man Did you hear? The coach quit after the match!

Woman 1 That was really unexpected. Especially after such a close game and his player won in the end!

Man Exactly. It was a thriller. I have no idea why he did it.

Woman 1 Well, it is a shame – they seemed to work very well.

Man Especially after that match. I thought he did a great job coaching Smith through the game.

Woman I guess we'll never know why.

Man Yes, I'm very confused.

Three. Listen to a boy and a girl talking about the boy's phone. What does the boy say about the phone?

Boy 1 I'm having problems with my phone.

Girl 1 Really? What kind of problems?

Boy 1 Well, first of all, the battery doesn't last very long, not as long as it used to. And sometimes the phone just switches itself off. Yesterday I was talking to a friend and – puf! – the phone switched off! And the battery was OK, I checked.

Girl 1 Have you had the phone a long time?

Boy 2 About four years. And I know, I know, you're going to tell me to get another one. But I can't. I haven't got enough money and neither have my parents.

Four. You will hear a boy and a woman in a shop. Why does the boy want to change the pullover?

Boy 2 Hello. I got this pullover as a present and I'd like to change it.

Woman 2 OK. Have you got the receipt, please?

Boy 2 Sure. Here you are. My grandparents gave it to me for my birthday. And you know … grandparents!

Woman 2 What's wrong? Did they get the wrong size? The wrong colour?

Boy 2 No. It's just that I don't usually wear pullovers. Can I change it for a T-shirt? I'd prefer to have something like that instead!

Woman 2 Sure. Have a look around and see if there's anything you like. Erm … the pullover was £25.00 so that's how much you can spend.

Boy 2 OK. Thanks.

Five. Listen to two friends talking. What has the girl done?

Caroline Hi James. How are you?

James Caroline – goodness! You look so different!

Caroline I know. Do you like it?

James Yes, I think so! It's a big change. Why did you decide to do it?

Caroline I just got tired of it being so long. You can't imagine how difficult it was to wash and dry two or three times a week. So yesterday, when I went to the hairdressers, I just thought – you know what, I'm tired of having it down to my waist. I want to make my life easier.

James Well, good for you. But I'm glad the colour's the same.

Caroline Oh, I'd never change that!

Six. Listen to two friends talking about music at a party. What did the girl think about the music?

Boy 3 Did you enjoy the party on Saturday?

Girl 2 Yeah, I did. It was OK. I just wish the band hadn't started playing and singing.

Boy 3 They weren't very good, were they?

Girl 2 Well, Mike's guitar playing is not so bad, but Jenny's singing … well, it's not very good, is it?

Boy 3 No, no it isn't. Still, they played some nice songs – I mean, songs that I like, anyway.

Girl 2 Oh, I agree. I just think, well, I'd rather listen to a DJ. To be honest, at a party, I prefer to dance to recorded music.

Unit 7

7.02

Interviewer We're talking to Marion Hyde as she's about to board the SS Marstrek. Marion, how are you feeling?

Marion Well, I'm looking forward to the trip of course. It's long, but I know everything will be very comfortable, so I'll be able to sleep.

Interviewer Is this your first time away from Earth?

Marion It is. I've never been to Mars, mainly because the journeys were so long. But this is a once-in-a-lifetime opportunity.

Interviewer What are your plans for the trip?

Marion Well, as you know, my family is coming with me so I'm going to spend time with them, and I hope I can use the different location to inspire me to write some new, great songs!

Interviewer Sounds great! And when are you coming back?

Marion I'm not sure yet. I think I'll stay at least a month. I want to see a bit of Mars, you know, do some sightseeing. I wanted to go skiing there but it's the wrong time of year, so I can't.

Interviewer Oh dear! Sorry about that. Won't you get bored?

Marion Not really. I'll probably take a couple of helicopter rides up there, too. Sadly, I can't use my helicopter pilot's licence on Mars.

Interviewer Well, enjoy your trip and come home safely!

Marion Thank you! Bye!

Interviewer So, Glenn, we heard about the experiment you're going to take part in. How do you feel about the tests that start next week?

Glenn Well, I'm very excited, of course. I think it's going to be very interesting, and quite hard, too. But I'll get a lot of support from the team, so I'm not worried.

Interviewer Do you know how long the tests are going to last?

Glenn Ummm, the idea is to do a week of testing, and if I'm OK, then we'll try a second week.

Interviewer I see! Do you have any worries before you start?

Glenn Well, yes, if I stay awake for 24 hours a day, what am I going to do? I'm taking a lot of books with me! I aim to read two books a day, at least. I'm going to miss my daily tennis training though!

Interviewer And how about your work?

Glenn Oh, I can keep on working, too. I can't take my phone, it's not allowed, so I won't be taking any photos. But I'm going to make notes all the time. Perhaps afterwards I'll write a book about my experience.

Interviewer But won't you get lonely?

Glenn Oh no. I'll still see my family and friends. I just have to use the charger once a day, and of course stay at the laboratory so they can watch me.

Interviewer Well, good luck, Glenn. We look forward to talking to you again afterwards.

Glenn Thanks a lot.

Unit 8

8.02

Mrs Roberts OK, everyone, quiet now. So, today we're going to focus on the importance of science and how it helps us challenge the way we think about the world and helps us explain how it works. Over the years science has helped change many of the things that people have wrongly believed about the world. For example, as I'm sure you all know, many people used to think that our planet was the centre of the universe. Everybody believed that the sun, the stars and all the other planets moved around the Earth. It was something they believed in places as far apart as ancient Greece and China. You can understand why they thought that by simply looking up at the night sky. We seem to be in the middle of it all.

It wasn't until the sixteenth century when people like Copernicus, Galileo and Kepler discovered that the sun was the centre of our universe. OK. So, what other things did people use to believe that we now know aren't true? Yes, Jessica.

Jessica Did people use to believe that the Earth was flat, too?

Mrs Roberts Yes, they did. Thanks, Jessica. Sailors used to be afraid of sailing out too far into the sea. They thought they'd fall off the Earth and into space. And you can understand why when you look out to sea. One of the things that Christopher Columbus, the explorer, did was proving that the Earth was round. How did he do that? He sailed around the world and he didn't fall off into space! I mean, these things seem crazy to us today, but you have to remember, people didn't use to have all the scientific equipment we have these days. They had to make up their ideas about how things worked from what they could see around them. Paul. Have you got a question?

Paul What about alchemists? Are they another example?

Mrs Roberts Yes, another very good example. Alchemists believed, among other things, that other metals could be turned into gold. It started in ancient Egypt where early scientists discovered you could take a substance, sand for example, and turn into another completely different one – glass in the case of sand. This led to people believing there was a way of changing almost anything into something else. In those days, gold was a symbol of great wealth and that's why so many people wanted the alchemists to be right. Yes, Daniel.

Daniel So do you think we now know everything there is to know about the world?

Mrs Roberts No, Daniel. Not at all. Our understanding of the world is changing all the time. Just because we believe something is true these days doesn't mean it definitely is. Maybe one day people will look back at the things we believed and have a good laugh about us.

Unit 9

9.04

Announcer And here we are looking at the world of work and jobs. Now, sometimes it's not easy to get a job, and it can be much, much harder to find a job if you have a disability – for example, if you need to use a wheelchair or if you are blind. But of course there are lots of disabled people who have very successful careers. We shouldn't forget that Britain once had a minister for education who is blind. Every day this week, we're talking to people with disabilities about their jobs, and today Mike Lawley meets Marina Stuart.

Man Marina, when you were born, you already had problems with your eyes – is that right?

Woman Yes, that's right. I could only see partially, and when I was 18 I had an operation to get rid of the problems. Unfortunately, the operation went badly wrong, and I was left completely blind.

Man So, what about your education?

Woman Well, I went to a special school for blind people, and then I went to college. But somehow, you know, the teachers at the college for blind people just didn't think we could get good, interesting jobs.

Man You mean, the teachers didn't think you were going to be successful? That's terrible.

Woman I know! And so I didn't really know what to do. I got a job in a shop, but I hated it. I stayed because I felt that, well, because I was blind, I really didn't have much choice.

Man But one day all that changed, right?

Woman Yes. I was in a café in London, and by accident I met someone who was in the theatre. We talked a bit, and I found out that he was the director of a group of disabled actors. He invited me to go to a workshop, and I went. I loved it, and soon I started doing real acting.

Man Then what?

Woman Well, after working in the theatre, I got an offer to work in television for the first time. I worked in two or three television films, and I'm happy to say that one of them won an award.

Man Acting isn't the only thing that you do, is it?

Woman No, I also love music, and I play the piano, and I give piano lessons at home to small children. It's wonderful, I love it almost as much as acting!

Man So, it looks like that teacher was wrong. It is possible for a disabled person to be successful in the world of work. Is that right?

Woman Yes, it is. When I was young, you know, when I was a child and a teenager, no one thought I could do much. And it was hard to imagine what jobs I could do. But I fought hard and the most important thing is, I didn't let being blind get in my way. I have always wanted people to think of me as Marina Stuart, that's all. I'm Marina first, and then I'm a blind person.

Unit 10

10.02

Lucas Hi Jackie. Fancy meeting you here! Where are you off to?

Jackie Hey Lucas. The gym at the shopping centre. I'm going to work out for an hour or two.

Lucas What? Running on the treadmill and stuff?

Jackie That's right. I love it. Put the headphones on and get running. Then some weights. I feel much better afterwards, so I go to the gym every week. Come on, Lucas. Walk with me a bit.

Lucas OK, sure. You know, I tried a gym a while ago – very expensive, to be honest, and I didn't really enjoy it. I just don't like exercise much.

Jackie That's OK. There are so many things you can do to keep in shape. What we're doing now, for example.

Lucas Walking?

Jackie Absolutely. You should walk as much as you can and sometimes walk quite fast, it's really good exercise. It's good for your heart, your legs … everything!

Lucas OK, let's walk a little faster!

Jackie Let's! But if I remember rightly, you like dancing, too.

Lucas I love it!

Jackie There you go – great for keeping fit.

Lucas And it's so much fun.

Jackie Right. It's a great combination – doing something you really, really love and working out at the same time.

Lucas I guess so. I'd never thought of that. Oh, here we are at the shopping centre. I'll come in with you, OK?

Jackie Sure. The gym's on the second floor. Hey, Lucas, no! Don't do that!

Lucas What?

Jackie Don't take the escalator; walk up the stairs. More exercise. And actually it's quicker! Come on – it's only two floors.

Lucas Well actually, Jackie, I think I'm going to have a coffee and a piece of cake. On this floor!

Jackie Well, then definitely use the stairs! But if you do order cake, eat it sitting down, don't eat and walk, that's one of the worst things people do.

Lucas Why?

Jackie Well, I read somewhere that if you eat and walk at the same time, the food doesn't do you so much good. And so, you feel hungry again before very long.

Lucas Oh? And actually it's nicer to eat sitting down, isn't it? But hey, Jackie, before you go, give me one tip, one simple thing to do to keep in shape.

Jackie OK. Every day, at least two or three times, do 'the invisible chair'.

Lucas Huh?

Jackie Start by using a wall – put your back against the wall and slide down a bit. Imagine you're sitting on a chair and the wall is the back of the chair. Hold the position for two minutes – if you can! And when you get better at it, do the invisible chair without a wall.

Lucas What's so good about doing that?

Jackie Well, it makes your legs stronger, and it helps your back muscles too.

Lucas Well, I'll think about it! Have fun at the gym – bye!

10.07

You will hear a man talking about summer jobs at the local newspaper. For each question, write one or two words or a number or a date or a time.

If you're aged 16 or 17 and would like a summer job, then listen carefully. The Daily Post newspaper is looking for young people to work in their office during July and August. So, if you are interested in a career in journalism, then this is your chance to get some valuable hands-on experience at one of the oldest newspapers in the world. There are a total of six jobs. They need three trainee journalists, two trainee photographers and there's one job for a junior assistant. No experience is necessary, and full training will be given on the job. Successful applicants will be expected to work a 20-hour week. Working hours will be from 1 pm to 6 pm on Mondays and Fridays and from 8 am to 1 pm on Tuesdays and Thursdays. So, that means you don't have to work on Wednesdays. You might have to work at the weekend sometimes. But the good news is that you'll be paid extra for weekend work! The paper is offering £5 an hour. Each position is for four weeks starting on 28th of July. And if you really impress them, you might be offered a part-time contract to work weekends during term time. This is an excellent opportunity to learn more about one of the most competitive careers there is. If you're interested, application forms can be downloaded from The Daily Post website, or you can find a copy in the newspaper itself every day this week. For more information phone Robin on 0184 6780, and he will give you all the information you need. Go on – do it!

Unit 11

11.02

Some journalists report on politics, some report from football grounds. Some journalists report from the law courts, others report on wars from the other side of the world. Warren Faidley is a journalist with a difference. He's an extreme weather journalist. Don't confuse him with a weatherman, who studies the weather and predicts what's going to happen tomorrow. Warren is a weather journalist. He's there when the weather is the news. For more than 25 years, he's been following and filming tornadoes and blizzards, giant hailstorms and floods. Wherever there is bad weather, Warren Faidley is never far behind.

An extreme weather journalist is always close to danger. Of course, Warren always tries to stay safe. He doesn't look for trouble, but trouble always seems to find him.

In his career, he's had many last-minute escapes. The closest he ever came to death, however, was when he was a 12-year-old child. He was by the side of a river with a friend watching a flood. Suddenly, the side of the river collapsed, and he found himself in the fast-flowing muddy floodwaters. He thought he was going to die, but luckily he managed to grab onto a rock and pull himself out of the water.

Warren's interest in extreme weather began when he was a small child. In his autobiography *Storm Chaser*, he describes several occasions when he came face-to-face with scary weather conditions. For example, there was one time when he and his father were chased by a huge storm while they were out sailing in a small boat. His father later told him he thought they were going to die.

Warren was always interested in photography and at college he worked as a part-time photojournalist. He reported from many dangerous places and quickly learned how to use a film camera in difficult conditions. His lucky break came when one day he took an amazing photo of lightning striking a gas farm. The photo was published by *Life* magazine and suddenly everyone was interested in his work. Warren was now able to follow his dream and become a weather journalist.

These days Warren is often seen on American TV news programmes reporting on incidents of extreme weather. He's also become an expert on how to survive in these situations and has written a book called *The Ultimate Storm Survival Handbook* based on his experiences. He's also started a charity called The Storm Angel Foundation which helps educate children about the dangers of extreme weather.

Unit 12

12.02

I want to talk to you today about my favourite game – chess. It's a game which was invented around 1,500 years ago in India. My father taught me to play when I was a little girl and I have loved it ever since.

So, how do you play it? Well, chess is a strategy game for two people. It is played on a square board with 64 squares – half of them black and half white. Each person has 16 pieces to play with. They each have eight pawns, a king, a queen, two rooks, two knights and two bishops. The aim of the game is to take the other player's pieces and to take the king.

So first of all, let's talk about the most important rules for chess:

The pawn is the weakest piece. It can move forward two squares on its first move. After that, it is only allowed to move forward one square at a time. It can only take a piece one square diagonally in front of it.

The rook, the one that looks like a castle, can move forwards, backwards and sideways, as many squares as you like.

The bishop can move as far as you like, too, but it can only move diagonally.

The knight moves in a different way. It can move two squares in one direction and one square in another direction, in an L shape. It is the only piece that can move over another piece.

The queen is the most powerful piece. She can move in lots of different ways. She can move forwards, backwards, sideways and diagonally, and she is allowed to move as many squares as she likes.

And finally, the king. He is the most important piece but he can't move very far. He can only move one square, in any direction. When a king is attacked, it is called check. When he can't escape, it's called checkmate and that ends the game.

Before you start, you have to decide who is black and who is white. The player with the black pieces lets the player with the white pieces move first.

There are some other rules to make the game more interesting. This is my favourite one. If a pawn reaches the other side of the board, you can make it into a queen, a rook, a knight or a bishop. Of course, it is best to make it a queen.

So who is the winner?

Well, the winner is the first player to take the other player's king and says 'checkmate'. Some games can last for hours and some games can be over very quickly. It depends how good the players are. If you want to be a better player, you have to play a lot of games.

12.07

You will hear a girl called Lucy talking on a TV programme about a competition she won. For each question, choose the correct answer.

Presenter Now, if you were watching the news yesterday evening, you probably noticed a new face in our team. 12-year-old Lucy Harmon won a competition to read the weather forecast for the day. She now joins us to tell us all about the experience. Lucy, welcome.

Lucy Thank you.

Presenter First of all, tell us, what did you have to do to enter the competition?

Lucy Um, I had to write a short letter to the producers saying why I wanted to read the weather on TV, and then I had to make a short video of me reading a news story. Then I uploaded it and about two months later I got a phone call saying I had won, and they wanted me to go to the studio the next Friday. I couldn't believe it.

Presenter So what happened on the big day?

Lucy Well, I got to the studio at about three o'clock. I met the producer and all the news team. They were really nice. Then I practised reading the weather a few times, for quite a while, just to get used to the cameras. The producer gave me some advice, and then suddenly it was time to go live on air.

Presenter At four o'clock?

Lucy No, it was actually at five. And I was happy for the extra time to practise! Someone else did the four o'clock news and weather. It was good to watch them as it helped me to prepare more.

Presenter And how did you feel?

Lucy It was such a good experience, and I was too excited to be worried. It was so much fun. I just loved it. No nerves at all.

Presenter So, what kind of forecast did you have to do?

Lucy Well, it had nearly everything: sun, rain, clouds, strong winds. Everything that makes British weather so interesting. The only thing it didn't have was snow, but then I suppose it's not that time of year.

Presenter But you wouldn't believe it if you looked out of the window.

Lucy No.

Presenter So what did you think of the day? Do you want to be a weather forecaster now?

Lucy It was great. I've always wanted to be a teacher, since I was a little girl, but I think that's changed now. I'm not sure I want to forecast the weather, but I would like to be some kind of TV presenter.

Presenter Well, Lucy, I think there's every chance of that. Your performance yesterday was wonderful.

Lucy Thank you.

Acknowledgements

The authors and publishers acknowledge the following sources of copyright material and are grateful for the permissions granted. While every effort has been made, it has not always been possible to identify the sources of all the material used, or to trace all copyright holders. If any omissions are brought to our notice, we will be happy to include the appropriate acknowledgements on reprinting and in the next update to the digital edition, as applicable.

Key: WL = Welcome; U = Unit.

All third party texts are reused from *Think Second Edition British English Student's Book 2*; **WL–U12:** All photographs are reused from *Think Second Edition British English Student's Book 2*.

Cover photography by David Sacks/The Image Bank/Getty Images; Alex Tihonov/Moment Open/Getty Images

Teaching Tip videos produced by Honest ideas Ltd